# MYSTERIE_
# FAR NORTH

"Jacques Privat revives the presence of the Scandinavians in Greenland during the Middle Ages. He sheds new light on contacts between Scandinavians and Inuit and on the premises of the great discoveries in Canada and North America."

JEAN-MARIE MAILLEFER, PROFESSOR EMERITUS OF
SCANDINAVIAN LANGUAGES AND CIVILIZATIONS AT
PARIS-SORBONNE UNIVERSITY

"The work of Jacques Privat forms a valuable contribution to our knowledge of the medieval history of the Scandinavians in Greenland. He introduces a new historical, geographical, and ethnographical vision. He offers new definitions of the relationship of this people with the church, the Inuit people, and the other nations of Europe. This book offers a new view of the disappearance of these Scandinavian settlers by freeing itself from the overly restrictive context of some earlier analyses."

PIERRE ROBBE, PROFESSOR AT THE
MUSÉUM NATIONAL DE L'HISTOIRE NATURELLE

"Privat's research is enticing because of the wide variety of fields it tackles, and the result is a truly original theory. Another new aspect is his examination of the evidence provided by Inuit art, whose value is obvious."

REGIS BOYER, FRENCH LITERARY SCHOLAR, HISTORIAN,
AND TRANSLATOR, SPECIALIZING IN NORDIC LITERATURE
AND THE VIKING AGE

"Having put together a vast and imposing collection of archival data, Privat was able to establish important parallels between the written source material, archaeological and ethnological evidence, and the contributions offered by ancient cartography."

JÖELLE ROBERT-LAMBLIN, RESEARCH DIRECTOR OF THE FRENCH
NATIONAL CENTRE FOR SCIENTIFIC RESEARCH (CNRS)

# MYSTERIES OF THE
# FAR NORTH

## The Secret History of the Vikings in Greenland and North America

### JACQUES PRIVAT

Translated by Jon E. Graham

Inner Traditions
Rochester, Vermont

Inner Traditions
One Park Street
Rochester, Vermont 05767
www.InnerTraditions.com

Text stock is SFI certified

Cataloging-in-Publication Data for this title is available from the Library of Congress

ISBN 978-1-64411-447-6 (print)
ISBN 978-1-64411-448-3 (ebook)

Printed and bound in the United States by Lake Book Manufacturing, Inc. The text stock is SFI certified. The Sustainable Forestry Initiative® program promotes sustainable forest management.

10  9  8  7  6  5  4  3  2  1

Text design and layout by Debbie Glogover
This book was typeset in Garamond Premier Pro with Americanus, Cinder, and Texta used as display typefaces

*In memory of my teacher, Régis Boyer, who guided me through this gold mine that has yet to reveal all its secrets;*

*And Madame Hedwige Vincennot, who always gave me steadfast support and especially shed light on my travels on the roads of the North, which have never since been closed to me.*

## ACKNOWLEDGMENTS

*Qujanarsuaq Kalaallit Nunannni tamanut, igamik Narsarmiumut Kali Karlsenimut*

Thanks to all those in Spain, Greenland, and Denmark (Hans Gulløv, and particularly Jette Arneborg of the National Museum, and the cartography department of the Royal Library of Copenhagen) who assisted me in bringing this book, which was originally my Sorbonne dissertation, to fruition; and my thanks to Jean-Marie Maillefer for his work on the Latin texts.

My special thanks to Claude Lecouteux for his unwavering faith in this book, his self-sacrifice, his help, and his lengthy revision work, without which this text would have remained in the dusty drawers of university research.

# Contents

# Foreword

A Danish, Swedish, and Norwegian translator, Jacques Privat is the first to have succeeded in retracing the history of Greenland in the Middle Ages from the time of the Viking arrival there. His work is truly pioneering. He has a thorough knowledge of this subject, having spent an entire year immersed in it coupled with many shorter visits to Greenland. Jacques Privat studied the Inuit language at the Eskimology Institute in Copenhagen and was even adopted by the village of Nassaq. Drawing on archives that have been overlooked until now and using every means at his disposal, this peerless researcher consulted the ancient maps; combed through the sagas, tales, and legends; and made good use of all the data from archaeological digs and set the record straight on many preconceived notions and even outright errors. Throughout his study, he brings in much information that will be completely new to most of us, whether it is the tribute paid to the Vatican in the form of falcons, furs, ivory, and eiderdown, or the presence there of the Germans, English, and Portuguese. It was these latter that gave this land the name of Terra Laborador—Labrador. He also cites the role played there by the Hanseatic League and the city of Bremen, as well as that of the Greenland Church with its many singular features.

Along the way, he solves a few geographical riddles such as the location of Estotilandia, Nurumbega, and the Illa Brasil and places Scandinavian colonies in North America (Maine, Newfoundland, Hudson Bay in Quebec).

It would take too long to discuss all the discoveries Jacques Privat shares with us in his book—a book that plunges us into a poorly known past that clearly deserves to be retrieved from the shadows where the dust of centuries has buried it.

Claude Lecouteux
Professor emeritus at the Sorbonne University

Claude Lecouteux is a former professor of medieval literature and civilization at the Sorbonne. He is the author of numerous books on medieval and pagan beliefs and magic, including *The Book of Grimoires, Dictionary of Ancient Magic Words and Spells, King Solomon the Magus,* and *The Encyclopedia of Norse and Germanic Folklore, Mythology, and Magic.* He lives in Paris.

# The Arctic beyond Your Imagination

The remote lands of the Scandinavian Arctic are still poorly known today. It is easy to imagine what the situation was like five centuries ago when there were much fewer sources of information, which I would not hesitate to describe as practically unilateral as they were primarily the work of the church. This helps explain the bias of numerous written sources and the preference long granted to certain alarmist theories about the fate of the Scandinavian colonists and their relations with the indigenous peoples of Greenland. The Arctic is the preeminent domain of the Inuit people (who were long called Eskimos, an exonym that still survives in citations from the ancient historical periods). Less numerous are the people who knew of the existence of this Scandinavian colony (which was originally Icelandic, then Norwegian and Danish) that inhabited Greenland and very likely eastern Canada for several centuries during the very heart of the Middle Ages, long before Columbus. Rarer still are the people who could conceive of the constant presence of a variety of European nations in these territories that will be described throughout this book: the English, the Germans, the Flemish, the Portuguese, and so forth were all drawn there by the magnetic pole formed by the medieval Arctic and its wealth. Contrary to longstanding notions, the Arctic was a source of precious goods: "unicorn" and walrus ivory, deluxe furs, royal falcons, and so forth. A quick glance through medieval source texts will give us some information about

1

the provenance of all these riches. During the Great Age of Discovery before Columbus, the Scandinavian Arctic would occupy a strategic position. For one thing, people then believed it offered a Northwest Passage to Cathay.*

My first objective is to dispel once and for all the longstanding isolationist theories about medieval Greenland. It offered the advantage of explaining the disappearance of the Scandinavian colonists of the Arctic as a result of their forced isolation after contact with Norway became increasingly rare. We will show that Greenland and the neighboring Arctic regions were frequented quite often by sailors, hunters, and European expeditions in the Far North long before Columbus. Consequently, I also reject any Inuit responsibility in the disappearance of the Northmen, as is commonly and too easily believed.

To some degree, the church's responsibility is accepted by many Scandinavian researchers. As I noted earlier, it was responsible for the source texts, and I shall strive to emphasize their one-sidedness. The Inuit were a perfect scapegoat for masking the disagreements that brought the church into conflict with the Greenland colonists. A good grasp of this situation, and of the weight of the church in Greenland and more generally in Scandinavia, can help us see the full scope of this situation. In fact, we can see that several elements tend to prove to the contrary that the Inuit and Scandinavian communities enjoyed fairly good relations. The hypothesis of an intercultural blending even takes on greater weight. So how do you explain the disappearance of the Northmen, one may ask? I will offer my vision of this in the last chapter but summarize it quite simply here: Inuit and Scandinavian, for good and ill, lived side by side for almost three to four centuries. A foreign element was introduced, and silence reigned fifty years after. This should inspire at least a little curiosity. Deciphering European maps can offer significant revelations in this regard.

We may initially believe there is no lack of existing research on

---

*Cathay is the ancient name for China, or sometimes part of China; for example, Marco Polo referred to North China as Cathay. It attracted many European explorers due its wealth, which was a much-desired economic stimulus for many nations.

this subject. That's true, but the holes characterizing the traditional approach to Greenland in particular, and the medieval Arctic in general, can be summed up as practically self-evident. It is a Scandinavian, if not to say Scandinavianist, vision based primarily on Scandinvian sources. In short, as the Inuit would say, the gaze of a white man using his own criteria: which has the effect of restricting the research. I am suggesting a completely different approach here.

I have chosen as the framework for this historical study the entire period of medieval Scandinavian colonization (from 982 to about 1560, spilling over the boundaries of the Middle Ages by a few years). The geographical context appears clearly in the book's title; restricting it to Greenland would have been to fall back into the error of traditional research. I have slightly expanded the geographical focus eastward toward Iceland because this subject cannot be restricted to a rigid context: the inhabitation of Greenland was launched from Iceland (Scandinavian colonization, of course). The same population, the same type of society and traditions, moved westward; I would even say very far westward. The history of the two countries often followed the same fortune and misfortune. What is the the final argument for using the Icelandic "factor"? Up to the present, no written source has been discovered in Greenland; all originated in Iceland or Norway—at least as far as the Nordic sources are concerned.

The Scandinavian population of Greenland had strong maritime traditions, which, I would like to remind you, ended up with the "discovery" of America and its temporary inhabitation. To get a better understanding of the Greenland colonizers means following their tracks to Hudson Bay, Ungava Bay, and Labrador. Proceeding this way is not really a mistake as the geographical notions of the time were fairly broad if not to say variable. We shall see, for example, that for at least half a century Greenland was confused for Labrador. This allows me to introduce another important axis of my approach: the use of all sources, even foreign sources, concerning the medieval Scandinavian Arctic and its population and the use of all concepts, even the ones proved to be erroneous. In fact, medieval history is rich in inexact notions touching on all the sciences. In my opinion, analyzing this world with data that has been corrected of their mistakes prevents the researcher from finding the thread of the era's various concepts and identifying the object of his or her study. The medieval Scandinavian Arctic's world offers very illustrative examples in this field:

> The mistaken placement of the Scandinavian colony of Eystribygð persisted for several centuries, because correct modern criteria were used instead of the flawed medieval concepts (the Scandinavian colonists believed they were living on the East Greenland coast).
>
> The geographers of that era long believed that Greenland was connected to Norway by a gigantic land bridge; this could explain some of the confusions about different peoples during the Middle Ages such as the commingling of the "Skrælings"* and the "Karelians,"† or even the scholarly confusion of Norwegian with Greenland "trolls." Similarly the notion of a western extension was equally real, the existence of the legendary "Norumbega" and so forth. As it is easy to see, there is no shortage of examples.

A total innovation that I will energetically defend is the use of European sources. We will follow the trail or European hypotheses concerning the fate of the Scandinavians in Greenland that I find extremely serious and increasingly consistent. I will make generous use of the European maps from the first explorations. As we shall see, the Europeans were not content, as long believed, with a discreet backstage presence in this medieval Arctic space. Their presence was far from temporary for various economic motives that we will examine in greater detail. Of even greater interest is the fact that the commerce of these sailors from various nations went hand in hand with the interests and presence of the church. We have the German period of the Hanseatic

---

*Skræling* is a Norse term given to the indigenous peoples of northeastern North America; see page 7.

†*Karelian* is a name used somewhat confusingly to refer to the inhabitants of northern Scandinavia, the Finns or Sami.

League accompanied by the nomination of German bishops and the confusion of Greenland with the mythical island of Friesland (according to Frisian sailors), an English period that followed the same process, and a Portuguese period that I suspect took the same path. This latter nation played a decisive and fatal role in the fate of the Scandinavian colonies in Greenland and Canada.

I will make broad use of the archaeological work concerning this subject, going from the past century to the present, and the most recent scientific studies from Scandinavian research. All the archaeological excavations of Greenland and Canada will serve—if not as a keystone—at least as a retaining wall for my research, permitting us to verify several axioms or hypotheses provided by the traditional background, such as Scandinavian written sources and so forth. Unfortunately, due to various factors (distance, the chronic isolation of the young researchers, and so on), the place given to Canadian studies is fairly reduced in proportion to the research performed there; but it was not as easy to contact Canadian researchers on site as it was the Danish researchers, which continues to be a source of great regret to me. As a good portion of my research was performed in Scandinavia and Greenland, I have deliberately given a significant place to Scandinavian studies.

In accordance with my desire to follow a dividing line from the older approaches, and pursuing the path of contemporary Scandinavian research (Danish in particular), I adopted a resolutely ethnographic approach, restoring the traditional Inuit source material to its rightful place (while recognizing its risks and limitations—interpretation and suggestion). In fact, what we know today is the official Icelandic version and the clerics' verson. This neglects another important player. The Inuit also memorialized the white man's presence in the Arctic for five centuries in their tales. Better than memorizing them, they carved them for posterity in walrus and narwhal ivory in the form of statuettes of white men whose trail can be traced from Greenland to Hudson Bay. These sources that have been common knowledge to all Scandinavian researchers for decades merit presentation to a wider audience.

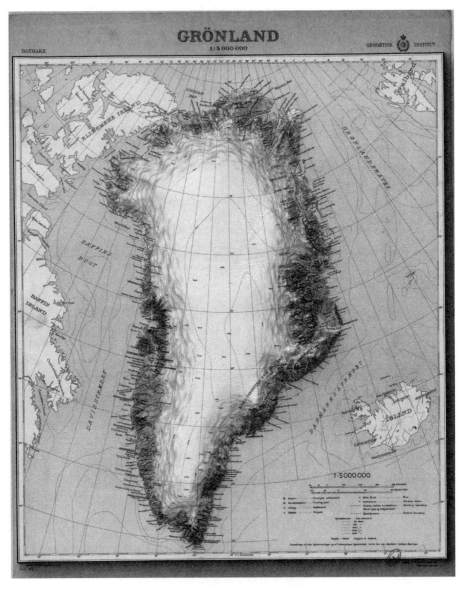

Fig. I.1. Map of Greenland, 1937. (See also color plate 1.)
*Courtesy of the Danish Geodata Agency*

## A WORD OF CAUTION

Because the Scandinavian population that colonized Greenland came
from Iceland, then Norway, I have made a compromise by grouping all

of them under the term Scandinavian or Nordic. I should stress that the name Norse could be the most appropriate as it includes all the Nordics of Greenland, Canada, and America.

I would like to draw the reader's attention to the risk of confusion surrounding the word *Greenlander*. During the entire Middle Ages, it was used to designate the Scandinavian population of Greenland; today it concerns the Inuit population (Kalaallit). Given the era under study here, and that neither Germany nor Italy existed as the states we think of today, the names "Germans" and "Italians" should be considered in quotes.

## SPECIFIC TERMINOLOGY

Sæter (plural: Sætar) translated as "shelter" or even "dwelling." In Latin it is "sessiones boréales." Often occurs in plural form combined with the term Nordr, such as Nordrsetur.

Skræling: medieval term attributed to the natives of Greenland, Canada, and America (puny or stunted being).

Kavdlunaat or Kavdlunak: name given to the Nordics by the Inuit; it probably dates back to the Middle Ages. Evolved into today's *kallunaat*.

Eskimo: an exonym that long served after the seventeenth century to designate the indigenous peoples of the Arctic, presumed to be of Algonquin origin (raw meat eater; other hypotheses exist).

Inuit: plural form of the word *inuk* (man, human being). This is the term used by all the inhabitants of the Arctic in referring to themselves, except for those of Greenland, who call themselves Kalaallit, untranslated until now; we'll give a possible explanation in chapter 5.

Eystribygð: the eastern Scandinavian colony in Greenland.

Vestribygð: the western Scandinavian colony in Greenland.

Brattahlið: meaning "the steep slope," a Viking site in the eastern colony where Erik the Red built an estate.

Independence, Saqqaq, Dorset, Thule, and Inussuk: the names of places where these cultures originated; for example, Independence Fjord in Greenland, or Cape Dorset on Baffin Island.

# 1

# THE INUIT IN GREENLAND

This subject could inspire an entire book of its own given its vastness and how much remains to be discovered. I will therefore confine myself to the entire Inuit culture contemporary to the Scandinavians; which is to say, from a medieval perspective.

Greenland's true past is slowly emerging, and in light of the research progress being made, existing theories will have to be revised despite the quality of the work put into them. It was long believed that the Inuit of the Thule culture were the most ancient wave of Inuit immigration, or even the Dorset people. We have, in fact, learned that the Inuit presence in Greenland goes back much further—some four thousand years (until the next discoveries). There were also periods when it was completely empty—for example, about seven hundred years between the Dorset I and Dorset II waves. The excavations made during the 1950s in Semermiut by Disko Bay provide an excellent illustration of this with clearly differentiated stratigraphic layers offering a perfect view of the various periods this area was populated. Let's make note of the cultures existing outside our historical context. We first have Independence 1 (2500–2000 BCE, some say a little before the year 2000 while others say 1800 BCE), which traveled over the North American islands with one group going down Greenland's western coast while the other traveled across the north. The Saqqaq (after 2000–1500 BCE, a little before 1000 for some and 700 BCE for others) followed on the heels of its predecessor, with whom they shared many points in common, settling in Greenland from west to east and absent from the Thule/Qaanaaq district. Independence 2

(1500–1000 BCE, some maintain a little before the year 1000 with others claiming 700 BCE), starting in the west, traveled over Peary Land and went down the eastern coast of Greenland. It shared a kinship with the Dorset culture, of which it was the precursor. But let's take a look at the groups who were contemporaries of the Vikings.

## DORSET CULTURE

The Dorset people were natives of Canada (Cape Dorset, Baffin Island), where their culture developed three thousand years ago. This culture has the distinctive feature of dividing itself into two branches; the most recent branch, which is contemporary to the Scandinavians, is called Dorset II. Its dates vary depending on the researcher. Some maintain it lasted from 700 to 900 CE, others say 800 to 1100.

This culture spread in two directions: Hudson Bay to the north and along the west cost of Labrador to the tip of Newfoundland to the south.

It was also present in Chesterfield Inlet, King William Island to the north of Baffin Bay and Devon Island, and in Ellesmere Island and Cape York in Northern Greenland. This culture developed north of the tree line. Caribou (reindeer) and walrus were the principal game animals. The Dorsetians had no dogs and pulled their sleds themselves. I have in mind a specific detail in the descriptions made by medieval Scandinavians: no allusion to Inuit dogs is ever made. Nor did they have kayaks. The first Inuit-Scandinavian contacts could therefore have taken place with members of this culture. After going through several phases, their houses adopted a quadrilateral shape. At the end of the Dorset Period, a system implementing construction of the foundation sunk beneath the ground was adopted to retain heat. Several features of the Dorset people make them comparable to the Saqqaq culture (2000–1000 BCE), and they both seem to have favored the same terraced sand or natural gravel sites by the capes backed by mountains. The question arises: Was this for defensive purposes?

They used an open fire surrounded by slabs of flat stone like the Saqqaq culture, but unlike them they did not have micro blades;

however, they did have comparable tools. They were also ignorant of the gimlet and dug summary holes with their tools. The Dorset tools such as the fish spear or trident with its many hooks and their much larger harpoons were more powerful than those of the Saqqaq culture. On the other hand, compared to the tools of the Thule culture, they were smaller and made from bone and flint, such as those found in Labrador east of Hudson Bay. The harpoon head is accompanied by a long cavity in the handle. Therkel Mathiassen discusses arrowheads whose back ends are hooked. Dorset culture material is much less developed than that of the Thule; they only have small harpoon heads, crudely carved stone blades, scrapers, knife handles, and needles.

This culture was particularly oriented around walrus hunting. The oldest Dorset encampment found at Kap Holbæk in Greenland (Danmark Fjord) is dated to within one hundred years on either side of 1000 CE. Remnants of this culture can be found along the western coast of Greenland up to Ammassalik on the eastern coast.

The first written account concerning this culture most surely comes from the *Islendingabók* (from around the beginning of Erik the Red's colonization of Greenland in 985) refers to traces of ancient settlements, stone tools, and the remains of hide boats found in the two Scandinavian colonies.

When we look more closely at Nordic source materials we shall see that the native inhabitants encountered by the Scandinavians during the earliest period of colonization avoided contact and fled. Was this why Jones concluded they possessed no long-range weapons or anything equivalent to those used by the Torngits (modern orthography: Tuniit), a mythical people of Nunavut who preceeded Inuit people and hunted caribou without bows, described in Inuit legends as very tall and very strong but very shy.*

The characteristic tools of the Dorsetians are the *ulu,* a woman's knife in the shape of a half moon, which is first encountered in this culture, and the snow knife, which also appears first in Dorset culture. They are also very likely the inventors of the *iglu* (igloo). Their oil

*See pages 17–18 for legends about them.

lamps were square and large. These lamps were generally smaller among nomadic peoples and oval in shape. Their typical artistic signature was ornamentation with carved diagonal lines.

Their powerful weaponry allowed them to take on formidable game animals like the walrus. This culture was primarily coastal, but they also made generous use of their inland territory. All researchers are in agreement about the strong Native American influence. Several Inuit stories show obvious resemblance to the bordering American Indian culture.

Finn Gad also found confirmation of Amerindian influence on mortuary customs: he cites the burial practice that first appeared in the Arctic and the ocher layer found in Inuit tombs as borrowed from Amerindian culture. These elements all seem to correspond fairly well with the descriptions of the first Norse-Inuit encounters described in the Sagas.

The Dorset migrated south from Cape York in North Greenland, during the period of Dorset II, and from Melville Bay down to Cape Farewell (Greenlandic: Uummannarsuaq; Danish: Kap Farvel), then headed back north up the eastern coast to Ammassalik. A new wave traveled toward Inglefield Land and Hall Land in northern Greenland.

In the area near Clavering Island, traces of the mixing of Dorset culture and later Thule culture have been identified: this took place around 900–1000 CE. The Dorset eastward migration may have taken longer.

Around 700 CE, another wave went southward from Cape York. The probability of a later migration toward East Greenland from the south also exists. Examples of Dorset dwellings from the fourteenth to fifteenth century (therefore at the same time as the Norse), also exist in East Greenland along Dødemandsbugten (Dead Man's Bay).

## THULE CULTURE

Just like Dorset culture, the Thule culture entered Greenland from Ellesmere Island by way of Smith Sound. Gad believes this represents a group of several cultures with specific features in common, but also differences such as the Inussuk culture. Gad depicts Ipiutak culture, which was established on both the coast and inland, as a transitional culture, a precursor of Thule culture. They had canoes but no specifically Inuit features.

The Thule culture appeared circa 800 to 1000 in northwestern Alaska, the Russian side of the Bering Strait.

The distinguishing feature of the Thule people was a powerful material culture, even greater than that of the Dorsetians. The harpoon is the characteristic tool of this culture, both the heavy harpoon for whales and, to a certain extent, the one used to hunt seals and walrus. Thule tools are large, equipped with blades of sharpened slate. Their main prey was the Greenland whale, which weighs 70 to 100 tons. Tools were a distinguishing feature of this people.

Their economy was primarily marine based. Their essential advantage was mastery of the sea, which allowed them to pursue game, as opposed to the Dorsetians, who hunted on solid land or at the edge of the ice pack. This did not prevent Thule peoples from hunting bear or caribou.

Their coastal economy depended greatly on large sea mammals and allowed larger concentrations of people to live in their settlements. Whale hunting was a group activity in small boats and kayaks, results of which could support large numbers. The Thule people brought a veritable technical revolution to Greenland. They introduced the sled, the kayak, the *umiaq* (a large boat made of sewn hides that could hold a good fifteen people with dogs and equipment), and other innovations. Specialists consider these three examples as wonders of their kind, from the technical point of view, and perfect examples of adaptation to the hostile Arctic environment. Mathiassen cites the following as technical innovations: drill bits, the three-pronged harpoon for birds, the salmon spear, the bola, the pickax for turf, pottery, and hollowed-out soapstone for use as stewpots or oil lamps. It was the Thule people who introduced the hunting of large sea mammals into Greenland. This culture with its highly developed technology was able to successfully compete with Norse culture: "The Thule people are dynamic and bellicose and either drove out or incorporated the Dorset people, who they had nonetheless learned the technique of hunting seals at their breathing holes in the ice from, as well as the construction of the *iglu*."[1]

# THE THULE CULTURE MIGRATIONS

The Thule traveled in two directions, essentially from Hudson Bay after crossing Canada from west to east. They either descended into southeast Canada by way of Baffin Island and Labrador or else northeast toward Ellesmere Island above Greenland.

## *The Southern Migration*
The native peoples currently living on the eastern coast of Canada are descendants of this culture and therefore closely related to the Inuit of Greenland. Compared with the central peoples west and north of Hudson Bay, coastal Thule culture was never really able to evolve. The ancient inland culture was therefore able to survive and perhaps mix with that of the Thule, bringing about the current paradox that, despite their obvious geographical proximity, today we find they are more different from their fellows on Canada's eastern coast than with the Alaskan Inuit.

## *The Northeast Migration*
It seems that the northeast migration took place quickly, which would explain why there are more points in common with Alaska. Around the years 900 to 1000, according to J. Meldgaard, this culture arrived in Greenland from north of Qaanaaq. It then went in two opposite directions: from Thule it went northeast before descending toward Ammassalik before going farther south, and from Thule toward the south going down to Cape Farewell and then moving up again following the eastern coast.

As evident, Qaanaaq was an obligatory transit point for the various waves of Inuit immigration. Thule culture is considered to be the oldest in Greenland. The discovery of an *umiaq* dating from 1440 in Peary Land, in the northern tip of Greenland, gives us leave to imagine a milder climate at that time as well as the possibility of sailing at a very high latitude for a period of a millennium.

It is possible and probable that Thule and Dorset cultures met and intermarried. The mixing of the two cultures of North Greenland seems to be a fact accepted by the Greenland artist Jens Rosing.[2] There is a high probability that the East Greenlanders (the Tunumiut) are descendants of the Dorset people, or at least a mixture of Thule and Dorset peoples. Several elements point toward this conclusion advanced by Mads Lidegaard: "There are common archaeological and cultural features between the Greenlanders of the east and those of the most northern areas of the west, which could easily be explained by such an old kinship."

## THE THULE HABITAT

Different kinds of dwelling shapes have been found; generally they are round but the bottom can be oval or in the clover shape, which is standard Thule practice. The size of the dwelling varies from a width of 10–11.5 feet, and from 13–16 feet by 16–19.5 feet deep. To hold warm air inside, a long entrance tunnel built at a different level served as a heat trap, something that is not found in the Saqqaq or Dorset cultures.

The use of whalebone for the building of homes is a characteristic feature of Thule culture, which goes hand in hand with their economy: whalebones and baleen formed the roofs or the frameworks of their houses.

A variant of this is found in Cape York: an entrance tunnel with a kind of reinforcement that probably corresponded to a "cooking corner." The Thule people didn't use the long hearth with an open fire like the Dorset people but instead large, triangular lamps with rounded and slightly curved corners. Finn Gad believed that the existence of different kinds of dwellings found from Disko bay to Qaqortoq (Julianehåb in Danish) in southern Greenland could be explained by an occasional lack of wood. I might add, because we are talking about Thule culture here and given the southern latitude, that it could also be an occasional lack of cetaceans. I would also like to point out that Gad avoids the possibility of the influence of the Scandinavian dwellings present at that same time, which we know were initially round and became square.

## INUSSUK CULTURE

The origins of this culture are vague. Various possibilities have been advanced such as the district of Qaanaaq in northwestern Greenland. Mathiassen places it near the Upernavik district at the lat 73° N in northern Greenland.

The Nordic histories in the Qaanaaq district reveal an influence from the south.* Inussuk culture is characterized by quite an advanced technology. In tandem with the hunting of large marine mammals, the hunting of seals and small whales by kayak stamps this culture so distinctively that it is hard to discuss it in terms of Thule culture. We should really discuss Inussuk culture as its own entity. This culture pushed a number of different Inuit techniques to perfection: the kayak with its bridge equipped for hunting, suitable tools, the water-proof anorak, a veritable hermetically sealed jumpsuit with a built-in buoy that allowed the hunter to climb aboard the back of a wounded whale and not drown.

Mathiassen is of the opinion that Inussuk culture existed around the beginning of the thirteenth century in northwestern Greenland. This culture rapidly spread in every direction, even going back to Qaanaaq. Modern research echoes this observation: Inussuk culture appeared in North Greenland under the influence of the Inussuk people of Upernavik.³

Inussuk culture also moved farther northward, extended into the east, then south. This is the culture encountered by the Scandinavians during the thirteenth and fourteenth centuries. If we accept the radical hypothesis of Helge Larsen, they were the ones who sealed the Scandinavians' fate: "When the Eskimos became a majority in South Greenland, the physically weakened Scandinavians could no longer match them. Vestribygð (the so-called western colony) was probably

---

*See chapter 3 for examples of stories on the origin of the white man and their comparison with dogs, placed in spots at a fair distance such as Staten Huk and Cape York. An even stranger fact, dogs were not used in South Greenland and almost never appear in either traditional Inuit or Scandinavian lore.

destroyed in 1350–60, and then again in 1379, the Eskimos ravaged Eystribygð (the eastern colony). It therefore was able to resist for a century."[4]

This quote nicely sums up the extermination theory that long dominated research. It is jazzed up here with the addition of Norse "weakening," if not "degeneration," which to this day has never been supported with any substantive evidence. We should recall that, in Larsen's defense, he did acknowledge the possibility of "alternating" peaceful and bellicose periods until the "final solution" of "total destruction, most likely around the year 1500."

Mathiassen thinks the Inussuk migration occurred in small isolated groups, which fits with their hunting economy following wandering game. Contemporary Nordic sources make no mention of large movements by the native inhabitants.

This culture dominated the entire country by the fourteenth century. Mathiassen places this Inussuk dominance on the southwestern coast of Greenland between the middle of the fourteenth century and the end of the fifteenth. Inussuk settlements were generally halfway up the fjords or along the coasts because their economy was based on marine life that required open waters, which was not the case with the inland areas of the fjords. Scandinavians had already settled in these areas.

There were two different kinds of Inussuk dwellings. Southern homes were small round constructions of earth clumps and stone. This habitat survived into the middle of the seventeenth century. A change took place in the northern dwellings during the sixteenth century when they adopted a square shape. Some homes even became double rectangles. The dwellings were still small and contained two corridors.

Gad noted that Inussuk settlements were distinctively divided in South Greenland. According to him, the Inussuk settlements were as compact as possible. Gad saw defensive reasons for this, "probably out of fear of the Scandinavians." He provides several figures concerning the area surrounding Eystribygð: "Of the 69 [Inuit] old style dwellings found in the 'southern' settlements, 55 were compressed together in only four spots,* which means they were compressed within very tight borders."⁵

This indirectly confirms the simultaneous presence of two populations, for it would otherwise have served no purpose for these Inuit homes and settlements to be so compact if Eystribyð was deserted. There are a small number of Inussuit ruins. Hunting conditions were far from ideal in this region; the climate was milder and both the Inuit and Norse populations were relatively higher. This could explain the relatively scarce evidence for Inussuk settled life. The migratory groups went to the tip of southern Greenland and began moving northward again along the eastern coast. Archaeology confirms an Inussuk presence after 1350 extending south from Kangaamiut on Greenland's western coast to the outskirts of Godthåb. Mathiassen's digs in the area of Qaqortoq revealed the presence of thirteen Inussuit houses dating from the end of the fifteenth century or early sixteenth century, the majority of which were placed halfway between the sea and the icepack. One of them was located by Prince Christian Sound in Anordluitsoq— the southernmost tip of Greenland.

I will give a quick glimpse of the Tuniit/Torngit question while discussing Dorset culture. This is a somewhat delicate issue as it remains far from elucidated and presents problems of classification. Should we classify it as an Inuit myth as is frequently the case in the Inuit stories referring to them, or should we rather include them as one of the cultures or Inuit culture groups that populated Greenland? This is more or less the solution I have opted for, albeit with reservations.

According to the legends, there was a robust, physically imposing people who once lived in Labrador and some parts of the Canadian Arctic. In Baffin Island and Greenland they are called the Tornit.⁶ Their physical strength seems to have particularly impressed their contemporaries: According to tradition, the Tornits of Baffin Island were gigantic. They dwelled on the northeast coast

---

*This comes out concretely as an average of thirteen homes per settlement, thus a population of about fifty-two to sixty-five people, based on a family unit consisting of four to five people. This concurs with the work of T. Mathiassen, which gives a density higher than five houses for the sites of Isua, Iglutalik, Uunartoq, and Anordluitsoq. (See map of Eystribygð, fig. 2.7 on p. 47.)

of Labrador, Hudson Bay, and the southern part of Baffin Island.[7]

Their prowess can be seen in the construction of their homes on impressive stone foundations. The Labrador Inuit say, "The Tuniit were able to build their houses with stones too heavy for the Inuit to carry. . . . They were able to build stone structures that the Inuit did not know how or were not able to build."[8]

It will be noted that while these regions all had a Scandinavian connection, as areas of Nordic exploration, or even outright colonization, they were also natural areas of the Amerindian people. The many physical feats and qualities attributed to the Scandinavians by Oleson and Duason are easily assumed by their Amerindian neighbors.

Citing Inuit legends, Oleson tells us that on Baffin Island and Labrador, the Tuniit were assumed to be from Greenland. In the western Arctic, they were believed to have come from the east. In Labrador, they were sometimes called Greenlanders but more frequently "Tornit." This word has never been translated.*

Oleson identifies them as the result of crossbreeding with the Scandinavians. He bases his position on several characteristic features of their material culture. For example, the long outfit typical of the Tornit would be a replica of the long medieval robe that was well known in the Nordic colonies of Greenland (great quantities of these robes were found in the excavations of Herjolfsnes). Oleson sees the Inuit habit of wearing their hair in a bun as a loan from the Icelandic hairstyle in the story of Bjorn Einarson Jórsalafari. I have offered the same hypothesis based on this same Scandinavian source from that time (fourteenth century), which can be clearly cross-referenced and authenticated. On the other hand, I refrain from mixing Scandinavians and Tornit together in light of the elements existing today.

The name caribou responds to the terms of *Tugtu/Tutu,* which we find, for example, in the description of a classic medieval place-name: *Tugtutôq*/Langey.† It is easy to see how worthwhile it is to compare terms

---

*A comparison should be made between Tuniit and Tunumiut, the name for the Inuit of the eastern coast of Greenland.

†Based on medieval sources, including Ivar Bårdsson's account, we know that this island had a large number of caribou.

such as the Inuit and medieval Nordic place-names as they can reflect the same subject. In this way a vanished word or concept can be rediscovered thanks to its still-existing Inuit counterpart. Moreover "*it*" has never meant simply "men." It is very simply only one of the most common plurals, which is why the plural of man (*inuk*) is "*it,*" meaning *Inuit.*

# 2

# THE VIKINGS IN GREENLAND

## THE SCANDINAVIAN COLONIZATION

In 982, Erik the Red, who had been exiled from Iceland for three years after his run-ins with that country's judicial system, landed in Greenland. According to *The Saga of the Greenlanders* (circa 1200), he would have made landfall on the eastern coast of Greenland at Miðjökul, the medieval Blåserk, then continued farther south. During his exile, Erik the Red explored the West Greenland coast, probably up to Disko Island. He also discovered traces of native settlements. He profited from his banishment, preparing for the colonization of Greenland by scouting out future settlements, thereby permitting colonists to establish themselves quickly three years later. This was toward the end of a period of warm climate characterized by vegetation dominated by shrubs. This climatic phase is also called "Betula glandulosa," "Salix phase" or even "the little optimum."

The figures concerning the total Norse population vary. For lack of irrefutable proof, I will cite the principal opinions on this subject:

> Thornvald Kornerup in 1900 dates the colonization from 985 to 1500 with 2,000 inhabitants divided among 190 tenant farms in Eystribygð, including 12 churches and 2 monasteries, and 1,000 inhabitants divided among 90 tenant farms in Vestribygð, including 4 churches.
>
> The Italian Corrado Gini (1956) gave the figure of 300 to 700 colonists at the beginning of colonization. During the most

prosperous period, the Norse colony numbered 280 farms and 16 churches: 190 farms and 12 churches in Eystribygð, 90 farms and 4 churches in Vestribygð.

The Danish Poul Nørlund believes that colonization began with 500 to 700 inhabitants, but Keller notes that he uses his sources in a less than critical fashion.

The Norwegian Kristian Keller (1989) advanced the figure of 1,000 inhabitants at the beginning. The maximum threshold of Scandinavian population would have varied between 3,500 and 5,000 inhabitants divided among 400 farms.

Knud Krogh (1982) opted for the figure of 4,000 to 6,000 inhabitants divided among 250 farms in Eystribygð and 80 farms in Vestribygð, giving us a total of 330 farms. On average, the density would have been 12 to 18 inhabitants.

Jens Rosing (1978) spoke of 500 to 600 men in the beginning and of 3,000 to 4,000 inhabitants later scattered among 190 farms at Eystribygð, which also included 12 churches and 2 cloisters, and 90 farms at Vestribygð, with 4 more churches. The total here is 280 farms.

In 1979 Thomas MacGovern gave figures of 4,000 to 5,000 inhabitants at Eystribygð and 1,000 inhabitants at Vestribygð.

The total population based on the most optimistic figures of the Danish administrator of Greenland (nineteenth century) Heinrich Rink, was 11,000 people. Norwegian explorer Fridtjof Nansen's more pessimistic figure was 2,000 people. Corrado Gini opted for a figure in between but closer to the maximum by basing his conjecture on the funds collected for Peter's Pence, the clerical tax sent to Rome. This, according to Gini, amounted to a tribute from about 7,000 people. The author notes that this tax included the Vinland* tithe, which has no effect on the number

---

*Name given by the Norse to a part of North America. Historians are still arguing about its identification and meaning. To put the two opposing theories as succinctly as possible, one opts for *vin* (wine) based on Adam of Bremen (original Cap. CCCIX/CCXLVI), also in G.H.M.III/406–7), the more recent one supported by the Swedish Söderberg (article of Oct. 30, 1919, in *Sydsvenska dagbladet*) opting for the translation of inhabitants as the people of Vinland generally came from Greenland.

As we are looking at the ancient sources, and as this allows me to demonstrate their value, let's cite the Swedish archdeacon Olaus Magnus, who in his famous *Carta Marina* gave the figure of 30,000 inhabitants. Could a churchman of his importance be so badly mistaken especially when using the very meticulous account books of the church? Per Lillieström's contemporary research reframes this tally and comes up roughly with the same figure as Gini. He rightly goes back to the earlier sources of the Norwegian archbishop Einar Gunnarsson of 1250. According to him Greenland represented one-third of a normal bishopric in Norway. In the thirteenth century the Norwegian population had climbed to about 560,000 inhabitants, divided into five dioceses of approximately 112,000 inhabitants each. So a third of a bishopric gives us 37,333, or something fairly close to the figure given by Olaus Magnus, which seems reasonable to me when including with the Greenland population those of its dependencies in the Arctic and to the west. The optimistic figures of 5,000 to 7,000 inhabitants in Greenland during its prosperous period no longer seem so unrealistic. Another major implication of this reasoning: about 25,000 Nordics would have populated the lands of the West spanning the area from the Far North down to the famous Vinland.

To return to Greenland, the colonists there were divided into three different colonies. The most prosperous, as shown by the figures, was located in the south at Eystribygð (or "Østerbygd," according to the contemporary official Danish administration)—in other words, the East Colony. This was where its leader, Erik the Red, lived in Brattahlið (Qassiarsuk today) but which also later served as the bishopric of Garðar (Igaliku today). Two factors played in this colony's favor: the gentler climate thanks to a branch of the Gulf Stream that allowed for more luxurious plant growth, and its relatively closer location to Iceland. This name, the "East Colony," would lead all archaeological and historical research astray, because for several centuries a fruitless search for this

---

(*cont. from p. 21*) "pastures, prairies." Ingstad (1982/82–83) notes that the term *vin* in Old Norse, meant "beiteland, Gressmark" and could be found in old Scandinavian placenames like Vinje and Vinås.

Fig. 2.1. Greenland, Brattahlíð ruins: this is at the spot known as "the steep slope," where Erik the Red settled as leader of the Norse colony at the very start of the colonization in 985. Over the centuries, the ruins have almost vanished, falling victim to their use as a source of building materials for the local populations. One notable historical irony: the current inhabitants are pursuing the same kind of farming activities as the Viking-era inhabitants. (See also color plate 2.)
*Photo by J. Privat*

colony was concentrated on the eastern coast of Greenland. It was only with the excavations of Daniel Bruun in 1894, that its location would be definitively placed in South Greenland (on the same latitude as Oslo).

Mellembygð, the central colony, had a reduced presence of twenty-five farms and no church, It is generally poorly known as it is often incorporated into Eystribygð, from which it is actually not so far away. Mellembygð has no historical basis: its name is purely technical.

Vestribygð is located in the vast complex of fjords of the Nuuk/ Godthåb region. This city is now the capital of Greenland. Vestribygð was located some 170 miles from Eystribygð—a sailing distance of six to twelve days. Its latitude is the same as Trondheim in Norway. Purely for reasons of navigation such as favorable winds and currents, this place was preferred for voyages west—which is to say, to America and Canada.

The density of the Scandinavian population in Greenland was

strongly influenced by the possibility of colonization inland. The division of most of the ruin groups seems to correspond fairly well with the distribution of plant resources. Contrary to the prevailing scientific behavior, I would consider with extreme circumspection all the alarmist sources—medieval or later—that suggest an impoverished Norse colony, or a material decline, for I suspect a certain bias of scribes or even that of religious or royal authorities. In fact, accepting the decline and penury of the Greenland colonies assumes and legitimizes the aid and intervention of the authorities. This had the special advantage of validating the dominant theories, notably during the medieval and post-medieval periods, finding in this economic explanation a means of passing over other versions in silence, such as frequent and extensive contacts with the indigenous pagans of Greenland. To the contrary, several tangible signs counter the prevailing view—such as the farmlands in the south with their irrigation canals; the imposing center of Garðar; the evolution of the Scandinavian dwelling from a simple longhouse to multiple dwellings; the interest shown by foreign sailors in Greenland, who were present there until the sixteenth century; the delivery of flourishing tithes to Rome; and the Scandinavian clothing that kept up with the latest styles in the second half of the fifteenth century. All of these elements testify, according to Corrado Gini, if not to a high level of life, at least to a normal, well-adjusted colonial lifestyle with "an underwhelming lack of dramatic features"[1] as noted by Keller in 1989. Both historical sources and the architecture suggest the presence of prosperous farms with large outbuildings.

The new lands were shared as follows:

Herjolf, wealthy Icelandic merchant who had authority over the cape of the same name as well as the neighboring fjords, Herjolfsnes and Herjolfsfjord.

Ketil, holder of Ketilsfjord, which bears his name and corresponds to the contemporary Tessermiut.

Hrafn, holder of Hrafnsfjord, which is Alluitsoq today.

Solvi, holder of the Solvadal Valley, which bears his name and is now probably Kangikitsoq.

Helgi Thorbrandsson, heir of Alptafjord, which is Sermilik.

Thorbjorn Gloria, holder of Siglufjord, which is Uunartoq today and home to thermal springs.

Einar, holder of Einarfjord, or Igaliku.

Hafgrim, holder of Hafgrimsfjorðr, or Eqaluit. The richest settlement of Vatnahverfi (a lake region) corresponding to the largest inland farm settlements of the colony.

Arnlaug, holder of Arnlaugsfjord, which was probably to the northeast of Eystribygð.

Erik the Red took as his holding the island facing Dyrnæs, which is Narsaq today, giving it its earlier name, Eriksey; then the settlement of Brattahlið (the steep slope), which is now Qassiarsuk and where farming is still practiced today. The neighboring fjord, Tunulliarfik, also carries his name in Eriksfjord.

Fig. 2.2. Reconstruction of the Brattahlið church (Qassiarsuk today):
with its low circular surrounding wall it is strongly reminiscent of the Celtic influence
discussed in chapter 9. It is consistent with the first generation of churches
with its incorporation of an insulating layer of peat. (See also color plate 3.)
*Photo by J. Privat*

Fig. 2.3. Greenland, reconstruction of the Tjodhild church:
Tjodhild, the wife of Erik the Red, converted to Christianity. The main entrance
looks out over the fjord. Notable is the extreme simplicity of the building (Qorlotoq
type), which contrasts greatly with the development of more impressive religious
constructions (Garðar, Hvalsey) inspired by continental models. (See also color plate 4.)
*Photo by J. Privat*

## GREENLAND'S SCANDINAVIAN ECONOMY

The Scandinavians imported a socioeconomic system shared by the rest of the Scandinavian world including the Hebrides, the Orkneys, Shetland, Faroe, and Iceland—a predominantly agrarian society. This is important, as we shall learn, for foreigners used it to describe the Scandinavians for several centuries not only in Greenland but in America as well. As strange as it may appear for a country like Greenland, the Scandinavians raised livestock. But remember that the climate was milder at that time. Hunting and fishing provided a secondary source of food.

The growing of cereal grains was quite limited for physical and climatic reasons: poor soil, salinity, higher levels of precipitation, and the essential need for a summer to be long enough to grow dwarf wheat were all factors that restricted the quantity and quality of the harvests.

To a certain extent, dairy production offered a non-negligible supply of high-energy products. We should not overlook the cultural factor: to varying degrees, Norway, the native land of the ancestors of the Greenland colonists, brings to mind the same characteristics with regard to climate and rugged terrain and offered the same dependence on live-stock raising and dairy products. This factor still exists and still poses some economic problems by virtue of the lack of competitiveness. These activities were highly sensitive to the climatic instability of Greenland, which led to the increased raising of sheep and goats. The disadvantages of poor conditions for growing grain are echoed in the medieval Norwegian book *Konungs skuggsía*[2] (*The Royal Mirror*) of 1240–1263, or again in the *Saga of Erik the Red* (*Eiríks saga rauða*), which mentions a complete lack of grain necessary for the baking of bread as well as the brewing of beer. This lack of wheat seems to have struck the author of the *Royal Mirror* quite soundly as in the space of a few pages he returns to this subject three times: "In this land, the majority [of people] don't know bread and have never seen it."[3]

However, in light of archaeological excavations, grain agriculture must have existed as several millstones have been discovered. The written sources should also be taken circumspectly because of bias. The author of the *Royal Mirror*—a churchman—could have intentionally exaggerated his dismal depiction of the Norse diet to encourage resumed contact with Greenland. This description offers a good illustration of the bias of sources I mentioned earlier and gives the impression of an impoverished community lacking even the primary foodstuff of that time—bread. The colonists' thriving livestock industry and the abundant game tones down this image of destitution. The archaeological excavations of Nipaitsoq provide a different image of penury. They attest to the supplementary contributions of wild plants as well as seaweed to the colonists' diet. Among them we find angelica (*Angelica officinialis*); Iceland moss (*Cetraria islandica*), which was once eaten in Iceland and Norway in a kind of porridge; arenaria (*Eiysus arenarius*), eaten raw or dried with milk or cream; and dulse or sea lettuce flakes (*Rhodymenia palmata*), a flat, deep-red seaweed that is highly nutritious and that Ingstad described as follows: "It has been used in Norway and

Iceland since time immemorial, and is even mentioned in the sagas and law books. Due to the high esteem it was held in it was even used as a currency in exchange for butter, wool, and meat. This seaweed was also used by the Eskimos."[4]

Nevertheless, several authors agree that all digestible flora, even seaweed, went mainly to animals—a habit still common. Livestock raising, which was thriving according to Corrado Gini, included cattle, sheep and goats; this latter species is surely responsible for the deterioration of the ecologically fragile terrain of Greenland's Arctic environment. Thomas McGovern is of the opinion that this livestock was intended for the production of dairy products and wool. Given how hard livestock replacement could be, I generally accept this claim with the observation that this primary function could change under the influence of external factors such as shifts in climate. McGovern surely made this same correction when, in 1985, he published the following table (cited by C. Keller[5]) concerning the Norse diet in the settlement of Eystribygð.

### 1. NORSE DIET

*(The numbers indicate the percentage of animal species consumed by the Scandinavians based on the total number of bones discovered.)*

| Species | Coastal | Inland |
|---|---|---|
| Livestock | 15.34% | 16.64% |
| Goats | 21.78% | 40.18% |
| Caribou | 5.87% | 1.21% |
| Seals | 56.80% | 41.28% |

This table listing the bone remnants found in six ruins allows us to draw several conclusions. First of all, we can see that the Nordic people living inland drew particularly from their goat stock, and that this stock was twice as large as that found in the coastal settlements, and we also see that caribou were more numerous on the coast. This is probably because the caribou were seeking protection from mosquitoes, which drove them to seek out the windier coastal regions as is the case in Lapland.

The consumption of seal is almost the same inland and on the coast; in other words, there was little difference between coastal and continental diet.

All these figures must be taken reservedly because the material analyzed here is limited in comparison to the large number of existing ruins. On the other hand, another analysis performed on the remains of the Vestribygð colony gave similar results.[6]

### 2. ANALYSIS OF A FARM BORDER IN VESTRIBYGÐ
#### (Niaqusat: listed under reference number 48)

|  | Domestic Animals | Caribou | Seals |
|---|---|---|---|
| **Deepest Layer** | 23.51% | 9.66% | 66.26% |
| **Surface Level** | 15.19% | 7.32% | 77.48% |

I will make several observations on these figures. First of all, it is logical to assume some kind of climate change compelled the colonists to begin eating their own working stock—the livestock intended to supply dairy products. The abundance of livestock bones corresponding to five head of cattle, illustrates a worsening of the climate and the consequent abandonment of the settlement.

Jørgen Meldgaard gives an opposite interpretation. He believes this is a sign of abundance. He also notes the presence of a barrel of curdled milk, mussels, a caribou carcass, a seal breast, four partridges, pieces of cow and mutton, an eel, three small fish, and the remains of a hare. There was an abundance of fuel for making fires. This gives us an image that is starkly opposite that of scarcity. Meldgaard offers two possible explanations for these remains—a battle with the Inuit or else a plague—but he provides no evidence and ignores the hypothesis of an intentional departure. Two Scandinavian skulls pierced by Inuit arrows found in Niaqusat are the sole confirmation of his hypothesis.

The consumption of the Scandinavian livestock is not necessarily illogical; the increasingly cold climate caused a reduction of pasture-lands and in this case the futility of a livestock solely for the purpose of dairy products. This behavior seems widespread as sheep, cow, and goat bones have been found in all the Norse farms. The substantial consumption of seals seems to confirm deteriorating climate conditions. Could the Scandinavians have adjusted so poorly to their environment? This notable consumption of seals could also be seen as a desire to not eat all the livestock that was, after all, their working capital.

Corrado Gini thinks along these same lines: "The populace did not only obtain its food from livestock raising, but also thanks to hunting at sea and on land. This was valid both for the coastal farms and for the farms located inland along the fjords."[7]

Knowing that the Scandinavians ate a particular category of seal—the hooded seal (*Cystophora cristata*), the bearded seal (*Erignathus barbatus*), and the harbor seal (*Phoca vitulina*)—because they were migratory, we must conclude rather efficient means of communication existed between the coast and inland: "These seals seem to have been caught by Scandinavians. This means that they were taken in open water during their migration rather than on the ice imprisoning the fjords."[8]

Table 2 indicates an 8 percent reduction in the consumption of domestic animals and an 11 percent increase in the consumption of seals.

The consequence of Scandinavian dependency on livestock was a sedentary existence inland by the fjords where the continental climate was favorable to a fairly luxurious flora conducive to farming and livestock. This is still the case, in an irony of history; these same Scandinavian settlements are now home to Greenland farmers and livestock raisers.

I would also like to mention Ketilsfjord/Tasermiut, the sole place in Greenland where trees grow: birch trees that are about 7 feet tall. Keller also mentions rich plant growth, citing a birch forest in the Scandinavian Eystribygð colony that grew at an altitude over 1,200 feet. This corresponds to the maximum altitude on which archaeologists have found Norse ruins. We also know that the report of the Norwegian bishopric of Bergen's envoy, Ivar Bårdsson (second in command to the bishop and nicknamed "The Greenlander" for his long stay), dating circa 1360,[9] mentions the presence of a forest in South Greenland. All of this concurs with archaeological findings that reveal high density inland by the fjords. McGovern believes haymaking was a major seasonal activity, with the harsh winters often beginning during the fall. The numbers of Scandinavian livestock had to be reduced, probably due to the difficulty in keeping them fed, which would explain the substantial number of dead calves—stillborn or ill—that have been uncovered in various excavations.

An agrarian economy requires an effective—if not substantial—material infrastructure like the large farms with outbuildings, barns, stables, storehouses, and irrigation canals found in Eystribygð, which forced the Scandinavians to adopt a sedentary lifestyle. Large game animals like caribou were not novelties to the Nordic colonists. Caribou bones can be found in all the Scandinavian sites. "The frequency of its consumption reached levels of 25–30% of total Norse consumption, indicating how intensely this resource was exploited."[10]

Fishing provided an important source of protein, but it did not play an essential role comparable to that in the seventeenth or eighteenth centuries. Based on the excavations, marine resources, especially seals, played a major role in the Norse economy. Even the farms in the most remote parts of the interior reveal a diet strongly based on seal consumption. McGovern offers the example of the e.167 farm in Eystribygð, a good day's walk inland, located approximately 700 feet above sea level. It shows that seals were 25 percent of this farm's residents' diet. The coastal farm of Niaqusat in Vestribygð (v.48) shows a level of 68 percent. Corrado Gini also notes the same thing with respect to the large sea mammals, as shown by the substantial remnants on the inland farms: "Even inland, the large sea mammals formed an important factor of the economy, which means that the farmers of the valleys must have gone hunting for whale and seal up to the open sea."[11]

Considered from an economic angle, this organization seems elementary, if we connect this with the fact that the best agrarian sites were located inland along the fjords, the prestige gained by this placement, and the factor of the riches provided by the sea. Seen in hindsight, it is obvious we should disregard deceptive geographical considerations, and, conversely, medieval sources (the written sources) tell us that only the large farmers owning bigger boats made expeditions to the north, toward the Nordrsetur. This affluence could only be procured from hunting large sea mammals rather than farming.

The primary seal species exploited by the Scandinavians were the harp or Greenland seal (*Pagophilus groenlandicus*), the harbor or common seal (*Phoca vitulina*), the hooded seal (*Cystophora cristata*), and the bearded seal (*Erignathus barbatus*). Keller and McGovern both believe they were hunted collectively using the same techniques found in the Faroe Islands and Greenland today: "As no harpoon (or even a trident) has ever been found in a Scandinavian site, these seals must have been caught by net or during group hunts in boats during which the seals would have been driven toward solid land or the ice field to be slaughtered."[12]

This technique is therefore very different from those of the native Greenlanders who hunted on the ice, which specifically required mastery of the harpoon and is adapted for the long Arctic winters. Numerous researchers share McGovern's and Keller's opinion on the absence of harpoons. On the other hand, Helge Ingstad and Vera Henriksen sing a very different tune, although apparently without any physical proof. They cite *The Saga of the Sworn Brothers,* which suggests the presence of harpoons: "The skald of Kolbrun was also there. He (Thormod) took a seal harpoon that others had cast on the ground."[13]

According to Henriksen, this harpoon was used in Norway and Iceland. Ingstad cites other even more plausible pieces of evidence such as Mathiassen's excavations in Upernavik (North Greenland) in which "pieces of metal blades from harpoons" were discovered. This weapon would therefore have clearly existed in Greenland. To boot, it was found in an Inussuk site (these Inuit people were heavily influenced by Scandinavians, as we saw earlier).

The absence of harpoons in the digs—according to McGovern— doesn't necessarily serve as proof they didn't exist among the Scandinavians of Greenland. If we consider the example of the Vestribygð bells that totally disappeared, but were certainly real, we can also suppose that a tool like the harpoon, as well as all tools and weaponry useful in hunting, would have been among the priority items taken by the Scandinavians when they deserted Vestribygð.

The Scandinavians were very dependent on the annual passage of hooded seals and other migratory animals: "These animals traveled along Greenland's southwest coast during the months of May and June on their way to the Disko region. On their return to Newfoundland, they would pass by again in February and March."[14]

The Inuit preferred, as they still prefer, the harp or Greenland seal, a sedentary species that lives in the fjords. There is no need to stress the advantages of a game animal whose presence is permanent. The role of fishing seems harder to determine. Nevertheless we cannot reject its presence as Inuit traditional lore (discussed in chapter 3) refers to the colonists fishing for salmon. The presence of foreign nations in these waters also emphasizes fishing's value. With regard to the Scandinavians, this can be seen as a supplemental activity, for they were known for their exports of fur and ivory, as well as high-quality homespun cloth, but not for their fish, unlike Iceland, where this resource even attracted British sailors. Whatever the case may be, the source texts glide over this point in silence. So we have no basis to speak of large-scale fishing operations, which would have presumed a Norse presence on the coast that is rejected by archaeology because of the rural economy.

In contrast to other bone remnants, few fish bones remain, probably due to their greater vulnerability to the acidity of the soil. We should, however, note the possible use of crushed fish remains for livestock. This still-existing technique also gives an unpleasant fishy taste to meat.

## OTHER ACTIVITIES

Large game hunting, from the perspective of the profits involved, played a certain role in the life of Scandinavians as a major export item. It is very poorly documented, but this may have been intentional. If we compare the problems of supply and competitiveness facing Norway, Iceland, and Greenland, the first two countries could focus on more profitable products, which at that time was fish. The Hanseatic Market was quite demanding and not far away, fishing was flourishing, and manual labor was available. The situation was different in Greenland. The sole source of big profits was found in Arctic products such as the gyrfalcon, ivory, leather hides, and furs. This was the sole trade worthy of the name capable of attracting foreign customers.

Several medieval sources refer to the riches of the Arctic such as the narwhal, whose ivory horn is the source of the unicorn legend, and the walrus, equally valued for its ivory tusks. This is made evident by its appearance in numerous medieval sculptures and religious objects. Walrus hide was also valued highly throughout Europe. Eugene Beauvois quotes the archbishop Jon Raude of Trondheim,[15] who noted that after 1270 the sole solvency for the Scandinavians lay in seal- and cowhides, and whalebone and baleen. Pope Martin IV (1281–1285) replied that it should all be converted into hard cash and sent to the Holy See as soon as possible.

Polar bear fur was greatly appreciated and deemed worthy of a king. Its value is perfectly illustrated by the reception of the Danish king Sveinn Ulfsson's court of the Icelander Audunn's gift of a live polar bear circa 1060. The king's gratitude was also very telling of this present's value: Audunn was thanked with a sum of money covering the cost of a pilgrimage to Rome and a ship laden with precious cargo such as rings and silver.[16]

This practice seems to have been fairly commonplace and greatly appreciated as it is mentioned on a variety of occasions. Norwegian kings were in the habit of giving polar bears to their royal peers to gain alliances or support. For example, the powerful king Håkon Håkonson gave King Henry III of England a polar bear as a gift and, no slouch in this department, also gave one to Emperor Frederick II. To continue this little story, this kind of bear currency must have enjoyed a certain success, as it seems another polar bear was next given to the Egyptian sultan El Kamil by the emperor.

Although no source mentions it, it can be presumed that the arctic fox, or blue fox, was not overlooked, even though its value did not begin to equal that of the polar bear. One possible confirmation is from Schledermann's excavations in the Canadian Arctic where he found fox and polar bear traps. Although Inuit identification is most likely, it does not remove the possibility that this technique was borrowed from the medieval Scandinavians as the Inuit had no need to capture live animals. The gyrfalcon was incontestably a valuable source of revenue. Here again, the medieval sources are fairly longwinded: these falcons were reserved for kings.*

The *Grønlands Historiske Mindesmærker*[17] also stresses the falcon's value: "From the time of Arild (until the present), the falcons (especially the white ones) were very popular in Iceland. In 1280, the king of Norway said that Icelandic falcons (regarded as the best) were worth a fortune." The falcon was holder of a powerful symbolism. Arab merchants even came to Bergen to put in their orders. Prytz cites Arab author Abdul Hasan Ali as giving white falcons a value of one thousand dinars as well as an Arabic proverb that a white falcon was worth twenty female slaves. As the overall theory would have it, these peripheral activities took place in the Disko region (Greenland). As no archaeological findings confirm this assertion, I reject it as do several other contemporary Scandinavian researchers. We will see from the traditional native lore, the testimony of outside Europeans, and various geophysical factors like polynias, that a Canadian identification is the most plausible.

Although more advanced than other medieval political systems (for example, the existence of a parliament), Norse Greenland society was far from democratic. Contrary to McGovern's contention, it would be extremely unlikely that all Scandinavians had direct access to the veritable manna that would be their reward for taking part in these expeditions. I am basing my objection to this claim on contemporary commentary taken from the *Hauksbók* (fourteenth century), which leaves no room for doubt: social rank determined who went on the remote Nordrsetur expeditions. It seems obvious given the material assets (boats, crews) that were called for. "All the wealthy farmers of Greenland had large ships designed for sailing toward the northern hunting grounds, equipped with all kinds of hunting items."[18]

It is clear that only the owners of large farms had the means to put together such expeditions. Keller sensibly arrives at the same

*K. Prytz cites the diplomatic sources of the *Diplomatarium Norvegicum* XIX, no. 167: "They [the falcons] are the most precious gift on the scale of values."

conclusions: "Most likely, these hunting expeditions were organized by the 'aristocracy'* or by the bishop."

The economic reasons were touched on earlier. A predominantly agrarian society—in an Arctic environment to boot—could not send all its laborers hunting during the brief Arctic summer. This agrarian activity has been duly established and confirmed either by archaeology or by the accounts of both the Nordic colonists and foreign visitors.† I will, however, share one important reflection: this observation seems to apply only to the eastern colony: Eystribygð. The disappearance of Vestribygð seems to show a democratization of this fortune hunting as suggested by the Swedish researcher Per Lilliestrōm.[19] In fact, Ivar Bårdsson's expedition only found livestock wandering free in the deserted colony. This livestock could not survive on its own in an environment like Greenland, if only for its need to be milked. Lilliestrōm concluded this demonstrated the overall absence of the colonists here in search of their fortunes in Canadian hunting grounds, leaving only a few old men and children to keep watch over the animals. These individuals avoided contact with Ivar Bårdsson's expedition in 1342, a conclusion I support (this point will be revisited in greater detail).

The widespread presence of ivory objects throughout the colony would be explained by the total absence of cash confirmed by all archaeological digs in Greenland. We know that the Scandinavians paid their tithes with ivory or swapped it in exchange for imported goods. It is completely logical to imagine the use of ivory as currency for external and internal transactions. What could be more normal than a rich farmer recently returned from Nordrsetur to pay the peasant who took care of his lands with precious ivory, which this latter gladly accepted knowing he would be able to exchange it for the rare goods on the next ship to make landfall there as "Arctic specialties" were highly sought after due to their value in the export market.

Given the scope of the ivory trade as either export product in the general market or delivered to Rome as tithes, there is legitimate reason

---

*I added these quotation marks.
†See chapter 11; accounts, especially those of the Portuguese, identified Greenland as the "Land of Laborers," or Terra Labrador.

to consider trade with the natives as its source. For the economic reasons mentioned above, as massive expeditions were not conceivable, small Norse expeditions to the north could return with far from negligible quantities of ivory as shown in the written medieval sources.* The tithes for the crusades of 1327 were anywhere from 900 to 1,400 pounds, depending on the sources. McGovern cites figures of 1,400 pounds of ivory intended for tithes and 34 pounds as Peter's Pence.† This offers a glimpse of the sums in play here. These figures represent the equivalent of six years' hunting for the payment of tithes. A distinguishing feature of the 1327 tithe is that it consisted essentially of walrus ivory, unlike that of 1282, in which walrus leather, seal hides, and the teeth and sinews of walrus are mentioned. Keller thinks it is hard to imagine the Arctic as some kind of El Dorado on the basis of the 1327 tithe, at least in the latter half of the thirteenth century. I would object that it is risky to take only the tithes the colonists paid in ivory as a basis as these individuals seem to have been more than reluctant to surrender these payments. In this case, a delivery of the smallest possible tithe—in the context of rebelliousness—is quite plausible. Without seeking to underestimate the Norse capabilities in the dangerous hunting of walrus (explicit examples can be found in Norway and Iceland) we cannot dismiss the appeal and value of collaboration with the natives. This hypothesis is taken quite seriously in contemporary studies, especially in Denmark and Norway.

> The Eskimos of northwest Greenland had ivory in quantity, as is shown by the archeological remnants of their settlements. If ivory and other products could be obtained thanks to the swap of small metal trinkets or worn-out tools, the exploitation of this lode would bring the Scandinavians excellent profits.[20]

---

*The medieval Norse source texts continue describing isolated Nordrsetur voyages (for example, that of 1379 in chapter 7). But keep in mind Lillieström's pertinent observations that the Vestribygð colony seems to have made many such journeys. This is supported by the written sources coming from Eystribygð, where the clergy was all powerful and apparently had little liking for the other colony that they thought dissolute.

†*Denarius Sanctus Petri,* an annual tribute to the church. —*Trans.*

Another reason for my support of this opinion is based on the implication that has so far gone unremarked of this famous tithe payment of 1327 with five hundred walrus tusks (in other words, 250 animals). What a jackpot, you may be thinking! Divided by six years, this equals about 41.5 walruses a year, which is far from the "scores" seen in Svalbard and implying a carnage that the natives would never have tolerated. I conclude from this that this was the fruit of a swap with them. A Roman source indirectly supports this hypothesis. We know that the *annuata,* or the annual revenue, of the Garðar diocese circa 1123 would rise to 250 florins during prosperous times.[21] If we can take the secretary of the Roman congregations at his word, the *annuata* payable during fifteen years by the new bishops and fathers superior represented only one-third of the annual revenues. This means that the actual revenues of the Garðar diocese would have climbed over a time to 750 florins. This is a considerable sum that is equivalent to the revenues of a bishopric like Venice and more than a third higher than that of the Orkneys.[22]

Also knowing that ivory served as the currency of exchange with foreign sailors, the quantity sent to Europe, if we judge it based on the frequency of the foreign presence there during the fifteenth century, must have been *much more* substantial. In fact, the figures given for the year 1327 have the flaw of completely concealing the possibility of exportation of ivory to destinations other than Rome. Keller acknowledges that "walrus hunting had become important not only as a source of profit, but as a means of transforming simple taxable products [for the church] into an exchange currency with advantages abroad."[23]

It is easy to see the value of collaboration with the natives, a theory championed mainly by Ingstad. To bring this argument to a close, I would like to say that I generally accept McGovern's conclusion that sums up the Greenland Norse economy as extensive annual exploitation of the land's resources in the continental zone and fjord borders and an intensive seasonal exploitation of sea mammals in the zone along the sea coast.

I would like to add here my own personal variant of a lucrative but discrete seasonal exploitation of the riches of the Far North in remote and "unknown" Arctic regions. The intensive but seasonal rural activities required a certain amount of settling down, especially in Eystribygð, that was different from Inuit activities. Vestribygð, located farther north and thus less suitable for agriculture, seems to have been more open to these remote, lucrative expeditions.

## THE SCANDINAVIANS AND
## THEIR ENVIRONMENT

In these remote times, environment played a considerable role as the Scandinavians learned at its expense. All the researchers are in agreement as to the destructive effect the colonists had on their environment. We must believe that they failed to learn from their Icelandic (in)experience, for they repeated the same devastating mistakes in Greenland. I am not seeking to present this as the decisive factor in the disappearance of the Scandinavians, but contrary to various other arguments that have spawned numerous theories such as the black plague, the destitution or degeneration of the colonists, an invasion of caterpillars, and so forth, that may have had more or less substantial but in no way fatal effects, the destruction of the environment by the Scandinavians was such that it cannot be passed over in silence. Before the arrival of the Scandinavians, Greenland's vegetation was dominated by birch and willow (*Salix*). This vegetation was quickly destroyed by the colonists, allowing weeds to replace it. Several experts have stressed this almost fatal destruction's connection to an activity such as livestock raising: "Referring to the climate fluctuations, pollen analysis, and recorded cases of soil erosion, he [Krogh] defends his theory that this decline must have been caused by overuse of pastures."[24]

Knud Krogh seems to favor this factor over all other explanations for the Scandinavian disappearance. All the researchers recognize the negative influence of an economy based on livestock in a milieu as fragile as the Arctic. I earlier described the scope of goat meat consumption by the colonists. Gini pertinently underscored the harmful consequences caused by large numbers of these animals.

In fact, as opposed to other ruminants, the goat has the singular feature or flaw of tearing out his food and not cutting it. The dire consequences of this in these latitudes is easy to grasp: reduced fodder from the practice of free ranging during the spring, ground erosion from wind and water, and subsidence of the terrain. "Leaves were collected for fodder and the livestock aggravated the damage by browsing on the tops of shrubs and small trees, and preventing their growth. In this way humans destroyed the essential protection of the other plants and allowed wind to erode the soil and sand to replace it."[25]

It is clear that human responsibility is beyond question. It can also be seen in the use of strips of sod and clumps of earth to build Scandinavian homes. The ravages caused by the livestock and the haymaking caused injuries to the biomass: the magnesium, phosphorus, potassium, sodium, and calcium in abundance around the farms increased soil acidity and delayed mineral dissolution, with the consequence of reduced productivity.

Fig. 2.4. Brattahlið: Reconstruction of a typical Viking longhouse completely covered with a layer of a natural insulating material. We also see here a traditional Viking characteristic, an overhang with a bird's-eye view of the entire fjord for obvious defensive purposes. (See also color plate 5.)
*Photo by J. Privat*

Geological studies confirm this destructive action: for example, the analysis of a small lake, Galium Kær on the outskirts of Brattahlið/ Qassiarsuk, reveals an increase in sandy sediments during Norse colonization, which gives the impression that the colonists accelerated the effects of climate deterioration.

Understandably, a comparison can be easily made between the ecological effect of the Scandinavians in Iceland and Greenland. It seems unfortunately established that the same errors were repeated, despite the same fragile environment characterizing the two countries: the cold climate of southwestern Greenland slows down all chemical processes and the vegetation is vulnerable. Since the Landnám (settlement) 1,100 years ago, Iceland has witnessed an 80 to 85 percent loss of its potential plant resources.[26]

Gwyn Jones is most critical on this issue of environment and overall Scandinavian behavior, accusing the colonists of criminal lack of foresight and wastefulness: "They [the Scandinavians] were the most careless farmers. They lived as squanderers, destroying the protective groves of birch trees by intensive pasturing, wood chopping, and accidental forest fires."[27]

This destruction of the Scandinavian environment went on for three centuries with all the effects we now know: erosion and desertification of entire districts. Jones views the Icelandic farmer as an exploiter. One-fourth of the six hundred farms mentioned in the *Landnámabók* (*The Book of the Settlement of Iceland*) were abandoned. The same worrisome signs and negative effects were seen on the western colony of Vestribygð.

The Norsemen's mistakes do not seem to have stopped there, as several authors unhesitatingly point out their inability to adapt. Again Jones has the harshest commentary. Their clothing was entirely inappropriate and closely modeled on European styles. The truth is that the long clothing found at Herjolfsnes, and that also appears in medieval-era native sculpture, seems poorly adapted to the unstable, mountainous environment of Greenland (though it was technically part of Europe then). Its value against the cold does not seem to have been a concern. "Icelanders never learned how to dress themselves against cold

Fig. 2.5. Greenland: Reconstruction of the interior of a Viking house with a central hearth. All the materials were of natural origin, the reindeer/caribou lived—and still live—in the wild. You will note the extremely abundant use of wood although it was presumably rare in Greenland, which did not have a single forest, and which also brings to mind the Viking's destruction of their environment in Iceland.
*Photo by J. Privat*

Fig. 2.6. Interior of a Viking house. This loom reminds us of the importance of this activity in this area of the world. The heavy Norse homespun cloth was extremely sought after throughout Europe, and even served as currency. This also reminds us of the importance of sheep husbandry in Viking colonies. (See also color plate 6.)
*Photo by J. Privat*

and rain. Their shoes were particularly poorly adapted to their climate and terrain."[28]

Taking a completely neutral stance, we can realistically ask ourselves if the Burgundy-style clothing unearthed at the Herjolfsnes cemetery met the needs of the country. An Inuit tale could have inspired Gwyn Jones's observations. This story tells how during clashes between Inuits and Scandinavians, the colonists would let themselves be torn to pieces on the ice—their shoes were too slippery for this terrain. As an exception I will cite this passage as it is quite in keeping with what I am alluding to. During a hostile confrontation between the two communities, the Scandinavians were compelled to chase two young girls over a frozen lake. "When they came out, the Kavdlunaat saw them and set off in pursuit. Because the ice was slippery, they could not keep their footing and fell on their butts or on their sides, while others were sliding back and forth. The angry father asked his folk: 'Did they all come out?' Someone answered yes. In great irritation, he headed out on the ice to pursue the Kavdlunaat. . . . He stabbed the first one he caught up to with his spear. The Kavdlunaat tried to strike him down, but he confronted them. Because they were all slipping and sliding, he was able to stab them. In the end all were slain before the little girls had even reached the edge of the ice cap."[29]

Jones's criticisms are just as severe on the Norse diet: "During times of famine, they had not even learned to eat all of the comestibles the country had to offer, and their fishing equipment was nothing to boast about."[30]

Jones's remark came immediately to mind when I read the story of Aqissiaq specifically helping the Scandinavians during their ill-starred attempts to catch salmon for lack of the appropriate tools. Jones offers a version that is diametrically opposed to that of Ingstad and seems a bit extreme. Vera Henriksen also completely disagrees with this theory of maladjustment. She bases her opinion on the excavations made at Niaqusat in the medieval Lysefjord that unearthed Scandinavian tools made of horn or bone. This reveals that colonists adapted local materials to their needs, thereby showing their intelligent adjustment to the environment. Another example concerning Scandinavian clothing in the *Greenland Annals* vouches for their ability to adapt. In it we learn that an Icelander named Jón the Greenlander during one of his many trips to Greenland discovered a recently dead colonist clad partially in European clothing, and partially in hides obtained locally: "They found a man lying dead on the ground. He was wearing a well-made hat, and clothes that were part homespun fabric and part sealskin."[31]

Thomas McGovern notes the relative frequency of wild and domestic animal bones in the middens, thereby confirming the consumption of their own working capital. This could also serve as a sign of adjustment to local climate conditions.

The environment depends on human activities as well as the ambient climate. A quick glimpse of this, and a brief digression about climatological research could prove instructive here. Modern climatological studies employ a variety of techniques for analyzing acidity, pollen, dust, and the proportion of oxygenated isotopes in the ice cap, but the best-known technique is core drilling. The glacial core consists of several layers of superimposed ice that go back (most likely) more than 100,000 years. Each layer corresponds to annual precipitation. In other words, valuable information concerning climate, atmospheric conditions, pollution or other adverse consequences due to human beings are stored in these layers of ice.

A number of drillings were made in Greenland in 1964. The core samples were taken from a depth of 4,300 feet at Camp Century in northwestern Greenland. The results agreed with those of palynology: the deterioration of the climate, which was becoming colder and wetter at the end of Norse colonization, and a variation of climate conditions in Europe.

In 1981, a core sample was taken from the ice cap at the meteorological station Dye 4 in southern Greenland at a depth of 6,200 feet. It revealed that worldwide volcanic activity was the cause of 27 percent of the temperature fluctuations during the fifteenth century. Comparison of Greenland temperature curves with other curves based on dendrochronology, sediment core samples taken from deep waters, variations of temperatures in the Alps, and historical analysis revealed that the Greenland climate changes preceded those in Europe.

To sum up: Scandinavian colonization of Greenland began under the good auspices of a clement period of weather and came to an end with the deterioration of the climate. Presenting these observations as the primary cause of the Norse disappearance from Greenland is not a stretch by any means.

## SOCIOPOLITICAL ORGANIZATION

This is reminiscent of the political structure found in Iceland. The Greenland colonists came from Iceland, so it is logical that they brought to Greenland their customs and habits such as power-sharing arrangements (no "chief of state," at least in the beginning of the colonization period before they swore allegiance to the Norwegian kingdom) and the Thing. An advanced governing structure not unlike those seen today, and indeed a predecessor to today's Nordic parliament, the Thing played a significant role in Norse society. This assembly of free men, often peasants, debated local issues and enforced laws. Keller shares this vision concerning the similarities of the Greenland and Icelandic systems. "During the period designated by the name of 'free state,' Iceland was not a veritable nation, but rather a federation of chiefdoms. We can assume that the organization of Greenland also consisted of chiefdoms, probably with a common Thing or central Council."[32]

At the start of colonization, the Thing was most likely headquartered in Brattahlið as all contemporary researchers believe. Then, at the beginning of the twelfth century, it was transferred to Garðar, which illustrates perfectly the transition of power toward the episcopal seat. At the end of the colonization, with the eclipse of the Greenland Church, the Thing returned to Brattahlið.

No political event of any importance seems to have occurred until 1261, the date Greenland accepted Norwegian sovereignty. The type of Nordic society that existed in Greenland differed greatly from traditional medieval society for several reasons: namely, the absence of any military authority like an army and regular troops; the lack of any urban framework, which is essential for any large-scale market economy, accompanied by absence of any monetary circulation as mentioned earlier. These are major differences with the medieval world.

Greenland stood apart from the types of medieval society in which the church held all economic and spiritual power with the traditional balance between royal power and clerical power. In contrast, the leaders of Iceland and Greenland held considerable religious powers until the church reform in thirteenth-century Iceland, and probably later in Greenland. This religious authority held by laymen is one of the characteristics of the remote Nordic colonies and surely one of the keys to the mystery of the Scandinavian disappearance, and to all the vagueness of the clerical written sources. There were definite differences of opinion between the church and Nordic settlers of Greenland, as well as those of Iceland and the Faroe Islands. To put this matter in a nutshell, let me briefly say that before reform, Scandinavian leaders and even—something that must have raised hackles during this era—free peasants controlled the local churches: "They enjoyed considerable influence over spiritual questions."[33]

The changes of ecclesiastical organization that took place later certainly sparked changes in the social organization, which in turn prompted opposition from the colonists. More than one written source supports this interpretation of events. Their opposition to reforms earned the Scandinavians of Greenland their reputation as pagans.

Confirming the church's monopoly of written sources, Finn Gad reminds us of the rural nature of Greenland's Norse society, which we can interpret by a dominant illiteracy, even if limited knowledge of the runic alphabet existed and was used up to the middle of the thirteenth century. This alphabet would be banned at the beginning of the fifteenth century for its magical pagan connotations. In passing, I would like to point out the late date of its disappearance; this is quite telling of the tenacity of the old traditional Nordic folklore. Gad underscores the oral importance of the oath and agreements made with witnesses, which can be seen in many of the sagas such as the *Laxdoela Saga,* for example. An even more serious matter is that this illiteracy could even be found among the governing class. As

Gad notes: "In Greenland, the peasants certainly had no trust whatsoever in the scribbles that the bishop Olaf of Garðar perhaps made them—we don't know for sure—sign. Moreover, this was what, only a signature?"[34]

To put it simply, we could say that the knowledge as well as the power of testimony (something we should remember with regard to historical analysis) fell into the hands of the church for want of any political or economic authority. But, as we shall see, this situation subsequently changed. To end this chapter, I would like to stress the distance we should take from the alarmist theories about the Norse colony such as debilitation, maladjustment, and so forth. Here, too, there are few concrete proofs that support these conjectures.

I plan to stress the Nordrsetur's extreme importance that may well have been underestimated until now. This is a major element on which commercial exchanges with the outside world rest and without which they most likely would never have taken place. It is also the basis for contact with the native peoples. These expeditions are vouched for by a variety of clerical sources including Rome, from where several churchmen took part in expeditions to the Far North and Canada. There cannot be any shadow of doubt about these expeditions. On the other hand, certain implications such as obligatory, repeated contact with the Inuit have yet to be assessed at their full value.

Scandinavian responsibility for the destruction of the environment cannot be denied, but it is my opinion that it did not play an essential role in the disappearance of the colonists from Greenland. Lastly, Greenland society stood out for its unique nature among contemporary medieval societies as more structured (state apparatus, organization, and so forth), as well as with respect to the balance (or imbalance) between the church and the little chiefdoms holding power at the beginning of colonization.

With my description of Norse diet, the colonists' economy, their choice of sites, and so on, I have taken the risk of granting greater importance to what could be taken as minor technical details but which I consider to be fairly revealing cultural markers. In this way I have sought to underscore all the differences between the Inuit and

Norse populations (dietary, economic, etc.) and provide some additional details that are often overlooked, helping to identify Norse
characteristics cited in written sources, or any mention of white
populations in Canada, North America, or any ambiguous settlements. This concern is also present in the chapter dedicated to the
Greenlandic Inuit. This knowledge will be a useful tool in the use and
crosschecking of information provided by the Inuit oral domain, written medieval sources, and even the accounts of the earliest explorers.

**Key**

(+ : church; △ : neighbouring inuit sites with less
than 5 houses; ○ : neighbouring inuit sites with
more than 5 houses according to T. Mathiassen)

Fig. 2.7. Eystribygð, eastern colony

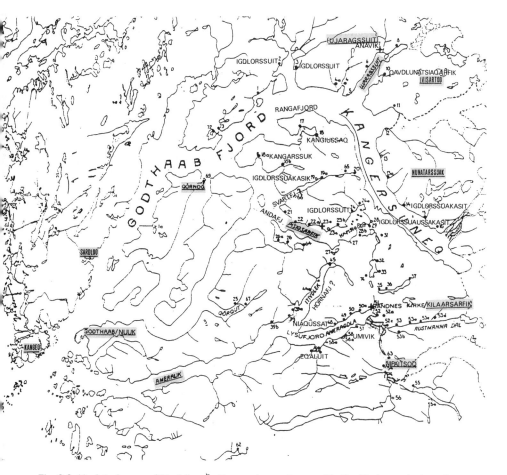

Fig. 2.8. Updated map of Vestribygð—the western colony—with the kind permission of Jette Arneborg (in *Hikuin* 1988). The sites mentioned in the tales are underlined and highlighted here. It will be noted that all the place-names allude to the Norse dwellings, in which the word for *house*, "igdlo," is declined in a variety of ways: the large houses, the very large houses, and so forth. The use of an Inuit lexicon could help to better pinpoint the location of Nordic sites.

# 3

## The Traditional Inuit Cultural Background as a Research Element

Long overlooked, the traditional Inuit cultural background could help answer many questions and confirm or reject obscure points related to a variety of subjects—namely, as testimony concerning the Scandinavians in Greenland, in the Far North in the vicinity of Qaanaaq, and in Canada, as a testament of relations between the two communities, or even as evidence of "Scandinavian isolation," or, to the contrary, reveal the presence of other nations—something that goes practically unknown to this day.

Attention given to this traditional cultural background is relatively recent, its credibility, its information value and true significance, and its possible use as analysis material have been studied by several contemporary experts like Jette Arneborg of the National Museum of Copenhagen and Inge Kleivan of Copenhagen's Institute of Eskimo Studies.

Attempts to use traditional oral cultural histories scientifically were initially launched in the nineteenth century. The great forerunner of this venture was the Danish administrator of Greenland, Heinrich Rink, with his *Tales and Traditions of the Eskimo* in 1875. He collected these stories from his contemporaries. As we shall see, this book still serves as a reference work.

Over these past decades, while still keeping the late date of these transcriptions in mind—and therefore their alterations—and the suggestions made to those providing the information, researchers have given greater attention to these neglected but still valuable source texts. They offer a non-negligible contribution to the study of the history of the Arctic regions and provide corroboration of several theories, like that of Viking/Inuit cohabitation or even another European presence in Greenland.

The great objectivity of some of the stories recounted is what distinguishes Inuit oral traition from that of the Amerindians. Heinrich Rink and the famous Danish/Greenland explorer Knud Rasmussen both remarked on this. Inuit stories are generally passed on in a certain category called *oqaluttuaq*, which these two specialists opposed to another genre called *oqaluppalaaq*.

Rink defines *oqaluttuaq* as "a clearly defined story that reestablishes ancestral events" and an *oqaluppalaaq* as an "element of discussion or entertainment, and normally a tale of events based on second or third hand testimony."[1]

The stories concerning the Scandinavians fall into this second category. An *oqaluppalaaq* obviously suffers from being of secondhand testimony as this means it could have been subjected to influences, evolution, or a historical graft while an *oqaluttuaq* is retransmitted in "a set oral form."

There are historical accounts describing a different population: generally Vikings but other visitors as well. H. Rink thought an *oqaluttuaq* was more historically reliable because of its set form. "We can presume that among each family and in different regions, new *oqalualarutit* flourished; older versions of the same genre were forgotten while the *oqaluttuaq* was preserved intact."[2]

Rasmussen describes an *oqaluttuaq* as "ancient myths that go back to a remote time when the Inuit still lived in their original homes west of Hudson Bay, probably all the way to the Bering Strait. Consequently they are known to all Inuit from Alaska to Baffin Island, and from western Greenland to Ammassalik."[3] These stories are part of the oldest tradition going back to the very earliest times of the Inuit emigration from Canada.

An *oqaluppalaaq* is defined by Rasmussen as a "story whose

subject are the people that lived during a very ancient time that is still remembered. They are *always local* and can thereby provide exact reflections of the places where they took place, but they have adopted the fantastical character of Eskimo stories and are no different from other myths."[4] For him, these Inuit myths and stories reveal events of more or less historical origin. The specific feature he underscores— precise geographical location—is one we should keep in mind for the story he mentions later.

I can also briefly mention the classification of the Danish anthro- pologist Erik Holtved that divides Inuit stories into three categories: those that tell of an event, those that are more informative or educa- tional and explain, for example, the origin of a place-name (they are therefore etymological), and epic histories. Because his classification is based on myth or story and avoids essential factors such as origin and time, they are hard to be used in my analysis.

I will only mention here the tales that directly concern the sub- ject of this book. The peaceful relations between Inuit and Viking are illustrated in two stories: "The Two Friends" and "The Story of the Good and Bad White People." The titles they carry are completely arbirtrary.

The history of these two people is so interwoven that we will start with four stories dealing with the original creation, which implies that these contacts are ancient. In fact, references to the Nordic people go back quite far in Inuit mythology. The story taken from the *Vocabulaire Français–Esquimau* (French-Eskimo vocabulary) of the French mis- sionary Émile Petitot (1876) cites them clearly as ancestors of the Inuit people. The other two stories offer a more nuanced and unfavorable vision of this common origin—whites being the descendants of dogs— but I would rather place this derogatory judgment in the turbulent, sometimes friendly, sometimes hostile, context that characterizes rela- tions between these two peoples. The image of the enemy brothers fits them perfectly. In my opinion, there is an overlooked reason that would explain the frequency with which this theme appears: the possibility of very early contact going back to the very start of the Viking coloniza- tion of Greenland.

## THE WOMAN WHO GAVE BIRTH
## TO THE *KABLUNAAT*

It is told that just north of the settlement called Staten Huk, the southernmost outpost of the country, a woman gave birth to some *Kablunaat* and some dogs. Her parents were greatly shamed by this and left their companions so they would not have to tolerate their presence. This extravagant progeny grew, greatly annoying their father, who had no love for them at all. This is why he took off. These brutal children decided to eat him if he came back. This happened quite quickly. One day he came by to feed them, bringing with him a piece of seal. One Kablunaak headed his way immediately and was given a piece of seal but as soon as he set foot on the ground, the dogs caught and ate him up completely along with the piece of seal. One day a Greenlander showed up paddling in their direction. On his way he cast his trident. A Kablunaak standing on a bluff thought the other man with the trident had no agility and missed his target. He snickered sarcastically: "Aim at me, I'm a guillemot, see if you can hit me."

The Greenlander immediately went toward him and killed him. This murder caused war to break out between Kablunaat and Inuit. Finally the latter gained the upper hand and exterminated all of them.[5]

This story was written by Poul Egede is 1737 while he was a missionary in Qasigiannguit/Christianshåb. It was published in Copenhagen in 1741. I won't write an entire essay in all the symbology that could have given birth to this identification. Let's simply say that if the Nordic colonists could label the Inuit as "stunted" and "puny" (one of the meanings of the word *Skræling*), it was fair game for the Inuit to pull them down to the same level. This interpretation can be found in various etymologies provided by de Vries[6] in Norwegian—*Skrælen*, "weak, feeble"—or A. Jóhannesson[7] tangibly offering the same interpretation and advancing another hypothesis that I find quite interesting starting from the verb *skrælna*, "to be shriveled by the sun."[8] Thalbitzer believes this word to be derived from the verb *shout* (*skråle* in Norwegian), because the Inuit approached strangers while making loud yells as a sign of welcome. It should be noted that the Amerindians did this as well, but as a hostile action.

It is also possible that the mixed-race Inuit-Vikings were not always accepted by the Inuit as it was a break from tradition—not to mention the cases of abuse of Inuit women as some stories at the end of the chapter suggest, hence this transfer to a completely derogatory level. In fact, just as the Nordic moral authorities (the priests) took a disapproving view of this kind of intercultural union, the higher Inuit authorities (the shamans, for example) would have been quite critical of this intermingling. In this sense, without trying to drag us into a Freudian analysis, it is interesting to see how the violation of this taboo is punished: the father is eaten by his children. What is left unsaid about the motivations for the distance established between the couples and their former Inuit neighbors implies a critical view from those around them and reinforces my hypothesis of a taboo violation. This is quite plausible between two communities that do not know each other and could tally fairly well with the beginning of the first Inuit-Nordic contacts. I would like to point out that the locale for this story is in South Greenland, the region that was most deeply marked by Nordic colonization.* The fact remains that this very ambiguous theme of a union between an Inuit woman and a dog, whose children were white men, pops up too frequently in the traditional cultural background for this to be simply a banal anecdote. As it can also be found in the serious works of Erik Holtved and Knud Rasmussen, it seems it should not be taken lightly.

During his sojourn among the Inuit of Cape York between 1906 and 1908, Rasmussen collected a story that deals with Europeans in the Far North. Its introduction bears a strong resemblance to

---

*Staten Huk has vanished today as a place-name. It appears on a map by Hans Egede dated 1733 at the southernmost tip of Greenland, Eystribygð. The people of that era viewed it as clearly located on the East Greenland coast. Graah, in his 1836 map, identifies it as identical with Cape Farvel, which seems to be generally accepted. The *Meddelelser om Grønland* of 1936 identifies it with Putulik Island.

this tale: "In the very first days, the entire world was Eskimo. Then it came about that a dog took a young woman for his wife, and from their coupling came the white man. The young woman was ashamed of her children and put them in a shoe* and cast it into the sea. This is how it made its way to other countries where these children became the parents of all the white people."[9]

As Staten Huk is located in the deep south of Greenland and Cape York in the extreme north, it is surprising to observe the resemblance of these two stories about the origin of white men. These two regions share in common the fact that they were visited or settled by Nordic people. The story collected by Eric Holtved in Qaanaaq falls into the same derogatory tone with regard to the Nordic people. Its location is also tangibly close to that in Rasmussen's tale.

A married couple had a daughter who absolutely refused to wed any husband. Finally, her father told her that she would do just as well to marry a dog. At that very moment the dog began howling because he wanted to come inside. He finally managed to get untied and take the young woman as his wife. The father then built a scaffold out of whale jawbones and placed his daughter there, out of the dog's reach. However, the dog began gnawing at the whalebones until they collapsed. After the dog possessed the girl again her father tied him in a way that he could not get free. He filled a bearded seal hide with rocks and tied it to the dog. Then he had his daughter sit in the back of his kayak and took her to Qingmiûneqarfik, where he abandoned her. The dog then began to speak magic words that caused the sack of stones to float on the water. Once he succeeded he swam all the way to Qingmiûneqarfik. There he found his wife and began copulating with her again. After a while, his wife became pregnant and gave birth to human beings and animals: two Inuits, two white men, two Vikings, two Indians, and two wolves.[10]

---

*Knud Rasmussen tells us in this same story that seen from above, the Scandinavian boat resembled the sole of a *kamik* (Inuit seal hide boot).

This text collected by Holtved has more detail but in its composition is also closer to the tale. One detail strikes me as particularly interesting: the allusion to magic. Is this an element generally found in the tales or a remote reference to the magic practiced by the Norse, a recurring theme as we saw with Aqissaq? The outcome of the story is tangibly similar to that in P. Egede's story, with the only difference being the father was eaten on the mother's orders. All her progeny were then cast into the sea. It will be noted that this story, echoing Knud Rasmussen's story we will soon look at, makes a distinction between white men and Vikings. It would be interesting to learn the reason. The reference to Indians allows me to introduce the final tale concerning origins. Although older chronologically (1876) I have set it aside as it distinguishes itself by the positive image given to the Vikings. Collected in Canada, it appears in Father Petitot's French-Inuit lexicon.* In opposition to the stories cited earlier, this tale seems to give star billing to the whites in comparison with the Indians although they are ethnically closer to the Inuit. "They [the Indians] are born in the West, on the island of the beaver, the nits of our lice. They are despicable, but Inuit and Kablunaat are brothers."[11]

Such affection for a people so different is hard to explain. Petitot's informant gave him some very pertinent information as a symbolic explanation: "Inuit and Whites are issued from the same family because they are the descendants of two brothers. To the west, on an island in the wide sea, the beaver created two men. Leaving for the opposing shore, they came upon this coast while hunting wood grouse. They violently grabbed up these grouse and began fighting over them. [After this quarrel] the two brothers parted ways. One was the father of the People [the Eskimos]; the other was the father of the Blowers [cetaceans; it was assumed the Europeans had descended from them because they came to the land of the People by sea]."[12]

The symbology of this tale strikes me as quite interesting. Were the relatively peaceful relations between the Norse and the Inuit

---

*See my article "Les relations entre Inuit et Norrois au Moyen-Âge, un faux mystère?" dedicated to this topic in the magazine *Il Polo,* vol. 4, 1991.

transposed—or even more accurately, sublimated—to this half-blood status? This could also be a reference to a long past intermixing of the two peoples. Another symbolic element: Did blowers or cetaceans have a large place in the Scandinavian economy, hence this association?

One thing is certain, the four stories refer to the element of the sea—whether it is the dogs cast out to sea on the seal-leather soles or the white sons of cetaceans arriving by way of the sea. The reference to the Nordic people coming by sea seems an underlying one. The final element I connect with this also refers to the Nordic people, the quarrel concerning the wood grouse. It could very easily illustrate some kind of rivalry with regard to natural resources or a cultural divide concerning very different hunting practices, with the ecologically unsound practices of the European sparking this quarrel.

While the stories on the origins of the white people—particularly the Nordic people—borrow greatly from the fantasy repertoire of fairy tales and are fairly vague concerning the people involved, the remaining accounts I am going to cite are clearly localized near Scandinavian settlements in Greenland (supported by Inuit place-names, references to Scandinavian habitat, and so forth) or close to their northern hunting grounds.

## THE FIRST ENCOUNTER WITH THE ANCIENT SCANDINAVIANS OR THE STORY OF THE TWO FRIENDS

This story is supposed to have taken place in the old Norse colony called Vestribygð in the Nuuk/Godthåb region.

An *umiaq* (a large Inuit boat) was sailing North from Nuuk. In their way they saw . . . to the west of Qoornok was a very large house that was apparently abandoned. When they stepped over the threshold, they did not recognize anyone for they were not Inuit. They suddenly found themselves face to face with the Scandinavians.*

---

*In fact the oldest Inuit word for the Nordic people is *Qavdlunaaq* (plural: *at*). Just as for the word *Tuniit,* no sure explanation has been provided. Petitot (1876) believed

These latter were very happy at the arrival of the *umiaq* because this was the first time they had met the Inuit, but they were scared of the Scandinavians despite their friendly welcome, so they rapidly took their boat back out to sea and left before the Scandinavians tried to keep them there. While going up along Kangersuneq, they saw many Vikings who lived in Ilulialik, Ujarassuak, Ivisartut,* and Nunatarssuak, but they quickly left them behind.

On their return to the fjord, the passengers of the *umiaq* told their compatriots everywhere about their encounters in the Nuuk fjords. No sooner had they heard this, some of them set off in search of the strangers, guided by their informants. This is why quite a parade of boats arrived in Kangersuneq. Seeing the friendly welcome of the Vikings, they began to trade. Later, other boats came to visit. The Inuit showed up in greater numbers and as the Scandinavians began *to learn their language,*† friendly relations were established between them. The Inuit saw there were Vikings in Kapisilik as well as Ameralik. Near Kapisilik, according to the story, there were two good friends, one a Greenlander and the other a Scandinavian, *who were always together.* They were in the habit of regularly competing at shooting arrows (at this time the bow was the only long-distance weapon) in order to see who could shoot the farthest, and their compatriots greatly enjoyed watching these contests as both could shoot their arrows a great distance. Being excellent archers, their arrows customarily fell next to each other, for they were of equal strength.

---

(*cont. from p. 57*) it applied to all whites, something I reject. The word comes from *kpablut* (eyebrow) and *kpablunapk* (frontal or coronal bone). According to Petitot, one of the major sources of the Inuit's surprise would have been the Europeans' headgear: "A hat must have been an object of odd shape to them because they saw it covering the forehead to the eyebrows whereas they always went about bareheaded or wearing a small cap." Some, like Keller, have opted for "long beards," but the debate is far from being closed.

*In the order they were enumerated, we have: "there where the houses were built," "the large stones" (the modern spelling gives a more logical "uit"), "sandstone with red and brown tones" (probably used by the Scandinavians), and "the wide land."

†I have italicized this information that I find extremely important as it is illustrative of good relations between the two communities.

During one of these archery contests, attended by many spectators, the Scandinavian said to his Greenlander friend:

"Let's climb this high mountain and let's first stretch a large caribou hide over this small island. We will then see who can hit the bullseye with his arrow from the top. The one who misses will be thrown off into the void, but the one who hits the target will be the victor."

That is what the Scandinavian said.

The Greenlander responded:

"I don't wish to do this for we are comrades and neither of us should die."

But the Scandinavian stuck to his position and despite all his Greenland friend's attempts, nothing could dissuade him. Finally, his companions offered their advice:

"After all, it's all the same if he is cast into the emptiness, since that is his wish.

These were their words in response to his stubbornness.

Although the Greenlander had initially refused, he set off toward the peak followed by a large crowd. When they reached the top and a large hide had been stretched out over the island, the Scandinavian shot first but missed. Then the Greenlander shot and his arrow struck the skin dead center. The Scandinavian who had wanted things this way went to the edge of the cliff and kept his word. . . . This is why he jumped, it was his decision, and no Scandinavian was upset about it as he had earned his fate. After this, the two communities continued to get along well and this summit was called Pisigsarfik (the archery place) because the two rivals competed here.[13]

The credit enjoyed by Heinrich Rink and the essential work he left behind only adds more weight to this story. It will be noted that according to this source that the Scandinavians learned the native language. So if cohabitation existed, then good communication was a must. It so happens that medieval observations make reference to the Norse knowledge of the native language. Even better, the language has Norse loan words for describing the Norse colony of Eystribygð in southern

Greenland. In any case this cohabitation is quite well illustrated by the episode of the archery contest that corresponds well with the traditions of both populations.

The Inuitologist Inge Kleivan has some reservations about all the place-names mentioned in this story, pertinently noting that these Scandinavian settlements were already known at the time this was written down and that Rink's informant could have purposely mentioned them to lend greater verisimilitude to this story. It should also be noted that the story of the two friends has a bellicose counterpart. In it we find a different scenario: Inuit and Scandinavian are at war, or fighting each other with bow and arrow.

## THE STORY OF AQISSIAQ*

This story also offers evidence of peaceful relations between the Vikings and the Inuit that included cohabitation. This detail is important because the clerical sources also mention this fact and viewed this situation quite dimly. The philosophy of that era viewed the natives as savages and creatures of the devil. Moreover, archaeology confirms this point by dating Inuit and Scandinavian settlements inhabited by both communities at the same time, and from a distance that is hard to overlook. The region of Dyrnæs/Narsaq is one of the best examples of the density of the Norse and Inuit population. Qaqortoq/Julianehåb a little farther south also appears frequently in native sources, but we will revisit this site later.

Something that was merely a hypothesis—prudish censure of the relations between these two people by the church—has become increasingly credible thanks to the respective archaeological dating that has since been made. This is how the story of Aqissiaq begins:

> Once there was a Greenlander named Aqissiaq who lived in the district of Frederikshåb with his father and four brothers. An old Scandinavian and his five sons also lived there. The boys often

---

*Pronounced "Akriksiak."

played ball together, but because the Vikings were stronger and always won, the Greenlanders grew resentful. Only Aqissiaq could hold his own against them without fear of losing. He was so strong that he could carry two of them on each knee. One day when the Scandinavians won again as usual, one of Aqissiaq's brothers quarreled with the Vikings and left in a rage.

One Scandinavian followed him and slew him without Aqissiaq noticing, then discreetly went back home. The two families then ceased all contact until one day when the mother of the young Scandinavians came knocking on the Greenlanders' door to ask Aqissiaq to come out and reconcile with them. But he refused.

Every night he went to check if the Vikings were sleeping. Every night he saw his brother's murderer sitting on his bed, watching the window. He had placed a knife between his two eyes to keep from falling asleep because he was so exhausted.

One time though, Aqissiaq found the Vikings asleep. He then told his brothers:

"Come, let's go kill our brother's murderer. Then we can flee to other lands."

They slipped into the house and killed the Scandinavian and threw him in the midden, then they all fled to the highlands. They were hesitant to take a break. The following day, they continued their journey and came to Tessermiut Fjord near Igaliku (Scandinavian Garðar), where they settled. In the meantime, they never dared go too far from their house out of fear of the surviving Vikings, so they had to be satisfied looking for food near the banks. This soon brought them to the verge of starvation and forced Aqissiaq to leave on a serious hunting trip.

This was when he encountered two Scandinavians who called him over to ask if a certain person was still alive. The younger of the two then said:

"I already saw you," and they gave him something to eat, advising him to pay attention to his hunting catch. These Vikings were great sorcerers; when they called to the sea animals, these beasts would come right to the shore.* They then called in a whale and when it drew near, the youngest one leaped over and struck it while inviting Aqissiaq to do the same. Once the whale was dead, Aqissiaq had a right to his share and his family was able to live on it for two years.

When their provisions grew low again, he had to go back out. This time he saw Scandinavians—young and old—fishing for salmon but whatever way they were pulling, their tools would break, preventing them from bringing their prey back to land.

Aqissiaq offered to help them. He jumped into the water and pulled so hard that his imprint can still be seen in the river. The salmon was killed and towed to shore, and Aqissiaq received half. This gave his family enough to eat for the winter.

One day when he was rowing in his kayak a violent snowstorm forced him to follow the shoreline. He reached a house inhabited by a Scandinavian and his son and daughter.

They gave him a friendly welcome, dried his clothes, and gave him dried caribou to eat. That same evening, a Scandinavian stranger knocked at the window and called to the daughter because he wished to marry her. The father, who opposed the match, went outside. A fight began. In seeing this, Aqissiaq got scared and fled. He then came close to being killed by a horned beast (is this a bull, cow, ram?) that chased him until he managed to rid himself of it by slaying it. After that Aqissiaq's family grew bolder and none of them were ever killed.[14]

This previously unseen story was collected in 1899. Setting aside a few exaggerations common to folktales in general (for example, a salmon that can keep a family fed for an entire winter), this story gives us some valuable and additional information with respect to the first encounter between Vikings and Inuit—namely an unambiguous account of Norse and Inuit cohabitation and something "new," the practice of magic by the Scandinavians.

---

*This cannot help but bring to mind the episode of Thorall Veidmadr, pagan hunter and friend of Erik the Red who used magic to summon a whale to the coast of Vinland (in *Erik's saga rauða,*" in *Islenzk fornit* IV; also cited by V. Henrikssen).

The two communities lived in close proximity, as has been confirmed by archaeology. They frequented each other's company regularly as can be seen in other Inuit tales concerning the Vikings. This cohabitation was friendly as games were involved. The murder is but one episode in the story. The Norse mother also took the trouble to try to reconcile the two families. Based on the tone of the text and the examples given, this was not an isolated case of good neighbors but, to the contrary, the general situation. Aqissiaq is given a friendly welcome by the Scandinavians every time. The difference with the sagas, in which hostile relations seem to prevail, is quite noticeable. Mutual aid can be seen in each episode (fishing for salmon, then for the whale). In passing, we should take note of the ironic native wink regarding the effectiveness of Scandinavian equipment.

An almost unnoticeable foreign element in Aqissiaq's story that could support amiable neighbors is the ball game played by the Inuit with a seal skin filled with clay and sand. Prytz compares this to the Nordic game *knattleikr*.* In his opinion, the Inuit borrowed this game from the Vikings. It is also illustrated in the traditional Norse cultural background with the *Eyrbyggja Saga*. This game was extremely violent, and all hits were allowed as is evident in the story of Aqissiaq. These characteristics of the game cannot help but bring to mind Olesen's observation concerning the reluctance of the Inuit to play ball games with the Tuniit. It is easy to see that the ludic domain could contain much information about Inuit-Scandinavian relations. It would even appear to me as the logical consequence of peaceful, friendly relations; one can imagine that good neighbors would play friendly games. There are then the Norse pagan practices. A quick allusion (with the episode of the whale) is made to Scandinavian pagan practices; namely, magic. We know that the church made the same complaints to the Scandinavians. One example among others is a 1342 commentary repeated by Gisli Oddsson in the sixteenth century: "The inhabitants of Greenland on their own initiative have abandoned the just Christian faith, after abandoning proper mores and customs in order to turn toward the peoples of 'America.'"[15]

---

*This game is described by F. Namsen in *Nord i Tåkeheimen*.

In another text with the title *Schondia,* published in Strasbourg in 1536—therefore one year before the Reformation—the mathematician Jacob Ziegler made similar commentaries: "As our Holy Mother the Church has paid no attention to the state of the faith in these regions [Greenland], the people of this country have practically fallen back into paganism and are otherwise very fickle in mind; they are particularly inclined to sorcery."[16]

His sources would be an old text by an archbishop of Nidaros. It could be Walkendorff. The written sources also tell us that a Scandinavian was burned at the stake for sorcery in 1407. Excavations have also revealed pagan practices, such as offerings to Norse gods, runic incantations carved to Thor, and so forth, in the midst of an entirely Christian period.

One final detail: what we have here is one of the rare examples that alludes to Scandinavian domestic livestock that would have been hard to slip past native eyes unnoticed but which—like the Skrælings in Vinland—must have surprised them. I will note the extreme popularity of Aqissiaq, which can be found in seven different versions in Rink's edition, in regions as far apart as Nuuk, Sisimiut, and Uummannaq. One story tells of, among others, Aqissiaq's fight against a monstrous serpent, an animal scarcely typical of these regions. I rather suspect this to have been lifted from the world of medieval Scandinavian fantasy.

## THE STORY OF POVIAK

This story was recorded by C. Pingel in *Nordisk Tidskrift for Nordisk Oldkyndighed* (*The Nordic Review of Archaeology*). It makes reference to a precise spot in the Frederikshåb/Paamiut district where Scandinavians had been buried. Published in 1833, it illustrates a universal phenomenon, the abduction of members of neighboring communities, which was suspected to exist in Greenland but on which there are few documents.

It is told how a Greenlander named Poviak (or Boviak) had gone into the mountains where he had met two supernatural giant women living in the country. They took him prisoner and carried him off. He lived with them until he had made both pregnant. A day came when all three of them had gone down to the beach when several Greenlanders arrived. Poviak called to his companions, who came to his aid.

The women tried to flee but only one was successful. The other was captured and the Greenlanders put her in one of their *umiaq/ umiat*. She was so large and strong that every time she moved the boat threatened to capsize. She then lived among them until the day she gave birth, which proved fatal to her. She was buried with her newborn in Ikerasarsuk.[17]

## THE STORY OF PISAGSAK AND THE OLD KAVDLUNAAT

This story only seems to have been recorded by Rink. His informant was Aron de Kangeq. It tells of the abduction of Nordic women by the Inuit and the attempted reprisals that followed. I am only going to cite an extract. Pisagsak was given shelter by an old *qiviatok** (sorcerer) who suggested they go abduct some women from the colonists.

"Tomorrow is the day when the servants of the Kavdlunaat come to fetch water," said the old *qiviatoq*. "Let's go there. I think there will be pretty girls tasked with getting water." They set off early in the morning and could see many houses overlooking a spring. They hid among the rocks. At sunrise a girl arrived to fill her pail with water, then left. Then several came there, one after the other. Some were quite beautiful, others walked very slowly bent under the weight of years. Then a young woman arrived who was pretty but rather

---

*I am making a distinction between *qiviatoq* (sorcerer) and *angaqoq* (shaman) as they hold two totally different positions that are often confused by the novice. The latter has an official, positive social function as an intermediary between the sky (spirits) and the earth (men). The former has an anonymous negative function (pure sorcery, crimes, evil spells, and so on). The Greenland professor R. Petersen has deeply examined this subject in the review *Folk*. See also P. Robbe's article in *Études inuit*.

young. Pisagsak noticed that his companion was trembling. When she went to take some water, his companion leapt out, grabbed her and fled gagging her with his hand. Pisagsak followed them. When they returned home, they took away her boots and kept watch over her because she tried to escape. They went off to hunt by turn, leaving one behind to keep watch over her. Finally the young woman abandoned all idea of fleeing. They could then leave her alone, and on their return their clothes were in order and a meal awaited them. In this way their sense of well-being improved. Later, Pisagsak and the "old man" returned to watch the young women fetching water.[18]

Pisagsak abducted an old Nordic woman because he did not want things to drag on and on at the sorcerer's home. The colonists mounted an attack, but the sorcerer caused the death of all the assailants. We know that Heinrich Rink had a reputation for being very serious about his work, which comes through in the writing, no commentary, no exaggeration (on the part of the speaker) for a subject that could easily lend itself to both. It seems that we have here a description of the southern colony during its best days (many houses are indicated). I can attest to the fact that examples of abduction or adoption* are found frequently in Norse literary lore as in traditional Inuit oral lore. The many European features of the West Greenland population noted by observers could be an illustration of this interbreeding, which was noted by the Norwegian pastor Hans Egede on his arrival in 1721, and noted by Pingel, who compiled the following story: "They must have spared a number of the defeated women [theory of the extermination of the Norse]. This is why we think we can better explain the particularly surprising European character of the inhabitants of South Greenland in comparison to those of the non-crossbred north."[19] It could be noted that the shadow of a peaceful commingling of the two populations never crossed the clerical mind of Pastor Hans Egede, which clearly illustrates the bias of many past Scandinavian theories.

---

*See Halldór's narratives in chapter 7 regarding the adoption of two young "Trolls" by the Icelander Bjorn Einarsson Jórsalafari.

# THE STORY OF THE GOOD AND BAD WHITES

This story, collected in 1906 to 1908 by Knud Rasmussen during an exploration among the Cape York Inuit in northern Greenland, is the sequel to the story on the origin of whites cited at the beginning of this chapter. It was published in 1925 in *Myths and Sagas of Greenland* (in Danish). It blends the Inuit fantasy and historical genres.

Rasmussen classified it among the *oqaluppalaaq/oqalupaalat* stories referring to a specific place. This history confirms the Viking presence in the far north, peaceful contacts, and a new element: the presence of other foreigners. Knud Rasmussen's text that I am citing here has the slight drawback of mixing Rasmussen's commentary with the story. I believe the entire introduction* is the work of Rasmussen based on the extremely interesting things he learned from the people he spoke with at Cape York, hence the use of the word *Vikings*. It would actually be very helpful to learn the real term. I personally believe that it was the word *Qavdlunat* that Rasmussen compulsorily translated as *Viking*.

[The ancients saw a difference between two kinds of whites: the *Qavdlunâtsiat,* who were considered as enemies and bellicose, and the *Qavdlunât,* who came as friends. The enemies had been landing on these shores since times that passed a very long time ago. It is told that they went as far as the islands north of Cape York in large boats called *Qaqaitsut,*† because they had no mast.]

All the accounts on this subject lie in the thick fog of the myths. I am speaking here of the Inuit who lived and still live in northwestern Greenland, from Melville Bay to the Humboldt Glaciers.

The "Vikings" had the custom of coming here during the first dark nights when the sea was free of ice. What then happened was the arrival of large boats full of many men, the *Qavdlunâsiat,* who were also called the *Nakasungnaisut,* meaning the "mapmakers." They were very

---

*I put this in brackets to distinguish it from the story that follows.
†Literally, "Those with nothing standing."

aggressive and attacked people wherever they found them. The following story is told about one of the very first confrontations.

> One winter, the sleds that had gone hunting for walrus* came across one of those large boats of the *Qavdlunâsiat,* which was trapped in the ice near North Thumberland Lake. As everyone knew they would eventually go on the attack, we attacked them immediately, armed with spears and harpoons. The ice was very slippery, which is why we had covered our soles with crafted sealskin.
>
> The "Mapmakers" were not familiar with this technique were and unable to keep their footing, thus quickly defeated. We pillaged the boat, and someone who saw a large chest brought it back home. When he opened it, he found a charming little lad who had surely hidden inside it to avoid being killed.
>
> The man let him grow up with his own little boy, and they quickly became great friends. The little white boy had the habit of trapping crows for his adopted brother and became a master of this form of hunting in short order. Everyone liked the little foreigner who received the same education as his little comrades learning how to hunt. People told how he would grow nostalgic on seeing the sky take on its flaming colors every twilight. He then began talking about milk and sweet things that he had become accustomed to in the land of the whites. After that he would grow very quiet. One day, when he had gone out hunting, he never returned. Not very far away, toward Cape York, some of his clothes were found, and the elders believed that nostalgia for his own land had become so strong that he had flown away to the land of his brothers.[20]

I would like to make several observations. This text, collected by an individual with the credibility of Knud Rasmussen, follows the same line as the earlier ones cited, by confirming the existence of intercommunity adoption and a Norse presence in the North. We already knew

---

*This detail about game confirms the northern location of the story, corresponding to the natural area for the walrus.

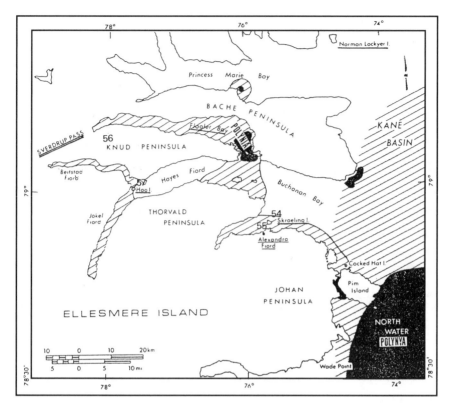

Fig. 3.1. Identified as a likely region of the Nordrsetur by comparative examination of the Nordic literary sources (including those of the priest Halldór in 1266) with native hunting traditions, modern scientific discoveries from glaciology, and archaeological discoveries. The numbers of the excavations cited in chapter 10 appear here as well as the place-names cited throughout the book (underlined). The convergence of all these very different sources highlights this region. The minor polynya (in crosshatching), which are free for some of the winter, and the permanent polynya (in black) must have formed a vast expanse that was very rich in game animals.
*Image by J. Privat*

of this presence through medieval written sources such as the letter of Halldór the priest circa 1266, which can be seen in the *Hauksbók*. Speaking to Arnald,[21] the priest aboard the knörr sent by Bishop Olaf of Bergen to Greenland (Arnald was then officiating at the court of King Magnus Håkansson of Norway; this was from 1263 to 1280), Halldór told him: "This summer people arrived from the Nordrsetur who had sailed very far North, much farther than usual."[22]

Thanks to the Inuit serving as our witnesses, we can more precisely pinpoint the location of the Norse presence in the Far North here at Cape York, which has been confirmed by archaeology. One specific detail is that the author speaks of Nordic voyages during the fall. There had been a general tendency to place these voyages in the spring, during the first thaw. The difference is important because the time needed to sail back to the southern colonies is quite short, if not impossible. This implies that the Scandinavians wintered over far from their homes or may have come back down by way of Canada. All of this agrees with the results of archaeological digs that revealed Scandinavian objects dating from the Middle Ages in the same places, particularly on Ellesmere Island and in northern Greenland. For example, there is the Kingittorsuaq runestone that has encouraged several researchers to advance the hypothesis of an overwintering by the Vikings in the North.

Another sizeable observation is the presence of other foreigners besides the Scandinavians in northern Greenland. We have confirmation of peaceful Inuit-Norse relations and evidence of belligerent relations with other European populations. One interesting detail has been provided: the foreigners' boats had no mast. If all the elements of the story are well founded, we should be able to quickly and more easily pinpoint who these new players may have been.

In fact, few nations during the Middle Ages could boast of excellent cartographical knowledge. Only the southern nations could put in a legitimate claim to that. Nor do others surpass their severity or hostility as described by the natives. Perhaps the ships of the galley type with removable masts correspond to the description given in this story. The hypothesis of Celtic boats should not be discarded; it is believed that the excellent mathematician and geographer Nicholas of Lynn made his way to the northernmost parts of Greenland and probably Canada in 1360. He was known for his mastery of the astrolabe. The—often violent—presence of the English in the northern lands is beyond doubt. However, despite an older presence in these waters (the Hereford map* from 1280

---

*Clearly visible on the map, from east to west, are the Faroe Islands, Iceland, and Ultima Thule.

Fig. 3.2. A detail of the Mappa Mundi of Hereford, 1289, which allows the
northern journey to be surmised: Faroe Islands, Iceland, and Ultima Thule
(better known as Greenland). (See also color plate 8.)
**Wikimedia Commons**

is there to prove it), the quality of their cartography is far from equaling
that of the southern countries. This is why I favor the southern theory,
particularly the Portuguese: it is by virtue of their advanced cartography, which was also noted by the native people; because of their geographical knowledge as they had already discovered the insular coastline
of Greenland; and for an entirely political context (the alliance of the
Danish and Portuguese crowns that will be examined in chapter 11,
leading to mutual expeditions into the Far North).

So this story provides us with a new element: the presence of foreigners confirmed in the traditional Inuit oral history. This long-suspected
foreign presence was due to the regular contacts between England and
Iceland, various voyages of exploration into the Far North long before
Columbus; for example, the Danish-Portuguese expedition of 1473
is more or less concealed by the Nordic written sources. Was this for
political reasons? In general, traces of this presence only appear at a

very high level (royal grievances and so on) but are unknown to the Scandinavian public at large of this time. There seems to be no written text on the Portuguese, for example. Would an admission be evidence of the Danish-Norwegian crown's impotence at dealing with these infractions of the Nordic monopoly? This "new" fact just toppled existing historical schemas that claim only an Inuit and Norse presence in Greenland. Several clues led some researchers to advance this hypothesis. Further study of this has revealed the existence of a number of troubling points: rather advanced foreign knowledge of the Arctic lands—mainly cartographical—and a sustained presence of foreign nations in Greenland, and in the Arctic in general, long before Columbus.

Inuits and Vikings were neighbors or even lived together in Greenland for better or for worse between two and four centuries with varying fortunes in a way that their traditional cultural background reflects it. My research will strive to show that this was more often for the better than not. Suddenly a new player arrives on the scene—and the testimonies concerning the Scandinavians start to dwindle before vanishing completely by the end of the fifteenth century. Couldn't a cause-and-effect relationship be found here? In other words, how could a small colony of farmers and merchants hold their own against the sudden flow of English, Portuguese, Basques, and so on who flooded into these regions during the fifteenth century, given the unstable medieval context with which we are all familiar? Whatever the case may be, the fact remains that in the space of one or two generations after their visit, we hear no more talk about the Vikings.

I would also like to emphasize that these foreigners brought with them techniques that the isolated Scandinavians were not able to match. This question of a foreign presence in the Artic in general and in Greenland in particular seems to be the theme of the story we are going to look at in detail next. The following account was collected in 1770 in Holsteinsborg/Sisimiut by Niels Egede, the younger son of the famous evangelist Hans Egede.

He [the shaman] told us what his grandparents had told him: their ancestors came from North America to end up in this part of

Greenland. . . . Some wished to settle with the Scandinavians, but these latter forbid that, only permitting them to trade with them. The Inuit were also scared of them for the Scandinavians had many kinds of weapons. Once they were settled with several families and they were gaining confidence, several sailors arrived in three small boats. They pillaged and killed several Scandinavians, but these latter were able to overcome them. Two of the boats raised sail and the third was captured, but we Greenlanders [the Inuit] did not have any fixed homes at that time. We got scared and ran away to the interior.

The following year, an entire fleet arrived that waged war, looting and killing, and taking their livestock and their furnishings before leaving. Those who remained took out their boats* and sailed south, leaving several Scandinavians behind. The Greenlanders [the Inuit] promised to come to their aid more often if such a misfortune happened again. The following year, the evil pirates returned. When we saw them landing again, we took flight, bringing some Scandinavian women and children with us inland along the fjord, leaving the others behind. When we returned in the autumn, thinking to find some of them, we had to accept the horrible truth that all had been pillaged and that all the houses and fields had been burned, leaving nothing standing. Seeing this, we took the Scandinavian women and children with us, fleeing inland far up the fjord. We lived in peace there for many years and took the Norse women as wives. They were only five in all, with several children.

Once our numbers were sufficient, we resumed our migrations, settling along the land without seeing a single one of these pirates for several years. Finally some adventurers arrived, English pirates. When they saw we had no fear of them and that we were many, they did not dare attack and only traded with us. The same type of men sometimes come here with Greenlanders [Inuit], and when they

---

*This is underlying in the story with the name "open boats," which the shaman applied to Scandinavian vessels. I deduce from this that the visitors were not Scandinavian. To keep the same image, the boats would have been "closed" or, more correctly, equipped with decks. These boats would effectively revolutionize sailing. The Danish term used by K. Rasmussen is *åbne båd,* meaning "open boats."

sense they have the advantage, they pillage everything. So it is likely that these pirates were the same and now owned some colonies that were hostile to us on the other coast, in American settlements.[23]

The importance of this account must be stressed, for the fact Niels Egede set down these words in writing—told to him moreover by a shaman, "the natural enemy of the evangelist"—only increases the importance he gave this story. This also appears in the very enthusiastic notes of the book. Several conclusions can be drawn from this story: relations between Inuit and Viking were peaceful if not to say close to a cohabitation based on mutual aid, and confirmation of the interbreeding of the two populations is given. All of these points have been touched upon in the previous chapters, yet it is interesting to see them confirmed by the descendants of eye witnesses who had unfortunately been ignored for a long time. Foreign pirates were frequenting the Greenland coasts.

This matches Knud Rasmussen's story at the beginning of the century in the Qaanaaq region. We find the same belligerent tendencies exhibited by the *Qavdlunatsiat;* the importance here is that this gives us an account going back to 1770. This presence contradicts the theory of Greenland isolation and supports the direction I'm taking. The harder task is determining the nationality of the pirate-merchants. Thanks to the traditional lore of the Inuit, we can identify these pirates: they are English, which verifies my claims in chapter 11—namely, the presence of marauders in boats in Iceland and Greenland.

This could give us an indirect explanation for the merging of Inuit populations in the south—that stands opposed to their economy based on traditional hunting—one of the consequences of which was the merging of the previously mentioned habitat. The defensive character of these concentrations would definitely have existed for serious reasons as we have seen. This was not because of the Vikings but other European visitors. As we can easily see, all these elements concur and appear much more plausible to me than a theory based on Scandinavian/Inuit aggressiveness that does not fit well with their status of neighbors or even cohabitants. It would be hardly logical if they were hostile to one another.

This text does not have the pleasure of belonging to Western noble, scientific, historical, or literary sources, and because it came out of the mouth of a "savage"—a shaman to boot—it fell into the garbage heap of history. It is a shame that not a single curious historian has compared it with another medieval source that relates the same unfortunate events and is highly difficult to refute: the papal letter of Nicholas V (at the Vatican Library), dated 1448, intended for two Icelandic "bishops."

> Christians were able to maintain for many centuries the Christian faith established by King Olaf in Greenland and erected numerous churches as well as a cathedral until about thirty years ago [therefore about 1418] pagans coming from neighboring shores came with their fleet to sow desolation across the land and its holy edifices, sparing nothing except the small remote parishes because the mountains and precipices prevented them.[24]

The phrase "neighboring shores" can be interpreted in two ways: the Icelandic coast or the American coast. In both cases, a foreign non-Scandinavian presence is confirmed, supporting the axis of my research that stresses the need of adopting a global view of the situation (and not isolated or restricted to Greenland alone as before). In fact, the second interpretation, in light of the commentary at the end, is the most plausible. Again I would like to stress that overlooking the situation with the neighbors of Greenland means sticking to a partial view of the issue, which amounts to enclosing it inside a rigid context that has no relation with reality. Unfortunately, this has been characteristic of Greenland studies for several centuries. The mystery surrounding the situation in Greenland and in the Arctic in general *cannot be limited to the two Scandinavian and Inuit players.* As we are beginning to see, there was no lack of foreign players. The renowned Olaus Magnus also mentions piracy in connection with a mythical pirate lair in Greenland called Hvitserk.

> On the high bluffs of Hvitserk, in the middle of the sea, there is a type of pirates who work using boats made of hide and during

their expeditions destroy merchant vessels by boring them below the keel.[25]

This testimony by Olaus Magnus is still thorny and has given rise to numerous controversies, and on several occasions he blended together things that took place in Greenland, Lapland, and Karelia. In addition, the Inuit or European identity of the "pirates" does not emerge from this account. Nonetheless the rocky hill Hvitserk appears on several occasions in Icelandic and Norwegian sources and is generally situated on the eastern coast of Greenland. We should also recall that another narrative written in the sixteenth century, but whose original dates from the fourteenth century, mentions the same facts. The Venetian Zeno family claimed to have been responsible for these deeds, describing them similarly to Olaus Magnus. The problem is that while Olaus Magnus could be controversial, researchers have vilified, the Zeno family, some even accusing them of duplicity although others believed their writings have merit. Further study of this would probably be most helpful.

However, we have an indubitable confirmation of Greenland's non-isolation during the fifteenth century, and what's more, the damage that was done there, making less and less credible the hypothesis that the Norse settlers were exterminated by the Inuit. These misdeeds indirectly confirm the substantial fortunes that were at stake in the Arctic world, as I mentioned earlier. These deviations from regular commerce into piracy are too well documented and too frequent to lend any credit to the hypothesis of isolated acts. We can state with no exaggeration that the remote Nordic dependencies suffered from the relentless attention paid them by foreign sailors/pirates for a century. F. W. Lucas even suggests the figure of 150 years for Iceland.

Because of its reduced historical value, it has only been recently that the Inuit cultural and historical stores have been given serious attention. All things considered, I would say that the medieval Nordic literary collections (sagas, poetry, and so forth), or those of Europe in general, differ in no way on the level of historical testimony from those of the Inuit. And if this is the case, I have a problem understanding the lack of interest in these sources. Could this be considered as a kind of ethnocentrism that has dominated history until the present? As the so-called primitive populations put it so nicely, history is often described as that of the white man, seen through his gaze and for his own ends.

Every choice means something else is excluded. It was necessary to select from the very wealthy traditional Inuit cultural holdings those that were most meaningful and—out of a simple question of time— use those that other researchers had already used or translated. So I would like to again thank Jette Arneborg of the National Museum of Denmark for having sent me her works on this subject.

Those who support the theory of hostility will maintain that there are other stories describing the conflicts between the two communities. I would refer them to my article concerning relations between the Inuit and Nordic peoples during the Middle Ages as seen through several well-know Inuit stories that were published in the review *Il Polo*[26] that refute the official position that has been so long dominant. This position reduces the contact between these two peoples to this bellicose pattern. I would note that all the traditional Inuit tales used by those holding the hostility theories (which end with the destruction of all or part of the Norse colony) sometimes start with sustained friendly contact between Inuits and Scandinavians (visits between the two communities, games, and so on), which belies or adds subtle shades to the official exclusively bellicose theory. The belligerent stories are long and plethoric, and often assume an epic style, so I will cite only a few extracts.

## THE STORY OF UNGORTOQ*

A man who had traveled in a kayak from Agpaitsivik arrived in Qaqartoq one day to try out his new trident for hunting birds. When he came to the spot where they fished for herring, he saw

---

*No meaning for the name is given, it is possibly a transcription of Ingjald (the sole close Inuit word would be *ungaartorpoq*, "to yell"; therefore someone who shouts or yells, or even the howler?).

a Kablunaak below his house busy collecting mussels. When the Norseman saw him, he said:

"Hit me with your spear."

"No, I don't want to," replied the man in the kayak.

The Kablunaak insisted:

"Yes, aim at me!"

The man in the kayak replied:

"We are friends, I don't want to cast my spear at you."

Then the [Nordic] leader, Ungortoq, came along and he said this:

"Go ahead, do it, since he is still asking you to target him, so just do it."

He picked up his spear. The leader repeated his order:

"So, throw!"

When the Kablunaak reached the edge of the promontory, he took aim and killed him. The leader then told him:

"I urged you to do it, that is why you did it."

Winter came, and the Greenlander lived in constant fear that the chief of the Kablunaak would get angry. But the winter passed, followed by summer, then two more summers went by. During the third winter, the man returned to Qaqortoq in his kayak followed by a companion. This person saw a Kablunaak collecting mussels in the same place. An idea popped into his head:

"I am going to kill him and not say anything [to the man in the kayak, who had been there earlier].

He picked up his spear and cast it so that it pierced the man still busy collecting mussels. Without saying a word to the chief, he took back his spear and returned home. There he told his companions:

"I killed one of those Kablunaat down there." He repeated the same thing every time a kayak returned. The Greenlanders asked if he had spoken to the chief and he answered no. They then asked him:

"Why didn't you say anything?"

Then the first murderer spoke:

"I killed because their chief asked me to. The way this last murderer did it, without speaking to the chief, will not make him at all happy."[27]

The story then continues with a series of bloody confrontations between the colonists and the Inuit, ending with the death of Ungortoq and many colonists. This history was used abundantly to support the Eystribygð destruction theory. It is well known in Greenland and throughout the Arctic. It was collected by Rink in the nineteenth century. The pastor Ulrik P. C. Nissen is said to have transcribed it again based on the story of a Greenlander named either Jonathan or Samek. Several variants exist, but all refer to the area of Qaqortoq— in other words, Eystribygð. The pastor P. F. Jørgensen, who was quite active, undertook several archaeological digs in this region and collected numerous stories about the medieval colonists. He states: "Ungortoq was chief of the Nordic colonists in the Qaqortoq region. They had long lived on good terms with the Greenlanders, until several events occurred that first caused dissent and finally the end of the Norse colony. [The kayak episode is introduced but with a few variations.] One of Ungortoq's people was sitting near the shore, and he saw the man in the kayak miss his target. He then began imitating a guillemot, calling out: 'Hit me, hit me.' The Greenlander did just that and killed him."[28]

A very similar variant exists in the work of Johan C. Mørch. One interesting point is that the story he collected was published for the first time in 1799. Quite noticeable is the common feature they share, the more or less stupid challenge that can be seen in the story of the two friends. I have selected the version provided by Rink because one detail from the story grabbed my attention: the confession of committing a crime. This particular feature, which was emphasized by all the companions of the second murderer, was typical of Icelandic society and even formed part of its legal code. All blood crimes had to be quickly declared, with the perpetrator at risk of being banned from society and being executed by anyone. Were the Inuit aware of these rules after long years of friendly cohabitation? The question is worth raising, for new elements appear in every story. This tends to indicate a rather good knowledge of each community's customs.

# THE STORY OF NAVARANAQ

This story may be even more famous than the previous one. It has spread throughout the Arctic. Because of its wide distribution I consider it with a few more reservations. There are variants in which the players can be Indians or Inuit. It is therefore difficult to know whether the precise origin of this story is in Greenland or America. It is one of the classic texts for supporters of the hostility theory and tells of the confrontations between the Inuits and the Vikings that were the consequence of the discord that an Inuit woman—Navaranaq—stirred up between them. Rink published it in 1872.

> The Nordic people of Ujarassuit [Vestribygð] had a Greenland woman named Navaranaq as a servant. They valued her highly. It was precisely at this time that that Inuit and Norse of Kangersuneq [the neighboring fjord] began to really understand their respective languages. Navaranaq frequently told her masters: "The Greenlanders are starting to get mad at you." When she visited her compatriots, she told them that the Nordic people wanted to make a raid and exterminate all of them. Obviously she was lying, for they were living together in the best possible harmony. However, the Nordic people began to get upset, for they still gave some credit to what she was saying. This is why they equipped themselves and set off to exterminate those people who were living at the mouth of Ujarassuit in Kusangassorssuak. Because the men were out hunting caribou, the Norse found only women there, and they slew them all.[29]

The story continues with the vendettas between the two communities. Navaranaq was killed by her compatriots in fairly epic fashion. These kinds of stories made the theory of ongoing hostility between the two communities child's play for its partisans. There is no question of denying their foundation or even their existence. Some technical details remind us only too easily of the Vikings' renown. One episode of the story describes the efficacy of the Nordic ax that reappears in several stories. This weapon was known as the Vikings' favorite weapon.

I do grant some credit to this testimony as the Inuit could have cited another contemporary weapon from the time these stories were written down. The medieval ax appears to have left the strongest impression on their memory.

Conflicts between the two communities occurred, but there were also peaceful times. This is what people tend to forget. The bellicose incidents are all that seemed to have caught the attention of the scribes. A positive image of the "barbarian" may not have conformed to the image crafted by the church. This could explain the accent placed on the tragic aspect of these tales, or on what that era's imaginations found sensational.* The story of Navaranaq, just like that of Ungortoq, begins during a period of peace between the two peoples. Just as in the story of the two friends, we learn that Inuit and Viking have begun to understand one another. We find the same element in the medieval story of Björn Einarsson Jórsalafari (the pilgrim of Jerusalem), the employment of Greenland natives as domestic servants and basically good relations.

The physical prowess of the Vikings could not help but be noticed. In the same story we learn that one of the Norse leaders, the great Olaf who was coming back from a seal hunt, upset at this Inuit attack, rushed back home, causing the seal he was dragging back from the fjord to bounce on the ground behind him. Another Norse leader from Garðar, also named Olaf, was so strong that he could carry a full-grown adult Greenland seal in each hand. Another detail that is worth pointing out as it practically never appears in the Inuit tales is the reference to livestock: "He [Olaf] owned a large number of animals."

The Inuit would therefore have seen the colonists' livestock, which means that they were not living far from the colonists, and their presence in the Scandinavian colonies could be relatively long-standing (the fourteenth-century date should thereby be pushed back). It seems to me that great herds of livestock could only correspond to the prosperous times of the colonies. This period extends

---

*We should recall that the procedure was the same for describing the Vikings in Europe. It can't be denied that they had several scores to settle with the church.

from the beginning of colonization to until the twelfth or thirteenth century.* The worsening climate then created a handicap for raising livestock. This situation was particularly obvious in Eystribygð going hand in hand with the multiplication of large churches. According to Pastor Jørgensen's informant, the bell of Garðar was of impressive size.

In this story, Jørgensen corrects Norwegian Aron Arctander's error in a very similar story published in 1793 that took place in the same region. In it Arctander had confused the name of the place Igaliku/Garðar with the name of the Nordic chieftain. The story goes on about the ruses conceived by the Inuit to achieve their ends. Igaliku managed to escape carrying his youngest son in his arms. The value of this tale lies in its relative antiquity. Arctander was sent to Greenland in 1777 by the company that held the trade monopoly in this land, Den Kongelige Grønlandske Handel (the former Royal Commerce of Greenland). His mission consisted of drawing up a list of the Norse ruins in the district of Qaqortoq/Julianehåb. We should note the frequent references to this region and keep them in mind when reading chapter 6, which examines the cohabitation or neighbor status of the Inuit and Nordic peoples. Here again, the size as well as the combat strength of the Vikings impressed the Inuit.

## THE NORDICS OF UPERNAVIK

I have selected this story because it is connected to a place of particular interest to me: Upernavik. This is the region in which the famous

---

*E. Beauvois limits it to the twelfth century, and Keller pushes it into the thirteenth entury, based on the intense activity involved in building churches, a sign of wealth. Could Beauvois have been influenced by a subjective factor like the Little Ice Age—associating the colder climate with poverty? This would overlook the fact that a colder climate would cause an increase in the most highly valued polar animals. I would therefore be quite hesitant to employ these subjective terms as they have long led researchers astray. For this reason, the fourteenth century could perhaps be included in this prosperous period even if raising livestock (a southern measure of wealth) was in decline as ivory, furs, and falcons were there to procure affluence and renown.

Kingittorsuaq runestone was found and where many of the Inussuk lived. The story was was written by Pastor H. C. Rossen in 1915. A variant that is ninety years older was written by a Pastor Kragh.

Once upon a time, the Northmen lived on the isle of Inugssuk, located to the southeast of Kingitorssuaq. There was still a cairn and a large [Nordic?] ruin on this island. Eskimos lived on Kagsserssuak.* One day, the angaqoq traveled through the air to Inugssuk where he told the Northmen to make themselves at home. He then returned to Kagsserssuak, where he told his companions:

"Tonight we will all go to Inugssuk, kill the Northmen, and take all they own. They immediately took *their sleds*†—because it was winter—and came to Inugssuk, where the inhabitants were already getting ready to retire for the night. Some had removed all their clothes, as they were in the habit of sleeping naked. Others were still wearing their *dog skin* small clothes and boots. The Eskimos burst into the house and felled everyone with their arrows, except for three Northmen who managed to escape. One of them, who was completely naked, headed to a nearby spot that is called Augpilatoq today. On his way there, the soles of his feet and his back froze solid. When he reached the Eskimo settlement by Augpilatoq Fjord, he took shelter in a house. But while he was crawling through the entrance, the frozen skin of his back fell off in pieces. The other two fugitives, a couple, fled to a steep mountain several miles south of Upernavik. They scaled the mountain and were transformed into stone. This crag was called Kavdlunarssuit [the crag of the Kavdlunnat or the Northmen]. Since that time these figures have fallen over, but they could still be seen one generation after this event, and the travelers passing that way were in the habit of throwing them a few offerings and asking them for fair weather during their voyage.[30]

---

*Around two and a half miles north of Inugssuk.
†I have put in italics the specific, significant information that research has neglected.

The story ends with the misfortune that befell the *angaqoq,* who fell victim to his own exorbitant greed. He had gone to great trouble to bring back the largest chest he could find, one he saw outside the house. This proved to be a coffin holding a Northman in a shroud. The location of this story is interesting, even if there is a risk of geographical error in things from the oral tradition. I consider it geographically plausible not because of the place-names (like Kavdlunarssuit), which are abundant in this area, but because of some technical details. In fact, this story gives us the first allusion to Inuit dogs (or sleds, rather). So what we have here are representatives of Thule culture, or its Inussuk branch, the one that was most advanced on a technical level. Upernavik and Inugssuk are known to be Inussuk names.

Another bit of technical information concerns the Scandinavians. They are wearing dog skin small clothes and not the long outfit, which means they were adapting to their environment, contrary to what Gwyn Jones says in his criticism of Scandinavian clothing in Greenland. We know of another example of clothing adaptation. Based on the Greenland annals, one of the last colonists of Vestribygð was found dead wearing small clothes made of seal hide Their presence here far from the colonies in the middle of winter seems to find confirmation in Inuit oral tradition. One final interesting piece of information in this tale is the presence of Nordic feminine elements. Was this an expedition to the Nordrsetur, or a colonization journey toward the western lands? Following the artistic testimony of the Inuits depicting the Scandinavians in the Far North, we have here a new tale placing them in higher latitudes. We should also point out, in passing, the confirmed practice of the Vikings to go fetch their dead—even in remote places—to bring them back to consecrated earth.

As a final example taken from the bellicose perspective, I would like to cite a fairly strange Inuit tale that was written between 1830 and 1840. Moreover, it is housed at the National Library of Iceland. The first edition was the work of Jøn Thorkelsson. Despite its obvious value (accounts of games between Inuit and Scandinavian children), it is difficult to use for analytical purposes because of the numerous commentaries woven into the text.

## THE ICELANDERS AND SKRÆLINGS
## IN GREENLAND

A man named Ingjaldur (the Skrælings called him Ingjili) once lived in Veidifjord.* He had many sons who all lived in the valley surround the [manor].† These folk were good Christians, enjoying the benefits of priests and churches, and all was going well.

During this time, the western coast of Greenland had a large populace of the folk we call Skrælings but who called themselves Innuk. . . . A number of them were living in [Nabaitsoq],‡ not far from Veidifjord, some even stretching farther south where the winters were less severe.

Relations were increasingly frequent between the folk of Veidifjord and the men of the north, although they had little in common because of the difference of customs between the Christians and the pagans who had no wish to convert to the true faith. However, some of them settled on the edge of Veidifjord, raising their huts

---

*This fjord is little known. The literal translation would be "the fjord of game animals/ hunting fjord." I will still make the connection with Dyrafjördur mentioned by H. Egede in a map dated 1733. In fact, another place-name from the story, Steinnefjord, also appears there. These places could be in Eystribygð or on the path to Mellembygð (between Midfjord and Thoraldfjord). I am using this conditionally as the only fly in the ointment is that this map is erroneous, not only for its location of the two colonies but also in how it distributes the sides within the same colony, particularly Eystribygð. It should be noted that C. C. Rafn cites B. Jønsson, who lists these sites gives the impression that either Eystribygð or Mellembygð are the starting points.

†I have bracketed all the terms that strike me as additions or exaggerations.

‡I also have doubts on the spelling of "Nabaitsoq" as "b" did not originally exist in the Inuit alphabet, but this does not seem to have been a source of concern to other researchers. It could be Napáitsoq, meaning the column in reference to a perpendicular rock formation, but this place-name doesn't (or no longer) exist in the region. Nipáitsoq is more plausible, in which case we would be carried far up Lysufjord not far from Sandnæs (Steinnes?) in Vestribygð. Another observation: this location is quite deep inland, basically at the source of the fjord, which is not in accord with Inuit custom. Could a valid reason (such as abundant game) corroborate this theory? Could it be the same as Napassut, an island located in the mouth of the Arsuk fjord? In this case we would be in the area of Mellembygð. This example offers an excellent illustration of the difficulties that come up when seeking to identify certain sites.

and tents, and living on fishing. Things proceeded this way for some time: tensions were high, but there was little outright conflict.

One day when the boys of Veidifjord were playing on the banks with their bows, the sons of the Skrælings were paddling along the coast in their kayaks, practicing with their harpoons. One of the Skræling boys came quite close. He told the boys they'd be better off practicing how to hurl their spears than airing their large bellies in the sun. They answered that they weren't about to be underestimated for their sport and that they [the Inuit] could surely not do as well with their spears as they could with their bows. The Skræling boy cast his spear among the group, and a boy of twelve fell down dead. Then the Skrælings all howled stupidly and left the banks. The boys raced off to tell their father of the incident. [Lord] Ingjaldur summoned all his people and said that he wanted to attack the Skrælings that very day, to kill them all or drive them out of the district. This was quickly organized, and sixty hearty men marched off in the direction of the coast. The Skrælings were not at all prepared as many had not yet come back from the sea. It is said that the farmers of the district killed them all, women and children, everyone they saw. A number of Skrælings returned then, and the work of the Veidifjord people upset them greatly. They readied to wage a ferocious battle. The Skrælings used spears with tips made of bone, but the men of the district had swords and halberds, so they slaughtered the Skrælings like flies.[31]

Reprisals soon followed on the part of the Inuit. One Easter morning all the people of Ingjaldur were burned alive while they were in the church. Those who escaped the flames perished under the arrows of the Inuit surrounding the church. This story echoes earlier ones completely, but it is harder to work with because of the scribe's numerous interjections. It is hard to say if the commentary is by Thorkelsson or by the scribe J. A. Jaltalin (1830–1840) or goes further back. I would have great reservations about this latter hypothesis as several details reflect periods that are too recent.

In this respect we can ask if the Icelanders' weapons are not exaggerated or anachronistic. Halberds never seem to have been found in Greenland, even though they appear in the illustrations of Greenland's national artist of the nineteenth century, Aron of Kangek. The tragic end of the colonists could be true if we consider that allusions to a church used to burn them alive recur frequently in Inuit traditional tales. This event would have left an imprint in memory. We also know from archaeological excavations that the church of Herjolfsnes burned down, and its Inuit name, Ikigait, means "the place that burned."

Nevertheless, applying this kind of episode to the entire Nordic population would be an exaggeration or an error in my opinion. I would point out that here again the children of the two communities have no difficulty (with respect to language) communicating, and a detail I underscored, the coming of the Skrælings to Nabaitsoq was quickly followed by the continuation of their migration farther south. A movement of expansion into the south had no reason to halt midway on the West Greenland coast, in Vestribygð, for example.

This would appear to be logically consistent with the information provided at the very beginning of the story: "the western coast of Greenland began to be inhabited by larger numbers of Skrælings." Could this be in the midst of the Inussuit migration? I would also like to point out that the word *skræling* appears in this tale preserved in Iceland but is absent from the mouth of Greenland speakers.

To conclude, I would like to stress one of the elements that has gone unremarked until now by researchers—the recreational aspect of games, a result of the friendly relations between Inuit and Northmen. It recurs frequently in several tales and concerns the children of both communities as well as the adults. This appears to me as the logical result of peaceful—even friendly—cohabitation of two peoples over such a long period. In fact, this aspect of play in the relations between these two peoples surely led to other consequences, such as loans. I will discuss this in a chapter specifically devoted to Inuit loans. We cannot entirely separate the heritage of a culture in the same way as the written sources in other cultures, although Inuit traditional lore is not one of the most robust elements of research. This remains the case despite the late dates that the lore was consigned to writing (eighteenth century for

H. Egede, nineteenth century for Rink), as well as the foreign influences and interpretations—namely, of the speakers—the stories may have been subject to. The conservative nature of certain stories plays in their favor, as well as what we might call the small, trifling detail that reflects or refers to precise populations, regions, or eras.

This is why the evocation of the *umiaq* evokes the Thule people (or the Inussuit), the absence of dogs brings to mind the Dorset people, and foreigners drawing up maps totally exclude the Vikings and can only refer to southern Europeans. During this era, two nations were the dominant players of maritime cartography, the "Italians" (actually the Venetians and maybe the Genoese) and the Portuguese.* Every technical detail gives us *a key* to important questions. To my mind it is much less likely that that detail underwent stylistic alterations on the part of the storyteller or the person collecting the story, seeing as the fact is a technical detail it plays a lesser role in the tale. I will defend this personal theory of the technical detail, which that has been utterly overlooked up to now. Understanding the significance of these little details would have surely made it possible for researchers to avoid making a lot of mistakes. This permits me to now introduce the next chapter devoted to medieval Inuit art in which these little details now appear tangibly and concretely (for example, the cross of a medieval figurine found in Canada) and have been handed down from the depths of the ages by the eyewitnesses, who in this instance are the artists who sometimes were ignorant of their meaning.

---

*Ironically, the English, whose presence in Arctic waters needs no demonstration, do not seem to have equaled these two nations in mapmaking, but we cannot completely exclude this hypothesis.

# 4

## Inuit Art as a Research Element

In the artistic domain, the Inuit have left evidence that leaves no doubt about the persons depicted: statuettes representing Scandinavians. These statuettes correspond to the Inuit style characterized by its simplicity of form and by its miniature size, which is quite practical for a nomadic people.

Inuit art obeys aesthetic criteria and extremely precise characteristics that are clearly visible in Dorset and Thule art. It can be stated that the examples cited here are definitely representations of white people—namely, because of certain clothing details, as we shall see. In my thesis, "Inuit Art in Greenland (1988)," I showed how this art falls into three categories: religion, utilitarian purposes, and the domain of play.

With respect to the first function, the statuettes often perform the duty of amulets and are predominantly small. The aesthetic has a religious connotation to ensure that game will be slain by a good weapon. In the Inuit world, all art has a purpose; art for art's sake is unknown to them. This mainly means that every carved or sculpted object is executed in a way to answer its purpose perfectly. We could say that a very high degree of functionalism characterizes these productions and there are no superfluous details (a cavity in a handle would be intended to give it a better grip, a bulge or protrusion on the end of an arrow would ensure that it adhered to the bowstring better, and so forth). Their philosophy could be described as centered on simplicity and efficiency. The bulk of Inuit carved objects (animals, miniature tools) were intended for children, like an initiation through play into their future lives as hunters.

All of these statuettes are now part of the National Museum of Denmark's collection. Obviously I am not looking to write a paper on Inuit art here. However, out of a desire to provide clarification and to allow the reader to follow my argument, it is necessary to present the two major Inuit styles, useful for dating the statuettes described in this chapter.

## DORSET ART

Older than the art of the Thule culture, Dorset art is characterized like all Inuit art, by its miniature size. However, Dorset sculptures have a rougher, heavier appearance* than those of Thule art. The features are less delicate and developed. Techniques and a limited selection of tools may need to be taken into consideration in this judgment.

In addition to these aesthetic criteria, another characteristic element of Dorset art will help to distinguish the two styles at issue here: the upper and lower limbs are always clearly depicted.

## THULE ART

This art also shares the characteristic miniature size, but it also stands out for an artistic perfection that would arouse the envy of a modern sculptor. Its comparison with modern and surrealist art has already been made. Except for the difference in size, some traditional Thule Inuit statuettes can't help but bring to mind the sculptures of the English sculptor Henry Moore. The simplicity of the forms in combination with a high aesthetic sense have given the impression they serve a fetishist function (amulets).

Except for the aesthetic nature, the great difference with Dorset art is the absence of upper limbs as well as feet and the extreme simplification

---

*It is quite difficult to present an account of a so-called primitive art without falling into the risk of an evaluation or judgment that lends itself to being taken wrongly as a value judgment. That is obviously not my intention.

of the people sculpted. Their faces lack features, which can appear as an outline in Dorset art, the heads are very stylized and generally oval, and the bodies are extremely simplified. The delicacy of the Thule line is surely connected with the technical perfection of Thule culture. In fact, this culture represents the height of the technical development of their adaptation to the Arctic environment. The statuettes in the Copenhagen Museum do not correspond with habitual Inuit norms—neither Dorset nor Thule—and cannot in this sense represent the Inuit. However, the crafting is native: the upper and lower limbs are not depicted, nor is the face. The Danish researcher Hans Christian Gulløv* of the National Museum of Denmark, whose work I am citing here, has worked extensively on this matter and shares this view.

### *Presentation of Scandinavian Statuettes*[1]

1. Statuette found during archaeological excavations in the Thule district in the so-called Comer's Midden (1935–1937).

   **Characteristics:** Carved in wood, height 3 cm. There are outlines of a hood and boots.

   **Dating:** Undetermined (Thule period?). The Danish researcher feels this is one of the less certain examples. Could this be a representation of a Scandinavian with several Inuit features?

---

*Out of all the figurines analyzed by H. C. Gulløv, I am only presenting twelve statuettes whose dating refers directly to the medieval period and whose connection with the Scandinavians seems more certain.

2. Statuette found by Therkel Mathiassen in an almost completely destroyed ruin (Kitorsaq) during archaeological excavations in the Upernavik district in 1929.

   **Characteristics:** Carved in wood, height 7.4 cm. The hood and two-piece garment appear clearly.

   **Dating:** Fifteenth to sixteenth century according to Gulløv. I would note that it corresponds to the short European style (level with the hips) from 1350.

3. Statuette found during the archaeological excavations of T. Mathiassen in the Upernavik district in 1929 in the midden of Inussuk.

   **Characteristics:** Wood carving, height 5 cm. The hood worn around the head and the long garment appear clearly.

   **Dating:** Thirteenth to fourteenth century. This statuette, which is one of the most realistic, unambiguously depicts the typical garment of the Middle Ages during the period of 1200 to 1350.

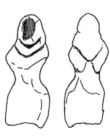

4. Statuette found in the Upernavik district during the 1929 excavations.

**Characteristics:** Wooden carving, 3.3 cm high. A large hood is depicted. No particular sign evident in the garment.

**Dating:** Between the thirteenth and fourteenth centuries.

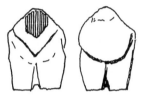

5. Portrait found during excavations at the same spot.

**Characteristics:** Wooden carving, 6.3 cm high. The clearly carved face is wearing a hood or small round cap similar to that of statuette no. 10 and those of the National Museum. There are two half keys carved on the back. The origin of this carving is much vaguer than that of the other examples as portraits are not, a priori, a characteristic of Inuit Thule art. There are less elaborate examples in Dorset culture. Might this be a Scandinavian self-portrait?

**Dating:** Between the thirteenth and fifteenth centuries.

6. Statuette found in Saarloq in the Upernavik district in 1967 during Jan Hjarnø's excavations.

**Characteristics:** Wood carving, height 3.4 cm. A two-piece garment and hood are clearly depicted.

**Dating:** Gulløv chose not to suggest any dates. I will simply note that it corresponds to the short style following 1350.

7. Statuette found by T. Mathiassen in Illutalik by Disko Bay, in a partially destroyed ruin.

**Characteristics:** Wood carving, height 3.7 cm. The hood worn over the head and the two-piece outfit appear clearly.

**Dating:** Between the fifteenth and sixteenth centuries. I would point out that the mid-length (down to the knees) clothing style (until 1150) is opposed to Gulløv's dates.

8. Statuette found in Aasiaat/Egdesminde district by Pastor P. H. Vibek before 1900.

**Characteristics:** Wood carving, height 5.8 cm. Hooded attire and long garment appear clearly. The hood has the same characteristics found in the other statuettes discovered in the Upernavik distict, although lacking the clothing detail.

**Dating:** Between the fourteenth and sixteenth centuries. Here again the long garment style (1200–1350) doesn't quite match Gulløv's dates.

9. Statuette found during the archaeological excavations of Hans Christian Gulløv and Hans Kapel in 1972 in Håbets Ø in a longhouse in Illorpaat.

**Characteristics:** Wood carving, height 3.4 cm. A hood is outlined. Indeterminate origin: doubts surround its location, presumably Illorpaat, and its dating.

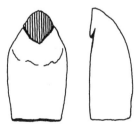

10. Statuette found on the western coast with no identified location.

**Characteristics:** Wooden carving, height 8 cm. Depicted on this carving is a short two-piece garment that is hip length,* with a high hood with what may be a plume. Gulløv believed this was inspired by the Burgundy style (short garment) of the end of the Middle Ages. The excavations of Herjolfsnes/Ikigait in southern Greenland that unearthed the greatest collection of intact, popular medieval clothing included several designs like this, although lacking plumes.

**Dating:** Between the fifteenth and sixteenth centuries. Note: there is a Dutch headpiece from the seventeenth century that is identical.

11. Statuette found during Peter Schledermann's digs on Ellesmere Island in 1979, in a ruin located on Haa Island.

**Characteristics:** Walrus ivory carving, height 2.7 cm. The local nature of the prime material in conformance with the location of its discovery in the Far North should be noted. The style is very pared down. What we see is the hood worn up around the head and the long single-piece garment.

**Dating:** Indeterminate, perhaps from the time of Thule culture (the long garment here could take us back to the style of the years 1200–1350).

---

*This is the short outfit style that began in 1350.

12. Statuette found during the archaeological excavations of George and Debby Sabo near the Hudson Strait in Baffin Island, Canada, in a ruin in Okilivialuk.

**Characteristics:** Wood carving, height 5.5 cm. A very realistic style indicating a long, single-piece garment, the hood is being worn, and the presence of a hem at the bottom of the robe can be seen.*

**Dating:** Thirteenth to fourteenth centuries.† This style is consistent with several written sources including sagas such as those of Erik the Red and the Greenlanders that mention the Scandinavian presence in North America.

The realism of this statuette 12 has inspired a variety of analyses. A cross appears quite clearly on the chest. Gulløv does not attach any particular importance to it, incorporating it with the placement of the soul in accordance with Inuit beliefs. This conjecture appears open to debate. If we go by native beliefs, souls are more likely to settle in specific areas like the joints, or in organs like the mouth, nose, and so forth—in short, in the sensitive areas of the body, which do not include

---

*It will be noted that the dates of these last two statuettes concur with Scandinavian written sources—namely, the priest Halldór in 1266 (see chapters 7 and 10).

†Given its importance, the soul cannot live just anywhere. The Dane Gustav Holm (1914, *Meddelser om Grønland*, vol. 39, 1–147), who discovered the Inuit population on Greenland's eastern coast in 1884, speaks of several small souls that reside in the human body. The larger souls live in the larynx and beneath the diaphragm. They are the size of a sparrow. The others are located in the limbs, hands, and feet. The Greenland professor Robert Petersen (1964) specifies that every joint holds a soul.

the chest. Even if we accept this hypothesis, this would be the *only* soul indicated on the amulet, which is quite a reduced number from the Inuit perspective.[2] Furthermore, this would be the only example of a carving representing a foreigner with a typically Inuit artistic approach (the marking of souls). As it happens, it is not in keeping with Inuit tradition to blend styles.

### *Observations*

The position of statuette 12's cross corresponds far too closely, in my humble opinion, to the place occupied by the crucifix over religious clothing for this hypothesis to be rejected out of hand. Medieval Icelandic sources also tell us that churchmen (Halldór, as we have seen, but also Bishop Erik Upse in 1121) set off with expeditions far into the north as well as into the west to Vinland.

An Inuit accounting of the hardly discreet presence of men of the church cannot be dismissed.

There is also one other clothing detail. According to Canadian researcher Guy Marie Rousselière, the horizontal line at shoulder level would symbolize a cape or a coat of mail.

Fig. 4.1. An Inuit statuette of the thirteenth to fourteenth centuries from the 1977 archaeological excavations of Debby and George Sabo in Okilivialuk on Baffin Island. It fits all the criteria of Thule art and has yet to receive the attention it deserves; indeed this style is characterized by its extreme purification. In my opinion, the artist stressed these clothing details, which must have left a strong impression on him. We are all familiar with the medieval church's taste for luxury, and a bishop clad in his most beautiful finery could not have helped but inflame the sculptor's imagination.
*Photo courtesy of History Museum of Ottawa*

This is not inconceivable when we recall that chain links from just such a coat have been found on Ellesmere Island. Rousselière asks if this might be an indication of the presence of a member of a martial religious order like the Templars.

We saw earlier the example of Björn Einarsson Jórsalafari, who came to Greenland on his return from a pilgrimage to Jerusalem. As we shall see later in chapter 9 concerning the church, this institution took great interest in the riches of the Far North (furs, falcons, whale blubber, ivory, and so forth), and we have every reason to think it may have sent its members—belonging to a military order or otherwise—to oversee the status of this wealth or to collect tithes. The priest Ivar Bårdsson's highly controversial report can be viewed in this sense, or even as a desire to keep a weather eye on everything concerning the Scandinavians as members of a flock considered overly recalcitrant.

This hypothesis is receiving increasing support among contemporary researchers. Recall, for informational purposes only, the numerous recriminations directed by the Catholic Church at its Greenland and Iceland flocks. The dispute was not so much spiritual as it was economical, basically based on different Nordic traditions concerning church property. In fact, for a long time the church did not own its physical buildings in Iceland and Greenland, or the taxes it accrued. The individual (or group of individuals) who had built the church was the owner of that church and all its revenues. Their role could even extend to the practice of the religion itself. Getting back to our "Scandinavian priest" statuette, other hypotheses have been advanced. It might be a Dorset statuette as depiction of the upper limbs are a Dorset-style characteristic. Another possibility is that it could be a carving done in the artistic style of Naskapi people (from the Hudson Strait in Labrador), which also possesses an open garment. The Norse hypothesis is nonetheless the strongest, corresponding to the period going from the thirteenth into the fourteenth centuries.

While confessing the greatest reservations, I would like to present here the very singular case of a portrait carved in wood of indeterminate origin. Is this of Scandinavian or Inuit manufacture? The beard carved into a point, the eyes seemingly more European, and a kind of cap (or else a monk's tonsure?) appear quite clearly. This carving was found on Skræling Island in a house belonging to the Thule phase of the habitation of so-called Ruin Island. The remnants found in situ reveal an impressive number of the typical tools of the Thule phase of Ruin Island, but the mark of a Dorset influence is visible. We should also note the presence of fragments of meteorite iron and a copper blade. The two homes on this site have been dated to about 1100, give or take fifty years. It should also be noted that this sculpture doesn't meet Inuit compositional criteria (as discussed at the beginning of this chapter) and might very well be a self-portrait carved by a Scandinavian.

However, there are examples of Dorset masks or portraits, and, for this reason, the hypothesis of an Inuit work cannot be dismissed. This is the position of Schledermann among others: "It is a fact that the carved face reflects striking Dorset elements, which is understandable when we consider the Dorset influence that characterizes the material culture of these homes."

Schledermann also stresses that the Dorset houses were strongly influenced by contemporary Thule culture. This enables him to advance the seductive hypothesis of a work resulting from an encounter between a Scandinavian group and a heterogeneous group of Dorset and Thule Inuit. His hypothesis is plausible and would explain the absence of typically Inuit characteristics.

To fully grasp the importance and utility of these new research elements, a rapid glance of medieval clothing proves necessary. Throughout the Middle Ages, women's garments were long. Until 1150, male clothing was short (knee length) and then became ankle length from 1200 to 1350. After 1350, male garments became short again (hip length).

Else Marie Gutarp provides some different dates. In the twelfth and thirteenth centuries, the long garment was a sign of wealth, even though styles had changed. The shorter knee-length style appeared at the end of the thirteenth and the beginning of the fourteenth centuries, and even continued into the fifteenth century. Gutarp bases her observations on excavations in Denmark, Norway, and Herjolfsnes from which items of clothing worn between 1300 and 1400 were unearthed.

This style had exceptions, and this quick overview of clothing styles is not always in agreement with the real facts because style could often run into the opposition of church morality, which condemned the short male garment. Furthermore, the excavations in Herjolfsnes, in southern Greenland, in the twenties contradict these dates because the clothing found intact in the permafrost dated from about 1400. The garments were long, which is in agreement with Gutarp's observations.

How should we interpret this fact? There are several possible explanations. It is possible that there was a time lag between the Greenland style and European style, something easily explained by the distance between them. Other clothing-style influences could have played a part. The weight of the church was very strong at a certain time because people could still be burned at the stake in Greenland in 1407. It may have been able to impose the long garment style for a longer period than was feasible in Europe. A rupture of contact with Europe would have led to the persistence of this longer clothing style, but I personally dismiss this hypothesis as there are a number of elements that have recently weakened this theory of Greenland isolation that has held sway far too long.

Poul Nørlund, who was responsible for the Herjolfsnes excavations of 1921, drew a comparison between the hoods they discovered there and the medieval hood (Lapûn) that was equipped with a long tail that fell down the back. This was a typical French garment of the fourteenth and fifteenth centuries that had the Latin name *liripipium*. This kind of headgear (*strutthœtter* in Scandinavia) was widespread among the lower classes at the end of the fifteenth century. In 1936, a similar outfit was unearthed in a southern Norwegian bog near Andøya. Analysis of the textiles in the headpiece showed it came from the middle of the fourteenth century. One thing seems increasingly clear, reflecting the contact between Vikings and Inuits: the hood of the Inuit anorak oddly resembles the medieval hood. This appears clearly in statuettes 2, 3, 4, and 6, all of which share the fact of being found in the Upernavik district. Nordic people frequented this region, and it is one of the preeminent sites of Inussuk culture. We thus have artistic evidence covering quite a long period of time from 1200 to 1500, which covers a part of the temporal context I'm proposing for the Nordic occupancy of Greenland.

The head coverings that are a kind of slightly conical shaped cap with a flattened tops (as can be seen in statuette 10) are dated by Nørlund and Gulløv as from the end of the fifteenth century. Citing as an example the Flemish Schools, particularly the paintings of Dirk Bout (died 1575), Nørlund emphasizes the fact that these caps are in the style of the time of Louis XI. He concludes from this that Greenland was frequented by foreign ships until a very late period. I completely share his opinion and support this statement in chapter 10 with discussion of the "British," Frisian, and Portuguese presence in Greenland.

Gulløv believes there is too much uncertainty surrounding the history of Greenland clothing; hence, there are difficulties in dating these figurines. We cannot use them as a historical reference, but their evidence concerning the presence of white men, Scandinavians in this instance, cannot be dismissed. The Danish researcher believes these statuettes confirm contacts between Inuits and Vikings. Some of them are quite surprising for their exactitude, such as example number 3, found by Therkel Mathiassen in 1929, and which cannot be explained unless there was direct contact.

To truly grasp the importance of these statuettes, we have to take into account that traditional Inuit culture is oral—which is to say, that this artistic evidence serves not as oral but as a material account, if I may put it this way, and serves as a kind of confirmation for the Icelandic written sources. In this sense, they are much more objective and offer no stylistic deviations. Only their interpretation is an obstacle as decoding them has proved to be difficult. What could they mean on a symbolic level?

If we take Inuit clothing under consideration, as well as their beliefs and taboos, several observations seem called for. These statuettes could only illustrate peaceful contact as depicting enemies is foreign to Inuit tradition. To the best of my knowledge, there are no pictorial representations of Amerindians, for example, in Inuit art, despite their geographical proximity.

The impressive number of statuettes, given the remote era and the conditions of archaeological researches, cannot reflect an episodic situation or an act of chance. The same is true for their location as each archaeological site (Ellesmere, Thule) was crosschecked with either Icelandic or Inuit sources.

All the statuettes are of Thule style with the exception of statuette 12, which has not been conclusively identified as belonging to the Dorset. Based on the data in our possession, such as the Nordic source texts, contact could have taken place during this period but surely not on the scale of the two people interbreeding. Contradicting this, however, the concordance of the dates of the traditional Inuit and Scandinavian folk history, and that of their artistic history, the dates when Thule and Inussuk culture appear tend to designate this culture as one the Scandinavians frequented long and diligently, with a strong possibility of interbreeding. I would deduce from this that contact with the Dorset people did not have to be so developed to allow for the creation of these statuettes. Given the enormous cultural gap that separated the two cultures—both technically and physically—it is almost normal that the Inuit could not refrain from leaving concrete evidence of a people they could not help but be impressed by. Examples can be seen in their dwellings if we consider the imposing buildings of Garðar,* techniques if we consider sailing, or even the proofs of physical prowess that are highlighted in some stories. Some foreign sources such as the Zeno brothers, which have been quite controversial but which are far from being uninteresting, testify to the Inuit deference toward Vikings "considered to be like Gods."

> The rude and savage people of these partes, seeing these supernaturall effects [the domestic use of hot springs], doe take these friars for Gods, and bring them many presentes as chickens, fleshe and divers other thinges, and have them all in great reverence.[3]

---

*This is visible in the use of all the comparisons combined in the word *igdlo* (house) mentioned in the Vestribygð map in chapter 2.

From this perspective, these amulets could have served as talismans. As a "religious" or "fetishist" use of Inuit art is one of its defining characteristics, this hypothesis cannot be dismissed out of hand.

As noted earlier, these statuettes have value as historical evidence, but they also offer a valuable testimony about the society of that era. Taken generally, the carvings of not only the Scandinavians but also of the Inuits, of animals, and of tools (miniature sleds, boats, and so on) illustrate the daily life of the Inuit people of this time and are thereby an element of valuable information.

At the beginning of this chapter, I mentioned one particular function of Inuit art: its role in games and play. Speaking plainly, Inuit children used Inuit sculptures that had no religious fetish value as toys. The admirably realistic examples frequently discovered in archaeological digs of carved kayaks and miniature sleds and seals and dogs carved out of ivory or driftwood were toys. This realization introduced a new hypothesis into my research. Because Inuit children were able to play with these Norse figurines, it offers another confirmation of peaceful relations between Inuit and Viking. Extremely strict taboos prohibited any similar kind of play with evil or enemies, which were mentioned as infrequently as possible. For example, it's hard to imagine figurines of Amerindians being used as toys by young Inuit children.

The last function of Inuit art, the utilitarian or practical function that is generally and quickly viewed as decoration of tools, for example, cannot be envisioned in the case of these Norse figurines.

The location of these figurines also fits in with the presence of other Scandinavian objects in the same sites. This Inuit visual testimony carved in wood or ivory explains the presence of Scandinavian objects and their owners at such high latitudes. As an example: Peter Schledermann's excavations on Ellesmere Island.

I found this hypothesis more plausible than that of trading: the objects found in the Canadian and Greenland Far North are laughable for their exchange value (pieces of nails, fragments of cloth, and so on) and would more likely be, in my opinion, things left behind by Scandinavians rather than objects of merchandise, unless we sell the native people short. I believe the insignificant objects the Vikings left behind and the statuettes carved by the Inuit are two facets of one phenomenon, the Scandinavian presence in the farthest northern regions (I am only considering here those settlements that are very likely Scandinavian and not Inuit settlements possessing "collected" Scandinavian objects).

These contacts are historically logical as we know the Thule migrations began circa 900 CE and are thus contemporary with the Scandinavian presence in this area. The presence of a Thule people is confirmed in Kangeq in the Nuuk/Godthåb region, where carbon-dated remnants of Thule winter settlements date to the first half of the fourteenth century. This would confirm the 1360 texts of Ivar Bårdsson. It can be seen that the facts match: the Thule migration from north to south and the written Icelandic sources mentioning Skræling incursions.*

Contact between the two peoples is increasingly accepted as a reality by contemporary researchers. Just like the Inuit oral traditional lore, their artistic legacy has also long slumbered in the dusty desk drawers of history. Yet its value as evidence of southern European or Scandinavian presence is beyond question. It offers the advantage by comparison to the oral or even written sources of Europeans to have not been subjected to any distortion such as the stylish variations and the additions of scribes. Here we have three-dimensional evidence of different styles of medieval European clothing, which we could describe as head to toe as different forms of headgear can be seen here.

The presence of Scandinavians or other foreigners at a very late period is confirmed in the southernmost sites, and to make it clear, these are not chance visits but respond to clear mercantile imperatives. This is fully visible in the fact that the clothing carved by the medieval Inuit completely corresponds to that depicted in the 1492 German globe of Martin Behaim illustrating the "mysterious" Arctic regions of the "four commercial trades,"† notions inherited from Nicholas of Lynn and referring to the specific riches of the Far North.

---

*Name given by the Norse to the natives they encountered in the remote territories, mainly those close to the Nordrsetur. It could apply to Amerindians or the Inuit of the Far North.

†These medieval notions will be discussed in chapter 10, which focuses on the Scandinavian presence in the Far North.

Fig. 4.2. A detail from Martin Behaim's globe, 1492, which talks of an "Eisland" whose inhabitants are Christians of imposing appearance and who sell their dogs for expensive amounts. This is intriguing as Iceland had been Christian for four centuries, a fact of which Behaim could not have been ignorant. Moreover, it also appears correctly spelled on this globe. And why would they sell their dogs for very high prices? Is this an allusion to another country of ice where dogs were used? (See also color plate 9.)
*Private collection, original Germanisches National Museum, Nuremberg*

All the statuettes that have been found (except for no. 5 and maybe no. 12) correspond with Thule art. This contradicts Duason and Oleson's hypothesis of Viking-Inuit mixed breeding at the onset of Dorset culture. Based on all the elements in our possession, such as Scandinavian source texts, contact could have taken place during this period, but surely not on such a large scale as to create cultural intermingling. To the contrary, the concordance of dates from the traditional Inuit and Scandinavian cultural stores, the dates of the appearance of Thule culture on Greenland tend to identify this culture as the one the Scandinavians diligently frequented for a long period, with a very strong possibility of cultural intermingling. Contacts with the Dorset people could not have been as elaborate as to allow for the creation of this artistic background (among other things, the general use of the term *Skræling* is placed in this period).

My focus on this artistic legacy is to highlight its value not only as evidence but also for its interpretive value. By restoring them to their natural context, it is possible to glimpse all these statuettes' implications, as well as the relationship between the ludic function of Inuit art and the peaceful contacts between the two peoples. This echoes my

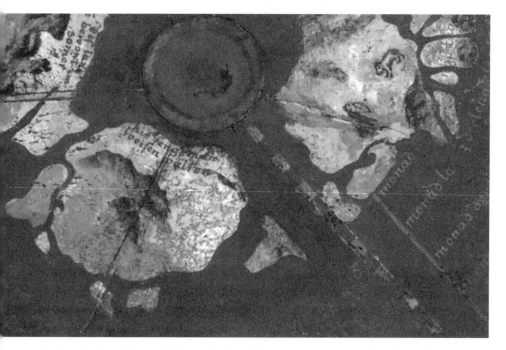

Fig. 4.3. A detail from Martin Behaim's globe: the Arctic regions bring to mind
Nicholas of Lynn's text in which the various commerces seem implied, such as
the polar falcon and the polar bear pursued by an archer wearing a long
medieval garment. This would be one of the first definite depictions of the
North American continent. (See also color plate 10.)
*Private collection, original Germanisches National Museum, Nuremberg*

observation in chapter 3 regarding the resemblance of certain Inuit and
Nordic games and the importance of play in these cultures. These statuettes deserve to be fully considered as the equivalent of written sources
of the Greenland and Canadian Inuit people who five centuries before
had carved three-dimensional records of the presence of the white man
in the medieval Arctic.

# 5

# Inuit Loans, Inussuk Culture, and the Vikings

Inussuk culture is the one that contrasts most sharply with those that came before it, including Thule culture. This culture left us a significant number of carved artistic evidence of the Vikings, and it is quite likely that a large part of the oral tradition referring to the Scandinavians, a.k.a. Kavdlunaat, had to have come from this culture. At least the historical dates and archaeology concur on this point. These are quite a few coincidences for a single culture. Several researchers don't shy away at all from the likelihood of close contacts between these two peoples. For example, Helge Larsen had no doubt whatsoever of this in 1950. Inuit people saw Vikings, hence the existence of these statuettes wearing Scandinavian clothes. Inussuk Culture reveals the newest objects that were unknown to earlier Inuit cultures. The statuettes depicting Scandinavians reflect direct and protracted contact. I will discuss three excavation sites geographically far from each other that confirm all the loans from Scandinavian culture.

## THE INUSSUK SITE
## (MATHIASSEN'S 1929 EXCAVATIONS)

These excavations took place in the Upernavik district of northern Greenland, twenty kilometers north of Upernavik. This was close to Kingittorsuaq, where the famous runestone that provided evidence of

Nordic trips in the north was found. An impressive quantity of objects was found here, both Inuit and Scandinavian, especially those made from whalebone. This is a distinguishing feature of Thule industry, particularly Inussuk.

The length of time this Inuit site was occupied seems to have been quite long as the midden was some two yards thick. Several Scandinavian objects were discovered there: two iron blades, a bucket made from wooden strips, a piece of wool clothing, a pawn, and a portrait carved in wood. The oldest layers were thought to date from the thirteenth and fourteenth centuries while the more recent are from the fourteenth and fifteenth. More recently (1977) R. Jordan revised these figures by giving the last half of the fourteenth century for the oldest layers and the first half of the fifteenth century for the most recent ones.

The technical borrowing from the Vikings is particularly obvious for several objects, such as the bucket made from wooden slats. This reflects cooperage techniques that were unknown to the Inuit of Alaska and Canada. Several researchers, like Gad in 1970 and Lidegaard in 1991, saw this as a noteworthy example of Inuit appropriation from the Scandinavians. Some specimens are very reminiscent of Norwegian barrel work. Helge Larsen viewed the tubs made from vertical slats assembled around a circular base as part of a technique that was absolutely not Inuit. This Norse influence is undoubtedly due to the fact that the Vikings made several trips into North Greenland during the latter half of the thirteenth century.

This completely developed and mastered technique recurs frequently in the finds at Inussuk sites and obviously reflects ties with Scandinavians. It should be pointed out that the Tunumiut (Inuit of East Greenland) pushed the art of cooperage to an extreme degree and are the only Inuit in the entire Arctic to have attained such perfection. As we know, the Inussuk moved back up the eastern coast after reaching the south. There is every reason to think that this technique borrowed from the Vikings followed the path of the Inussuit migration and that the Tunumiut who lived in isolation for a long time (the Danish captain Gustav Holm only contacted them in 1888), the originality of this technique was preserved and more importantly given the chance to fully blossom.

This loan was not the only one, other examples exist, such as the bone spoon whose long, delicate handle is remarkably similar to medieval European spoons, or the spoons with the handle end in the form of a circle. I should also mention the brooches with crosswise ribs, the baleen saw, and the whalebone knife that takes the form of a dagger or dirk totally foreign to the Inuit craftsman and interpreted to be a copy of Scandinavian tools or weapons. Lidegaard believes the dagger confirms a desire to imitate European models.

We should recall that the Inuit, even those of Thule culture, had no warrior traditions, even though this culture is clearly characterized by the power and efficacy of its tools/weaponry. This means that Inuit tools are conceived for one specific purpose: hunting. In Inussuk culture we find as many items of Scandinavian provenance such as cloth ends, pieces of bronze, and pawns as we do those made by the Inuit showing an obvious Norse influence or loans of aesthetic motifs (dotted lines, circles, etc.).

## THE SITE OF ILLUTALIK
## (HOLTVED AND MATHIASSEN'S
## 1933 EXCAVATIONS)

This site is in the Disko region of northern Greenland. Objects close to Inussuk culture were found in one of the deepest layers of the first part of an excavated midden. One of the most surprising was a seal fishing net that amazed many scientists, as net fishing was not an Inuit specialty originally, and this technique wouldn't appear until much later among the neighboring Inuit of Canada and Alaska. We know that the Vikings used this technique, which apparently did not go unnoticed.

Another curiosity was a small tub made of a baleen hoop. Arrow heads with screw threads at the end greatly surprised the experts—as it happens that the screw was unknown to the Inuit of this time. The same is true for the large tips for bird-hunting spears, which also had a screw thread at their back end. A statuette in short clothing and of recent fabrication (sixteenth century) could reflect a change in medieval styles, thereby confirming the later presence of Scandinavians or other Europeans.

In addition to these Inuit imitations, this site offers the presence of numerous typically Scandinavian objects, which given the immediate proximity of the two populations is quite logical and is another confirmation, if needed, of contact and exchanges between the two communities. Among these I'd like to point out the wooden dagger hilt similar to a medieval European design (between the fifteenth and sixteenth centuries), a walrus-ivory statue of two stylized dragon heads, a weaving loom weight found in all Scandinavian settlements, and a piece of wood carved with a zigzag pattern unknown to the Inuit.

Both Inuit and Scandinavian objects likely refer to a period a little more recent than the fifteenth century, during the presence of Thule culture. The deeper layers of the midden in which Scandinavian objects were found are assumed to date from the 1400s, during the occupation of this site by the Inussuk. The oldest inhabitation of Illutalik goes back to about 900 to 1100, which would mean Thule culture.

I should quickly mention that the site of Illorsuit in this same region of Disko was also excavated by Mathiassen and Holtved in 1933. Fifteen Inuit homes were unearthed. A bronze cooking pot and an iron knife blade were discovered in a house dating from the thirteenth or fourteenth century. This was the oldest dwelling on this site. Both objects were attributed to Scandinavians.

## THE SITE OF KANGAMIUT

The Kangamiut site is located 300 kilometers north of Nuuk/Godthåb, thus in the Vestribygð colony. Only a few Scandinavian objects were unearthed: several pieces of bells and a small model of a Scandinavian boat. All the Inuit and Scandinavian objects date from about 1350 to 1500 and support the notion of a later Norse presence. This site was heavily populated, which Mathiassen attributes to strategic or defensive motivations. This interpretation eludes, as we have seen, the collective nature of their economy based on the hunting of large marine mammals, as well as another factor: the foreign presence. This brings to mind the distinctivly gregarious defensive nature of the Inuit habitat seen in the story of the shaman collected by Poul Egede.

Based on these different sites, the evidence of the Viking statuettes, and the copied Viking tools, Mathiassen comes to the conclusion of a simultaneous presence of the two populations in southern Greenland and in the Upernavik district. The Kingittorsuaq runestone and the bell pieces from the Inussuk midden permitted him to provide relatively firm dates from about 1350. A slightly older date of 1250 cannot be ruled out if we compare it to the substantial runic background existing in the Hanseatic merchant quarter of Bryggen in Bergen.

Several clues are very useful for dating the arrival of certain objects in Greenland. The game of chess is supposed to have appeared in Scandinavia during the twelfth century, but its earliest traces found by archaeologists date from the thirteenth century. In Nipaitsoq (Vestribygð) chess pawns very similar to those of northern Greenland are viewed as connected to the last phase of Norse habitation, the four-teenth century.

Mathiassen was surely the first, following his excavations, to so clearly recognize the possibility of Inuit loans from the Scandinavians, as these latter had a strong influence on the material culture of the Greenland natives. Ironically, his conclusions were detoured onto some unfortunately eccentric paths.

A truly technical revolution and rich flowering took place in these wealthy regions, and on this level contact was positive: "contact with the Vikings gave them [the Inuit] new impetus."[1]

There is no lack of examples of technical transfer or innovation spanning the gamut from aesthetic details to true technological changes. In the first category, we have the loan of aesthetic motifs—for example, the use of dots or circles in decoration. There is an example of acanthus leaves (completely foreign to Greenland) carved on a piece of ivory. This motif refers to an older Gothic era. In the second category, technologi-cal innovations, we have in the fifteenth and sixteenth centuries the replacement of the old harpoon point with flattened points that hold prey more tightly, the disappearance of the oil lamps with a wick on the ledge, and the tips of weapon heads equipped with a grooved end similar to a screw, which allowed a better grip by the spear thrower than the former pommels.

Mathiassen believed the influence began in the twelfth century with, for example, the cooperage technique. The screw, unknown at this time to the neighboring Inuit, shows up in Inussuk culture around 1500. This novelty is not a coincidence or a technical caprice. Lidegaard describes a specific and intentional technique: "In the old Eskimo culture, arrow points had been equipped with two to four lateral incisions or bulges, but now the points have been threaded. This is a new element in Eskimo cultures, which must have come from outside."[2]

It was during the Inussuk culture that the kayak evolved to reach its current perfection, as well as the spray skirt, a kind of raised cylinder that allowed the hunter to use his craft in rough seas.

Quadrilateral houses replaced the former round houses; they were smaller but more solidly built. They were also sunk into the ground. This kind of construction began about 1500 and could be a copy of the

Fig. 5.1. Kayak: Greenland evolved quickly. However, the past is never far away. The old traditions persist in the capital Nuuk/Godthab, the most Westernized of all Greenland towns. This father teaching his son how to use a kayak is a fine example of this.
*Photo by J. Privat*

Scandinavian model. Ironically, in southern Greenland, where the phenomenon of proximity (and thus cohabitation?) was stronger, the Inuit continued using the round house, whereas the four-sided house was the one adopted in the northern regions of Greenland.

Should we see this as a kind of exacerbated "nationalist" sentiment at work here inspiring the Inuit to cling to their traditional habitat? The question was different in the north, because the Norse presence was fairly random: copying in this case no longer had the same symbolic value. It was not the abandonment of a cultural feature in favor of another belonging to a strong, foreign culture so much as the incorporation into its own cultural reserves a temporarily interesting foreign element; but this is only a personal conjecture.

I would give more weight to a socioeconomic reason as a possible explanation. Because there was a greater quantity of sea mammals in the north, a quadrilateral house might better fill the needs of the larger population required for this kind of maritime hunting activity.

T. J. Oleson clearly leans to the side of an Inuit borrowing of the Scandinavian habitat as he considers the rectangular dwelling to be a Scandinavian import and the round house an older type. He supports his belief by citing Mathiessen's excavations in Disko Bay. Everywhere contact existed between Dorset and Thule cultures, he saw the presence of a rectangular dwelling that he considered equivalent to the Icelandic *skáli*. He also cited similar observations on the rectangular Inuit home by Thalbitzer and Mauss. Because Oleson viewed the legendary Inuit people, the Tuniit, as Inuit-Scandinavian mixed bloods, his argument can almost seem too perfect: "The square house of the Tuniit and the later Eskimo square house simply represent the Icelandic dwelling."[3]

We shall see later that his approach is not proof against criticism. It should also be noted that Oleson sees a similarity between the Scandinavian tent and that of the Thule people. What we do know for certain is that several explanations are yet to be discovered and a number of unknown factors still cover a variety of points today.

Again rejecting the hypothesis of coincidence, Gad bases his position on the early presence of all these Scandinavian objects in Inussuit sites to dispel the hypothesis of recuperation at work on Viking sites at the end of the fifteenth century or beginning of the sixteenth century. "Several of these objects were found in (archaeological) layers so deep and beneath very thick layers dating from Inussuk culture, they must have been thrown away at the very beginning of this culture, at least the thirteenth century."[4]

More generally, as supporters of a theory of Viking loans to the Inuit, I can cite André Leroi-Gourhan. He believed that the Inuit may have copied the Viking ship: "The umiaq, the large Eskimo canoe, could perhaps have been inspired by the Norse drakkar."[5]

Leroi-Gourhan believes that both ships behave the same at sea. I share his opinion that the form of the sail used on the *umiaq* is practically identical to that of Scandinavian boats. Without seeking to pick a side, I earlier mentioned the non-maritime nature—in the full sense of the term as exemplified by the Vikings—of the Inuit who sailed within sight of the coastline but avoided crossing large expanses of the open sea. One element could offer support to Leroi-Gourhan's assertions, the fact that the *umiaq** and the Vikings appeared in Greenland at practically the same time. However, for the reason stated above (the Inuit people are not sailors) I would keep my distance from his hypothesis that "the Eskimo could just have easily sailed it [the *drakkar/umiaq*] from the coast of Europe to their current habitat.[6]

Here we see the old theory of a shared origin of the Sami and Inuit peoples. Furthermore, traditional Scandinavian lore recounts cases of the construction of hide boats by the colonists, which means the two peoples used a technique common to both of them. One example concerning boat upkeep is dealt with here:[†] "It was customary to prepare seal fat over there [in the Nordrsetur], as hunting was generally better there than at home in the colonies. Melted seal fat was spread over the hide boats, which were then hung facing the wind in isolated drying sheds until they were dry, then they were prepared as was called for."[7]

---

*See the second part of chapter 1 on the arrival of Thule culture between 900 and 1000. In fact, the case of the *umiaq* is much richer and more complex than one might think.

†In chapter 7, where we discuss *Flóamanna saga,* we shall see a case of a loan in the full sense of the term where east coast natives (according to the *Grønlands Historiske Mindesmærker*) borrow the skin boat of this saga's hero, Thorgil.

This description of the preparation bears a strong resemblance to that of the *umiaq* as practiced in some regions. Here again, the theory of the Vikings' inability to adjust to the Arctic is seriously roughed up. Would these drying sheds have any relationship to the isolated ruins unearthed by various excavations in the Canadian Arctic that still remain an enigma?

One thing is certain, the Vikings enjoyed the benefit of extensive knowledge of the sea. They were also in contact with the Celts, who used coracles (*currach*), which distinguishes both these cultures from the Inuit, who had no seafaring tradition.

Up to the present, the prevailing theory was that the Inuit (Thule culture) had introduced the *umiaq* to Greenland during their migration from the American continent. All these accounts complicate the theories in vogue quite a bit.

The question I raise is: Just how extensive was the loan of this ship-building technique and who was its author? Did both people copy each other, borrowing their neighbor's strong points? In this case the Inuit would have borrowed the sail of the knorr, and the Vikings would have adapted to their environment by using local products such as walrus and sealskins like the natives. Should we regard the Scandinavians as the sole inventors of the *umiaq*? The idea is less absurd than it may appear, for the Nordic people were known for their worked walrus hide, which was highly sought after because of its quality. This was one of their exports to Europe and was even used to pay their tithes to Rome.*

Leroi-Gourhan sees Scandinavian loans to the Inuit in two domains: that of the harpoon with the current Scandinavian fish gig, and that of making fire. Following are his observations on the first case.

It is equipped with a female harpoon head on each of its three teeth, the profile of which is identical to that of Greenland. It's not

---

*"The collection of tithes from Iceland, the Faroe Islands, and Greenland are difficult to sell or ship to Rome or the Holy Land: Greenland merchandise consists of cow hides, walrus tusks, and walrus leather rope, which are difficult to sell for an appropriate price." In *Regesta Norvegica*, vol. 2, April 4, 1282, with a response from Pope Martin IV on April 15, 1282. The extreme rapidity of the pope's response is notable.

attached to the line by a channel, but simply knotted to the socket, which forms a kind of transition from the unperforated male harpoon and the female harpoon of the simplest Greenland type.[8]

Leroi-Gourhan sees a technique in the second case that has been confirmed as existing in Sweden's Värmland province until the nineteenth century with a point-by-point resemblance with the stringed brace of the eastern Greenland Inuit (just like the needle case of Tunumiut women would be a Scandinavian loan in his opinion).

Anne Stine Ingstad believes the rudimentary ironwork of the Thule Inuit would be a technological loan from the Vikings: "The Thule culture in Greenland was not a pure Stone Age culture for these Eskimos had learned the use of iron from the Vikings who arrived in Greenland during the tenth century. Sometime before the Thule, the Dorset Eskimos had lived in Greenland and must have also been in contact with the Scandinavians."[9]

The author notes that examples of ironwork were discovered in two Dorset settlements: in Hall Land, where a piece of meteor iron that had been cold forged was discovered by Mathiassen; and Inglefield Land, where a complete tool, a knife blade apparently forged from meteor iron, was discovered.

Ingstad's observation about earlier contacts with the Dorset people is of interest to me because it reinforces my observations concerning the Scandinavian description of the different Inuit peoples. Most importantly, it places those researchers who use the Dorset people as a referential element concerning Viking influence on the Inussuk Inuit in an awkward position. They claim that the elements found in Inussuk culture that were previously present in Dorset culture allows them to discard the idea of Scandinavian influence.

But if Dorset culture was not entirely free of contact with the Vikings, the axiom falls apart as the Canadian Dorset Inuit could also have borrowed material features from Greenland's Scandinavian culture. This gives us a better grasp of the full value of Schledermann's hypothesis concerning the mysterious portrait found on Skræling Island, which could be a piece of Dorset evidence. We will revisit this question of loans also touching Dorset culture with the Inuit objects provided by Mathiassen.

For several decades these objects have formed an important element in the theory of contact between both populations, if not an actual merger of the two peoples, particularly for those defending the notion of Inuit borrowings. This position tends to arouse challenges today. The objects mentioned from Mathiassen's digs in the thirties, mainly in the Upernavik district, have been the subject of countless discussions, and the question of Scandinavian loans to the Inuit will not be settled anytime soon.

Mathiassen believed that the spoons with the stylistic handles could only be the result of Inuit borrowing. All come from Thule sites. Identical models have been found in Norway, particularly in Bergen and Trondheim, which are known for their maritime relationship with Greenland. These many spoons whose style appears so refined to us seem to have a uniquely aesthetic function that is not really proper to Greenland in the sense of a search of art for art's sake. If Vikings and Inuit were indeed neighbors and cohabitants, I would consider this a result of the proximity of the two peoples, a desire to imitate a completely gratuitous ornamentation that must have seized hold of them, for their own aesthetic sense, on the other hand, was quite real.

However, over recent years research has been prone to increasingly distance itself from these objects, arguing they are present throughout the Arctic. They maintain that these spoons as well as the pails we shall soon discuss could have been invented by the Inuit themselves (thus without any Scandinavian influence) or even have originated with Dorset culture. This position leaves me doubtful as it starkly contradicts the functions of Inuit art in which there is nothing superfluous. As it happens, the sophistication that characterizes these Inuit spoon handles doesn't reflect any function.

The same aloof attitude can be seen in study of the saw and dagger. Here we again find the argument of the Dorset antecedent mentioned earlier, and I would oppose it with that of Anne Ingstad—shared by other researchers such as Oleson—of contacts between Vikings and the Dorset people during the first years of colonization. Technical confirmation can be found in Scandinavian descriptions or in those of Adam of Bremen concerning weapons, the absence of sleds, and so on. In other words, Scandinavian influence may have already been at work on this older culture in Canada. This would explain the presence of objects with a pronounced Scandinavian imprint in Inuit craftwork.

Just as has been done with the medieval spoons, some contemporary researchers are beginning to distance themselves from the Inuit pails. R. H. Jordan, J. Meldgaard, and H. C. Gulløv have all noted the existence of these pails among the Canadian Dorset. Jordan hypothesizes that they originated in these regions. All three now reject the introduction of this technique by Scandinavians. We should recall that Thule culture had prolonged contact with the Vikings and had every opportunity to copy Scandinavian models. They spread southward or back toward the north to come back down Greenland's eastern coast. It is therefore logical that we would find these pails in Illutalik in southern Greenland and not outside of Greenland for the Thule people. Because this technique can also be found among Dorset peoples, as contemporary research seems to show, it does not appear necessarily contradictory as this culture was also equally present inside and outside Greenland. For this reason, it seems to me that the hypothesis of the Scandinavian introduction of this technique should not be rejected completely.

An example of a wooden bucket found during Mathiassen's excavations in Illutalik could provide more elements than we might guess. In fact, this bucket is clearly made from wooden slats, like the traditional uniform model, but this bucket has the singular feature of being curved. The diameter of the bottom is narrower than the opening at the top. I would suspect this could be a non-Inuit technique originally as this kind of result is obtained by working with heat, a technique the Vikings had mastered perfectly to obtain the perfect curves of their long boats (*langskip*). As the Inuit were not part of an Iron Age culture, they consequently did not forge iron with heat. To the best of my knowledge, working wood with the heat or steam necessary to curve it was unknown to them. This means that this bucket of Inuit manufacture (Inussuk) found in an Inussuk site would therefore be the product of a technical loan. If my hypothesis is correct, this technical detail would clearly confirm the borrowing of this technique by the Inuit, with everything that implies: long periods of peaceful contact and cohabitation, and so forth.

The case of the Inuit net found in Mathiassen's excavations is no less mysterious than that of our wooden buckets. This net was found in a very deep layer (between the seventh and eighth layers of the dig) at the Illutalik site in the Disko region. The question of its origin arose: Was it Inuit or had the Vikings brought it? Given the depth of the archaeological layer, which has not been contested, Mathiassen excluded the hypothesis that it had been brought there by European whalers. All that remains, therefore, is a Scandinavian hypothesis as this site has been clearly classified as Inuit (Inussuk)—the notion that this technique was borrowed by the natives, if not something they were taught by their neighbors during the time of a long and peaceful cohabitation, clearly must be considered. In fact, according to Mathiassen, *no equivalent is to be found* in the central Thule culture, and the net only appeared at a relatively late date in Alaska. We have seen that net fishing was a favorite technique of the Scandinavians, and one also used for hunting seals. It is still practiced on the Faroe Islands. Conversely, it was not characteristic of the Inuit.

## LOAN WORDS FROM THE VIKINGS

This particular subject still requires further exploration. The hypothesis was maintained primarily by the Norwegian evangelist Hans Egede and then his sons, particularly Poul Egede in his 1750 Greenland dictionary. As a principle, Hans Egede's position makes sense. Indeed, if we accept the theory of peaceful cohabitation, which archaeology appears to confirm, there was much close contact for commercial reasons. We then have to consider a minimum of verbal exchanges, which are reflected in several Inuit tales like that of the two friends. They tell us that the Vikings even learned the native tongue. One of the supporting arguments for this, ironically, went unnoticed in Bjørn Jónsson's thirteenth-century description of Greenland based on an older source;[10] in fact, in his list of place-names of the Eystribygð colony we learn that one of the fjords, Utliblikfjordr, is not named after a Scandinavian colonist but is instead based on the native word *Itiblissoak*.

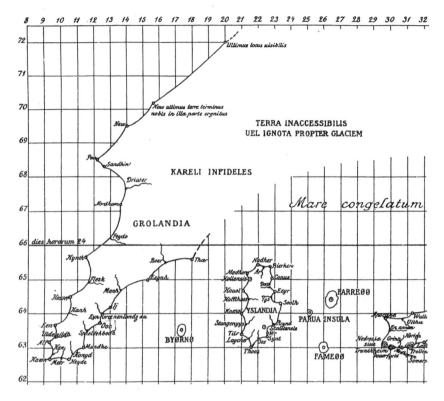

Fig. 5.2. A sketch uncovering the deception in Claudius Clavus's map. In 1904,
Carl S. Petersen and Anton Bjørnbo of Denmark extracted all the alleged places-names
from their "poetic" embellishments (visible, for example, in the 1569 Mercator map), like
the "Thaer Promontory, the Boer River," and so forth. Placed end to end by following
the entire Greenland coast from east to west, they reveal the lyrics of a medieval ballad.
*A. Bjørnbo, "Cartographia Groenlandica," 1912*

This practice is quite odd as it doesn't conform with tradition and
allows us to assume that the Vikings had a basic knowledge of the
native language. This use of native vocabulary indirectly gives us confirmation of a good Inuit-Norse relationship. Another ambiguous word,
*Alba,* classified until now as a medieval invention, could have originated
the same way. Numerous medieval maps of Greenland based on those of
the Venetian Zeno brothers and of Claudius Clavus (1424, for example)
provided completely made-up place-names (see fig. 5.2).

Among other speculations, this has been presumed to have been a plagiarism of a Russian place-name. But I would like to point out that Alba in the Latin of antiquity refers to the color white (or rather "the white garment" according to the Gaffiot dictionary). Oddly enough, there is an Inuit settlement located roughly in the same place on the European maps with the name Qaqortoq, which means more or less the same thing, perhaps the name of a mountain that is heavily snow-covered. Could their Nordic neighbors have known or been able to overlook—depending on the position you take—this meaning? Let's recall also the place-name that recurred throughout the whole of Norse colonization: Hvitserk (the white shirt), which appeared on all the maps and in all the source texts from before the Nordic arrival (982 was the first voyage of Eric the Red). It was apparently a very handy physical landmark for navigation.

There is a strong likelihood that this word *Alba* could be a new example of Inuit-Scandinavian contacts. For Europeans or Scandinavians to adopt Inuit concepts would be a novelty. This would not be in accordance with tradition. The origin of the place-name seems to have gone entirely unnoticed by contemporaries. But let's go back to the reverse phenomenon of Inuit loans from the Scandinavians.

The quasi-contemporary French translation (1763) of Egede's work by Des Roches de Parthenay will be very helpful to us here. The following terms are presented as medieval loan words from the Scandinavians (I cannot take a firm stance on either side of these statements, and it is the same for other authors): *neeriok,* "meat," which gives us the Inuit *nerrivoq,* "to eat" (probably "meat eater" originally), comes from the Scandinavian *norrie* (to eat) in Norse according to H. Egede.[11] Let's note that in his own dictionary[12] his son Poul says that *nérryok* means *æder, spiser.* In fact, the ad hoc term for that time would be *noera* (to feed),[13] which became the contemporary Norwegian *noere* and even the medieval *naera* (which is the contemporary Norwegian *naere*). The word also exists in Canada, *neqi* (meat), and *neqivoq* (in which meat is implied),* which inevitably evokes the medieval Scandinavian *naering* (food), which is even older but still current.

---

*Scandinavians also knew this connotation: to eat (meat).

As the Vikings also haunted these lands, it is difficult to take a firm position as their influence could have also been at work there. If this were the case and the word came from the continent like the Inuit migrations, this would also contradict Egede's hypothesis. Did Des Roches transcribe something incorrectly? The fact remains that in Old Icelandic (medieval or earlier)[14] *næra* clearly means "to eat," and *næring* means "food." The similarity to the Inuit word *neqi* could not be anymore striking when it is known that the letter "r" did not exist originally in the Inuit alphabet and that the "q" is phonetically quite close to it (thus from their arrival in Greenland) until the recolonization by Hans Egede in 1721, quite a bit later. In fact, the letters "r" and "q" are completely absent in the dictionary compiled by his son Poul in 1750. I'd like to point out that in the contemporary Greenland dictionary *Ordbogi* from 1977, the space occupied by the letter "r" is symbolic (a half page) and primarily includes words derived from foreign languages, especially Danish. Inflexions, on the other hand, are quite present although oddly absent during Egede's time.

*Arkset* would come from *aske,* meaning "cinder or ash."

*Kollek* (also found in Poul Egede's dictionary) would derive from *kolle,* meaning "the lamp." The current Inuit word is *qulleq.*

*Kuaneq*[15] would come from *kvane* or Old Scandinavian. It is *hvönn* (plural *hvannir*) in Old Norse (Erik Jonsson's dictionary: 1863, 263). It is therefore medieval or earlier and means "angelica" or "*angelica officinalis* or *archangelica* in classical Latin, which takes it back to antiquity. Helge Ingstad was totally of this opinion. This plant appears to have played a role in the Norse diet as illustrated by the use of the medieval place-name "Kvannerset"[16] in the Ketilsfjord region (Tessermuit), one of the most prosperous Scandinavian settlements as three monasteries are cited as being there. (I have put it in quotations because apparently Pingel and Graah adjusted the spelling.) I would actually connect it with the medieval or earlier word *Saetr,* which is touched on often here. This and the word that follows are among the most likely loan words. We have to believe that it was truly adopted by the Kalaallit because its traces are again found in the

1836 map of Lieutenant Graah of the same site: Kvannersaet. It should be noted that it is located at least ten kilometers from the Augustine cloister cited in medieval source texts such as that by Ivar Bårdsson (so mid-fourteenth century).

*Kona* would come from the Old Norse *kona*[17] and at that time would have designated a married woman. It went on to enjoy a long life as it is still present in Poul Egede's colonial lexicon.[18] We should note that the Norwegian and Danish *kone* still exists. The fact that the word has (almost) completely disappeared in Greenland could be a sign that the older and stronger Inuit cultural tradition got the upper hand (with the word *nuliaq*) over the foreign word. However, this word is present in the Egede dictionary (1750, 293) and spelled as *nullia,* meaning "his wife." This appears to be a more solid example. It can be found in Poul Egede's dictionary and in that of Otto Fabricius in 1804. It had already been recorded in 1656. If I say it has almost vanished, that is because it hasn't totally disappeared. In fact, while its meaning has been taken over by an Inuit word, it seems that the medieval word has managed to stay alive with a certain deviation that still has a feminine connotation. It is now used to refer to a certain kind of necklace.

I would like to point out that all the terms looked at here have a relationship to women as they all form part of a vocabulary that we would label as "domestic." In Inuit society women were in charge of maintaining the lamp, seal oil, the cooking fire, and, as in many cultures, food preparation. According to some theories, such as that of Gini in 1956, it was on the initiative of Norse women that peaceful contact was made between the two communities. According to Inuit tradition, they hosted them otherwise abductions would have occurred. A loan of Scandinavian words with a domestic connotation is therefore possible. It is unsettling to see the persistent presence of this medieval Scandinavian feminine vocabulary into the time of Hans Egede, so much later.

In Des Roches de Parthenay's translations of Hans Egede, we also find examples of Latin loan words such as:

*Ignek,* which would come from *ignis,* "fire" (present in the Latin of
Christian authors as well as in the Gaffiot dictionary of French
and Latin). His son Poul spelled it *ingek.* The word reappears
in his son's dictionary[19] with all its derivatives such as *ignekpok,*
*ignem concipit* (113), *ignengniarpok,* and *ignem producere.*
*Appa* would come from the Greek or the Hebrew word for father.

We are in the domain of the hypothetical here, and while some words
seem to reflect certain loans from Scandinavian vocabulary, these last
examples from Hans Egede's list are subject to greater reservations.

He also cites the Inuit words:

*Sava,* coming from *saudr* (plural *saudir*), "the sheep." This
hypothesis is possible as the animal was not native to
Greenland and its name could have been borrowed from the
Scandinavian lexicon.

*Kalaaleq* (plural *Kalaallit*) in the old spelling, is, with the word
*kona,* one of the most interesting.

*Kalaaleq* is the word the Greenland Inuit use for themselves.
Contrary to all the quick statements that sometimes pop up, although
contemporary Greenlanders consider themselves to be Inuit, this word
has never meant "man." The southern Greenlanders told Poul Egede
they had inherited this name from the former Scandinavian colonists
whose word it was for the Inuit. A hasty explanation claims this is a
derivative of *Skræling* (which appeared with the Norse colonization and
its expeditions during medieval times), but the phonetic and meaning
relationship is far from obvious. I would reject this hypothesis and offer
another in its place.

If we assume that the relationship of the two communities was peaceful and relatively friendly—based on Inuit tradition and Nordic written
sources—it is impossible for the word *Skræling* to have been used in this
instance for it is extremely pejorative. The word *Troll* was largely used
by the clerics, it seems, for an outside audience. So can we ask ourselves
what word the Vikings used to describe their neighbors? It was in fact

the nitpicking of the medieval scribes in Nordic source texts describing the natives who put this idea in my head, not calling things (or people, rather) by their names as can be in seen in the story of the shipwreck of Björn Thorleifson and his wife in Greenland where they were rescued by a Tröllkarl and his wife, in short a man who was also a Troll. This leaves a fairly amusing impression of the scribes' discomfiture. If we consider the name by which all the natives of the Arctic region from Siberia to Inuit Greenland called themselves—men—and that used by the people of ancient Scandinavia, we see that they used the medieval (and probably age old) term of *karl* [*kadl*] meaning "man" (free, married, old, and a variety of other meanings).[20] We also know that in Old Scandinavian the medieval word *lid* means, among other things, "the people" or "the folk."[21] Knowing the Vikings enjoyed frequent and rather peaceful relations (with the exceptions we looked at earlier), it seems logical that they would call them by this old Scandinavian name—*karl/a,* or even the people of men—by coining the medieval compound word *karlalid.* In this case, we are extremely close to the Greenland word recorded by Hans Egede, *kalaadleq* (*kalaadlit,* plural). The contemporary form is equally evocative: *kalaallit.* This personal hypothesis seems more plausible to me than any comparison with *Skræling.*

The theory of Inuit loan words from the Vikings suggested by Hans Egede has been long criticized because it is quite fragile. His detractors underline the late date of his observations (he arrived in Greenland in 1721). However, I would not reject this possibility entirely because it has been proved that older lists of Inuit vocabulary reveal the same similarities for several words. I will briefly mention them: the list of the explorer Davis that contained 40 words and was collected during the expeditions of 1585 to 1587[22] and the list of Olearius of about 108 words published in 1656. The historian Finn Gad[23] cites three words listed by Olearius with a Norse connotation:

> *Mamad:* "food" (connected to *mad* by Poul Egede and carries the same meaning today), with the closest medieval word being *mata,* the contemporary *mat* and *føde.* It should be noted that the word *matr* exists in Old Norse. De Vries also cites *mata.*

*Kona:* "the wife." This was used until the end of the eighteenth century to mean a married woman. Here it appears one century before Hans Egede, therefore during a time closer to Norse colonization, which gives a certain consistency to Egede's theory.

*Posak:* "the bag" (connected to the contemporary Norwegian and Danish *pose* and to the Old Scandinavian *posi* by De Vries, who notes an older form: *possa.*

Bartholin's list* contains 291 words and dates from 1673 (in *Acta Medica*).[24] In it we find the eternal Scandinavian *kona* with a different spelling:

*Cona:* "*uxor ex Danica kone.*"

*Igne:* "*ignis, ex Latino derivatam hanc vocem, manifestum est*" (classical Latin from the Gaffiot dictionary).

*Kuan:* "*Rad Angelicæ.*" Did Bartholin alter this? The fact remains that Heggstad, Hødebo, and Simonson speak of the *Angelica archangelica* from medieval times.

All of these words can be found in the dictionary of Hans Egede a century later. One technical term on sailing—the preeminent domain of the Northmen and not really a prerogative of the Inuit—appears in this same list (and in Hans Egede's work as well):

*Nau:* "*Navis latinæ originis,*" the boat, in other words, in classical Latin.

In 1776, Egill Thorhallasson suggested several Inuit words as possible Old Norse derivatives. Among others we see the traditional *hvanni/hvonn* and *kollek/kola* but also *nisa/Hnisa* (which also appears in P. Egede's book on page 287 and on page 28 of volume 2 of Frisner's book, published in 1891), "the dolphin" (*Delphinus phocaceus*). We

---

*Reference is made here to the word *Kablunaak* (with an obsolete spelling), designating the Nordic colonists. *Kablunarsui peregrinus qui Groenlandiam patriam non habet* (1673, 74). The word reappears in Poul Egede's work (1750, 57).

also have *nuuk/Hnukur* (the point, the cape) and several first names: *Terkelin, Olak, Uttuk, and Sunnilik,* which could correspond to Thorkell, Oli, Otto, and Gunnhildr.[25]

Let's finally look at the list of the Reverend Father Émile Petitot. In the introduction to his *Vocabulaire Français-Esquimau,*[26] Petitot used Egede's examples—namely, *quaunek/quaun, kollek/kollè, apkse/aské,* and *nisé/nise.* Volume 3 of the *Grønlands Historiske Mindesmærker* had also pointed out the similarity of this last word for dolphin or porpoise, which is quite close to the Icelandic *Hnysá,* the *Nuisa* of the Faroe Islands, or the Norwegian *Nisa* (*nise* today). On the other hand, I have found no confirmation of what he says in regard to the language of the Faroe Islands. The *Grønlands Historiske Mindesmærker* sees a loan from the Norse language to the Inuit here. Petitot also cites *Ignek* (fire) as a Latin loan word from *Ignis,* as well as *Gutté* (drop) from the Latin word *gutta,* and *kappa* (summit) from the Greek *kapa.* Just like Egede he mishandles the Inuit and Nordic languages (there are no accents in Inuit), and he repeats Parthenay's error by translating *nörrie* as equivalent to the Norwegian verb "to eat" when it should be "to nourish." He perhaps follows Egede's example too blindly. Among other things, Petitot sees the word *imapq* as an Inuit loan word from the Latin *mare,* meaning "the sea" in classical Latin.

Possible Scandinavian loan words are very hard to get the most from, and this is even more so with Inuit loans to the Scandinavians, which cannot be rejected 100 percent, as the example of Utbliksfjord,* derived from *Itblissoak,* which appeared in Björn Jónsson's *Greenland Annals,* is there to remind us. We should recall that the official position of the church was that the two communities did not frequent each other. This loan word is fraught with consequences. It seems to have appeared during a later time corresponding to that of the colonists' almost total rupture with the church. If we follow the words cited by Rafn, Graah, and Andersen, we could deduce from this that

---

*If we go by the ancient sources cited by Rafn, this fjord would be located in Eiriksfjordr and not Isafjordr. The author of the final composition (in Jón Gudmudsson) could have been led astray by the very loan word given to the Inuit place-name. In fact, a map of Lieutenant Graah dating from 1837 shows Iitiblissoak connecting Isafjord

the colonists used this loan word to "rebaptize" a site under Garðar's jurisdiction. This would give us an example of their deteriorating relationship with the church or even its removal. At the same time, I see this loan of an Inuit place-name as a reflection of prolonged, peaceful contact (it is the name for the loan of the concept Alba meaning *qaqortoq*, discussed above). Contrary to the majority of contemporary researchers, I would refrain from rejecting this hypothesis.

## LOANS IN THE WORLD OF PLAY

This point will be discussed quickly for it is still under-analyzed or too weak from a scientific standpoint. It doesn't prevent me from repeating what I said earlier about the possibility of loans and influences being completely defendable and working in the sense of peaceful cohabitation. K. Prytz speaks of the loan of "ball games" (*knaattleikr*). I believe contemporary Inuit games and other activities entering into the ludic domain such as dance or music deserve more careful study. The first people to frequent the Inuit during the seventeenth and eighteenth centuries noted these similarities. With respect to games, Oleson mentions the Icelandic game *heljarbru* (bridge of hell), a kind of hop scotch game played on stones set a certain distance apart from each other.

The Tuniit are supposed to have played this game. Games of strength still popular today (like arm or finger wrestling) had their equivalents in medieval Iceland. Oleson sees the Inuit games like this as similar.

T. Kornerup gives credence to an Inuit loan in the field of music. He bases his position on Thuren's 1911 book (*On the Eskimo Music*),

---

(*cont.*) and Reiksfjord. In this case it was the Inuit root *itivi* that had to have been kept (as b existed) and which can be seen in *itivipog:* "to go by a land connection from one fjord to another." This corresponds with its geographical position and the Latin translation provided by Rafn: "*Hoc nomen ab Eskimoico (Skrælingico) Itiblik o.e. osthmus derivandum es videtur.*" The *Grønlands Historiske Mindesmærker* also underscores this particular feature. *Itiblik* means "a spit of land." Would members of this people (the Inuit) lived or wandered in these regions? More interstingly, E. Langer Andersen shows that in the *Grænlendinga þáttr, Garðar* means "*eid,*" "spit of land, isthmus."

according to which the combination of round dances and drumming dances of the West Greenlanders would very likely be a survival of the medieval Icelandic round dances of the thirteenth and fourteenth centuries. Oleson also says: "There are many clues that tell us Eskimo dances and songs are derived from medieval Icelandic dances."

This still fragile hypothesis cannot be rejected out of hand if we consider Inuit culture's great ability to adapt and appropriate as shown by the confirmed cases of Inuit borrowing of European dances dating from the time of the whalers, as well as their incorporation into Inuit cultural tradition. Fans of musicology can also discover old polkas and other dances in Greenland that are perfectly preserved but are regarded as a typically Greenlandic cultural element.

## CONCLUSION

It is fairly difficult to draw a definitive conclusion about Scandinavian influence or Nordic culture's loans to the Inuit. Even contemporary Scandinavian research is still hesitant to do so in a categorical manner. However, it seems that many elements from the fields of archaeology, technology (cooperage, nets, screws), and artistic motifs (acanthus leaves) appear quite early, if not to say too early, in Greenland, and the only explanation would appear to be Scandinavian influence. This observation compels me to draw the logical conclusion that an Inuit loan from Scandinavian culture would presume long periods of contact, or lengthy periods as neighbors, as well as fairly good relations for these exchanges to take place. All of these elements point to one culture and one alone, the Thule culture, particularly its Inussuk branch, whose techniques seem to bear numerous features belonging to Scandinavian craftsmanship. These exchanges seem to have been so fruitful that some theories should perhaps be reexamined, such as that about the *umiaq*. Should this give us reason to believe it was a copy of Scandinavian boats? Which culture was truly getting the loan? It seems obvious that Vikings were masters of the sail, but their traditional history informs us they also constructed boats made with hides similar to the *umiak*. Should this let us deduce that the *umiaq* was a copy of Scandinavian boats? Remember that this means of transport only arrived in Greenland about the years 900 to 1000, the end of this period corresponding with the arrival of the Vikings. I still lean toward an Inuit paternity for the *umiaq* as it sailed from the Canadian Far North to reach Greenland. However, the loan of the Nordic sail does not seem incongruous to me. The Northmen, on the other hand, had all the time in the world to be inspired by the Celtic coracle.

Finally, a variety of fields—technical, linguistic, ludic—reflect these intercultural contacts and go hand in hand with peaceful, friendly relations. The theory of loan words has long been subject to criticism; however, it doesn't seem entirely devoid of foundation to me, and the examples I've analyzed here go far back in time.

One domain that has scarcely been explored until now is the domain of play and games. With extensive examination by experts (musicologists, medievalists, and so on) it could also reveal some very interesting information concerning the occupations and leisure activities—that must have been mutual—of the two peoples. This aspect of the Inuit-Scandinavian relationship is a logical corollary of peaceful, friendly relations that have been concealed until now by the preference long granted to the theory of bellicose contacts that would not allow such relations to be imaginable. Earlier we saw how all the warlike stories began with accounts that included games between the two communities. They had calm and peaceful periods that sometimes soured. In sum a history not much unlike the neighboring countries of Europe.

I should make clear that in speaking of Inuit borrowings, I am not claiming any kind of alignment of their material culture with that of the Nordic colonists.

In fact, contemporary research more or less accepts the theory of Viking loans to the Inuit. I would say, rather, that the problem is knowing how these loans took place. By underscoring the duration of contacts and their relative tranquillity, I have tried to provide partial answers to this, for it is of paramount importance. It gives us the key to the relationship between the two peoples.

# 6

# Prolonged Contact or Cohabitation
# of Inuit and Vikings

In 1953, Mathiassen laid out the issue quite clearly, basing it on three major axes: archaeological evidence, Nordic source texts on the Inuit, and Inuit traditional lore concerning the Vikings.

We looked at this last axis earlier. I will follow this chapter with one on the official medieval commentaries, after an exhaustive look at what archaeology and architecture has to tell us. This will allow us to have at hand concrete elements, many of which have been crosschecked. In short, we will have solid material with which to weigh the objectivity and value of these sources.

## ARCHAEOLOGICAL EVIDENCE

Earlier we saw how Mathiassen's excavations in South Greenland provided evidence that the Inuit and Norse populations both lived in the same regions. Mathiassen believed that the Narsaq region had the largest Inuit population, drawing up an inventory of four dwellings on the island of Tuttutooq/Langey, including two Norse houses several kilometers from the Inuit settlement of Isua. The two editions of K. Krogh's book, *Erik den Rødes Grønland* (*Eric the Red's Greenland*) in 1967 and 1982, include maps that show numerous Norse settlements on this island. This appears logical as medieval sources—Ivar Bårdsson's description among others—show that

Fig. 6.1. Greenland: icebergs in Eriksfjord (Tunulliarfik). This was the magnificent landscape that greeted the Norse colonists of Dyrnæs. Archaeological excavations have revealed an Inuit presence in the region. Today this is the site of the small village of Narsaq. (See also color plate 11.)
**Photo by J. Privat**

Langey had a large number of caribou. They belonged to the bishopric.

Near Narsaq/Dyrnæs, immediately across from the Inuit settlement of Illutalik, there was a Norse farm with old-style houses (ruins ø17 and ø17A). Other contemporary researchers have confirmed this and done even better thanks to new discoveries—sixty-nine Inuit houses discovered in southern Greenland. Finn Gad pointed out the proximity of the dwellings: "Two of the largest (Inuit) sites are located on the island directly across from the the church of Dyrnæs, the contemporary Narsaq Avangnardleq* and around the strait between this island and solid land where there are four Eskimo settlements."[†]

------

*Literally, "the farthest north of Narsaq."
†See the map of Eystribygð (fig. 2.7); Ø corresponds to the Danish standard for Østerbygð.

The site of Illutalik[1] contains four old-style houses, but no Scandinavian settlements have been recorded in Illutalik by modern researchers. Archaeological excavations were made here by Mathiassen and Holtved in 1934.[2] Twenty-four Inuit houses were recorded as being from the Thule Inussuk culture. The first settlements go back to 1350. Scandinavian objects are connected to this culture: three weaving loom weights, two metal knife pieces, two pieces of unidentifiable iron, and an indeterminate sharpening stone made from soapstone.

All these observations are confirmed by Inuit traditional lore: the two communities coexisted as neighbors, if not necessarily living together, at least within the geographical boundaries of the islands.

The site of Isua includes eight houses of old design containing two pieces of a bell, a bronze fragment in the shape of a fleur-de-lis, a four-sided soapstone container, two iron knives, a sharpening stone, two weaving loom weights, a piece of wool, and two indeterminate pieces of iron. These discovered Norse objects were seen as having a connection to the Thule Inussuk culture.

Based on the form of the Inuit homes, the first inhabitation would date from 1350. The settlement had been entirely Inuit. Mathiassen connects it to an early phase of Inussuk inhabitation. Almost half of the local Inuit population of the early Middle Ages lived in these four settlements.

Similarly we find three Inuit ruins of the old style in Uunartoq, about ten miles upstream, at the mouth of the fjord.* The sixty-nine Inuit houses are connected to the old Inussuk culture, twelve of which date from an ancient Inuit settlement of the early Middle Ages.

They are little, round, or square with rounded corners (the earlier observation about their shape, therefore, seems to suffer some exceptions and could perhaps add an additional argument in support of Inuit loans). The dwellings are sunk in the ground. Some have an extension or a kitchen. Two or three complete houses have been found.

In the light of all these discoveries, the allocation of the Inuit and

---

*See fig. 2.7 for the map of Eystribygð. I recommend that the reader consult it for all the sites (Nordic and Inuit) cited in connection with the eastern settlement.

Scandinavian houses is made clearer. It could be said that as a general rule, the fjords, regions typically inhabited by the Norse, provide evidence of very few Inuit settlements. Einarsfjord has no Inuit ruins from the fifteenth century. At the very tip of the Qaqortoq/Julianehåb peninsula, in addition to the Scandinavian sites, we find one Inuit settlement. This is a bit of a surprise as the testimonies from the era were rather stingy, if not completely silent, about nearby Inuit populations.

Thirty-six miles to the south, we find the following Inuit sites: four settlements are distributed around Ippik (northern tip of Uunartoq), and in the northern part of Alluitsoq/Hrafnsfjord. However, eight Norse ruins have been found by this fjord, a monastery (Uunartoq is cited in medieval Nordic texts for its thermal springs), as well as twelve Norse ruins in Alluitsoq.

The reason for a small Inuit presence in a typically Scandinavian place seems obvious. It seems difficult to claim that one existed at this already occupied site, and we know that the economies of the two communities were heading in different directions. For this reason the Inuit settlement of Ippik seems logical. Mathiassen and Holtved recorded twenty-six house ruins in their 1934 excavations. Based on the settlement's layout, Mathiassen placed the first inhabitation at about 1350. He cites the same parameters: the Vikings settled inland and at the back of the fjords while the Inuit settled on their banks about halfway up. Mathiassen gives the fifteenth century as the time of Inuit-Scandinavian cohabitation, and notes the existence of a small Inuit population in the Qaqortoq/Julianehåb district.

The southern population according to Mathiassen (in keeping with the migrations discussed in chapter 1) was frequently strengthened by the waves of Inuit migrations from the north, although they arrived in small groups.

Citing archaeological evidence, Arneborg places these contacts at roughly 1200 to 1250, quite far from the Scandinavian settlements and more specifically in northern Greenland and Canada. To be clear, she connects them directly to the Nordrsetur.

It is obvious that the first certain contacts verified historically or archaeologically date from this period. But to note the proximity of the two populations in southern Greenland without imagining or accepting the consequences, including trade, among other things, is not a realistic position in my opinion. While archaeological proofs are more or less lacking, the thirteenth-century date suggested by Arneborg seems completely fanciful to me if we consider the date of the Viking's arrival in Greenland first in 982 with Erik the Red's expedition and then in 985 for the combined colonization and trade expedition of the Vikings (Erik the Red had already explored Greenland as far as Disko Island). Likewise, the accounts of northern voyages toward Greipar and Kroksfjordarheidi confirmed by 1211 sources and the first voyage to Vinland all contradict this theory. These first contacts were more likely during the eleventh century according the *Grønlands Historiske Mindesmærker*.

Based on all available data, a date as late as the thirteenth century seems to be completely ruled out. One thing is certain, this contact did take place as attested by traditional Inuit lore, Norse influence on the natives, or quite simply Inuit objects found in Viking houses, likely the result of trading. Mathiassen also mentions the following irrefutable examples:[3]

An oval box made of whale baleen of typical Inuit craftsmanship was found lying beneath the skull of a Scandinavian in a tomb of Ikigait/Herjolfsnes. The grave was located within the very walls of the church according to Arneborg. She did not see any difference here with any of the examples found in several Thule Inussuit sites. There is no doubt that contact existed between the two populations. "The whale baleen container from Ikigait/Herjolfsnes was found in what all evidence tells us is a Scandinavian context and must have circulated in Norse hands before ending up in a Christian grave."[4]

An ice knife made of baleen (for building an igloo, an essentially Inuit technique, if there ever was one) was found in a midden in the medieval Vatnahverfi. These two objects are typical of Inussuk culture and have never been discovered farther south than Sukkertoppen. The ice knife is a pure Thule product that has even been found in Canada. These objects could easily have been the result of a swap between Inuits and Vikings in the Far North.

Another object that was unearthed is the walrus-ivory handle for a hauling line used to drag large game. This tool dates from the end of the Dorset era and the beginning of the Thule era. Similar examples exist in Canada and North Greenland. The one from Vatnahverfi has two bear heads carved at the ends and two cross motifs on the lower side. A twin example has been found in Baffin Bay. The ice knife and the hauling line handle could only have been brought there by the Scandinavians. "Neither of these two cultures (Dorset and Thule) have been recorded in southeastern Greenland, and for these reasons it is reasonable to conclude that this object was brought by the Vikings themselves."[5]

What was the symbolic value of the Scandinavian objects acquired by the Inuit? A prestigious connotation may have been associated with this trade. (Recall the Inuit story of the two friends citing the enthusiasm of the natives for going to find the Vikings.)

What at first glance is only a detail could have an importance and more consequences than we can currently imagine. Some researchers have advanced the hypothesis of a migration (or an increased number of Inuit migrations) due to this trade. Basically, the Inuit deliberately sought to establish contact with the Vikings. This point will be revisited. The excavations really show an abundance of insignificant objects whose commercial value is difficult to establish. They could have represented a more or less symbolic value such as those seen in the *Vinland Saga* with the trade of cloth strips to the Skrælings.

> The discovery of useless Scandinavian objects such as weaving loom weights, sharpening stones, or even game pawns (checkers most likely) in Eskimo settlements in western Greenland far from the Norse colonies, gives the impression that these *curiosities* with no utilitarian value were objects of great interest.[6]

It is quite striking to note after more than half a century the persistence of old narratives restricting Inuit-Viking contacts to the Nordrsetur despite the archaeological discoveries and all eminent work preformed by not only the Scandinavians but also by Canadians and Americans.

These objects can be found in Inuit settlements of northern

Greenland like Inugssuk, Illutalik, and Illorsuit,* as well those we just mentioned in southern settlements such as Ikigait and Herjolfsnes and Vatnahverfi. "Mathiassen's position is that the Inuit and Vikings were in direct contact in the Upernavik region in 1300 on connection with the Norse hunting expeditions in the north. Mathiassen believes much earlier and more frequent contacts took place in the Disko region farther south.[7]

D. Brunn identifies this region with the Nordrsetur. I have made note of a more reserved view of contact dates with regard to Disko. Even though some Scandinavian objects could have been passed on by hand from southern Greenland to end up in the Disko region, Mathiassen expresses doubt that such a large number could have made this journey. I would personally add that it is equally astonishing for such a large quantity of Norse "curiosities," fruits of exchanges between the Inuit following the disappearance of the Scandinavians, to all end up in the same place. The impression it leaves is rather that of a substantial Norse presence in this northern site—a prolonged presence if we follow the conclusions drawn concerning the Kingittorsuaq runestone,† in the Upernavik district. Its translation reads: "Erling Sigvatsson, Bjarni Thordarsson, and Eindridi Oddson, on the Saturday before 'Gangdag' [April 24] erected [these] cairns."[8]

Given the northern latitude and the given date, any departure before April 24 from the Scandinavian colonies would seem risky in this season. We have to believe that the members of this boat wintered far from their home regions, either in northern Greenland, but that is not an absolute. It is perfectly logical and imaginable that they wintered farther west under more clement skies, which would fit in very well with a return to Greenland in the spring. Another reason could be a "forced" wintering over for the Vikings far from their colonies, a theory that Prytz[9] has pertinently advanced. The valuable furs the Vikings were hunting absolutely had to be caught in winter as the summer furs

---

*These two Inuit place-names mean, respectively, "there where there are houses" and "large houses." Could this be a reference to the Norse? An extensive study of place-names could be helpful.
†Literally meaning "what was raised very high."

were worthless. Because of the difficulties that would be involved, a far northern presence of the Norse during the winter has been given scant consideration. I must also point out that the performance, with regard to the tools of that era, was also a factor. We can see that the knowledge of all these technical details is a very valuable aid.

These contacts are also acknowledged by contemporary researchers, especially those who recently distinguished themselves with their discoveries in the Canadian Arctic: Paul Schledermann (1976 excavations) and Robert McGhee. In Schledermann's case, the Inuit objects reflect direct contacts between the Inuit and Vikings in the Smith Strait region between 1200 and 1400. I make note here of the late date but also his categorical opinion concerning direct contacts.

The presence of copper and iron from very remote times (corresponding to the beginning of Scandinavian colonization of Greenland) in Cape Garry on Somerset Island has been recorded. While the Norse origin is confirmed, the hypothesis of the pillaging of deserted Scandinavian sites cannot be supported, which obliges us to accept the possibility of a direct contact based on trade between the two peoples as the sole explanation for the presence of these metals in this site. The dating of these objects thereby shows itself to be quite helpful in my analysis of contact between the two populations.

The fact remains that the objects discovered in northern Greenland are connected to classic Thule culture in the Ruin Island phase and the Inugssuk phase. Based on the discoveries made on Skræling Island in Canada, contacts between Inuits and Vikings would have occurred between 1200 and 1350.

Robert McGhee seems alone in assuming a wide view that matches my observations on the generally accepted late dates. Indeed, the Canadian researcher resolved the matter by quite simply summing up exchanges between the Inuits, the Indians, and the Norse as taking place throughout the entire duration of the Norse colony. In addition, he situates them in southern Greenland. McGhee also shares my viewpoint (presented in chapter 2) concerning the utility of an Inuit-Viking collaboration: "These relationships are considered as a form of dependency that manifested itself in the establishment of commercial ties. The Vikings were particularly dependent on this exchange, as this meant they could obtain walrus tusks and narwhal horn for their trade with Europe."[10]

McGhee could not be any clearer in his depiction of what was at stake. His theory is worth serious consideration due to the considerable fortunes represented by ivory exports, but he did not stop there. He believed that the Vikings had made contact with the Dorset Inuit and various Amerindian groups of Newfoundland, the Labrador coast, and Baffin Island. The Scandinavians also encountered the Thule Inuit of Ellesmere Island migrating to Greenland, where they then traveled south toward the Norse colonies.

Basing his position on the presence of Scandinavian objects and the evidence provided by the Inuit statuettes, Mathiassen came to the conclusion that the two populations were simultaneously present in southern Greenland and in the Upernavik region. His trustworthy reference points are the Kingittorsuaq runestone dated to about 1300 based on its runes, as well as the bell fragments found in the upper layers of an Inussuk midden heap.

Knowing the extreme conservatism of Arctic peoples*—researchers would be the last to complain about this—it seems very unlikely that foreign techniques could have been borrowed from Vikings who were just passing through. It is not customary for the Inuit to abandon ancestral techniques to copy the first stranger to pass by. In this respect, during a more recent time, we know of no loans as significant as the objects cited for Inussuk culture, for example, with the transitory populations of the seventeenth and eighteenth centuries.

To the contrary, these objects strengthen my hypothesis of prolonged Viking-Inuit cohabitation. It is necessary that the two populations were rubbing shoulders together for a long enough time (as the archaeological findings seem to indicate) that their relations were primarily friendly for these changes in technique to take place. By way of an anecdote I would like to cite an example that is entirely foreign to

---

*I have cited the Thule artistic styles that survived into the present, or quite simply the persistence of thousand-year-old tools like the sled and the kayak.

the time period we are looking at. After a year's stay at Ammassalik, the Inuit abandoned their thousand-year sled model to adopt that of Paul Emile Victor.

Jette Arneborg advances the possibility of an encounter between Inuits and Scandinavians elsewhere at some unspecified time before the Inuit settlement in Inussuk, but without going into any detail. She calls back into question Mathiassen's argument for the first contact taking place sometime between 1200 and 1300. Based on Scandinavian objects unearthed in the excavations of Inussuk and Upernavik (North Greenland), she concludes contacts took place in a more recent period.

The scant number of Scandinavian objects found in Nuuk compared to Inuit settlements has also been emphasized. However, if we consider their location, this should come as no surprise, as the Vikings settled inland by the fjords. The presence of Inuit objects (the largest number) at Vestribygð, mainly in Kilaarsarfik (Sandnæs) in the medieval Austmann Valley, and in Nipáitsoq has also been noted.

The first digs in Kilaarsarfik, the medieval Amerella Fjord, took place in 1930. Among the objects of Inuit origin I would like to mention a knife, cleaver blade, and comb all made from caribou antler. Schledermann noted the absence of Inussuit dwellings near the Scandinavian sites inland by the fjords. Ironically, McGovern acknowledges the presence of ruins and middens in the costal region of Kangeq, Qoornoq (halfway to the coast), and in Saarloq, which are probably Inussuit.

Some objects go back to the occupation of Norse ruins after they were abandoned, but several objects belong to Thule/Inussuk culture, for example a typical bow. Similar examples were found in Illutalik near Ilulissat and on Skræling Island near Ellesmere. Carbon-14 dating puts it anywhere from the end of the twelfth, beginning of the thirteenth century to the fifteenth and sixteenth centuries (therefore contemporary to the Vikings). The oldest Inuit settlement of Vestribygð would be that of Kangeq in the islands across from Nuuk. Scandinavian objects have been found in a midden on Kangeq Island at the mouth of the Nuuk/Godthåb Fjords: a soapstone pawn and a piece of wood with a zigzag design. This is one of the sites Gulløv uses as a base for his argument.

Its carbon-14 dating provides a margin covering the thirteenth and fourteenth centuries, which leads Gulløv to suggest that Inuit-Viking cohabitation in Vestribygð lasted for several generations.

Similarly, the Kilaarsarfik arrowheads with bulges on the handle are known in other settlements like on Skræling Island or the Comer Midden in Uummannaq dating from the fifteenth century. The dates suggested for Kilaarsarfik are at the turn of the twelfth to thirteenth centuries. Based on Greenland National Museum's digs in 1984, the Vikings were not the first to settle on this spot as stone tools of the Paleoinuit were found.

Explaining the presence of the objects found far from the excavations is not always easy. Jette Arneborg made the following observations about the Inuit objects found in the Scandinavian settlements of Vestribygð: The objects of Nipaitsoq and Austmann Valley were initially connected to these farms. Some Inuit objects at the Sandnæs farm at Kilaarsarfik are connected with these establishments; others belong to no stratigraphic layer. The first excavations of Nipaitsoq were made in 1952. An ax blade made from caribou antler and two Inuit arrowheads were found there. The ax blade dated from the last period this area was inhabited (toward the end of the sixteenth century). A piece of meteorite iron was found in Nipaitsoq; its shape resembles that of an Inuit arrowhead (cold forged). Most strikingly, this metal came from meteorite iron in the Thule region. This confirms the importance of this northern area as a source for iron. Andreasen even goes so far as to advance the notion of "a possible swap of iron between the Inuit and the Vikings."[12]

Two explanations are possible concerning the existence of these objects in typically Scandinavian settlements: these objects were in Viking possession, or else there was an Inuit presence after the farms had been abandoned but before their walls had collapsed. All the Inuit objects of Ameralik/Ameralla go back to Thule Inussuk culture, which agrees with the written sources that mention a native presence during this time.

Based on the carbon-14 analyses done in the Scandinavian dwellings of Nipaitsoq and Niaquassat, the two settlements were deserted relatively late, respectively: 1405 ± 65 years, and 1395 ± 50, years (based on the corrections that were made), which call into question the written sources, especially Ivar Bårdsson's work including a description of the "disappearance" of Vestribygð. We should note that the margin of error of 50 or 65 years puts us in the period of 1340, which is in agreement with these same sources. Gulløv gives 1405 ± 50 years for Nipaitsoq and places the abandonment of the farms between 1355 and 1455, which is to say long after Ivar Bårdsson's visit. The archaeological layers of the Kangeq midden reveal an Inuit presence in the fourteenth and fifteenth centuries. These would be the oldest dates for these regions. "There has been no earlier Inuit settlement observed in the inland regions by the fjord near Nuuk."[13]

Nevertheless, a seasonal presence for hunting caribou or fishing is quite conceivable. This detail takes on full importance if we consider the various Inuit migrations and the changes of the climate. Considering the Inuit winter economy (hunting seal and fishing through holes in the ice are activities requiring a certain level of cold temperatures), it is a cause for some surprise to only see the appearance of this Inuit culture during the fourteenth and fifteenth centuries, which corresponds to a climatic warming, whereas the Little Ice Age would have been more conducive to their activities.

We know that carbon-14 measurements are rather broad and cannot be considered for their scientific precision, yet the margin given remains interesting. Other purely material factors can also step in, such as one stratigraphic layer accidentally bleeding into another (landslide and so on), the so-called reservoir effect in which water-sourced dates of the Arctic are too old, or lastly human interventions. For example, during Mathiassen's excavations, Scandinavian objects were found in connection with newer houses—for example, in Tuttutup Isua/Langey and Illutalik/Eriks Ey. The dating of the houses is 1650, which hardly fits with the Norse period. At Uunartoq and Narsarsuaq, Scandinavian objects have been found associated with houses whose dates generously range from 1350 to 1650.

We must keep in mind the pillaging of abandoned Scandinavian settlements that can even include medieval-era stones for the building of Inuit homes. In these cases it is easier to understand the fanciful dates. The presence of bell pieces in Tuttutup Isua confirms the hypothesis of pillaged farms. This practice had a long life as the same behavior was described in 1654 with the natives digging up old Scandinavian settlements in search of iron and nails. However, we should refrain from seeing this as a general practice at all the Scandinavian settlements. A stark difference appears to exist between the sites of Eystribygð and Vestribygð, where it is much harder to suggest with the support of archaeology that Inuit pillaged Vestribygð settlements, for very few Scandinavian objects have been recovered there. This echoes what we have already seen was the case for Nuuk/Godthåb. Here the observation applies to the entire region. Nevertheless, the possibility of a limited reclamation should not be rejected outright, even if we have no direct archaeological proof. What seems to be the sole known example of bells in Inussuk in the Upernavik region, dating from the fourteenth to fifteenth centuries by Mathiassen, would have been connected to the Eystribygð colony and not Vestribygð, even if we cannot entirely exclude this hypothesis.

It is strange that modern research has not drawn the connection between the rarity of Scandinavian objects in Inuit sites and the intentional departure of the Vikings as everything leads us to believe. If we go by Ivar Bårdsson's report, the Norse colony of Vestribygð was discovered entirely empty, apart from the presence of livestock. An intentional departure suggests they took everything they could when they moved, and all the necessary evidence seems confirmed by archaeology. Although, Jette Arneborg pertinently presented a small detail that archaeologically distinguishes Vestribygð from Eystribygð: the absence of bell fragments from the first colony while they are legion in its southern counterpart. Confirming my Inuit reclamation after the Scandinavians left hypothesis, there are no lack of sites in Eystribygð: Ikigait/Herjolfsnes; Kujalleq/Undir Hofda; Qaqortokulooq/Hvalsey; Igaliku/Garðar; Qassiarsuk/Brattahlið; and Narsasuaq. This is an important observation by the author, except for one case that is absent here: "All the fragments of the Eystribygð bell were found around the church in which they were presumably used."[14]

This is an extremely important detail for study as it counters the keepers of the dominant theory of "wandering" Scandinavian objects discovered in archaeological digs. I feel obliged to mention that in the specific case of the bronze bells, they haven't budged an inch from their place of origin. We should keep this in mind when reading the chapter on the archaeology of the Norse presence in the Far North. There is no proof that the Vikings broke these bells themselves (the sacrilege is too obvious). We also cannot imagine the Inuit had free access to objects of worship; all that thus remains for a hypothesis is an Inuit reclamation after the Scandinavian departure.

With the acceptance of the Inuit "appropriation," the mysterious case of Vestribygð raises questions. How are we to explain the archaeological inexistence of these objects of worship in Vestribygð? The answer seems obvious, going hand in hand with an intentional departure from Vestribygð; in other words, a deliberate relocation by the Scandinavians. The Vestribygð colonists would have taken their bells with them. The scenario implied here is one of emigration or colonization of the Western lands, or America. The fragments found in the south come from native reclamations in Eystribygð. The older research performed by Corrado Gini in 1956 came to the same conclusions with regard to Scandinavian tools: "Nothing in the expedition report [by Ivar Bårdsson] seems to indicate that hunting or fishing tools were abandoned on the spot, no more than the most important household tools. . . ."[15]

In other words, the tools essential for life in an Arctic environment were brought along, which reinforces my theory of the Vikings' voluntary departure, if not outright joining the natives. A look at the Scandinavian tools abandoned at Vestribygð could prove instructive in this regard.

# 7

# The Testimony of the Nordic Source Texts

shall use Krogh's observation about the sagas to get started. He
believed they could be considered as historical novellas. The genealogies were complicated, bursting with details, and the scribes were
interested in major figures. As he points out, they do not necessarily
describe what happened but what might have been able to happen: "The
shape in which the sagas are handed to us can be compared with broad
rivers into which many sources have poured their waters. It is hardly
possible to separate these waters again, to point out the exact origin of
the tradition, and its accurate course."[1]

The current official position concerning the sagas could be summed
up as follows: their core could be considered to be the expression of
historical oral traditions, but (unfortunately) this tradition was subject
to countless transformations and distortions long before they were set
down in writing.[2]

In short, we can consider them for a certain image they give us as
context. I will stress an a priori benign aspect of the sagas, the details and
technical information that appears relevant. For example, in the *Saga of
the Sworn Brothers* (*Fóstbrœdra saga*), we are given information about the
Vikings arms and techniques. They therefore allow us to reconstruct the
facts in a period of time. With regard to certain mentioned or omitted details concerning the natives living, for example, "in holes in the
ground" or again the absence of sled dogs, and so forth, these would

imply certain Inuit peoples or certain periods of inhabitation.

Classification is always arbitrary and in this case taxing, given the number of sources involved. There is no room here for a detailed examination of these studies, as there is material here for many books. In the interest of convenience for the reader, I will adopt a simple chronological order and be satisfied to simply show the connection to the subject at hand.

I am convinced that a wealth of information slumbers in the old written sources, even the most legendary, lying low beneath these little trivial details, but of high cultural value and evocative of techniques and various forms of knowledge.

Until now, the keys necessary to decode them were missing. An ethnological look can help us better interpret them, because these technical elements that we have arbitrarily called mere details carry meaning.

As an introduction, and an exception to my list as it is a non-Scandinavian source, I will cite a later scolia found in a manuscript of Adam of Bremen[3] describing the countries of the north, the content of which is quite troubling. This text offers several clues on sailing in the Arctic and an account concerning the natives or the Vikings.

> From Iceland to Greenland, there are 14 *duodenae leucarum* (14 dozen miles) and in Greenland there is a cape "Hverf" with a glacier called "Hvideserk."[4] From there to "Suderbondt"[5] (the south bay) it is 10 dozen miles [369 nautical miles according to Prytz]. From there to "Norderbondt"[6] [the north bay] 11 dozen miles [400 nautical miles] and finally 17 dozen miles [612 nautical miles] from "Nordenbondt to "Hunenrioth" where people go to kill the white bears and the long-toothed whale [narwhal].[7]

Aside from Hvideserk, which researchers place in Greenland, all the other place-names are quite mysterious. Hunenrioth has never really been located. Canada has been given as a possibility, and Bjørnbo compares this word with "Himinrad," which often appears in Nordic source texts. The Norwegian Kåre Prytz stresses to the contrary the German origin of the word *Hunenrioth,* and draws a comparison between the German *Huhn,* "chicken, rooster, and by extension, fowl," and the Scandinavian *Höne*. He identifies its location as Upernavik in Greenland, at lat 73° N, considering this as the best site for game such as birds, walrus, narwhals, bears, and fish. I would personally ask if the bird snares and nest boxes found in the Canadian Far North in Ellesmere might not have a connection with these place-names. We know that these regions are quite rich in game (bear, narwhals, falcons). We should remember that the location of the Norse islands appearing in the written sources—Eisunes and Aedanes—have never been identified.

The second quote from Adam of Bremen is better known and corresponds more with his repertoire that is more evocative of fable than history: "There are numerous islands in the ocean among which Greenland is not the smallest. There, the salty sea gives the inhabitants a bluish-green appearance, hence the name of the country. They live the same way as the Icelanders, but they are crueler and harass the sailors by attacking them."[8]

Adam of Bremen's very free interpretation shows he had not mastered his Nordic sources and that he took literally the break made frequently in that era in transcriptions of the green country, or "grøn land." Ingstad and Gad sum up the nature of Adam of Bremen's Nordic sources quite nicely: "The things he says are things that only he hears."[9] We should note that Adam of Bremen acknowledged he got his information from the Vikings—namely, the Danish king Sven Esthrithson.

Adam of Bremen's final observation is quite ambiguous. Who are the people he describes, natives of Vikings? The Inuit didn't live like the Icelanders, and the Scandinavians—in theory—were not supposed to have attacked foreign ships. We cannot rule out an error of interpretation here for a reading of the sagas dealing with this period at the beginning of colonization such as the *Saga of the People of Flói* refers to internal quarrels and "vendettas." One of the pirate leaders is named Thorstein, a name that could hardly be more Nordic. "It happened that winter that several robbers caused many problems. Their leader was named Thorstein. There were thirty in all, and they had all been banished. The colonists suffered heavy losses from their constant raids and they asked Erik [the Red] for help. They had their lair on several islands in the Eriksfjord."[10]

In this case, we can see an internal matter to Greenland with the foreign pirates arriving later. At a time as remote as that of Adam's (or more to the point, that of his older sources) that brings us back to the beginning of colonization; there is no testimony of conflict. We must wait several centuries for descriptions of aggressions. So the question remains open: I will simply point out that these kinds of observations can be found in the work of other authors.

Despite its many failings, a total rejection of Adam of Bremen's sources would be a mistake. The difficulty lies in selecting what's valuable out of the more or less farfetched tangle of information provided by the German. I would note in his defense the limited state of geographical knowledge during his time. One fact is certain: Adam of Bremen is describing polar regions. The problem lies in knowing which ones. Lapland? Spitzbergen? Greenland? Or someplace farther west? Perhaps it is a generous blend of all these lands.

One question primarily interests me, that of contacts between the natives and the Vikings. It so happens that Adam of Bremen's text cited above (chapters 40–41, 247–48) provides us with some particularly valuable information. The fantastic nature of his description has allowed this information to fade into the background as part of the fable. I would therefore suggest we reread this text:

> After leaving the Orkneys behind them, and Norway on their right, at the end of a long voyage [the Frisian merchants] made their way to ice-covered Iceland, then carved their way by sea to its northernmost point. After a long streak of bad luck (fog, gulfs, and terrible currents) they arrived in the kingdom of cold (*provinciam frigoris*) on an unknown island. They landed and found men there . . . hiding in subterranean holes (*antris subterraneis*). There was a quantity of gold or metal containers in front of their doors. When they had taken as much treasure as they could hold, the joyful sailors set off again. They then saw those men of an amazing height, which our folk call Cyclops, were chasing them. Dogs larger than ordinary ran before them. The giants pursued them shouting all the way to the sea.[11]

In contrast to Adam of Bremen's other sources, this paragraph appears—despite the initial reservations a critical reader could not help but have—as one of the more realistic. Despite its superficial fantasy veneer, two readings are possible. One, which has prevailed up to the present day and prevents us from going further, is the fantastic tale of Cyclops and troglodytes. The other is an analytic reading that for the sake of simplicity I will call ethnological. In this case, all the earlier references seen in the beginning of the book will now prove helpful to us. Outside of Adam of Bremen's natural tendency to exaggerate, we can find some very interesting data here.

Once we have removed the fantasy veneer in his description (the Cyclops and the giants), his story cannot help but bring to mind certain Inuit populations. Just as Gwyn Jones suggested the existence of confusion between native clothing that included a long train on the back and the fantasy beings called unipeds, we can see the same kind of confusion made by Europeans here.

The characteristic of the true Inuit parka hood is to completely enclose the head while extending it forward to an exaggerated degree, while narrowing it. There is a hole at the end lined with wolf or dog fur that serves a dual purpose: windbreak and holding in warm breath, thereby creating a bubble of warm air that keeps the face as warm as the rest of the body. The effect is fairly striking, the head being extended by a kind of narrow sleeve with a fur-lined hole at the end. What could cause greater surprise in the medieval imaginal realm, or in an Arctic fog such as that described by Adam of Bremen? Confusion is easy and, in this case, very comprehensible. As we have seen with the narwhal, the medieval imagination was very easily ignited.

The description talks of figures of amazing height (*homines mirae altitudinis*). We know that among the different waves of Inuit populations that one of these peoples stood out for their height and physical strength: the Thules. They were an energetic, robust people who, covered in furs, could reasonably be expected to command a certain respect. We have a clue here that illustrates my remarks concerning the importance of certain details: the reference to dogs, which has not yet been considered at its just value.

Among all the Nordic written sources, both clerical and secular, not a single text alludes to the Inuit dogs, although they are the first detail that strikes the stranger passing through their villages. Sled dogs (and sleds) appeared in Greenland with the Thule culture that migrated there about the year 900.

We probably have here a description of Thule cultural elements—or Dorset culture, for no mention of a sled appears. However, the Dorset dog that served as a pack animal could assume impressive size. This would therefore be the oldest text written about the Inuit, whether it is the powerful Thule culture or Dorset culture.*

We recognize it again for its underground dwellings (*Homines in antris subterraneis meridian tempore hatitantes*). This is either an unintentional distortion or an exaggeration by Adam of Bremen describing the native dwellings that were not underground but steep-sided and terraced.

The long entrance corridor was always located in front of the entrance for the same purpose of trapping warm air inside. A person entering had to crawl before reaching the main room. Their structures made of clumps of dirt and stones could only add to the confusion. In fact, their houses were easily confused for underground cavities. My view is reinforced by the fact that the same exaggerations were made concerning the dwellings in Iceland.

The flight of the natives also supports their identification as Inuit. What we could have here is not only the first duly dated allusion to Dorset or Thule Inuit but also to Canada. In fact, the reference to gold and metal containers is an invention or has a basis of truth. As supporting evidence, we have Erik Walkendorff's 1516 list, which also mentions precious metals in Greenland.

We know thanks to several explorers and geological studies that the Canadian Arctic has a wealth of minerals, which also formed one of the reasons for the rush of Europeans into these regions. Greenland was not lacking in these, as contemporary research bears out. In sum, what we have in this very brief passage are some highly condensed bits of information on the natives and their geographical location, which have gone unnoticed until now.

---

*In my opinion, the case for an Amerindian identification is very weak, given the far northern latitudes described by Adam of Bremen.

## *The Book of the Icelanders* (Islendingabók)

This book was probably written in the twelfth century by the Icelander Ari Þhorgilsson, who was born in 1067 or 1068. As indicated by its title, this book discusses the history of Iceland's colonization from the end of the 800s to 1200. Several copies exist that date from the seventeenth century. With respect to our subject, this is one of the oldest written sources that refers to the Arctic natives, albeit a brief description. Gwyn Jones's translation tells us that

> the country which is called Greenland was discovered and settled from Iceland. Erik the Red was the name of a man of Breidafjord who went there from here. . . . Both east and west in the country they found the habitations of men, fragments of boats and stone artifacts, from which it may be seen that the same kind of people who passed that way as those that inhabited Vinland, whom the Greenlanders call Skrælings (*skrælinga*).[12]

Greenland is the subject of chapter 7. Ari Þhorgilsson's information came from an uncle, Thorkell Gellisson, who had heard them from a man who had been a follower of Erik the Red. The information regarding the Greenland natives is quite scant. They were supposed to have once lived in the two settlements set up by the Vikings and emigrated elsewhere after a certain time. One interesting fact here from the meager data provided is that the Vikings connected them with the remote Skræling populations and to Vinland. No date of any encounter is provided.

The date of the *Islendingabók* writing gives us 1130 as *terminus ante quem* for contacts with the Skrælings. Ari Þhorgilsson is considered a reliable source. In his time, information on events in Greenland were of fairly qood quality.

### Historia Norvegiae

The *History of Norway* was probably written in 1170. This book describes the history of Norway from the time of the Ynglingar kings, including the beginning of the *Saga of Saint Olaf* in Norway in 1015. The author counts among his sources Ari Þhorgilsson and the island descriptions provided by Adam of Bremen (1075). His sources on Greenland were obtained directly, or indirectly by way of Iceland (Ari Þhorgilsson most likely), as well as perhaps other sources of information. The book contains information about the Skrælings not found in the *Islendingabók*—for example, the way the Skrælings bleed).

> This country (Greenland) that the Icelanders, discovered, built, and governed under the Christian faith, is at the Western boundary of Europe. It almost touches the African islands that the ocean pounds with its waves. Farther north, the Greenlanders (Vikings) and some hunters have encountered little men called Skrælings (*scrælinga*). When they are slightly injured, their wounds turn white and they do not bleed; but if they have serious wounds, their blood flows without stopping. They do not know the use of iron but use *walrus teeth* as throwing weapons, and sharp stones as knives.[13]

No date is given concerning this (or these) violent encounter(s).* Written copies of the *Historia Norvegiae* existed in the Orkneys circa 1450. The author was presented as a Norwegian cleric, but the original is supposed to have been written in Denmark during the latter half of the twelfth century. The historians agree that one of these sources would be the *descriptio insularum aquilonis* from about 1075 and are in accord as to the historical trustworthiness of the work. A priori, we have as little information as in the preceding case, but we shall see that a more meticulous analysis using the smallest scrap of seemingly innocuous details can offer up some valuable unsuspected information. Here the accounts are based on actual experience: the Vikings encountered the Skrælings. This is more or less consistent with the *Islendingabók* concerning the location of this people, which is clearly underscored. McGhee translates it as "farther north." Storm's Danish translation is interesting as it is more faithful to the original

---

*According to Mathiassen, this would be before the thirteenth century. If we go by the source texts, no Norse-Inuit contacts took place at this time.

Latin. What might seem to be repetitive text represents, in fact, the scribe's emphasis of the remoteness of these meeting places.

> They are far from the Scandinavian settlements.
> They are even farther north.

I might add that this contact took place very far north as we can see from the scribe's anodyne note "walrus teeth as throwing weapons," which was not deciphered as it should have been. In concrete terms, this leads to the Far North, the natural habitat of the walrus (I will leave a door open for the possibility of the Disko region, Upernavik). The context of these voyages is a little better circumscribed.

Another piece of valuable information gives us dual confirmation of my working theories: "Some hunters" indicates an isolated presence of Scandinavians during the Nordrsetur journeys. "Little men" indicates a small native presence, which goes without saying in a traditional hunting economy. We will see the damage and mistakes that our anachronistic Western outlines can bring about such as the invasion "of Eskimo or Karelian armies" as noted by Danish cartographer Claudius Clavus and echoed by Olaus Magnus.

This mention of the natives and their weaponry causes us to lean strongly toward Thule culture. But the possibility of lingering Dorset people is not to be dismissed, either. Nor should the more detailed hypothesis of the author of the *Historia Norvegiae* that may well have benefited from other information on Greenland that is now lost be rejected. This is certainly possible, but I would like to venture another hypothesis. Couldn't we simply see in these different descriptions a difference between the people under consideration, which would be more historically consistent with the dates? The *Islendingabók* would therefore be referring to a description of Dorset people (or even older populations) and the *Historia Norvegiae* to one of the Thule or northern Inuit (Inussuit). I will, however, keep in reserve the theory of lingering members of Dorset culture because of the mention of stone weapons, and especially the lack of references to dogs. An Inuit identification in the case I have to make is sure: the anecdotal detail about native wounds has been presented by some scientists as a particular Inuit characteristic (concerning blood coagulation). We also have to conclude that violent contacts took place. As several researchers have stressed, the responsibility would seem to be attributable to the Vikings (cf., *Flóamannasaga* and the episode of the mutilation of a native). On the other hand, I would warn readers to be wary of the frequent extrapolations and confused accounts. For example, McGovern carelessly introduces an element that was not present in the original: "people who resembled trolls."[14]

This interpretation did not appear in the original, which only mentions the *Scraelinga,* which (for several decades now), could pass for a mere detail (a certain physical identification finding its niche there), appears today from the perspective of several works* as a misinterpretation. Generally speaking, *Skræling* refers to remote populations (in the Far North or in Vinland) or at least those that are far from Scandinavian settlements. This can be seen in almost all the texts of that time. *Troll* (still in accordance with these works) refers to neighboring native populations who are peaceful, if not friendly and helpful, as seen in some sources.

I will later cite the story of Björn Thorleifsson and his wife, Olöf, who were rescued by a couple of old Trolls, taken from the Annals of the Bishops. However, later texts send these Trolls into remote (probably Canadian) regions. The *Grønlands Historiske Mindesmærker* also recognizes this neighbor status: "In many places, it has been shown that at the time of the author [of the *Bárdar Snæfells Saga,* so the fifteenth century] the Nordics called the Eskimo 'Trolls' and they surely lived on the same coast."[15]

We shall later see the repercussions of this kind of clarification for this distinction made by the Vikings of this era (I suspect even the church of being the author of this learned subtlety worthy of a cleric) helps us better understand the relationship between the two populations. Let's say for the moment that no Nordic source in general depicts these Trolls as aggressors, which is not the case for the Skrælings. It is

---

*Jette Arneborg (1991) pertinently notes the difference in the use of the two words, *Skræling* appearing during the Nordic expeditions (namely, the Nordrsetur) and *Trolls* in the vicinity of the Nordic colonies. I would add that these sagas were written several centuries later by religious men ever ready to employ a biased and Manichean terminology.

easy to understand in this case the importance of clearly distinguishing the cases. It would be illusionary to seek to limit the use of this word to a later period, first because it is part of traditional Nordic lore and next because even at the time of Saxo Grammaticus the term was applied to the natives of the eastern coast of Greenland, called Tröllbotnar.* The *Grønlands Historiske Mindesmærker* likens it to the Scorebysund region. This means that the Vikings knew Trolls were living on Greenland's eastern coast during this time. An explanation (or at least part of one) could be provided regarding the native/Troll mythological spirits amalgamation.

> These lands (*Tröllbotnar*) were peopled by Trolls who were imagined in olden times to be wicked supernatural spirits. But later, it was believed that the wild Laplanders of Finland, the Eskimo, and so forth, were their descendants and worshippers.[16]

This explanation could actually be admissible during the medieval era. What particularly interests me is that even the *Grønlands Historiske Mindesmærker* recognizes this Scandinavian name attributed to the Greenland natives, whereas until now, only the name Skræling was known and poorly used: "In Iceland, even during the fourteenth century, and in the part of Greenland inhabited by the Vikings, the Eskimo were called Trolls."

To clearly grasp the tone of these accounts, a short summary of trolls appears to be called for. Trolls are grotesque-looking deformed creatures belonging to the world of fantasy. In folk belief, these supernatural beings live in the Norwegian mountains of Jötunheimr (the Land of Giants), a freezing empty wilderness. In Nordic mythology, Útgarðr† was inhabited by giants and Trolls who warred with gods and men by sending winter and its torments upon them. In such a context it is normal that Vikings would have immediately thought of giants and Trolls in these regions that fit so well their own mythological lore.

---

*Literally, Troll Bay, the polar bay between Greenland and Norway.
†The outer world located beyond the world of men, the dwelling place of the giants.

However, this doesn't explain the subtle difference that was made with the most desolate regions of Canada or northern Greenland. Why did some see Skrælings and others see Trolls? This is what I wish to focus on here.

Despite their physical disadvantage, Trolls do not always seem to have been such evil fellows, they could have their good sides. This is especially visible in the Icelandic definition of the word: "The old Icelandic troll refers to the notion of oversize creatures like giants and titans, generally in a negative sense, but also in a more positive sense."[17]

In Scandinavia Trolls are synonymous with magic; they are not necessarily evil, simply strange and are sometimes good. Their negative image exists—for example, that of wicked ogres—and Trolls were even used recently in the Scandinavian countryside to scare children into behaving. I suspect other, more southern influences. All the ambiguity distinctive of the Troll seems to fit perfectly—in both shape and spirit—to the Greenland natives.

## Gesta Danorum

I cite here with great reservation a passage taken from the book of Saxo Grammaticus, written during the period 1200 to 1220, in which a boreal land is described. No clues exist to make it possible to identify this land as Greenland, but in the interests of objectivity, I would like to include this short passage: "There is in the north a country whose position and name are unknown to me. It is not inhabited but swarms with strange and monstrous creatures (*sed monstrosae novitatis populis abundantum*). It is separated from Norway by an immeasurable ocean."[18]

Its northern identification is obvious but limited. Would it be Lapland, Greenland, Canada, or Spitzbergen? The latter seems more plausible if we take Saxo Grammaticus literally when he speaks of an uninhabited land as all the other sites were already inhabited in the twelfth century. The allusion to monstrous, supernatural creatures supports this position, as the waters of Spitzbergen were teeming with marine mammals in a way that should have kindled the imaginations of that era (see Olaus Magnus's illustrations in his *Historia de gentibus septentrionalibus*). However, two restrictions should be kept in mind:

It is possible that Saxo Grammaticus's informant only saw—as is most likely—a portion of the countries cited. And the informant or Saxo Grammaticus could have read something classifying the natives as misshapen creatures. But, in hopes of more concrete data in the future, I will hold on to the first identification with Spitzbergen as seeming the most realistic.

### *The Saga of Snorri the Goði* (Eyerbyggja Saga)

The original saga dates from about 1250.* There are several medieval copies, with the most complete version dating from the last half of the fourteenth century. The saga mainly tells the stories of different families that colonized western Iceland from about 881 to 1031. The allusion to Skrælings is extremely brief and refers to a warlike situation in Vinland outside the scope of this book: "Snorri went to Vinland the Good with Karlsefni and died like a man in battle with the Skrælings."[19]

Although the episode concerning Guðleifr's shipwreck in "Greater Ireland" is very interesting from a historical perspective, and seemingly confirms a very early Celtic presence in Western lands, it has nothing to say about the Inuit populations.

> At last a land came into view. It seemed a large place, but they had no idea what country it was. Guðleifr and his crew decided to put in, not wanting to battle against the sea any longer. They found a safe harbor, and after a while some people came down to meet them. They did not know who the inhabitants were but they seemed to be speaking Irish. Soon a great crowd gathered there, hundreds of them, attacked the crew, took them all prisoner, shackled them, and marched them some distance inland, where they were taken to a court to be tried and sentenced. Guðleifr and his crew understood that some of the people wanted to put them to death, while others proposed to share them out as slaves.[20]

---

*Not all the experts are in agreement here. Finnur Jónsson has suggested before 1200 and Einar Ó Sveinsson before 1222.

To this day, no trace of the Celtic tongue has been found in the Inuit language, and slavery was no part of this people's traditions. An identification with Amerindians seems more logical as it is consistent with the widely accepted location of Great Ireland farther south, among other things.

## The Saga of the Greenlanders (Grœnlendinga saga)

According to Jón Johannesson, the original saga dates from the end of the twelfth century. It was recorded in the *Flateyjarbók,* written in Icelandic—and I would say for an Icelandic audience—in 1387 to 1394. It deals with the colonization of Greenland since Erik the Red (thus the end of the tenth century), as well as the voyages from Iceland and Greenland to Vinland.

> A large group of men came out of the woods close to where the cattle were pastured. The bull began snorting and bellowing very loudly. This frightened the natives, who ran off with their burdens, which included all sorts of fur pelts and sables and all kinds of skins.[21]

Although one of the classic texts of this genre, it is extremely miserly about our subject area: contacts with the natives. The mention of Skrælings refers to Vinland and probably to the Amerindians of Labrador and Newfoundland (with a slight possibility of Dorset Inuit). In fact, all the peoples cited are North American forest dwellers. I earlier pointed out the difference of game animals hunted by the Inuit and Amerindians. The group of indigenous people came from the forest, which the saga appears to describe as their natural element.

## The Saga of Erik the Red (Eiríks saga rauða)

The original dates from about 1285. It resembles the previous saga in many respects with its colonization of Greenland and Icelandic and Greenlandic voyages to Vinland. There are two manuscripts for this saga, the oldest appearing in the *Hauksbók* shortly after 1300. The more recent one can appears in the *Skalhóltsbók.* The two texts visibly diverge, but it is clear they share the same source.

The episode regarding the Vinland Skrælings is basically the same. It should be noted that there is a more epic-like cast to it (for example, the episode of Freydis). This is easy to understand as the books purpose was to more or less shower the lineage of Erik the Red with praise. But this also gives distortions an opportunity to enter. The Freydis example seems to illustrate this perfectly.

> She [Freydis] came across a slain man, Thorbrand Snorrasson, who had been struck in the head by a slap of stone. His sword lay beside him, and this she snatched up and prepared to defend herself with it as the natives approached her. Freeing one of her breasts from her shift, she smacked the sword with it. This frightened the natives, who turned and ran back to their boats and rowed away.[22]

The saga includes some more or less fantasy-like episodes that not only reflect the reality but also the notion of reality that prevailed during the Middle Ages. In support of my identification made in the *Groenlendinga saga* of Skrælings as remote populations (probably Amerindians), I would like to point out the physical features described in *Eiríks saga rauða* (large eyes, broad cheeks) that are more reminiscent of Amerindian physiognomy than Inuit.

> A woman entered wearing a black tunic. She was quite small and wore a headband, her hair was light brown and her pale face was set off by large eyes, so large that no had ever seen their like before. . . . These people were brown and rough in appearance. Their hair was tangled on their heads, and they had large eyes and broad cheeks.[23]

Oddly enough, the *Grønlands Historiske Mindesmærker* saw this as a description of the Inuit people. To the contrary, I would see this as rather Amerindian features (for example, the eyes, cheeks, or even the hair-do). Likewise, the slingshot, a typical war instrument* never mentioned in con-

---

*The Inuit of Greenland and eastern Canada had no machines or weapons of a warlike nature. Their techniques were intended for hunting, even if they were used in battle on

nection with the Inuit, does exist among some Amerindian populations.

> Karlsefni's men saw that the Skrælings had a large ball on a pole, which looked like a bluish-colored sheep's gut. They brandished it at Karlsefni's band. It made a terrible noise when it crashed to the ground.[24]

Gwyn Jones also advises an identification as Amerindians. Jóhannesson (1962) believes *Eiríks saga rauða* is later than the *Grænlendinga saga* and even suggests that its author was familiar with the earlier work. As is evident, the Skrælings of these two sagas have very little connection with the natives we are interested in, and even less with the Trolls of Björn Einarsson Jórsalafari's story, or that of Björn Thorleifsson and his wife, Olaf. We can now more easily see why all the studies seeking to clarify Inuit-Viking relations had so much trouble making any headway given the paucity of materials available.

In fact, at a given moment, confusion was destined to arise as the same word *Skræling* was used to describe remote peoples some distance from the two Norse colonies in the north and the peoples of Vinland (this region was most likely believed to be an extension of the remote northern lands).* It turns out that these are two different peoples.

I have to stress the gap that separates the date of the transcription of the actual facts and the more than probable transformations they gave birth to. This involves the Icelandic tradition of adjusting facts dating from the tenth century to a thirteenth-century reality. We should also remember that these Icelandic sagas were written with Icelandic readers in mind (long genealogies and so forth). All efforts to find any scientific

---

(*cont.*) occasion. This contrasts with the Native Americans whose culture had a strong martial imprint (education, warrior class). A similar weapon was used by the Ojibwe people near Lake Superior: "Such war clubs were anciently made by sewing up a round stone in a green skin, and attaching a long pole to it. After drying, the skin assumed great hardness and the instrument, which performed some of the offices of a battering ram, was one of the most effective weapons of attack." H. R. Schoolcraft, *The Indian tribes of the United States* (Ed. F. S. Drake, Philadelphia: 1891).

*This was notably shown in several maps that depicted a land bridge to the West.

basis for the natives would be futile here, and it may well have been merely an exotic patina.

The core of historic truth is difficult to extract from the overabundance of facts, but I will note that each bit of "technical information" belonging to the era allows corroboration of these facts. The scribe may have felt little motivation to change a material detail whose meaning escaped him and which, in the worst-case scenario, gave some local color. On the other hand, it is not necessarily the case of a genealogy whose most beautiful flowerings are cited while the others are discarded. The trivial technical details of Skræling trade (martin skins) reflects forest dwellers who are therefore Amerindians and not Greenlanders.

## *The Saga of the People of Flói* (Flóamanna saga)

This saga is presented by the *Grønlands Historiske Mindesmærker* as the oldest saga concerning the history and geography of Greenland. It was written circa 1300 by a scholar who used several of the known source texts. It was preserved in the form of copies. The *Flóamanna saga* is about Icelandic and Greenlandic events at the beginning of the year 1000. Although it takes its name from the story of people in Flói, Iceland (chapters 4–12), this saga focuses primarily on a certain Thorgils, whose voyage is described so realistically that his presence there is presumed.

The passage on the Greenland natives is brief, but it allows us to appreciate the subtle difference with the Vikings seen earlier. Thorgils was shipwrecked in Greenland.

> Thorgils and his men began fishing enthusiastically. They constructed a boat made of hides over a wooden frame. One day, when Thorgils had gone out by himself, he saw an impressive animal that had been pulled out of an ice hole and two Troll women* (wild women)† who were tying together large pieces of the animal's meat.

---

*The *Grønlands Historiske Mindesmærker* says they were clad in *skynnkyrtlum;* in other words, hide tunics.

†This is absent in the original *Ok Þarhjá tröllkonur tvær . . .* (*Grønlands Historiske Mindesmærker*).

Thorgil leaped upon them with sword unsheathed and struck the one who was hefting a sack over her back in such a way that she lost a hand, and her burden fell to the ground, but she managed to flee. They then took the sea animals and they had enough provisions.[25]

This short paragraph tells us several things: the first contacts—because of the Vikings and their prejudices—were violent and that the natives of the regions neighboring the Vikings were not Skrælings but Trolls.

Two details have passed unnoticed in this narrative: the building of the boat and the theft of the hunting booty from the Troll women. The description of the boat built by Thorgils is strongly reminiscent of that of the Inuit *umiaq*. This is also the interpretation of the *Grønlands Historiske Mindesmærker*: "Thorgils's boat could be compared to the contemporary Greenland 'women's boat.'"* This would imply that the Vikings knew Inuit techniques during this time. We saw in the previous chapter that Leroi-Gourhan also drew a technical comparison regarding the *umiaq* (borrowing the form of the boat and the sail by the Inuit). Here we have the opposite example: the borrowing of the *umiaq's* very structure by the Vikings. The question was raised earlier concerning the Irish *currach* and in no way excludes the possibility of a Nordic borrowing. Strong presumptions exist regarding the presence of Greenland colonists as well as monks driven out of Ireland in the western lands. In both cases, these two peoples would have been in contact with the indigenous North Americans. It is quite plausible that this contact included loans of techniques. It is easy to see that a lot of interesting questions hover about this famous hide skiff, the *umiaq*.

The theft of the game from the two Troll women illustrates a complaint found in several Inuit tales.

In fact, this saga is much richer in information concerning our subject than may be suspected. These bits of information (like that of the construction of the *umiaq* by Scandinavians) seem to have passed by practically unnoticed and reveals the cultural gap separating the two peoples on such things as the notion of loan or theft. This is

---

*This was its traditional name as it was Inuit women who paddled the *umiaq*.

quite interesting as we have two entirely different concepts at work in Thorgils's theft of the game and the example that follows. In fact, shortly after this misdeed, Thorgils's hide boat disappears—it is easy to imagine his predicament in such a country—to reappear a short time later at the same place from which it had vanished. The event is recounted so quickly in the saga that it is easy to pass over it without noticing: "He heard a loud shout, saying they should take their boat. They came out and saw two women [Troll women] who vanished immediately."[26]

The *Grønlands Historiske Mindesmærker* offers a very interesting explanation that appears quite plausible to me. The natives had borrowed this boat and then brought it back from where they had taken it, something that is quite normal in Inuit society. If we consider how Thorgils "borrowed" his hunting booty, we can easily see the gap that separates them. I would also draw another conclusion, this borrowing by the "female Trolls" amounts in a certain way to showing honor to Thorgils and his crew. What I mean is that the craft must have been particularly well made for specialists in this kind of boat to borrow it. Indirectly, this example shows that the theory of Nordic maladjustment (mainly technical) is more than fragile.

We can assume that the scribe possessed other documents that explain the note on the hide clothing of the Troll women or his comparison with "wild women." This is of particular interest to me as it provides a good example of that Nordic phenomenon consisting of blending ancient Scandinavian mythological tradition with the reality of the Arctic world. For the *Grønlands Historiske Mindesmærker* there can be no doubt: "It is beyond any question that only wild women, and not the standard 'Troll women' or giantesses are involved, although they are called *fœminae gigantœ* or even *dœmones montani*."

The *Grønlands Historiske Mindesmærker* opts for the theory of a description of Greenland natives colored by Nordic mythology elements: "These Troll women were not witches who used magic to unloose the wind, or forest nymphs (*faunœ*) or aerial Trolls (*striges noctivagœ*), *kveldiriður,* although in the *Eddas* and fables they are often called female Trolls. They are clearly actual women of impressive size and strength. These people were the descendants of giants some of whose families remained in mountain caves living on hunting and fishing, and, sometimes, on human flesh. They appear now and then in stories that are trustworthy in Finmark."[27]

We can see to what extent reality and mythology were commingled and how they complicate the work of researchers trying to decode these sources. Without seeking to look further for an explanation, it seems to me that this impressive physical nature corresponds rather well with the Thule people. As we learned earlier (chapter 1) the *umiaq* first appeared with this culture.

We have noted throughout Nordic traditional lore the repetition of numerous elements referring to the native Arctic peoples: cave dwellings, clothing made from furs, an economy based on hunting and fishing, and so forth. Even if the colonists gave free rein to their imaginations drifting through mythological tradition (but couldn't this be the work of the scribe?), they also clearly described the peoples they met either in their vicinity or in the Arctic.

J. Kristjánsson interpreted this saga as one of the most colorful and fairytale-like of the fourteenth century, resembling portions of the *Book of the Settlement of Iceland* (*Landnámabók*). However, the voyages and sojourns in Greenland seem quite credible. The meeting with the natives is generally accepted and placed by some on Greenland's eastern coast about the year 1000. Personally, I would be less critical than Kristjánsson and put emphasis on the misunderstanding of several factors—mainly cultural—regarding the native Greenland populations that prevent seeing the full value of the information transmitted here. In this respect, this brief passage is most interesting as it describes fairly well an episode occurring at the beginning of colonization. The placement some have made on the eastern coast should be replaced in the context of its time. It is in the east, yes, but in the eastern colony that until the nineteenth century was believed to have been located on the eastern coast.

## The Greenland Annals (Grœnlands annál)

This saga represents a compilation of narratives about the Vikings in Greenland. According to Icelandic philologist Oláfur Halldórsson, they were collected in Iceland circa 1623, probably by Jón Gudmusson, known as the wise man (1574–1658). The original work is lost but several copies remain, among them that by Björn of Skardså from about 1643. It includes two texts (the expedition of the Scandinavian priests to the Nordrsetur and the episode of Björn Eriksson Jórsalafari), that provide the most interesting information if not the most reliable about Inuit and Viking contacts. The completely different tone from that of earlier narratives, especially the *Flóamanna saga,* is quite noticeable.

The first text I would like to mention is the story of the Greenland priest Halldór. We will also look at this text in the chapter on the church because its information is very useful. I would like to open with a citation of one of the earliest discrete accounts dealing with the natives: "Pieces of wood were found in the sea that had been carved with small axes or adzes; one of them was inlaid with ivory and bone."[28]

It is clear that what we see here is an implicit allusion to the craft of the Greenland natives that had washed ashore at Hitarness on the Icelandic coast.

Halldór's second allusion to the natives/Skrælings is connected with the Nordrsetur. Although they never appear in his text, the Skrælings are still the object of the priest's attention: "That summer, men returned from the Nordrsetur. They had sailed farther north than usual. They had found no trace of the Skræling's passage, except on the Kroksfjord mountains."[29]

Here we find a confirmation of my premise: the remote location of the natives (implication the Skrælings) and the meticulous search for them by the Vikings, which is fairly surprising: "We can see how carefully the Greenlanders (Vikings) of that time paid attention to the places of Skræling dwellings."[30]

This commentary most likely dates from the seventeenth century. The tone of the text has led several researchers to give credence to a theory of a deliberate search for the natives for commercial purposes. We cannot help but see the care with which all the settlements with a Skræling connotation were reviewed. Didn't the Scandinavians have anything better to do, or did they already have a kind of tacit alliance with proven suppliers who they actively sought out during the Nordrsetur expeditions?

This is certainly the impression given by the end of the text: "They arrived at the bay. . . . They came upon several signs that the Skrælings had occupied these settlements earlier. They then sailed for several days and there they found some bits and pieces left by the Skrælings."[31]

Halldór's letter is taken from the *Hauksbók* and does not appear in any other source text. Here I need to make a short digression concerning this book. The *Hauksbók* is a compilation written by the Icelandic lawman (*lagmann*) Haukr Erlendsson, who died in 1334. Born in Iceland, he spent his childhood there and practiced there from 1294 to 1295. He was then in Norway from 1302. So what we have here is an interesting, practically firsthand account. Unfortunately, Halldór's writings on Greenland are lost, but a part of the original is preserved containing one version of *Eiríks saga rauða* and the *Landnámabók*.

The events described by Halldór are attached to a narrative of a shipwreck that took place at Hitarness, Iceland, an event noted in the *Icelandic Annals* (the *Konungsannáll,* among others) for 1266. These royal annals are part of the oldest Icelandic annals and were probably written at the same time as the *Hauksbók*. The reference to Bishop Olaf, sailing to Greenland circa 1271, and to King Magnus Håkansson (1262–1280) provide very specific reference points and dismisses any later date for the initial Inuit-Scandinavian contacts. Other sources will show us they go back further.

Among all these sources, Halldór's letter is perhaps the only one to give a straightforward account, meaning one not addressed to a foreign audience, which is notably visible in its style. This is of double interest for research. The second text is equally interesting, if not more so. It is one of the rare Nordic accounts—from the time, moreover—that unambiguously describes normal relations between Vikings and two Troll children.

> It happened that he rescued two young Trolls on a rock that the sea was about to submerge. They swore him loyalty and from that moment he never lacked for anything because they were skilled at

hunting a variety of game. The little girl Troll considered it the highest favor the possibility of carrying and cuddling the little boy that the lady of the house had just given birth to. She also wished to wear a headdress similar to the lady's. In its stead, she made one from whale gut. The brother and sister killed themselves by jumping into the sea when they learned they could not accompany their dear farmer Björn to Iceland.

The *Icelandic Annals* tells us that the account concerning Björn Einarsson known as Jórsalafari (the pilgrim of Jersualem) was taken from a voyage that is practically unknown today. None of the known texts are prior to the time of Jón lærði (the wise man) Guðmundsson (1574–1658). The event recounted took place in 1385 after a pilgrimage to Jerusalem. Björn Einarsson's wife, Solveig, accompanied him. For two years they lived in Eiriksfjord. This provides us with an extremely interesting confirmation (for it is duly dated) of the simultaneous presence of both peoples in Eystribygð. Surely the two Troll children were not on their own there.

I will make another observation here: as 1385 is practically certainly the date when this event occurred, that clearly says the Inuit were in southern Greenland some forty years after Ivar Bårdsson's* visit to Vestribygð as both incidents have been precisely established. It is easy to see how valuable traditional lore placed back in its proper context and corroborated can be for our investigation. Here we have two well-established temporal benchmarks, recorded by clerics, that support the theory of Inuit-Norse cohabitation during the fifteenth century.

It is historically proven that Einarsson, known as Jórsalafari, lived

---

*It is presumable that as a representative of the authority that long held sway there, Ivar Bårdsson would have mentioned an Inuit presence in Eystribygð. However, his report is so ambiguous and full of holes that all doubts are permissible. B. Jónsson's description from the first half of the seventeenth century mentioning the place-name Utiblikfjord, borrowed from the Inuit "Itiblissoak" cutting through Isafjord in the middle of Eystribygð can give us some maneuvering room for placing this Inuit presence in southern Greenland. The sixteenth century is sure while the fourteenth and fifteenth centuries are quite likely.

in Greenland toward the end of the fourteenth century. Indeed, the *Icelandic Annals of Flatey (Flateyjarannáll)* mention a Björn Einarsson among the passengers of four boats arriving in Hvalfjord, Iceland, in 1387 after two winters spent in Greenland, which is consistent with the 1385 date. The *Flateyjarannáll* are generally dated from 1388 to 1390. The same event is confirmed, but with no mention of the passengers, in the *Lögmannsannáll.*

> This is the same figure who was tried with his companions in 1389 in Norway for illegal commerce in Greenland. Based on several decisive elements that are often absent from other accounts, I can underscore:
>
> The very short period of time for the writing of the account (*Flateyjarannáll* dating from 1388–1390), it is probably the closest thing to a "live broadcast" during the Middle Ages in our possession.
>
> The neutral nature of the text (especially regarding the young Trolls) and the absence of the exaggeration that is often inherent to adventure narratives.
>
> The fidelity of the account* (the hunting skills of the Trolls, survival in difficult regions).

In short, we have one of the rare faithful accounts of the era and what more of European—Scandinavian—origin. All these elements contribute to a quality of the given information that can be seen with a different approach from that of Halldór's letter. All those who uphold the theory of peaceful coexistence and other researchers who take a more middle of the road opinion see this episode as proof of peaceful Inuit-Norse relations.

Now that we know the range of these solid references provided by

---

*I would personally add that this fidelity could even help us solve a riddle about an Inuit women's hairstyle (Tunumiut) on the eastern coast consisting of an impressive bun adorned with pearls. No other Inuit people adopted this hairstyle. Could this have been a borrowing of the medieval Norse hairstyle? Fittingly, the famous necklace adorning the hairstyle cited in the chapter on loans was called kona.

the relatively precise historical dates, we are able to place our subject better. I am striving here to select the most lucid documents that are objective, historically speaking, and not necessarily "great classics." We can all acknowledge this is not always the case with literary sources. The four following source texts—with the exception of that of Ivar Bårdsson—have the advantage of being solidly dated. Contemporary research tends to group them together because they could well be the different faces of the same event.

## The Note of 1342

This is surely the most important text for both the meaning and consequences of the Scandinavians fate; it was issued originally by the bishopric of Skálholt (Iceland): "The inhabitants of Greenland voluntarily abandoned the true faith and the Christian religion after turning their back on all the good customs and true virtues, and turning toward the peoples of America. Consequently, Christians began to abstain from any voyages to Greenland.[32]

Unfortunately, the original is lost. Today's existing copy comes from a Latin book, *Annalium in Islandia farrago, hinc inde descripta,*[33] dating from July 24, 1637, in Skálholt and written by the bishop Gisli Odsson. This later date (three centuries later) explains the anachronism concerning America. Risks of revision, therefore, are possible. Gisli, son of the bishop Odd Einarsson, had access to the bishopric's archives and library when he was growing up. So it is quite likely he had access to a written source that vanished in the 1630 fire. Storm believes Gisli could have taken his information from the *Oddverja annáll,*[34] circa 1580, in the 1606 *Greenland Chronicle* of Lyschander as well as local Icelandic histories. Corrado Gini also cites the *Greenland Chronicle,* which is actually fairly strange as it refers to the year 1340 as the year Greenland abandoned civilization.

## The Mission Order of King Magnus Eriksson Smek of 1335

"It is our wish that you [Powell Knutsso] take all the men the Knarr can carry . . . among my guard. . . . We ask you to accept this command for the salvation of our soul and those of our predecessors who brought Christianity to Greenland and have kept it there to this day and would not suffer its fall now."[35]

Only a single copy of this letter from King Magnus Eriksson Smek survives. It appears in a confused sixteenth-century translation from Danish to Swedish.

## Ivar Bårdsson's Description of Greenland (circa 1360)

This text is quite controversial. Crosschecking shows that the dates of the events would have fallen after 1341, the date Ivar Bårdsson's passport was issued by the Bergen bishopric (August 8, 1341).[36] I am only citing a passage from the text—which is moreover quite vague—concerning the Greenland natives. "Now the Skrælings possess all of Vestribryð; nevertheless there are horses, goats, and sheep wandering freely, but not a single living soul, neither pagan nor Christian."[37]

"Ivar Bårdsson, known as the Greenlander who was administrator in Greenland for many years . . . was one of those named by 'the higher authorities' to leave for Vestribygð to drive out the Skrælings."[38]

This text is only known for copies, most of which date from the seventeenth century, with the oldest going back to the end of the sixteenth century. The original would date from the fourteenth century. In her 1998 booklet, Jette Arneborg cites 1360, the date I've used as it concurs overall with the various factors that will be examined later. The oldest copy dates from 1608 based on a Norwegian original translated into High German in 1560, then into Dutch, and lastly into English. The original was found on the Faroe Islands in an accounts book from one hundred years later, which gives us 1460. A copy was made for the Archbishop Erik Walkendorff circa 1515 (*Grønlands Historiske Mindesmærker*). His higher title would correspond to a Protestant translation of the "officialis" Catholic title (*forstander/officialis* in the original Nordic and Latin text), as a person could replace the bishop for certain duties, particularly economic ones. It should be noted that the bilingual version by C. C. Rafn uses the term *procurator*.[39]

## *Note from the* Icelandic Annals *of 1379*

This document tells of a conflict between the Vikings and Inuits that turned to the latter's advantage. Several researchers have been prone to making this a generality, something from which I refrain.

> The Skrælings attacked the Scandinavians, killing eighteen men and taking two boys captive.[40]

This footnote can be found in two different copies, one from the seventeenth century and a more recent one that reflects an older source, one that is unfortunately impossible to verify. The 1379 footnote is given by three annals cited by the Gottskálks annáll circa 1550 to 1560. Two other annals confirm it: the Holenses Annals (AM 412) "written at the beginning of the seventeenth century," and the Annals (AM 410), which are supposed to have been written by the bishop Thorlak Skulesson of Holar circa 1640. No other written source confirms this event, but there is no a priori reason to reject this source said to be from 1379. Let's look at how these four written sources were used.

## *The Note of 1342*

This source is only known through Bishop Gisli Odsson's 1630 retranscription. Because of its clerical origin, it is flawed for its lack of neutrality, visible with the emphasis placed on the abandonment of the Christian faith. However, it still shores up several theories.

### Theory of the Crossbreeding of the Two Populations

F. Nansen saw here proof of a "forced" crossbreeding between Inuits and Vikings and emigration to America. "They turned to the beliefs and customs of the American populations (i.e., the Skrælings), and they were obliged to adopt the Eskimo lifestyle, crossbreeding with them."

P. Nørlund limits this Inuit-Scandinavian crossbreeding to Vestribygð. It is one of Gwen Jones's hypotheses, and he explains this abandonment in detail. It is possible that the Vikings emigrated to Newfoundland or Baffin Island, alone or with the Inuits (a hypothesis not shared by Jones, who instead believed the Norse fled to Eystribygð, to which I raise the objection that no other annals tell of an event this serious).

Among the fans of this theory cited by Jones are Helge Ingstad and Corraldo Gini, who even talks of apostasy. Jones sums up the questions: "Some believe that the Greenland Scandinavians mingled with the natives, adopting their customs and religions. It was probably to examine the nature and extent of this apostasy that Bishop Håkon of Bergen had send the priest Ivar Bårdsson one year earlier."[41]

## Simple Theory of Emigration
The new theory entertained by contemporary researchers suggests a divergence of masking of the reality. This is why Gisli Odsson evaded the real questions: the rejection of reformation of the Nordic Church. All he could do was present the church's official version: "We do not clearly see (in Gisli Odsson's text) who was threatened: the Christian faith, the colony, or both?"[42]

## The Mission Order of 1355
Until now, this mission has been considered as proof of hostile relations between the two communities at Vestribygð in the first half of the fourteenth century. The king's planned expedition has never been confirmed and nothing is really certain about its motivations. It is likely it never took place due to the very serious problems facing Magnus E. Smek.* The most widespread (and simple) hypothesis of a punitive expedition against the Inuit is not the most certain, far from it. Others have seen a connection between the 1355 command and Bårdsson's 1360 report, whose visit is presented as a logical consequence of this order: "The direct cause for sending a boat was probably the sudden advance of the pagan Eskimos toward the Western colony."[43]

---

*This will be tackled in the same chapter. We should note that H. R. Holand supports another opinion. The expedition would have taken place about 1362 to 1363 and returned to Scandinavia in 1364. Holand bases his position primarily on the works of G. Storm (*Studier over Vinlands reisene*), and A. Bjørnbo.

An interesting point of view is shared by Ingstad and Prytz who see primarily economic motivations:

> We are right to presume that this was an expedition of exploration and tax collection including Sweden, Norway, Iceland, England, and where the (Scandinavian) Greenlanders should be looked for.[44]

H. Ingstad connects King Magnus's mission order to another falsely trivial piece of news, that of 1346 in which the Icelandic annals tell of the arrival in Bergen of a Knörr from Greenland: "The knarr of Greenland arrived in good condition with a quantity of merchandise."[45]

The following year (1347) the same thing happened in Iceland, this time the boat had wandered off its Markland*-Greenland course. "A boat also arrived from Greenland; it was smaller in size than the Icelandic ships. It came outside of *Strömfjörd*. It had lost its anchor. Its seventeen men had gone to Markland, but on their return they were detoured here."[46]

Here we have a completely different image from that of a poor and isolated community. To the contrary, the Vikings give the impression of maintaining a prosperous commerce with numerous voyages west. Drawn by this wealth, the king planned the expedition discussed in the 1355 letter. It is even possible that he had made the journey to Markland. I would also emphasize the tacit alliance between the royal

---

*Markland designated the land to the west of Greenland (therefore North America). The most common translation was "wooded land" (D. Bruun, 1931, and H. Ingstad, 1965). Researchers are in agreement that it refers to Labrador. Today the hypothesis of a translation of Markland by "pasture lands" appears more and more frequently. The matter becomes more complicated if we consider the original meaning of the term: "Mark, plural Mörk, a word common to all Teutonic languages (German, Swedish, Danish). The original sense is an outline, a border, whence are derived *mörk*, borderland; also *merki, merkja*" (R. Cleasby, G. Vigfússon, 412). The relationship with the forest would therefore have come later: "forest land with the notions of march land, border land" (413). Restored to a medieval Scandinavian context, this would mean that Markland could also mean "the frontier land" and that the reference to Vinland is implicit because according to the sagas that is the country located just beyond Markland.

house and the church, each finding their own benefit in this planned expedition—bringing the unruly Scandinavians back to heel, collection of their taxes, and bailing out the royal treasury.

The historian Finn Gad connects the four source texts together, particularly the order of 1355 and the 1373 note, which, in his opinion, reveal a latent state of war between the Norse and Inuit communities. Gad doesn't believe that the Inuit or Scandinavian stories apply specifically to Vestribygð but concern the Norse population in general.

## Ivar Bårdsson's Description (1360)

Grafted to the problem specific to the interpretation of this source is the additional riddle of the author's identity and his stay in Greenland. According to the generally accepted version, Ivar Bårdsson would have been an official representative of the bishop of Bergen.[47] In the last part of "the description of Greenland," Ivar Bårdsson is introduced as a kind of steward of the Garðar bishopric who could have been an aide or a replacement to Bishop Arni. Ivar Bårdsson is supposed to have replaced the bishop when the post was vacant from 1348 to 1368 but returning to Norway before 1364. His signature appears on a canonical document of the Bergen apostolic church in 1364. According to C. Keller, this chapel was one of the most prestigious of the kingdom of Norway, which could mean that Ivar Bårdsson was in the king's service. Some even see this as proof of an alliance between the clergy and royalty in Greenland.

The date his passport was issued (1341) doesn't necessarily indicate his presence in Greenland a short time later, something to which both Gini and Keller raise objections. Citing extremely serious sources (the *Regesta Norvegica*), Keller gives a clear, precise date for Ivar Bårdsson's departure for Greenland: August 11, 1341. We know that he remained in Greenland for quite some time (twenty to twenty-seven years according to Keller), and because of this was nicknamed the Greenlander.

Henriksen mentions a Bergen priest named by Clement VI (1342–1352) in connection with a post to be filled. According to the Norwegian author, it is more than likely that this priest would have gone to Avignon. In this case he would not have left for Greenland before 1345. Henriksen suggests 1347 as the more probable date, which means while Bishop Arni was still alive, and excludes his presence in the 1370s as this would be meaningless.*

Ivar Bårdsson's report concerning the Norse colony of Eystribygð is, on the other hand, quite vague on the subject of the natives. It is surely not enough to supply a basis for an Inuit attack on Vestribygð, or even further, its extermination. I will note that Ivar Bårdsson speaks of Skræling possession of all Vestribygð without providing the slightest detail or any description of them, or even a single solitary proof for his statement. Most contemporary researchers are in agreement that his expedition did not encounter any natives.

The presence of Ivar Bårdsson could be the result of an earlier attack against the western colony. The sole reliable benchmarks provided by the text are an Inuit presence in the region of Vestribygð circa 1340, which is confirmed by archaeology. Contemporary researchers made the following observations: What are Bårdsson's criteria for his term: "going to hunt the Skrælings?" Isn't there an interpretation at this stage of the text?

Indeed, Ivar Bårdsson is no warrior, but I will admit that the presence of a man of the cloth in a punitive expedition is not exceptional. Recognizing his administrative responsibilities, his presence in the western colony is explicable. It was a subsidiary of the church and not under Norse jurisdiction. A possible alliance between church and crown is not to be dismissed. In fact, several researchers view this as a punitive expedition against the colonists. Ivar Bårdsson would have sent them to bring his flock back to order, in which case his expedition should be connected to the 1355 source text. The gap is only thirteen years, after all.

This very serious hypothesis is placed in a very awkward position by the hitherto prevailing theories. It has received more and more attention in contemporary Scandinavian research that rejects an Inuit attack on Vestribygð just on the basis of Bårdsson's text, a view I share. Yet it

---

*Vera Henriksen believes it is quite likely that Ivar Bårdsson was present in Norway when he wrote his report. Given its inconsistencies (in the descriptions, the sites that were confused or omitted) nothing could be less certain.

does not reject the possibility of disputes between the two communities, which has been confirmed archaeology as we have seen in the Sandnæs excavations.

The 1342 letter or the 1355 letter cannot be considered proof of Scandinavian extermination and clearly sum up the ideas that prevailed until the onset of the twentieth century. Finn Gad notes quite relevantly that no source including the *Icelandic Annals,* speaks of problems between the Vikings and Skrælings (with the exception of the 1379 note). In tandem with Bårdsson, we cannot pass over in silence an even more mysterious figure, the English monk and astronomer Nicholas of Lynn, who was allegedly present in Greenland during the 1380s, the same time as Bårdsson. His relationship with the latter's report is only known through sixteenth-century source texts that are impossible to verify.

As a source of the hypothesis of a shared journey of Ivar Bårdsson and Nicholas of Lynn, I can cite, among others, this passage from the latter testifying to the gift of an astrolabe from a minorite friar of Oxford to a churchman. (Remember, the Scandinavians sailed without compasses or maps.)*

> He had been bequeathed this astrolabe in the will of a minorite friar. . . . The priest mentioned had explained to the king that in the "commerce"† in which he had lived the rain hardly fell more than six times a year. [48]

The hypothesis of a more or less long encounter of these two figures in Greenland or at the Norwegian court of King Magnus (in 1364) has been suggested. Jacob Cnoyen, Mercator's source, was at the court. According to Prytz, it was Ivar Bårdsson who would have given the minorite friar's gift of an astrolabe to the king. Bårdsson is thought

---

*A 1457 map by the Italian Mauro tells us that the Scandinavians sailed by sounding the depths not with map or compass: "*per questo mar non se navega cum carta ni bossola, ma cum scandaio.*"

†See chapter 10, especially the 1492 globe and my identification using the geographical divisions of Nicholas of Lynn (trading businesses) in accordance with local products.

to have borrowed the information of Nicholas of Lynn on the polar regions. Mercator states that the English astronomer and mathematician had traveled to Norway five times, following his polar expedition. We also know that during this time Ivar Bårdsson may have been in Norway as his report is dated 1360. Barring the discovery of more solid information, this hypothesis cannot be dismissed, knowing that this report is characterized by much obscurity.

Questions persist concerning Ivar Bårdsson's presence after the writing of the report. Was he still alive? For Keller, the description of 1360 was told based on official documents that Ivar Bårdsson had either written or carried, but he is more reserved as to the second possibility. I would personally add that the numerous inconsistencies appear in his descriptions (location errors, churches like that of Herjolfsnes omitted). They are hard to accept based on his long stay in Greenland. I would tend to doubt that he was present for the final writing of his report.

### The 1379 Note

This is by far one of the least ambiguous pieces of information, although precise details concerning the location are lacking. It obviously supplies grist to the mill of the hawkish theory supporters. Yet it would be somewhat expeditious to try to limit this source to a banal account of conflict between the two communities: some see it as confirmation of an Inuit presence in Eystribygð. This means that the Inussuk migration would have gone beyond the Nuuk region (and the western colony) would have already spread into southern Greenland by the end of the fourteenth century. Ingstad and Krogh offer a totally opposing analysis that sees this as an isolated incident rather than a proper battle between the two communities. The number of Norse losses (18 men) corresponds precisely to the crew of an exploration boat, like those to Markland. And we should also not overlook the presence of two *trælle* boys (slaves) on another boat to Vinland. All of these details corroborate Ingstad and Krogh's hypothesis that this event took place during an expedition to the Nordrsetur. Krogh even makes a sound observation, given the late date. Vestribygð would have been deserted; consequently the Scandinavians mentioned in this text would be from the eastern colony.

I would also add that, despite the widespread rumors of the supposed animosity of the Inuit now living in Vestribygð—according to Bårdsson—the Scandinavians were continuing to mount expeditions that traveled through Vestribygð into the Far North. This seems most illogical to me, or maybe we should admit that the alleged "state of war" didn't exist.

I would also note that the Icelandic scribe speaks of Skrælings and not Trolls, which in my definition refers to remote populations, excluding Eystribygð.

Catching the hawkish theory completely off guard, Jette Arneborg sees to the contrary an exceptional fact worthy of note: such quarrels and minor conflicts were ignored.

> While there were small incidents between Vikings and Eskimos, by all evidence, they were not serious enough for the Vikings to make them worth telling. Because this information dating from 1379 did manage to make it into the Icelandic annals is surely due to the gravity with which this event was regarded, so that the Vikings deemed it worth recording.[49]

As can be seen, her position is more nuanced and doesn't exclude minor conflicts. Several experts accept them as inevitable because of the large gap separating Scandinavians and Inuits.

### The Story of Gunnar Keldugnupsfifl

This story seems to have been written in the fourteenth century, and F. Magnussen and C. C. Rafn classify it among the tales. During his youth, Gunnar had to flee Iceland for having committed blood crimes. After sailing for a long time, lost in the fog, he arrived in a land almost totally covered by glaciers, with broad fjords and large capes.

> An abundance of fish, seals, and whales were there, and even many polar bears. The land is inhabited by Trolls who live in holes.

Gunnar killed several of them, but the others flattered him and offered him a lot of gold and silver.[50]

The fauna is typical of the polar region, and the minerals could indicate Canada. The native dwellings, gold, and silver cannot help but recall the episode of Adam of Bremen. This is one of the rare cases in which the remote populations are called Trolls, but this word still retains its "pacifist" connotations, in contrast with the Skrælings, for the Trolls here are properly cut to pieces by Gunnar. Here we see confirmation of my position (Trolls in clerical sources concerning Greenland are the equivalent of peaceful populations). The Trolls described in a Greenland context are far from shining at the art of war. The text offers few exploitable elements and has remained almost practically unused by researchers overall. Under these conditions, it is hard to extract useful information.

### The Maps of Claudius Clavus

During the early Middle Ages, cartography was still based on the work of Ptolemy (second century). Scandinavia did not figure in it. Starting from the fifteenth century, several maps appeared still based on Ptolemy but including Scandinavia. It is generally accepted that this addition comes from Scandinavian sources—namely, the Danish Claudius Claussön Swart. His name often appears in Latin as Claudius Clavus if not sometimes distorted and Latinized as Nicolaus Niger. He went on to produce two kinds of Scandinavian maps: the relatively correct Nordic maps known as "Type A" (Greenland occupies its normal place) and the Nordic maps known as "Type B" in which Greenland is placed north of Norway.

Although its production gave rise to much commentary concerning the author's actual knowledge, several elements are no less undeniable.

The date of 1420 on these maps confirms the vouched-for presence of Claudius Clavus in Rome. Keller identifies him with Nicolaus Gothus, cited in Rome in January 1424, idem for F. Nansen, who found him under the name of "Claudius Clavus Nicolas Niger." This is where he was initiated into the art of mapmaking, which was not really a prerogative of the Vikings.

A direct consequence of Clavus's sojourn is the appearance of the first correct representations of the geographical position of Greenland, even though only the eastern coast is drawn—to the west of Iceland. During the Middle Ages Greenland was commonly depicted as an extension of Scandinavia with a giant land bridge connecting the north of Norway to Greenland. Unfortunately the quality of his work or approach stopped there. With respect to the subject at hand, contacts between Inuit and Vikings, the testimony of C. Clavus is of an entirely different caliber.

The Latin text of his second map (1424), found by chance in 1900 by A. Bjørnbo, in fact gives us a disparate and very vague account of the natives through evoking their techniques. We also have an illustration of the earth bridge connecting Greenland and Scandinavia.

> After them (the Sami) we find far to the west the small pygmies, one ell in height, and who I saw after they had been made prisoners in a boat made from skins, it is hanging now in the Trondheim Cathedral. One day a long boat made of skins was also captured with the same pygmies on board. The peninsula of Greenland extends north toward a land that is unknown and inaccessible because of ice. However, as I was able to see, the unbelieving Karelians come down continuously in large hordes and probably come from the other side of the North Pole.[51]

Several source texts actually mention the presence of Inuit craft that were probably kayaks (long leather skiffs) in the Nidaros Cathedral. Sometimes it would happen that unscrupulous sailors would "bring back" natives on their ships. Unfortunately, it seems that the knowledge of Claudius Clavus on Greenland or the natives stops with secondhand knowledge acquired from Trondheim Cathedral, and that contrary to what he says, he never set foot in Greenland. Keller shares this opinion because Claudius Clavus would not have confused Karelians and Skrælings. It clearly seems that he cites Nordic source texts reporting on fairly serious clashes in northern Scandinavia. These lasted for two centuries. In 1278, a group of Karelians and "Kvens"* kidnapped the governor of the Troms district, Torbjørn Slane, killing thirty-five of his men. Other attacks were launched during the years 1322 to 1326. In a circa 1323 letter, the Norwegian-Swedish king Magnus Eriksson described these attacks and asked Pope Jean XXII of Avignon for financial aid to fight the "infidels." The pope answered on August 30, 1326, with promise of support for a crusade to expel the Russian and Karelian pagans.

Claudius Clavus—among others—greatly contributed to the spread of erroneous notions, casually combining the population of northern Scandinavia with that of Greenland. The most eminent figures of the time, such as Olaus Magnus and Adam of Bremen, were not innocent of this.

> From this cape (in Greenland) an immense country extends eastwards to Russia. The northern part is inhabited by "infidel Karelians" (*Careli infideles*) whose land goes from the North Pole to the Eastern Sere (the Chinese).

This ethnographical confusion could have a connection with a purely linguistic confusion. In fact, some researchers are of the opinion that Skræling could be a corruption of (S) Kareli. Bjørnbo sees an allusion to China in this quote, hence this digression: "A polar continent on the outskirts of Greenland extends all the way to 'Cathay.' Such notions are surely not foreign to the search for the Northwest Passage. Other more serious elements support the reservations I recommend concerning Claudius Clavus. If his position of Greenland is correct, then all exactitude stops there.

> The Greenland place-names indicated (Thær, Bœr, and so on) are *entirely fictitious*. In fact Claudius Clavus pulled off one of the most audacious impostures in the annals—unless like R. A. Skelton we

---

*Word used by northern Norwegians for the Finns.

interpret it as "scholastic joke of genius." Claudius Clavus managed to have all his contemporaries (in fact up to the twentieth century) accept his random places names that are truly only the words of a popular medieval song.* His names extend from the eastern to the western coast of Greenland (see my illustration number 6). Under these conditions it is difficult to give blind credit to all the information supplied by Claudius Clavus. Furthermore, even his Scandinavian place-names are subject to question. In the same incriminating map Coventer appears for northern Norway. Let me simply add that his sources are the same as those for all this era's mapmakers, Ptolemy brought up to date with Italian maps—with an obligatory stay in Rome—and travel accounts from the fourteenth century such as the Bruges Itinerary (a geography book focusing mainly on pilgrimage routes). Bjørnbo sees fairly blatant borrowings in the announcement: "From Bergen, Norway to Iceland . . . From Iceland to Greenland by crossing the sea; Then Greenland until the Karelians."[52]

Let's also mention the medieval author who seems unavoidable and who I refuse to dismiss: Nicholas of Lynn and his book *Inventio fortunate*. Bjørnbo finds resemblances between the pygmies of Claudius Clavus and those of Nicholas of Lynn: "23 individuals who no higher than four feet, 16 of whom were women."[53]

## The Anonymous Letter Addressed to Pope Nicholas V (1447–1455)

Oddly enough, the text was translated from French into Latin. It describes the wonders of Norway and includes this passage on Greenland: "Over there, (live) pygmies who have the shape of little men, only an ell in height. When they see people, they gather together and

---

*Placed end to end, the place-names form the following ballad: *Thær bær eeynh manh ij eyn Grænenlandzaa / Ooc Spieldebodh mande hanyd heyde. / Meer hawer han aff wide sild. / een hanh havwer flesk hynth feydh / Nordh um driver sandhin paa new.*" (Over there lives a man by a Greenland river. / His name is Spieldebodh, and so forth). Cited in Jens Rosing. See my illustration.

hide in holes in the ground, just like a swarm of ants. They cannot be defeated because they don't wait for anyone to attack them. They live on raw meat and cooked fish."[54]

The original of this letter, found in the Oxford Library in 1892, is believed to date from the first half of the fifteenth century. According to Storm, the source of this description must have been further back. He connects it to Nicholas of Lynn's account. Helge Ingstad connects it to Jacob Cnoyen. In the meantime, the text by Claudius Clavus was discovered (in the Vienna map), which bore a great resemblance to it as the author of this letter uses almost the same words and turns of phrase straight out: "some pygmies in the shape of little men, the height of an ell."

For Bjørnbo, Claudius Clavus's work was either used or plagiarized, or the two authors used the same, older source. The fact remains that some elements of the letter to Pope Nicholas V are new in comparison to the text by Claudius Clavus. We could even say they offer a certain ethnological value, as several features of Inuit culture shine through:

> The refuge in caves could be a distortion of the native habitat as seen by European eyes.
> The flight of the natives responds well to the generally non-aggressive nature of the Inuit noted by all explorers (this reminds me of another older contemporary source, that of Adam of Bremen with the flight of the unipeds).
> The diet based on raw meat and boiled fish also fits the same people.
> The small size of the people.

I will not discuss the use of the term *pygmy,* which is obviously inappropriate in a scientific context. I would criticize the modern interpretation that sees a blend of notions with fanciful connotations such as pygmies from India, Picts from the Orkneys, dwarfs from the domain of mythology, and Trolls.

I will obviously not simply dismiss this hypothesis. The possibility of confusion is obvious but entirely explicable in the medieval context and imaginal realm. Is this reason enough to reject this source? I will offer a simpler and to me more appropriate vision. A witness from the common folk like sailors could very well have used this—incorrect—word, but illustrating perfectly the message he wanted to transmit—namely, the small stature of the Skrælings/Trolls/Inuit. My interpretation is supported by this caption appearing in a map of the yet very learned Mercator:

> Here dwell pygmies, commonly called Skrælings. *Hic habitant Pygmei vulgo Screlinger dicti.*[55]

If need be, we should recall that medieval accounts describing the unicorn were false but began from a true postulate, the narwhal, quite distorted by the era's imagination. The words used by Claudius Clavus to designate the Inuit of Greenland reinforce this hypothesis: "Karelians," and "pygmies" for the oldest map of Vienna.

The map of Claudius Clavus, known as the map of Nancy and copied by Cardinal Fillastre, is even more confused for we find griffons, giants, and unipeds in addition to the already mentioned populations. This generous mixture by the cartographer finally convinced the experts that he had never set foot in Greenland and that he had sowed a great deal of confusion thanks to his reputation as a good mapmaker.

The pygmy definition smacks me as a similar kind of confusion as the word *uniped*. These fantasy creatures that the Vikings encountered in a saga of Vinland were small beings with only one foot who could move at great speeds. All the singular fantasy creatures listed earlier (narwhal turned into unicorn, Inuit natives into pygmies) were quickly distorted by eyewitnesses or scribes seeking inspiration.

### *Pope Nicholas V's Letter to the two "bishops" of Skálholt and Holar (dated September 20, 1448)*

This letter has the advantage of providing precise reference points in time: 1448, the date it was written, and 1418, the date the events it describes took place.

> Complaint that has been submitted to us on the part of our honorable sons, the natives and community of inhabitants on the Isle

of Greenland, situated as we are told at the extreme limits of the ocean in the northern regions of the kingdom of Norway in the metropolitan province of Nidaros. . . . It was thirty years ago [1418] that pagans from neighboring shores came there with a fleet (*classe navali*), attacking all the inhabitants of this place and devastating with fire and sword this land and its sacred sanctuaries, sparing nothing save the parishes that we are told extend to the frontiers, which they were not able to reach due to the obstacles of mountains and precipices.* They mistreated the pitiable natives of both sexes, primarily those who were apt to endure perpetually the burden of servitude.[56]

The important event here is the devastation of the Scandinavian settlements by barbarians from neighboring lands. Another detail: Greenland is described in 1448 as an island whose original spelling I've kept—*Insule Grenolandie*—which implies Rome had rather good geographical knowledge of Greenland.

Greenland had always been considered to be land attached either to Norway or America, or both continents. Very few source texts consider Greenland an island. I will note that Nicholas pushes back the conversion of Greenland to Christianity by some six hundred years; that is, the year 848, which puts us squarely in the time of the Hamburg-Bremen bishopric. Was Nicholas V fooling himself as well? For those upholding the falsification theory is this just perfect or should we reconsider the dates of Greenland "colonization" or instead the presence of Irish monks?

A lot of ink has been spilled over this letter, and it was very controversial, for while the author and the date are clear, the figures described are much less so. The upholders of the bellicose theory quickly saw this as confirmation of Inuit-Viking conflicts, but nothing is established. The most prominent researchers credit this theory. Nevertheless, several inconsistencies in this account have been pointed out.

---

*The extract from the *Grønlands Historiske Mindesmærker* states that only six parishes remain: "*solis in insula novem relictis ecdesiis parochialibus, quæ latissimis dicitur exlendi terminis.*"

The barbarians arrived with a fleet, which doesn't square at all with the Greenland natives; nor are they, incidentally, called Skrælings as they should be (this source text was adopted by the supporters of the bellicose theory). I would add that the Inuit do not have, strictly speaking, a maritime tradition; the word *fleet* in this case seems surprising and even a euphemism for the native boats, unless other persons were involved here.

Another detail that I believe would totally exclude the Arctic natives is that the broadsword (or simply sword) was never an Inuit weapon. I am amazed at the facility with which the Greenland natives were held responsible for all the ills befalling the Scandinavian colonists. Slavery is not an Inuit tradition. As we saw, the barbarians took the unfortunate inhabitants of both sexes as slaves, bringing them back to their own land.

I would also see in this last detail an allusion to an external people for the natives of Greenland lived there. It would seem that Nicholas V, to the contrary, was indicating a destination some distance away.

In Pope Nicholas V's letter the Skrælings are clearly called *Homunciones* (dwarfs), so there is a degree of difference with the word *barbarian*. Exaggerated importance may have been granted to the words *pagans* and *barbarians,* too easily assumed by the indigenous people.[57]

I would simply suggest that the church did not require much prompting to award this label to its enemies, or enemy brothers during a time of rupture, which is why I oppose limiting this word to the indigenous people of Greenland. Given this example, in the context of this time, the bias of the scribe who was an interested and injured party any attack against their property or "flock" could only be the work of a barbarian or pagan in the eyes of a cleric or pope.

Bjørnbo casts serious doubt on an Inuit war expedition, seeing this as inconsistent with Inuit traditions. The value of this papal letter to the two self-proclaimed bishops Marcellus and Matheus has also been contested. It could simply be a fake, but Gwyn Jones supplies no argument in support of this contention. Keller suggests that these two figures could have had access to a source that contained this information. According to him, Pope Nicholas V wrote this letter to two

German "adventurers," Matheus and Marcellus, who had introduced themselves to him supplied with false papers. They managed to get themselves anointed as bishops of Iceland. Marcellus had already been convicted of fraud before. This episode needs to be restored into the troubled context of the Great Schism when Norway supported the pope of Rome.

Nicholas V's letter has long formed the basis for two theories: that of pirates and that of Inuit responsibility for the disappearance of the Greenland colonists. Knowing that the concept of the Type B maps (in which Greenland is attached to Norway) was widespread in Europe, Keller connects this letter to a tragic event that struck the Finmark. In a letter dated September 5, 1420, to Bergen, the inhabitants of the Finmark and Hålogaland lodged a complaint with King Erik of Pomerania about the abuse inflicted upon them by the Russians and pagans who were sowing destruction and abducting their women. These alarming deeds are quite well documented as twenty-four years later, about 1446, a Swedish-Norwegian reprisal raid in the White Sea put an end to these acts of violence.

Keller sees strong similarities between these two events in Greenland and northern Norway, which could have led the pope astray: "Could the pope or the people who drew his attention to this matter confused the attack on northern Norway with an attack on Greenland?"[58]

Russian-Karelian misdeeds were well known in Rome. King Erik of Pomerania visited the city personally during his pilgrimage of 1424. Claudius Clavus's Type B maps only contributed to the confusion. This is visible in the geographical position Nicholas V attributes to Greenland: "*Que in ultimus finibus oceani ad septentrionalem plagam regni Norwegie in provincia Nidrosiensi dicitur situate.*"[59] Keller concludes from this that Nicholas V confused Greenland with the Finmark: "The 1448 letter is not a source text concerning Greenland, but a source text concerning Norway." In this case, the the pirate theory would be seriously shaken.[60]

However, we would be less categorical than Keller. It is obvious that Nicholas V is illustrating here a kind of syncretism reigning during the Middle Ages, blending a variety of more or less scientifically solid notions. Nevertheless, it would be dangerous to reject this source text for this reason alone. As we have seen with Claudius Clavus, the geographical error concerning Scandinavia was almost the rule in this era. Indeed, it seems that Keller underestimated one bit of geographical information: Greenland's insular nature is mentioned four times. I wonder where Nicholas V could have obtained such good information? This "detail" concerning Greenland's physiognomy was not yet known. To the best of my knowledge, only the Portuguese would realize this at the end of the fifteenth century. Furthermore, while Greenland's configuration was poorly known in the fifteenth century, I strongly doubt that this also held true for the Finmark, and as a consequence was mistaken for an island.

A second piece of information adds additional support to my identification with Greenland: the reference to the return of slaves (*ex captiuitate predicta reduntes*). There are several other sources, namely Roman, that mention the return of Scandinavian slaves to Greenland.[61] This would not be the case of Russia. In my opinion, these two arguments escape Keller's Norwegian identification, even if a certain geographical confusion reigned among the learned.

The three short sagas that follow are not so well known. The *Grønlands Historiske Mindesmærker* classifies them as tales and dates them as probably sixteenth century. Nevertheless, they often borrow elements from the traditional folk lore.

## The Words of Bardr Ase of Snaefell
### (Bárdár Saga Snæfellsáss)

The text, which was probably written during the fifteenth century, is confused, tangled in several geographical notions as well as dates,* but I am compelled to cite it for it is one of the rare sagas that alludes to the abduction of indigenous females by the Vikings (which supports the idea of the crossbreeding of the two populations). On his father's

---

*For example, the references made to Harald Hårfagr refer to 874, and those concerning Erik the Red are a century later. According to the *Grønlands Historiske Mindesmærker,* this saga was probably written in the fifteenth century, borrowing from old folktales and *kvædi* (Nordic songs and poems).

side, King Dumbr descended from a line of impressive and solidly built giants, while his mother was descended from Trolls.[62]

The reference to King Dumbr's paternal ancestry connected with giants could refer to Vikings (in chapter 3 of Poviak's story, the Scandinavian women were spoken of as giantesses). This somewhat agrees with Oleson's theory that identified the "Tornit giants" from traditional Inuit lore with Scandinavians. This intercommunity marriage made with a Troll and not a Skræling reinforces my conviction about the non-aggressive nature of Trolls in general, and thus my identification of them with the Inuit populations.

Analysis of this text is rendered more difficult as the plot locations vary in the various copies. In P. E. Müller's edition, the father of the hero Bardr is a counselor in the bay region extending southeast from the Risaland (the country of the giants).

The copy 158 in the folio of the same saga speaks of the north of Helluland. In this case, the allusion to the aboriginal populations of North America is flagrant. This brings us back to Amerindians or Inuits. Now, as we have seen with other sources (the story of Björn Einarsson Jórsalafari), the term was especially used for the Greenland Inuit. Here is one of the rare cases where this word is applied far from the Greenland colonies, unless we should be taking a different approach. I can suggest a possible explanation: because the Vikings had established sufficiently stable colonies north of Helluland—connected to Greenland in the medieval imagination—this word recovered its descriptive function of the neighboring Inuit populations bordering the colonies. Confirmation for this statement appears during the early Middle Ages when it was imagined that in Iceland as in Helluland (the land of the large flat stones of the sagas) this area was located on either Greenland's eastern coast or in a land on the western border of Greenland. In contrast to the authors of the *Grønlands Historiske Mindesmærker,* I don't see any big problems here. The place described in the mind of the original anonymous author being located between a northern point (Risaland—correctly or incorrectly placed) and a southern point (Helluland).

Other manuscripts use Kvaenlandi instead of Greenland (in other words, the Finnish Lapland Kveners land). It is easy to see that the identification of the saga's context is of primal importance for my argument. I can glimpse some resemblance between Dumbshaf (the Sea of Dumbr) and its numerous little islands with the Canadian archipelago. This sea lies precisely south of Dumbr's kingdom.

Rafn and Magnussen lean instead for identification on Greenland's eastern coast that was sometimes called and confused with Svalbard (Spitzbergen) during that era. The information that most interests me is the marriage of the father of King Dumbr with a woman of Troll origin (*Tröllakyni*). This shows that Vikings did not reject intercultural marriages. They even seem run of the mill as the saga informs us that King Dumbr did the same with a virgin native: King Dumbr took a wife who he abducted from Greenland (which had not yet been discovered).

King Dumbr's subjects are a kind of Troll who end up murdering him. In his flight, his son Bardr brings with him people who had been raised north of the sea of Dumbr as well as Trolls. He avenged his father but had to take refuge in Iceland due to the growing power of Harald Finehair (therefore about 874). We have one other piece of information about this place: "It was difficult to get homespun cloth there but seal hide was used in its stead."[63]

Both of these elements, the proximity to Iceland and the use of seal hide, could take us back to Greenland (although the second one is applicable to other Nordic countries). After his arrival on the Snæfellsnes Peninsula in Iceland, Bardr and his retinue performed a great sacrifice in a cave that since that time has been called *Tröllkirkja* (Troll church). It is hard to lend much credit to this saga as it later mentions Erik the Red, no less, who lived a century later. We cannot deny a slightly exaggerated touch worthy of the epic for the saga ends with the murder of three creatures (Trolls based on copy 158).

### The Story of Jökull Búason

This story only goes back as far as the fifteenth century. It was published in Björn Marcussen's book *Soguþaettir Íslendinga*. It also bears a strong fantasy stamp, but we cannot rule out a core of truth. The plot takes place in Greenland, identifiable by clearly provided place-names.

Jökull, son of the Icelander Bui Andridsön, was shipwrecked in Greenland in the Öllumlengri Fjord, one of the largest fjords in the southeast, near Cape Farvel. An unequivocal allusion is made to Trolls [the plot is therefore in areas outside of Scandinavian settlements] as well as to giants: "This part of the coast was heavily inhabited by giants (Jötnar) who when counted in a group with females were called Trolls (Tröll). Their clothing was made from animal pelts. Their king was named Skramr."[64]

The saga also speaks of the complicity of a female Troll in the murder of King Skramr. Could this be a new allusion to the relationshop between the Nordic people and the aboriginal people of Greenland? "She [the female Troll] was smitten with the son of Skramr, Grimner, this is why he was spared by Jökull and named king in his father's place."[65] The description could fit the natives if we consider the clothing and location, the southern tip of Greenland, which was the obligatory passage point for the Inuit migrations going back up the eastern coast. In its current state this saga offers few useful details.

### *The Lay of Halfdan the Protégé of the Giantess Brana* (Hálfdonar saga Brönufóstra)

This saga is found in C. C. Rafn's *Fornaldar Sögur Nordrlandr* and in the *Sagabibliothek*. Rafn and Magnussen classify it as one of the tales. Halfdan, son of a Danish king, leaves for Bjarmaland with four ships but is blown off course by strong storms and fog. He lands in Helluland.

> He washed up in the deserted regions of Helluland invaded by icebergs and solely inhabited by Trolls who lived in caves. They were cannibals. There was much driftwood on the shores.[66]

This saga can't help but bring to mind that of Gunnar Keldugnüpsfifl as the circumstances are the same, Helluland is overrun by glaciers,* the

---

*This allusion interests me because Nordic accounts on the difficulties of sailing because of icebergs or pack ice are very rare, which is surprising on the part of a people of sailors.

Trolls live in caves, and so on. Is this borrowed or the description of the same reality? One piece of additional information makes me lean toward the latter: the presence of driftwood. Another novelty is that cannibalism is not an Inuit feature (cases have occurred during periods of famine as they have among many other peoples). Did the scribe exaggerate or was he alluding to populations farther south? This saga, which is one of the legendary sagas (*Fornaldar sögur*), is not very useful in its present state.

## The Lay of Handsome Sansom (Samsons saga fagra)

It was written in the fourteenth or fifteenth century, and P. E. Müller classifies it among the more or less romantic fables. It contains a brief allusion to Trolls and to the geography of the time in which Greenland was connected to the continent by a land bridge. "Risaland is located northeast of the Baltic, farther northeast is the country called Jötunheimr (the land of the giants) where dwell the Trolls and the demons (dangerous monsters); from that place to the wild Greenland regions there is a land called Svalbard where different populations dwell."[67]

Here we see again the concept of a land bridge linking Jötunheimr to Greenland and what would seem to be confirmation of the medieval belief that Svaalbard was Greenland's eastern coast. The text is practically of no use in its current state.

## The List of Bishop Erik Walkendorff (1516)

This prelate was first dean of the Roskilde chapter in Denmark, and at the same time personal friend and chancellor of King Christian II. With the king's support, he was elected bishop of Trondheim, but this idyll did not last long as he was forced to flee abroad (Holland, Germany, Rome) in 1521. His knowledge of the northern lands was not lost in Rome as it is believed he was an information source for many cartographers.

Walkendorff is also known for his attempts to resume contact with Greenland, collecting much information about this land abandoned by the crown. This was his motivation for compiling the following list of products supposedly native to Greenland.

These products come from Greenland: antelope, marten, ermine,*
gyrfalcon, [seal fat, whale blubber, walrus ivory, gold bearing ore,
and silver] also salmon, moose, and all kinds of furs, lynx, fox, wolf,
and wolverine.[68]

Ending his list, Walkendorff noted the need "to bring axes [we
presume for the purpose of cutting wood] and to make a large fire."[69]
Now wood is rather rare in Greenland and forests are to be found
rather farther west in America. In fact this could be an allusion to
America. It would be interesting to know where the information used
by Walkendorff came from originally. Greenland most likely [and in my
opinion] exported these highly sought-after products. But this doesn't
mean they existed there. In Walkendorff's list six products or species
are native to North America:

The marten, the ermine, the lynx, the wolverine, and the antelope (probably confused for deer), and moose are forest-dwelling
mammals. We know that there is no forest worthy of the name
or such animals in Greenland.

Gold and silver were reputed to be in certain North American
regions. I have in mind some of the more fantastic sagas looked
at earlier that allude to these riches. There should be some basis
in truth for this widespread belief.

The value of this non-literary text is revealed to be even greater
when reading the following bits of information that seem to have been
passed over unseen until now. In fact, Walkendorff tells us that it was
customary "*to erect large cairns* and numerous strange works, and *to
carve large crosses* [in wood or stone]."[70] It is known that these remnants
were seen in several regions of Canada by the first explorers such as
Jacques Cartier (this will be revisited). They appear clearly drawn in
Mercator's map of 1569,† and numerous Scandinavian and Canadian

---

*These first species are highly unusual for Greenland.
†See fig. 7.1.

Fig. 7.1. A detail of George Mercator's 1569 planisphere (Nova et Aucta Orbis Terra Descriptio ad Usum Navigatium Emendate). The mysterious Grocland—written here with a t—can be seen on it (which we've identified with Devon Island), whose inhabitants were Swedish according to the map description, and whose numerous crosses echoed what the indigenous inhabitants told Jacques Cartier.
*Wikimedia Commons*

studies (the 1898–1902 "Fram" expedition, Thomas Lee in 1966) have revealed the existence of such works. According to traditional Inuit lore these are the work of foreign peoples. In this letter by Walkendorff we have a rare contemporary account of these Scandinavian customs. What's more is that they existed before 1516 (the date this letter was written) as Walkendorff only gathered existing Nordic source texts.

## *The Bishops' Annals* (Biskupsannáll)

These were written by the Icelandic priest of Reiphól, Jón Egilsson (1548–circa 1636) during the 1600s. In it we find an account about a captain of King Christian I in Iceland, Björn Thorleifsson and his wife, Olöf Loptsdatter. They were shipwrecked in Greenland in the middle of the fifteenth century. This account is based on oral tradition according to Halldórsson. Because of its age, it is of particular value, as it allows me to advance several observations and trails for research.

> Now, we shall speak of this couple. One day it happened that they were shipwrecked in Greenland for they were lost at sea. A couple of old Trolls* arrived. The old Troll woman tied three ells of leather around her own head but only two ells around that of the old male Troll. They were carrying large chests on their shoulders and arranged them to their liking. The male Troll helped Björn into his chest and the female Troll put Olöf in hers. They then carried them until they reached the fence of a farm. They were in Garðar, location of the seat of the Greenland bishopric. This couple stayed there all winter and returned to Iceland the following spring.[71]

Here we have another confirmation of the peaceful relations with these fantastic Trolls. One particularly interesting point is that it was noted by churchmen and addressed to a learned clerical audience.

---

*This is a particularly interesting detail. The original text says: *"Tharat kom Tröllkarl ok kerling."* This somewhat matches the theory I presented in chapter 5 on the *karlalid.* Here we have the use of the word *karl* by men of letters to designate the Troll/Men (the Inuit, in other words). I highly doubt the colonists used the word *Troll* (at least no source reveals its use), so only the word *karl* would have survived?

According to the *Grønlands Historiske Mindesmærker,* this narrative could be the sequel to a chronicle of Icelandic bishops, the *Húngurvaka,* which gives another dimension to the story.

With the story of Björn Einarsson Jórsalafari, we have here the second reliable example dated and compiled by clerics illustrating the peaceful and rather helpful relations of the neighboring Inuit populations, a.k.a. the Trolls (I have intentionally left aside the little sagas classified by research as folktales).

This "made to order visiting card" of the Troll* appears to me as a skillful and may I say totally brilliant subterfuge of this era's scribes, or the church rather, as it allowed for contacts with "savage" pagan peoples without causing too much of a shock to the dominant Christian morality (remember, this is during the time of the Crusades).

Thus, although not displaying all the forms of Christian "respectability" it was possible—occasionally—to have some contact with them and to be rescued by them (like our Icelandic couple), basically as occurred with the good spirits of the Scandinavian mountains. Thanks to this Inuit/Troll conflation, a very concrete situation, Inuit-Viking relations that led to a status of mutual aid was suddenly transferred to another level and displaced into another dimension: that of the fairy tale, if not something totally imaginary.

What reasons are hiding behind these quibbles. Couldn't this be a very lyrical form of denying this reality? Could the very knowledgeable clerical elite really confuse the indigenous peoples of Greenland with fantasy creatures? I strongly doubt it. This confusion between the imaginary world of Trolls and very real facts (the intercommunity contacts) can only be the work of a subtle clerical ruse.

---

*De Vries, 1962, 598, gives some interesting interpretations of the word: *Riese* [géant], *Maikäfer* [June bug], *lappisch* (Norwegian) *truölla. ruölla. mittelhochdeutsch: Trolle/Trold =* *Unhold* [demon, evil spirit, monster]. *Unhold* [gnome, sprite]. *Tölpel* [lout, oaf], *vergleich* *trollen: mit kurzen schritten laufen, vergleich trylla.* This definition, to run with little steps, cannot help but bring to mind the figures of the sagas (Trolls and unipeds) described this way. While supplying the customary definitions of Trolls, R. Cleasby and G. Vigfusson underscore the absence of the devil in pagan thought: "the heathen creed knew of no 'devil,' but the Troll; in modern Danish, Troll includes any ghosts, goblins, imps, and puny spirit." They also acknowledge their positive connotation in ancient Iceland.

This subterfuge was remarkable, we should remember, as it long passed unnoticed. It has only been pointed out recently in Danish research that is very advanced in this regard overseen by Jette Arneborg. She pertinently notes that in all the cited examples in Greenland and particularly in the vicinity of the colonies, the Vikings never encounter Skrælings but Trolls (for example, Björn Einarsson Jórsalafari or Björn Thorleifsson). Why was this subtle distinction made?

We have to believe the Scandinavians held a different appreciation of the neighbors—cohabitation oblige—that didn't precisely correspond to the criteria of the church. Skræling is generally pejorative, and we only hear of the Skrælings in the context of distant journeys such as the Nordrsetur of northern Greenland or into North America (with the exception of the story of Bardr Snæfellsás). We also know that the relations between the two peoples were more lukewarm if not outright hostile, which is never the case in the narratives mentioning the Trolls, who are often helpful (the story of Björn Einarsson Jórsalafari, the story of Björn Thorleifsson and his wife, Olöf), peaceful, or openly fearful (episode of Thorgils in the *Flóamanna saga*).

This lexical difference has to be interpreted as the reflection of a difference in behavior substantiating again my theory of generally positive and peaceful contacts. A detail that could turn out to be important, the geographical representation of that era connects northern Norway—thus the land of the Trolls—to Greenland. From this perspective, we clearly have the same fantasy beings with whom some relationships are permissible, a little bit like home. "It is believed that this country called Jötnaland or Trollbotnaland is located northeast of Iceland, and even touches Iceland."[72]

## CONCLUSION

Quickly summing up this chapter, and unfortunately quite arbitrarily, I stress the vagueness in the Norse description and terminology concerning the natives of the Arctic as the name Skrælings can be applied to a variety of peoples. The vagueness of the word *Skræling* is only equaled by the same lack of precision characterizing Vinland: "The misreading of the data, can mean that all the lands located to the north and west of the Scandinavian settlements (in Greenland) were seen as part of Vinland, just like all the indigenous populations were merged into Skrælings."[73]

I would note nevertheless that in the oldest original sources, Skræling is used for countries far from the Scandinavian settlements. It would become quickly and copiously used (particularly by the clerics and foreigners) for all the natives commingled into one. In fact, I would consider a more complex version regarding the name of the Greenland natives, reflecting the moral or ethical dilemma they posed. This could explain the still current fuzziness that characterizes the real meanings of the different medieval names for aborigines. It is certain that *Skræling* was broadly used, probably intended for remote "savage" peoples as proposed by Jette Arneborg, but over time it became mixed up with other peoples. It appears to me that the word *Troll* was used by the church at the beginning of colonization, if not by the first colonists still steeped in Nordic mythology with its spirits dwelling in the mountains and so on, to describe the neighboring and peaceful peoples of the two colonies. They must have had frequent relations with the colonists, especially in Vestribygð as both Inuit and Nordic sources seem to indicate. The words *Troll* and *Skræling* have disappeared today, which would tend to show their limited use. On the other hand, I can see a recollection of this medieval name in the word *Kalaallit: karlalid,* the people who were sufficiently widespread and tenacious to overcome the barrier of time. To this day, no explanation has ever been found for the origin of the Greenland name Kalaallit.

This artistic vagueness concerning the natives goes hand in hand with the vagueness—thick as fog—concerning place-names. We've experienced this already with the riddle of Vinland; it seems that Markland could be equally contestable if we take as our guide the studies by Cleasby and Vigfusson and their interpretation of Märchland meaning *graenseland.* Having long studied the avatars of the word *Labrador* (a.k.a. Laborador), I am inclined to give some credit to this observation for we must confess that until now the parameters used have failed to identify these sites that have been sought for so long.

From the perspective of the oldest Nordic source texts (*Íslendingabók* and *Historia Norvegiae*) the Vikings' knowledge of the Greenland natives goes back long before 1200. The written sources are in agreement as to the first meetings in the Far North, which is confirmed by both archaeology and traditional Inuit art. These contacts are generally listed in the context of the Scandinavian Nordrsetur.

Knowing that starting with the first years of his banishment (982), Erik the Red explored Greenland up to the Disko region, and that other sources mention the Norse presence, including the clergy (1121 expedition of Bishop Erik Uppse, a.k.a. Gnuppson) in the Far North—probably Canada—I will react quite critically to the idea of a late encounter in the thirteenth century. I accept McGovern's theories suggesting very early Nordrsetur toward the eleventh and twelfth centuries, in accord with the well-known explorative nature of the Norse, and especially a strong impetus or economic demand for polar goods.

Archaeology has recently confirmed intercommunity contacts on several occasions mainly revealed by the presence of Inuit objects—particularly those of the Thule culture—in Scandinavian sites, or Nordic objects of Eystribygð in the northern communities of the Inuit. The carbon-14 dating in an Inuit Thule midden in Kangeq (Nuuk region, i.e., Vestribygð) support this. The dating from other settlements—Avigaat, Torsuut Tuna in Paamiut (therefore Mellembygð or "central" colony)—also indicate Viking-Inuit proximity. The most plausible contacts, and the earliest and most frequent (during the first years of colonization), seem to reflect the Disko region in the Upernavik district, which has sites typical of Inussuk culture. Such relations were not absent in the Thule areas of the Far North and later the southern colony. A certain proximity of both populations (Inuit site of Isua in the south or Illutalik) follow in the sense of the traditional bases of both cultures.

A serious question has been raised by the findings of C. Andreassen, H. C. Gulløv, and J. Møhl providing the dates of inhabitation in Nipaitsoq and Niaqusat (Vestribygð) after Ivar Bårdsson's visit. While a dating error is always possible, the fact remains that Bårdsson's report is very ambiguous and confused. Should we add the label of slacker one day? Did Bårdsson neglect to visit some remote farms like that of

Nipaitsoq? We are given no information on the scope of his inspection at Vestribygð. Seen from the angle of a more or less coercive expedition or a tax-collecting mission, it should come as no surprise if the colonists of Vestribygð avoided all contact, which could also explain the farms abandoned at Bårdsson's arrival.

Archaeology in no way confirms the scenarios of massacre and wide-scale destruction or of reoccupation of Scandinavian sites by the Inuit. Let's add that the bellicose theory has often suffered as many research-ers acknowledge today the phenomenon of suggestion: "We cannot be entirely sure that the stories told were not suggested by the European investigator."[74]

So we can rightfully ask if the Inuit-Viking relations were as bel-licose as people have claimed, and especially—perhaps an even more important question—what could the motivations of this hawkish the-ory have been? Today we can see that this attitude of the church was not entirely innocent. The connection made by the church (or its scribes) between the decline of the Norse faith and the native presence makes it possible to mask, if not flush away, the Norse people's overly friendly attitude toward the Inuit/Skrælings laying the blame on these latter for the decline of the Christian faith. This is how the church exonerated itself of its quarrels with the colonists, pushing the religious decline into the background. Keller shares this viewpoint, a kind of (false) cause and effect relationship being presented by the clerical source texts as follows: "As the Skrælings advanced, Christianity declined."[75]

The postulate is quite simple and quick to incorporate. Even the greatest names in research have been satisfied by this made-to-order explanation. The essential lesson of this chapter is that the Nordic writ-ten sources are not sufficient to conclude that or forge a connection with the disappearance or extermination of the Vikings in Greenland. They are characterized mainly by their great lack of precision. Generally their underlying bias is easily detected.

Nevertheless, an intermediary position that considers the possibil-ity of episodic conflicts is generally accepted today. This matches with the archaeological excavations that sometimes reveal traces of minor disputes between Inuit and Viking (Niaqusat seen in chapter 2) but never, absolutely never, proof of substantial confrontations. Quite the contrary; the way the two populations were neighbors makes it easier to imagine good relations. Too much exaggeration has gone into the hawkish theory. Consequently, the theory of Norse extermination at the hands of the natives should be rejected: "The interpretations made by fifteenth century scribes, just like those of more recent authors, according to whom the decline of Christianity (in Greenland) was the result of Skræling attacks, should be, for the most part, rejected."[76]

On the other hand, the Scandinavian written sources are too extensive to go over with a fine-tooth comb and allow us to reveal these technical bits of information betraying a Nordic knowledge of and contact with the native populations. I am in fact convinced that a priori trivial information slumbers in many texts. This is how certain "classic" sagas like *Flóamanna saga* can surprise us with their content of such highly sought-after information.

Another observation to be taken into consideration is the imprecise nature of the source texts, their bias if not the quick mapping out of Inuit-Viking relations are perhaps the reflection of—or should I say the veil masking an entirely different problem with no connection to the indigenous people—the relations between the Scandinavian colonists and the church.

# 8

# The Different Theories on Inuit and Viking Contact

Theories on Inuit and Viking contact go from one extreme to the other, from the friendliest relationships—including a theory of integration— to the most violent relations, encompassing a theory of Norse extermination. Overly entrenched positions are not necessarily the most appropriate. There is every reason to believe, as does contemporary research, that the relations alternated between peaceful and bellicose moments. However, given the archaeological, artistic, and mythological elements we discussed earlier, it is quite plausible that they leaned more to the friendly side than to that of war. Recall the confirmed and uninterrupted presence of the two populations involved for four centuries until the appearance of a new element that we will revisit: foreign populations. To illustrate my position I will cite Danish historian Finn Gad.

> A certain tension was undoubtedly present in the beginning, but their relations had to have been rather peaceful just like the first encounters with the Skrælings of Vinland. This peaceful coexistence was possible judging by the numerous tales of Greenland legends recounting the relations between the two races who differed so much from each other both physically and behaviorally.[1]

Some discretion is called for regarding excessive use of the traditional Inuit sources because of their later composition (in the eighteenth century at the very earliest), alterations, suggestions, and so on. They cannot form the sole working material for this subject. To simplify the problem posed by the abundance of theories concerning Inuit-Viking relations, as well as the fate of the latter, I will classify the various existing theories into three trends of thought.

## THE PACIFIST THEORY

This theory consists of various subscribers and offers a number of variations. It cannot be considered as a homogenous bloc. The same is true for the so-called hawkish theory. In practice this translates into fairly elastic theoretical positions; this is how researchers defending the hawkish theory will in certain cases be able to accept completely opposing positions (see the final part on the written sources concerning the contacts and cohabitation between Inuit and Scandinavians). Basing his position on the 1342 source text concerning Norse apostasy, the Danish ethnologist William Thalbitzer sees no proof for blatant combats between Inuit and Vikings. He stands out as one of the preeminent defenders of Norse emigration into America. Jette Arneborg pursues the same course: "The text of the 1342 source leads us to believe that the population of Vestribyygd freely abandoned their farms to settle on the other side of the Davis Strait in American to take their chances."[2]

### *Helge Ingstad*
Norwegian researcher Helge Ingstad, who was responsible for the discovery of the Nordic site of L'Anse aux Meadows in Newfoundland, was an enthusiastic supporter of the pacifist theory: "The population of Vestribygð emigrated freely to America and not because of Eskimo attacks."[3] Ingstad bases his case mainly on the seventeenth-century commentary of Gisli Odsson repeating the oldest and now vanished source text from 1342 on the apostasy of the Greenland colonists and their emigration into America. Ingstad quotes this bishop: "The Greenland colonists had willingly lost their Christian religion and the true faith; having abandoned all healthy conduct and true value, they turned to the inhabitants of America."[4]

He rejects the assimilation theory. It is true that this name is poorly formulated for it allegedly designates the forced assimilation of the Scandinavians by the Inuits and takes no account of a consenting integration. Ingstad suggests that some Vikings had abandoned farming life to adopt the Inuit lifestyle.

The frequency with which Nordic objects are found in Inuit settlements should nonetheless be considered more attentively. It should be acknowledged that this question of a Norse acculturation is harder to demonstrate scientifically. On the other hand, the Inussuk technological traditions we saw earlier present pronounced signs of borrowing from Norse culture. The objection will be raised that this doesn't prove any Norse acculturation, but I would like to point out that, quite curiously, one aspect of this hypothesis has not been considered: If there were technical loans from the Inuit, how did they occur—simply plagiarism on the part of the natives?

In this case, we should admire their talent at reproducing if not outright mastering techniques that were unknown to them such as the net and the pail made from slats of wood discovered during the Upernavik district excavations. Just as I suggested in chapter 4 on Inuit art, such precision of the Inuit artistic testimony leads to presumption of contact or even closer cohabitation over an extended period of time. This contact is also explanatory of technical loans such as cooperage using heat. So we cannot dismiss the hypothesis of a Norse presence (if not acculturation)* that permitted the transmission of this knowledge. Catching this argument on the wrong foot, McGovern (rather defending the maladaptation theory) says that it would be interesting to consider the Inuit tools missing in the Scandinavian context (such as the harpoon) as proof this cohabitation was nonexistent: "There is no indication that the Vikings adopted such an effective tool as the Inuit harpoon."[5] I would be less categorical than McGovern and raise the following questions.

---

*This brings us to the hypothesis of an Inuit-Norse crossbreeding, the claim that isolated Scandinavians in the north gradually melted into the native world, losing their own culture and adopting that of the Inuit. This must have been the case with the exiled Scandinavians appearing in *Skáld-Helga rímur,* but also during an era as far back as that told by Adam of Bremen (*Grønlands Historiske Mindesmærker*).

Could there have been such references to such loans, considering the church's dissuasive presence and its censure of any such loan, which would have been presumed as apostasy? A borrowing from the natives would have had to be discreet, far from the eyes and ire of the church; I could say the same kind of discretion that surrounded the Scandinavian departure from Vestribrygð. In fact, I am starting from the simple postulate that during this era, the "savages" were generally considered creatures of the devil, and all that was part of their culture fell under the same judgment. The fact remains that Scandinavian source texts have given us the interesting example of identical Inuit and Norse techniques—namely, the boat made from skins.

Contrary to McGovern's statements, there are allusions, or at least foreign accounts of whites in kayaks committing acts of piracy (for example, Olaus Magnus, the highly controversial Italian sailors and authors of the Zeno family, and even the illustrious Christopher Columbus). I do share McGovern's opinion that these were not loans but outright adoptions, something we will revisit.

### *Corrado Gini*

This Italian researcher who is scarcely known to the public at large presented an interesting thesis in Bergen in 1956 concerning the Vikings' disappearance from Greenland. He tackled his subject from an economic angle and, what was quite original at this time, a genetic one. Unfortunately, his study is limited to small groups, and he does not seem to have had anyone to pick up where he left off. While several points of his theory are debatable, it nonetheless offers many very interesting axes of research. It can be placed in the pacifist camp without hesitation, as the author unreservedly subscribes to a Norse migration into America. He gives special emphasis to the appeal of these very promising lands to the Icelanders and clergy: "It is well known that the Scandinavians emigrated from Greenland to Vinland. That they were followed by other colonists not only from Greenland but very likely from Iceland cannot be doubted, if it is true that a half century later, a bishop named Jonas went there from Iceland in order to support the colonists in their faith, and that one century later, the bishop of Iceland himself, Erik Gnupson,* abandoned his episcopal seat for the same reasons."[6]

Gini restricts this emigration to the eleventh and twelfth centuries, which is consistent with the written sources (thus 1121 for Bishop Erik Gnupson, also named Upsi). The Italian researcher explains this emigration because of a population saturation threshold reached by the Norse at this time with all exploitable settlements now occupied. This argument is quite plausible, but I reject his following conclusion in which he maintains the numbers emigrating were limited due to a lack of the boats necessary for the trip. This is something that is far from proved. In my opinion, this overly widespread argument of the lack of wood for construction is not admissible, if we consider the generous use (or reckless use as Gwyn Jones puts it) the Vikings made of it. For example, Prytz tells us that some Greenland churches had at least one wooden wall. Some passages from the sagas leave the impression that wood was far from being deficient, such as the episode of Sigurd Njållsson[7] appearing in *The Lay of the Greenlanders* (*Grænlendinga Þáttr*), who burned the boats that had washed ashore, keeping only the nails. There are also the Icelandic sources speaking of the wood found in Markland. For it is definitely in the famous Markland that the answer to this supposed shortage question lies. In fact there is a contradiction in Gini's position: How could the Vikings be short of boats while making regular journeys to Markland or worse, emigrating there as the Gini suggests? There is something illogical here. I have already underscored the bias of the theory of the destitution of the medieval Greenland colonies and the absence of any real proofs to support it.

Gwyn Jones is also difficult to pin down. He accepts the notion of peaceful cohabitation between the Scandinavians and Inuits at Eystribygð: "So long as the Vikings could stick to the decision to stay together, the two races had enough space and no need to try out their neighbor's life style."[8]

Jones also bases his position on Inuit traditional lore relating the encounters between the two communities and, a rare phenomenon in

---

*See the summary list for years 1112 to 1121 in chapter 9.

this research, traditional Inuit art. Research on this subject has evolved considerably over the last decades. Major progress was made thanks to the excavations organized in the Canadian Far North under the name of the Inuit-Scandinavian project of 1976. I will give special examination to McGovern's theory, which I think sums up quite well the new directions being followed today in response to the progress made by contemporary research. The other "classic" theories will be quickly introduced as they have been surpassed today and are even regarded as inconceivable by some. McGovern classifies the cultural contacts between Inuits and Scandinavians in four phases. His classification has the advantage of including the earlier theories.

### The Phase of Nordrsetur Contacts (circa 1050–1300)

According to McGovern, the first contacts were made in the Disko region. This is still the old classic outline limiting the destination of the Nordrsetur expeditions to Disko. On the other hand, McGovern gives a much earlier date (and in my opinion realistic) as he places these inter-cultural contacts connected with the Nordrsetur in the years 1000 to 1100. This position is shared by Schlerdermann: "It seems to me more difficult to explain why the Vikings would not have explored the Greenland coasts as far north as possible after settling in the south. An Inuit-Norse encounter in the north circa 1100 seems quite likely to me."[9]

I have in mind the later dates (thirteenth century) advanced by T. Mathiassen, and even the fourteenth century (J. Arneborg). McGovern supports the idea of trade with the Inuit: "In the beginning, the contacts were in the form of an occasional trade, in which Scandinavian metal but also little trinkets were swapped for walrus tusks and polar bear furs."[10]

McGovern doesn't exclude the possibility of native ambushes of isolated Scandinavian groups during these remote expeditions. He believes that these objects were the fruit of trade or theft, and passed from hand to hand until Thule, then to Canada in the years 1050 to 1300, which is opposed to Mathiassen's position. Until today, the defenders of the wandering Scandinavian objects theory have not found these remnants throughout the Arctic but only in very specific, identified sites that do not in any way correspond to the extent of Inuit dispersion. I opt instead for the increasingly plausible hypothesis that the Inuit were drawn to these sites solely because of the Norse presence.

Archaeological sources substantiate this first phase of contacts, mainly the sites of

> Kingittorsuaq, in the Upernavik district, where a runestone was found.
>
> Ruin Island on the outskirts of the Thule area in northern Greenland. There the dating of objects varies from 1020 to 1070 (with a margin of error of one century).*
>
> Semermiut near Ilulissat/Jacobshavn. Peat samples taken from the layers dating from the Inussuk culture period give dates of 1010 ± 120 years, and 1240 ± 120 years. Mathiassen prefers the latter date.

McGovern recognizes the importance of Thule as a site where Scandinavian objects brought by the Inuit passed through, and considers the possible passage of Vikings from there to Canada, which seem to me rather timid conclusions in comparison to the reality. Too many medieval source texts and various sagas, such as *Skáld-Helga saga* from around 1022, Eirik Upse in 1121, Halldór's tale from 1266, and the Markland boat in 1346 and 1347 all make reference to the western lands—northern or not—to remain in the limited context of what's possible according to McGovern. However, he does acknowledge their occasional presence in Newfoundland and Labrador.

It remains to be seen if the Scandinavian's chronic poverty in metal can be confirmed by archaeology. Without seeking to underestimate a certain degree of isolation for the Norse colony, couldn't this destitution be exaggerated? We have already seen a similar case with wood.

---

*H. C. Gulløv notes the importance of this location, whose name would be given to a specific phase of Thule culture. According to him and Schledermann this "Ruin Island" phase is directly related to the Norse objects of the Canadian Arctic and northern Greenland.

The question is worth asking for metal. There is the analysis by Keller presenting the colony as offering "a deceptive deficiency of dramatic features." The defenders of this thesis of an isolated populace in chronic need do not seem to have offered much proof supporting this conjecture. Moreover, the frequent presence of iron, namely meteor iron forged by heat according to Norse methods has been observed in various spots in Greenland, including the Far North.

Archaeologists have not been able to prevent themselves from emphasizing the impressive quantity of iron objects that the Vikings left behind them in the Far North of Canada and Greenland. "Why were so many useable iron utensils abandoned when this material was so valuable?"[11]

The answer (cold-worked iron by the Greenland natives as seen earlier) is given by E. Langer Anderson. The Scandinavians had ample benefit of this meteoric iron: "The results of metal analysis show that the bulk of the iron was of meteoric origin, a large part of which came from Cape York. In other words, the iron was important (and came from the Far North) but could not be considered a rare product."[12]

Another example provided by Schledermann supports this theory: among the ship nails found on Skræling Island, the vast majority showed little wear, they thus had spent little time in their owner's hands. A swap of still new objects doesn't really illustrate the scarcity of these products. This example totally contradicts the episode of Sigurd Njålsson collecting the nails from shipwrecks. This is a major rebuttal of the destitution of this metal essential to the Scandinavian colonists. The origin of the ore confirms the Nordic travels in the remote Far North, as well as the major economic interest of the polar regions.

McGovern himself admits the trade imbalance visible in the swap of Scandinavian trinkets for highly sought Inuit goods (ivory and so forth). It is hard to see how the exchange of glassware (broaches, pawns, weaving loom weights) could cause any kind of deprivation to the Norse community. As it happens, archaeological excavations seem to echo my hypothesis precisely by turning up so many objects of little value. So I would not support McGovern's argument that sees the Vikings at a disadvantage here after already stressing the considerable benefits provided by this trade. The presence of foreign nations in Greenland and the Arctic strengthens my own hypothesis. Their primary motivation being profit, these sailors should have found this trade to their advantage in order to make such voyages. Secondarily, the Scandinavians could take advantage of this European presence to restock their supplies of the allegedly scarce metals or of trinkets. I also reject the hypothesis explaining the presence of Scandinavian objects in the Arctic as the result of an Inuit raid against an isolated group. "In fact, all the Scandinavian objects coming from Thule and Canada could represent all the goods of a single Scandinavian group scattered across the far north."[13]

I feel this view is an extreme simplification of the matter. Even by adopting the hypothesis of a bellicose confrontation between the Inuit and Norse that ended to the advantage of the Inuit, we could expect to find more worthwhile objects such as weapons rather than trinkets resulting from a trade with scant advantages for the Inuit. The victor, on the other hand, would have been faced with an embarrassment of riches. Furthermore, the evidence of Inuit art allows for the assumption of other contacts that were much longer than a simple murderous raid. The American researcher sums this position up well when he says: "Such commercial relationships—even sporadic—should have resulted in the widespread presence of Scandinavian objects among the Eskimos of Greenland and the Canadian Arctic during the twelfth and thirteenth centuries rather than a couple raids of isolated Scandinavian hunters."[14]

The sum total of Scandinavian objects found in the Smith Strait region, which is not many, could have also come from a Scandinavian shipwreck in these waters. While this is a plausible hypothesis, it doesn't explain the presence of Vikings in such remote and perilous waters. The only substantive reason would be all the economic reasons we've suggested. The wealth of the traditional Inuit cultural and historical base, and its artistic base, would suggest to me quite the opposite: this Norse presence had nothing to do with chance. McGovern doesn't trouble himself about contradictions as he acknowledges the presence of Inuit settlements throughout the entire Nordrsetur route. I would think this rather confirms the postulate advanced throughout this book of a deliberate search of contacts with the Scandinavians and consequently peaceful relations between the two peoples. "The possible hostility of Viking hunters seems not to have prevented the establishment of Inuit winter settlements throughout the *entire* Nordrsetur zone."[15]

McGovern places Inuit presence in Disko between 1010 and 1240. Knowing that the northwest Greenland coast—namely, the location of the Nordrsetur —was occupied by Inussuit Inuit hardly frightened by possible Norse hostility described by McGovern, we should conclude that the Scandinavians passed through theoretically hostile sites over an expanse covering some 1,300 kilometers. In an environment as unforgiving as the Arctic, this is quite an achievement by itself. The kinds of feats possible in Europe were not necessarily a given in northern Greenland where havens, ports, and areas where game could be hunted—and thus resupply the expeditions—were limited. The frequency and duration (several centuries) of these expeditions seem to reveal a tranquil situation. In support of this theory, let me stress that all it took—based on the Icelandic sources—was one single conflict with the Skrælings (or a very small number of them in my opinion) for the Vikings to halt their voyages to and colonization attempts in "Vinland." If this was the case, how can we explain several centuries of expeditions into the Far North, if not for the peaceful situation made possible by the Inuit?

I will lay out the question differently:

Either the Inuit avoided contact, which is partly possible, some written sources mention minor conflicts that cannot be denied, which were dictated by cultural divides and medieval prejudices. In the most extreme hypothesis, the natives would flee at the approach of representatives of Christian civilization. This is strangely reminiscent of the letter sent to Pope Nicholas V during the first half of the fifteenth century. Given the details provided, I would lean toward this letter representing the Dorset people. In this case, the Inuit presence along the entire Nordrsetur route isn't explained, unless as evidence of a certain masochism or the more improbable desire to play hide and seek with the Scandinavians, by settling there when the Norse were absent and leaving on their arrival. There is no element supporting this interpretation.

Or the relations between the two communities were much more peaceful than people have wanted to say, and the Vikings traveled these 1,300 kilometers every year without hindrance. This theory comes with additional support from the hypothesis advanced by several researchers who saw both people seeking each other out for commercial purposes. It seems to me that this version agrees better with the apparent facts, the accounts at our disposal, and the conclusions drawn from excavations made in the Arctic.

I follow the trend in contemporary research that asserts the two Inuit and Norse communities were aware of each other's reciprocal existence and even sought prosperous contacts as implied in the medieval source texts. We will revisit the possible location of these contact in Disko Bay, but I would like to stress that no archaeological proof has yet been presented that would clearly identify this island with the Nordrsetur location.

## The Phase of Contacts at Vestribygð

According to McGovern, after the first phase (Nordrsetur contacts) the natives established contact with the Scandinavians of Vestribygð (in other words, with the northernmost Norse colony in the region of Nuuk/Godthåb) circa 1300. The contacts were initially peaceful then deteriorated into a state of direct competition, in the author's view, particularly concerning the division of natural resources. This situation would have led the church and King Magnus Erickson Smek to react. Unfortunately, I feel compelled to express several reservations about this theory, and even purely reject some of its conclusions. It is possible that some errors in McGovern's postulates, such as the placement of the Nordrsetur, could explain several inconsistencies in his theory. I have already pointed out several contradictions earlier. As McGovern sees it, the second phase of contact would result from the (alleged) end of the Nordrsetur.* With the support of archaeological proofs, I reject this assertion. We also know from the written sources (mainly tithes

---

*We should note that Keller sees the end of Vestribygð as presaging the end of the Nordrsetur, attributing this colony with a monopoly in these expeditions. This, to my eyes, overlooks the fact that Eystribygð took its wealth from these lands.

to Rome) and archaeological excavations that the Nordrsetur expeditions were used until 1400, if not later. If the expeditions toward these colonies continued well after the "discovery" of Disko, it is because this island was not their final destination. This reinforces my belief that Canada was the location of the Nordrsetur. Furthermore, Disko doesn't offer such a concentration of game "with added value."

McGhee provides a larger range for the dating of the Nordrsetur and advances a pertinent but legitimate question with respect to North America: "If such trade was occurring, especially during the eleventh through fourteenth centuries, would it have been only limited to Greenland's west coast?"[16]

### The Phase of Contact at Eystribygð (circa 1350–1500)

For McGovern, this phase begins in 1350, the date of the supposed disappearance of the Vestribygð colony. The basis of this theory are the excavations of Mathiassen and Holtved in the Julianehåb district in 1936. Both deduced a simultaneous Norse-Inuit occupation of these sites, with the Inuit settling there a century before the Vikings' departure. McGovern identifies the incriminating Scandinavian sites with the following farms: Ø* 17a, 17, 18 (this last number is the Dyrnæs Church). While adopting the condition for a simultaneous Inuit presence, McGovern deduces the existence of strong pressure from their Norse neighbors. This is what clearly appears through Finn Gad's works in which we can see the heightened density of Inuit locations bordering the Scandinavians. Sixty-nine Inuit dwellings are piled up on four sites,[†] which scarcely corresponds with Inuit customs nor corresponds to the elementary requirements of hunting, which rather require them to be scattered. We are compelled to somewhat support Gad's hypothesis of defense—the Inuit grouped together for more safety against their neighbors, unless we might be obliged to consider other players? To dismiss

---

*Ø for Østerbygd and V for Vestribygð is the archaeological norm adopted by international research. See the map of Eystribygð in chapter 2.

†This would therefore give us an average of seventeen houses per site, which is between 68 and 85 individuals if we go by the Inuit family unit of 4 to 5 members. Gad, *A History of Greenland,* 167.

once and for all the doubts concerning the simultaneous close presence of both populations, I would like to point out that McGovern was able to lift these hesitations by approaching the mater differently.

This hodgepodge of Inuit dwellings is for me—without considering the archaeological excavations—the logical culmination of simultaneous Norse-Inuit cohabitation. Indeed, why would the Inuit feel a need to pile their homes atop one another if they had moved there after the Norse left or disappeared, with all the inconveniences that posed for hunting? There would have been no lack of space. This therefore confirms a simultaneous presence of both populations, and implies that the natives were looking for the Vikings. What would in fact be the Inuit's interest to come down from the north to crowd into already fairly crowded lands like Eystribygð? It is easy to see that the hypothesis of fruitful trade—or even a reciprocal dependency of both parties—enlivened by peaceful, friendly coexistence, is a serious trail to pursue. Nor should we underestimate the phenomenon of acculturation. We know the speed with which so-called primitive populations can adopt new techniques and adjust to new needs (economic, dietary . . .) leading to a certain dependent status for them. More recently, this phenomenon was the same in Canada, also based on hunting for deluxe furs (white fox and so on). In response to needs of the Canadian economy some natives broke the balance of their own food-based economy and adopted a more sedentary lifestyle close to white exchange centers.

Revisiting the description of the Inussuit settlements' "strategic position" for cutting the food lines of Eystribygð, I come to the conclusion that its author is exaggerating. Game animals and sea mammals cannot be guided with a staff like some flock! It is difficult in this case to imagine how the natives could have starved the (besieged?) Scandinavians.

I see instead good intercommunity relations, the Vikings visibly not worried by the native presence in a "strategic place" (with the same subtlety given those words by the church).

Like for the Vestribygð colony, McGovern cites traditional Inuit lore, while underscoring the reduced number of stories concerning

Scandinavians. He also uses the Icelandic source concerning the pilgrim Björn Einarsson Jórsalafari.

Puzzlingly, McGovern concludes that this third phase, the arrival of the Inussuk, is difficult to date, which is not at all the case. We can see that the process of Inussuit migrations underwent a change that is revealed by a rapid passage of the migrant populations to Eystribygð to continue further south before going back up the eastern coast of Greenland. There is no need to revisit the relative overpopulation of Eystribygð to explain this change.

Even taking McGovern's dates as our basis for the second phase of Vestribygð (1300–1350), it is fairly easy, by counting broadly, to place an Inussuk presence in southern Greenland from the start of the fourteenth century, knowing that one of its characteristics is its expansionism and nomadic nature. For greater precision, a simple dating of Inussuk sites in southeast Greenland could give us an even more precise range of their passage to Eystribygð knowing that Inussuk culture—among others—migrated by way of Cape Farvel.

We should recognize in McGovern's defense that he saw a difference in the fate of the two Norse colonies, which is the most frequent position in contemporary research. Despite the sometimes-odd conclusions he adopts, McGovern even goes so far as to dismiss the theory of Norse extermination by the natives (a theory that was long shared and widespread), a dismissal I completely share. He underscores the marked difference of the population of Eystribygð, which was prosperous, numerous and unisolated, unlike Vestribygð. "No indication exists that the much larger and more prosperous population of the Eastern Colony vanished as a direct consequence of the Inuit presence."[17]

### The Phase of the Exploitation of the Ruins

This is the period following the disappearance of the Norse and the use of their sites by the natives, which would explain the recuperation of numerous Scandinavian objects. The best illustrated case is that of metal obtained from the bells of Eystribygð. The immense clerical activity in Rome during the entire fifteenth century with an eye to sending bishops to Greenland implies that the colony was not yet deserted. Foreign accounts, such as the maps almost completely ignored by researchers, also go in this direction; although the date of 1500 advanced by McGovern is doomed by its pessimism, Portuguese cartography confirms that Greenland was deserted toward the middle of the sixteenth century, as shown by the map of Diego Homem (1558) showing Greenland as *Desertibusoz terra agricole.*

Nevertheless, I believe this later date has the advantage of pushing back the generally accepted fifteenth-century cutoff date. The end of the eastern colony is poorly documented. I would caution against an overly rigid view strictly imposed by a fixed date. Contrary to Vestribygð, the fate of Eystribygð did not end with a single blow as seemingly confirmed by archaeology. The "extinction" of the colony was gradual, which differentiates it completely from Vestribygð. No proof of massive massacres or a mass return of Scandinavians to Iceland or to Eystribygð has been provided, either in Icelandic source texts or Inuit oral tradition, or even by archaeology. I believe this difference in the fate of the western colony confirms the voluntary nature of the Scandinavian exodus from the colony there.

Recall that until now not a single researcher—or almost—has seriously considered using neutral foreign sources, which is vexing, for there are several source texts provided by foreign navigators (German, Portuguese) testifying to a partial Norse presence. Pushing the dates for the "Norse disappearance" to the middle of the sixteenth century could open up a new path for study. For example, Gini cites the dates of 1520 or 1534 for when a foreign ship saw the livestock in a pasture (in Herjolfsnes, it seems). The latest known date would be 1540 as it is when a Scandinavian was found dead in front of his house.[18]

To finish, I would like to share an observation concerning the late date of the appearance of the English and Dutch in 1620 provided by McGovern. It could be that commercial whaling activity was beginning at this time, but that doesn't prevent the fact that the regular appearance of these two nations in Greenland waters began much sooner, about two centuries earlier in fact. I would therefore heed his recommendation to only consider his four-phase model as a temporary working arrangement that does, it is true, provide some landmarks for this subject.

To sum up, my strongest criticisms are:

The arbitrary date of the establishment of the Nordrsetur; their
halt having no reason, at least not during such an early period.
Lowered European demand for "luxury products" from the
Arctic toward the end of Scandinavian colonization is a possible
consideration and probably connected with the decline of the
Hanseatic League.

The underestimation of peaceful Inuit-Norse relations in the Far
North. However, they allowed the continuation of these same
Nordrsetur, if not to say their very existence.

A logical consequence is McGovern's fixation on outdated models:
the bellicose model. This seems to prop up a large part of his
four-phase model (the third phase in particular).

The alleged destitution of the Norse in metal and wood.

His silence on the foreign presence in Greenland.

In short, despite his proposed model's purpose of simplifying the
subject, the author seems to get muddled up in numerous contradictions, spotting interesting points but not drawing their conclusions
(alluding to my second observation above) or advancing, to the contrary, completely opposing conclusions. The author ends with a very
interesting question: Was the commercial relationship between the
Vikings and Inuit akin to a patron-client relationship? I earlier mentioned the case of Canada with the fur industry (for example, the
Revillon Frères establishments). A relationship of this type would
explain better the reasons for an Inuit presence in a highly populated
area (Eystribygð) and economically unstable for reasons of hunting and again migration (or movements) of the Inussuk people to
Vestribygð. This kind of economic dependency is in any case in perfect accord with the proximity of the two populations, it is even a
sine qua non for all good businessmen, as the Nordic people generally were. Quite relevantly, McGovern notes that among the Nordic
people in Scandinavia such (commercial) relationships have actually
existed in northern Scandinavia between the Norse leaders and the

Arctic hunters."[19] However, this does not prevent analysis of the situation from a more or less hawkish angle of hostilities, which seems to me to be in contradiction with a situation like this.

## The Theory of Norse Assimilation

If we remove the medieval sources of information that vaguely allude to it, we find in this category (at least partially) the Norwegian pastor Hans Egede, who set off to preach the gospel to the Scandinavian descendants in the eighteenth century. In fact, he couldn't help but notice the extremely mixed features of the entire West Greenland population, which is still valid today. A genetic study of the most isolated populations could maybe supply some interesting elements.

Unfortunately, this highly interesting hypothesis has not been the object of serious, extensive study. Egede presumed no more nor less that the Inuit were in part descendants of the Scandinavian colonists. Coming on behalf of a representative of the dominant culture of the eighteenth century, we have to believe there was some foundation for this conviction for Egede to suggest an observation that his time and milieu certainly would have found shocking. It is a legitimate question if this crossbreeding was restricted to the moralizing and biased mind of this missionary,* or if it corresponded to a quantified reality. It is a shame that Hans Egede didn't make a statistical study of these mixed elements. He was far from being the only person to remark on this strange singularity, which in this case gives us grounds for presuming a phenomenon spread throughout the western coast of Greenland, which, let me remind you, is the traditional region for Scandinavian movement.

Egede would later be joined in this view by Norwegian historian Eilert Sundt, who rightly lays emphasis on the external obstacles and environment (mainly intellectual) hostile to this line of thought. However, it helps us give a better grasp of the impasse in which pure research found itself with the proliferation of theories and hypotheses

---

*Recall this is in a colonial and missionary context (dominant/dominated) directed at a pagan aboriginal population by a representative of "civilization."

on this subject: "Generally speaking, people are hesitant to accept the idea that a higher, Christian, and reasonably civilized population would be able to descend from a more barbarous tribe or disappear by melting into it."[20]

It seems clear that the bias of the critics had the effect of deliberately shunting aside certain scientific working hypotheses. However, if we consider all the Scandinavian colonizations, every single one of them without exception met the same end: assimilation, the disappearance of the Nordic minority into the native majority whether it is the Swedish Vikings in Russia, the Danes in Normandy, or the Norwegians in England. Only the scarcely scientific criteria seen above have dismissed this possibility for the case that concerns us: the Vikings in Greenland / Canada and may it be said in passing, in Vinland/America.

Nevertheless we occasionally come across neutral analysis considering this possibility. At the beginning of the twentieth century, Eugène Beauvois rightly stressed the common points of these two populations, which was quite rare: "*Scarcely differing* from the Eskimos whose land they occupied, they did what their own Christian ancestors had done alone in the midst of Iceland's pagans, they put up with the influence of the new environment in which they found themselves: some of them surrounded by the aboriginal population adopted their ways and superstitions."[21]

Such an intellectual stance, even at the beginning of the century, must have been shocking (we have seen the case of Mathiassen forty years later). Perhaps with the benefit of hindsight this aspect will be considered with more attention and an open mind. Beauvois's judgment is far from being wrongheaded, aside from the Scandinavian cultural tradition that is curiously missing in Greenland, not a single book has been written nor any library mentioned that should be food for thought, although there were few things opposing the Scandinavians to the natives.

We have seen that animal raising, agriculture and sailing techniques differentiated them and curiously enough, it was animal raising—reflection of a certain kind of civilization—that was abandoned at Vestribygð. On the other hand, many centers of interest like hunting, fishing, an explorative nature, and enterprising, adventurous spirit brought them together. In fact, I have only one observation concerning Beauvois and that is that the Vikings had no need to abandon or renounce much of anything as all these characteristics were not foreign to them. Additionally, the Scandinavians' faith seemed quite limited and fickle, often combing paganism and Christianity. We should not forget that this kind of assimilation is fairly banal and has occurred in more recent times:

> The French fur traders sent to Canada among the same Arctic people allegedly to work for the crown but who wholeheartedly joined the "savages."
>
> In the eighteenth century, Hans Egede and his son echoed the same phenomenon when the new colonists embraced the natives and their lifestyle too quickly.

As we see, the case is far from exceptional. A simple look at the status of the lower-class members among the colonizers and the freedom of the natives gives an idea of the temptations offered the newcomer to become a turncoat or disappear into the wilds like Canada.

Fridtjof Nansen is another who supports the theory that the Norse were assimilated by the Inuit; he is certainly one of this theory's more eminent spokesmen. He totally rejected the theory of Norse extermination at the hands of the Inuit in his classic book *Nord I Tåkeheimen* of 1911. Nansen bases his position mainly in the Icelandic written sources concerning the pilgrim Björn Einarsson Jórlsalafari, who was shipwrecked in Greenland about 1285 to 1387, and the annals of the bishop Gisli Oddsson, seeing confirmation in the latter's work regarding crossbreeding with the Inuit. This is supposed to have taken place in the fourteenth century.

Kaj Fischer Møller in 1942 was one of the rare individuals who, after examination of Scandinavian skeletons coming from the two churches of Vestribygð (Anavik/Ujarassuit at the end of Godthåb fjord, and Sandnæs near Kilaarsarfik, at the end of Amarella), concluded that crossbred Inuit-Viking individuals were present. He worked with the discoveries from the excavations of Aage Roussell* at the beginning of the 1930s: "The Eskimo imprint is so pronounced on certain skulls, that it can only be from cross breeding of the Eskimo and Nordic races, although in relatively limited proportions."[22]

Unfortunately, no other analysis seems to have been made that confirms this either in Vestribygð or Eystribygð, or any other analyses of Greenland skeletons. McGovern cites the craniometrical studies by Laughlin and Jorgensen (1966) refuting this hypothesis. Even Corrado Gini, a fervent defender of the assimilation theory, goes along with this: "We find practically no pronounced Eskimo imprint among the Scandinavian skeletons as could have been hoped for among hybrid populations."[23]

This conclusion doesn't prevent from keeping such a possibility in reserve, stressing that generally in this case (contacts between two foreign populations) the mixed-race individuals remain among the native tribes. Morality and religious conventions surely play a role here: "We must assume that the hybrids among the colonists remained with the Eskimo tribes as was the case and is still generally the case with contemporary hybrids born from contacts with outsiders."[24]

We have to believe that these hybrids maintained an appreciable distance from the Scandinavians, because Gini cites cases of hybrids on the American continent, particularly among the Inuit of Baffin Island (this was part of the Norse area of influence as shown by several source texts): "The stature of the Eskimos, their features, pigmentation, and blood group composition, their clothing and their customs revealed a European influence that according to the traditions of the natives was even more pronounced in the past among some Baffinland residents."[25]

According to him, Inuit traditions echoes this, speaking of an emigration of tribes with Nordic character from Baffin Island. Unfortunately, Gini gives almost no further information. Some explorers mention their descendants in Coronation Gulf and Victoria Island as having pronounced Nordic features, but anthropologists don't support

---

*1930 excavation of Vestribygð in Kilaarsarfik (ruins of farm V.51) and excavations of 1932–1934 (ruins V.7 in Uparassuit; V.5 and V.52 in Umiviarssuk).

their claims. In fact, there are abundant examples since the arrival of the first explorers to Canada of Inuit peoples with European features surpassing the geographical area cited. This is easy to grasp when we know these are nomadic peoples. Gini emphasized one important point: the absence of Norse traces found by Scandinavian archaeologists in no way invalidates his theory, as Vikings had adopted an Inuit lifestyle. It is certain that this hypothesis requires more extensive study.

Gini maintains that a blend of the two populations would have given the natives typically Nordic qualities: "The qualities of enterprise and energy native to Scandinavians, and most notably, the warrior qualities* that Eskimo tradition described for its champions in their encounters with the colonists."[26]

This more or less brings us back to Inussuk culture. All these features described by Gini can also be found among the Inussuk people who differ the most from their peers both in technical abilities and—it seems—physical abilities (for example, in the story of Aqissiaq being able to carry two men on his knees). Beauvois and some written sources say that in the sixteenth century whites using native martial techniques (kayaks, harpoons) attacked foreign ships and sunk them by holing them below their water lines (Olaus Magnus and the Zeno brothers).

In contrast to McGovern, Gini draws precise conclusions from his hypothesis, which I should say, considering the era of the composition—are judicious. In fact he perfectly grasps that any union between Viking Christians and Inuit pagans could not help but bring down upon it the wrath of the church with apostasy as a possible consequence. "It seems improbable to me that the union between Scandinavians and Eskimos was not accompanied by the apostasy† of the first group. In this case, the higher echelons of the Catholic hierarchy would have had difficulty crediting an account of events

---

*Here Gini is alluding to certain stories used by the supporters of the bellicose theory telling of sparring matches between the two communities like that in the story of Ungortoq.

†Gini's argument is defensible if we believe, for example, that the Scandinavians lived in isolation with the Inuits. In the strict sense of the word, this is apostasy: abandonment of the faith and the Christian religion.

that obviously hardly conformed to the respect due to the authority wielded by the Church."[27]

The Norwegian professor Knut Fægri, who directed the Botanical Institute of Bergen University, brings a maximalist variant to this judgment. He favors the hypothesis that the Scandinavians were excommunicated for apostasy. I personally believe that the two hypotheses are correct, defendable, and in no way contradictory. Without truly realizing it, Fægri put his finger on a certain historical fact: the Greenland colonists were definitely excommunicated by the church but primarily for mercantile reasons—and this occurred several times.

This possibility is extremely interesting when we think of anthropologist William Thalbitzer's work in the origin of the name Eskimo: "The name first appeared at the beginning of the seventeenth century namely among the accounts of the French Jesuit missionaries of 1611, but originally in the form 'excominquois' that has only a remote resemblance to the word we used today: 'Eskimo.' Several years later, it was abbreviated to 'excoumins.'[28]

An example cited by Thalbitzer is a village that preserved the name "Les Excoumains."[29] This village is on the north shore of the Gulf of Saint Lawrence. It was not until 1640 that the word *Esquimaux* appeared in Jesuit accounts, and then cited by Thalbitzer in its current form, *Eskimo*. He explicitly states that in the orthodoxy of the missionaries, *excommunicere* means "to excommunicate." The pagans are punished for their stubbornness and hostility by banishment—in other words, excommunication.

This view appears quite plausible to me and even logical in light of the strained relations between the Scandinavians and the church. "There must have been some form of excommunication by the Church for although they hadn't foresworn their religion, they [the Scandinavians] had adopted the Eskimo lifestyle and joined with them."[30]

As we have seen, any kind of more or less friendly relationship with indigenous pagans could only shock the medieval clerical mind, with little inclination for tolerance, especially during the intensely expansionist period of the Crusades. The church's behavior toward the Scandinavians (and vice versa) was sufficiently ambiguous, so this excommunication hypothesis is far from being unfounded. Gini raised another original question: the imbalance of the Norse population weighed heavily in women's favor. His conjecture is based on skeletons exhumed in the eastern colony, but he doesn't cite his sources. These are his figures:

| AGE OF EXHUMED SKELETON | RATIO OF FEMALES TO MALES |
| :---: | :---: |
| 50–60 years old | 50 women per 100 men |
| 40–50 | 116 per 100 |
| 30–40 | 400 per 100 |
| 20–30 | 500 per 100 |
| 20–25 | 1,000 per 100 |

If these figures are correct, there was a definite imbalance to the detriment of the generations most likely to renew the Scandinavian population (from 20 to 40 years). Unfortunately, Gini seems to be the only one to assume this position. In the particularly hostile Arctic context it is safe to assume that the male populations of both the Norse and Inuit peoples were actually more vulnerable to accidents, if we consider that they were responsible for hunting, exploring, and protection. Based on this imbalance, Gini defends his novel hypothesis that assimilation occurred under the impetus of the Norse women. "As Norse women had no or few males of their race at their disposal, and as their religion forbid any marriage with pagans, they recanted their religion to contract new marriages with the Eskimo whose customs they had adopted. In the end they left with them for lands better suited for their new lifestyle, putting the sea between them and the other Scandinavian settlements."[31]

This hypothesis—just like the one concerning the gender imbalance—does not seem to have been picked up by any other researcher except to refute it. Jones notes: "Gini . . . advances the indefensible suggestions that it was primarily under the impetus of the Norse women that the Whites would have left to join the Skrælings."[32] Oleson totally rejects any female emigration with the natives. His arguments are equally moral and cultural (and in fact colored by anachronism as medieval Norse women enjoyed a certain status). For this reason, they seem partisan to me and limit his approach: "There is no possible way to claim that Icelandic women would have accompanied the Nordrsetur hunters. This would have meant a loss of both their language and their religion."[33]

This statement allows us to emphasize its contradictions. Historically, the schema criticized by Oleson is what actually happened—namely, the disappearance of the Icelandic language and culture from Greenland, as well as the Christian religion. The extent of the role of Scandanvian women is a digression. As noted elsewhere, the religious decline of Greenland is relatively well documented.

Oleson rejects any female participation in Nordrsetur expeditions, which is arguable. In fact, this would be untraditional, and no text concerning these polar journeys makes any reference to it—but if an ordinary fact, should it be noted? I would note, however, that Freydis, Leif Erikson's half-sister, and five Norwegian women were part of the Vinland expedition, and Portuguese professor A. Cortesoào (1954) mentions a woman of high rank (noble or royal?) accompanying an expedition in these regions. Above all, we have seen an Inuit story that mentions a Nordic couple in northern Greenland (Upernavik district), therefore far from the colonies; in other words, during a Nordrsetur trip and in a commonplace context that held no interest for the scribes. This phenomenon seems to have been repeated fairly often. So Scandinavian women were not entirely absent from the northern journeys. It is just as possible that other women could have been present but were not considered worth recording for history. Slave women (*trælls*) could have served on the supply chains of long expeditions.

Reading T. J. Oleson leaves the impression that the Scandinavians who left on expeditions into the Nordsetrar didn't return because he speaks of their abandonment of the Icelandic language and religion. This is not at all the case. He is merging two entirely different facts: Nordsetrar expeditions for trading purposes and colonization expeditions. The latter do actually amount to a one way journey, which would lead to abandonment of the Christian religion.

On the strength of his hypotheses, Gini could have tackled the archaeological digs from another angle. As I noted earlier, the tools essentially intended for hunting and fishing do not seem to have been discovered—by neither archaeologists or Ivar Bårdsson—on the other hand, an impressive number of Scandinavian objects have been recovered from Vestribygð such as spindles, distaffs, shoes, cutting boards, combs, shovels, and spades. The last two tools illustrate the Vikings' sensible adjustment to their environment as they are made of whalebone or caribou antler. All these objects have in common a certain value in typical Norse agrarian economy, but in a typically Inuit Arctic economy their value is practically nil. In this perspective, we can note the scant interest the natives seem to have had in farming or weaving objects. Gini takes this as a verification of his postulate, which will be weakened presently by the restricted confirmation of voluntary Scandinavian emigration, while waiting for more proof concerning these Norse women: "When leaving, the Norse women left behind them the utensils that Eskimo didn't know, taking with them those that were better suited to their lifestyle."[34]

Gini has come up with several highly original—if not comical—hypotheses, which I will present here without taking any position. Archaeologists were surprised by the presence of purely domestic objects (like those described above) in a Sandnæs stable. Gini regards this as a completely symbolic illustration of the rejection of a certain lifestyle, a hypothesis that would be confirmed by a second even more symbolic example on the Umiviarssuk farm. Here Scandinavian objects were found that had been outright tossed into a midden—namely, many game pieces. Gini offers two explanations: a puritanical ecclesiastic hand would have cast these objects there in a fit of rage, or else the Norse women threw them away. "Norse women, adopting Eskimo custom, threw away the pieces of the Scandinavians' favorite games."[35]

All the context of the end of Vestribygð (voluntary departure) can fit such a scenario that I will keep on hold for lack of other explanations.

To return to the theory of assimilation by the Thule people, the Vikings would have been overwhelmed by the "inferior Skrælings" and become acculturated.

## *The Bellicose Theory or the Theory of Inuit-Scandinavian Confrontation*

In this category I include all the varying hypotheses that end up with a Norse disappearance due to the Inuit. This is the theory that has prevailed longest and extensively, having the advantage of easily responding to the patterns of the time or to accompanying ethnocentric biases: the representatives of Christian civilization were massacred by savages. Even McGovern takes his distance from this position: "The simplest model is also the oldest. Hans Egede's contemporaries believed that the Inuit had invaded and exterminated the Scandinavian colonists."[36]

This model is based on traditional Inuit lore and stories collected by Poul Egede (son of the famous pastor Hans) and cited by several researchers: Inge Kleivan, Knud Krogh, and so forth. The bulk of these stories share:

> Conflicts or bloody encounters, an abundance of stereotypes such as "Conflicts between the resource rich Inuk and the unfortunate, unhappy, and violent Scandinavians."[37]
>
> The later date of their composition (the middle of the nineteenth century for the essential works of the Danish colonial administrator Heinrich Rink). These stories were collected after many years of contacts with Dutch and English whalers or Danish missionaries. Just like Kleivan or Arneborg, McGovern underscores their bias and the many flaws that are characteristic of them: suggestions of the speaker, feelings of "national pride" or "revenge" among the Inuit too happy to exhibit a model that valorizes them as vanquishers of the mighty Vikings.

Just like the pacifist theory, the bellicose theory combines various trends, even a single author can draw from several viewpoints. Let's quote a few proponents of this theory going as far back to Hans Egede, C. C. Rafn, T. Mathiassen, and P. Nørlund.

I would also like to quickly mention the former existence of a variant of the Norse disappearance theory, that of degeneration—which had its glory days in the 1920s and 1930s. Some of the most eminent researchers gave it their support: "The last colonists of Herjolfsnes belonged to a race doomed to extinction. The lack of new blood was very likely a major factor."[38]

This theory was very widespread and popular because it had the advantage of rationally explaining the Norse disappearance; better, it excused it in a way that spared the national, if not overtly racist pride of that era. "The dramatic description of the last weakened colonist was used to substantiate the racist ideas of the twenties and thirties in the Western world."[39]

The scientific basis for this theory was the discovery of Scandinavian skeletons in Herjolfsnes in the 1920s and the hasty conclusions that were drawn from them: Scandinavian weakness and degeneration. The people of that time did not take into consideration the possibility of the deformation of the skeletons during their long stay underground but even more importantly, as is recognized today, the damage they suffered during their journey to Denmark. In 1924, preservation and freight techniques were not as evolved as now, and everyone acknowledges that mistakes were made during transport, such as desiccation with its well-known consequences. Unfortunately, Mathiassen provides a very good illustration of this kind of thinking when describing Norse extinction in Greenland this way:

> The Scandinavians were already in pronounced decline thanks to their abandonment by the mother country: a degenerate, underfed, sick, and weakened race who the energetic Eskimo had no trouble of avenging themselves.[40]

A corollary to the extermination theory is that of Inuit-Norse competition for natural resources, which would naturally have led to conflict between the two communities. Daniel Bruun is a strong supporter of this position that is also shared by McGovern: "Competition over rare resources could had led to conflicts."[41]

McGovern offers an example involving seals and caribou. Regarding the hooded seal, he notes that strong concentrations of this species are found in the outer regions of the fjords, thus sites that are generally Inuit. Inspired by contemporary scenes in which he saw the natives driving seals into narrow passageways to kill them, or placing nets in these same passageways, McGovern concluded that their Inussuit ancestors used the same techniques, which he believed would have aroused Norse hostility. McGovern also notes that Scandinavian traditions (notions such as property ownership, for example) would have been foreign to the Greenland natives. I will make several observations in response.

First, this species of seal is not a major part of the Inuit diet. One major detail, as we are informed by Mathiassen, is that the net is not an Inuit technique. McGovern assumes the practice of a technique involving concealment and net fishing would be similar to that of our time, without advancing any concrete proof. I nonetheless do not dismiss this hypothesis as an Inuit net was discovered by Mathiassen in Illutalik in the Disko region so we can accept that it saw use, as there is nothing in Inuit culture that serves no particular function. This hypothesis leads me to entirely different conclusions than McGovern's. In chapter 5, we saw that the net is entirely foreign in origin. As a net was found at the Inuit site of Illutalik, it seems that the Inuit borrowed this technique from the Norse, which would have involved learning how to use it. In other words, a certain amount of collaboration was called for. Mathiassen's net is too old to be a vague copy of the Scandinavian model made after their departure or extermination, depending on which position one supports.

Another question arises: Why would the Vikings have taught the natives this technique if they were hostile to each other or engaged in economic competition?

To the contrary, I see this as a result of friendly and commercial Norse-Inuit relations. In my opinion it is hard, if not unrealistic, to try to reduce the medieval situation in the Arctic into discrete and isolated regions in which trade was the only reason for Inuit-Norse contact. In fact, I feel obliged to note that all the elements unearthed by research fit together remarkably well in the sense of frequent and extended contacts. The situation could be summed up as follows:

The feverish Norse quest for Arctic riches (ivory, gyrfalcons, furs...) would inevitably bring them into contact with the natives present.

The no less feverish Inuit quest for Scandinavian trinkets, likely encouraged movements by Inuit populations.

Due to the intensity of trade and once the introduction and assessment phase was over, the two communities became neighbors.

In the resulting stage of Inuit-Norse relations, the reader can draw the conclusions themselves, which seem obvious to me and were already embryonically present in the second stage. Two totally different populations becoming neighbors can lead to two major consequences: either they are good neighbors or conflicts erupt. We know that conflict wasn't the goal in mind, rather, commerce required it (even if the possibility cannot be rejected—for example, because of episodic quarrels that happen everywhere). Nevertheless, archaeology confirms this prolonged proximity, or even cohabitation. It is difficult to imagine relations stopping at the second stage, meaning a neighboring situation that had no concrete results, especially if you take into consideration the specific features of the two populations: the peaceful and curious nature of the Inuit, and the Scandinavians' ability to adapt, their enterprising and "commercial" spirit noted wherever they traveled, and lastly, for both populations, the conditions specific to Greenland and the Far North—isolation and the absence of other population groups. Anyone who has spent time in these lands cannot help but see the humility of their inhabitants with respect to the environment, which was incidentally deified as animism, was still a potent force then. In short, the extreme conditions of the Arctic require a certain degree of wisdom—in this case "civilized" relations—or otherwise run the risk of dying sooner rather than later.

While the competition for the possession of game animals between the two populations is plausible, that for livestock is much less. I would consider it as irrelevant and having no connection to the Inuit context. McGovern offers no proofs for his assumptions of Inuit theft of Scandinavian livestock. As noted in chapter 3, and in a fairly ironic way,

Scandinavian livestock is almost never mentioned in Inuit tales if we make an exception for the Aqissiaq episode in which he runs away from a horned animal. Livestock seems to have been unknown or perhaps I should say uninteresting with respect to the cultural difference, which could translate into different culinary traditions.

Gini and Fægri both strongly contest the theory of economic rivalry. The latter sees no basis for any rivalry between Vikings and Inuits over fishing. We should recall that Greenland Inuit society was primarily a community of hunters, not fishermen, in contrast with the Scandinavians, who were also sailors. Summer fishing existed in Inuit life but primarily as a temporary activity or one engaged in by women.

Gini takes the same position regarding the exploitation of sea mammals and underscores the excesses or obsessions of many researchers with this subject. As few people have done before him, he emphasized the maritime nature of Norse fishing, even for the remote farms far inland: "The diet of the colonists, even those in the most continental farms of the western colony, *was largely based on the marine fauna of the high sea.*"[42]

However, I will insist on a long-underestimated phenomenon, briefly mentioned earlier when describing the Inuit's lack of interest in livestock: the cultural divide is a possible factor of problems, or even conflicts. McGovern tells us that the Vikings killed walrus in great numbers—and we have a written account supporting this—which conforms with their commercial logic of racing after profit, and is easy to believe in view of the quantities exported. While recalling that precedents for this are known in Norway, such a practice leaves the impression of very non-ecological hunting with little respect for the environment. McGovern tells us that the Scandinavians killed young walruses—both male and female—without distinction, "suggesting massacres of entire herd in a single hunt."[43]

McGovern deduces this had a certain effect on the preservation of the animal in these regions. What I see is an enormous waste. As the Scandinavians were first and foremost interested in the ivory, no written source material gives us the impression that they took any concern for the tons of wasted meat that would also have reduced their valuable ivory cargos. Here I part from the principle that the Vikings would have hunted the walruses themselves as appears in some source texts (see chapter 9). In the opposite case (because there is no talk of major conflicts), they could have obtained these quantities of ivory thanks to trade. These two scenarios are not in any way contradictory and should even have co-existed for the all-important sake of profit. The minimalist theories have too much of a tendency to underestimate Norse adaptation. In the French edition of his book, Prytz sums up the Norse hunting technique as a dozen hunters *harpooning* the walruses closest to the bank, thereby blocking the rest of the herd. Even better, we learn that in 1327 a cargo of 1,100 kilos of walrus tusks were unloaded in Bergen. It sold for 12.7 kilos of silver, a veritable fortune at that time. We can ask how much meat this represented. I doubt the sailors would have taken on such a heavy cargo.

This underestimated phenomenon that long passed unnoticed had negative consequences, creating problems between the two communities. There were vast differences between the Vikings' hunting practices and those of the Inuit who were animists, as mentioned earlier, and therefore much more respectful of their game animals.

The cultural and especially religious sentiments, the lack of respect for taboos and for game animals, for their souls and for the balance of souls and nature according to Inuit spiritual beliefs, each of these could have been important factors in the misunderstanding and discord, if not outright confrontations, between the two cultures. We have long given too much weight to the Scandinavian perspective in this question of competing for natural resources. One thing is sure, practices such as the wasteful massacre of game animals—which, in addition, took place in very difficult conditions at high latitudes where food sources were limited—must have shocked the natives greatly. Kleivan cites an Inuit tradition mentioning such practices on Greenland's eastern coast: "The Scandinavians were burned because they frightened away the game with their fires."[44] She cites other tales where they were killed for wasting game: "The Scandinavians near Kulusuk (East Greenland) were burned because it was impossible to keep winter stores safely around them."[45]

One last example cited by Kleivan is that they brought the wrath of the natives down upon them because of their (Scandinavian) interest in Inuit women: "The Scandinavians near Kuummiut (East Greenland) had taken a Greenland couple as servants, but because they had taken his wife the Greenlanders set fire to the house."[46]

All these examples taken from Inuit tradition should support my hypothesis of a cultural divide, played out on a small scale, for no excavation has revealed evidence of any large-scale conflicts. I will end this section on Keller's observations, clearly emphasizing the context that was particularly recpetive to biases in which this bellicose theory evolved, wearing blinders based on notions of racial superiority crafted during eighteenth- and nineteenth-century periods of economic and colonial expansion. It is obvious that in this context the bellicose theory had a number of advantages over those of assimilation or cohabitation. Keller sums up the bias and blindness that gave free rein to a number of clichés such as the sneaky savage versus the valiant European: "In no case could the Inuit have defeated the Vikings in open combat. The explanation was that they had killed the Scandinavians by underhand means like ambushes and intentional fires (forgetting that these techniques were all too familiar in the Iceland of that era)."[47]

To sum up, I insist on the necessary precautions we need to take with regard to various theories in vogue during the period of 1920 to 1940 (Scandinavian weakening and degeneration, and so on). I reject the idea of the Inuit extermination of the Norse as, to this day, none of the hawkish theories have advanced any decisive arguments on their behalf. Moreover, they are flawed by their lack of objectivity. The pacifist theory seems to currently correspond better with the various elements provided by contemporary research. I would also stress the value lying in further study of the relationship between the church and the Scandinavians, which are the key to the existing accounts. In short, are these accounts biased or not? Circuitously, the trail opened by William Thalbitzer on the "Excommunicated" deserves to be extended.

# 9

# THE CHURCH IN GREENLAND

There is no need to insist on the weight of the church during the Middle Ages. A power in its own right, if not a counterpower, the church was inescapable. "The Roman Catholic Church was beyond any possible comparison the most prosperous economic structure in medieval Europe, and perhaps the most effective economic organization that ever existed."[1]

P. Jeanin rightly notes that prelates and the high aristocracy were a political force in their own right and presented an obstacle to the expansion of royal power. Before looking at Greenland's specific case, a brief overview of the church's power in Scandinavia described by Jeanin will allow us to properly contextualize the matter.

> In Sweden, one-fifth of the land belonged to the church. The reduction of the powers of the church by Gustav Vasa, King of Sweden, occurred about 1527 and was a reaction to this power.
>
> In Denmark, one-third of the land belonged to the church. A similar reaction, but one more turbulent, occurred.
>
> In Norway, the archbishop was the highest authority in the land. The church owned more lands than the crown and the nobility combined. Keller's excellent studies show that during the fourteenth century, a priest could own 45 times more land than a peasant, and a bishop 500 times more. Resistance appeared here as well, with the peasants protesting the tithe, and a political and religious opposition in 1537 with the bishop Engelbrechtson.

In short, the church was well represented in Scandinavia, though not without some friction. This helps us get a better grasp of the same discord in the remote Nordic dependencies (Iceland, Greenland, the Faroe Islands) and also its hostility when the crown clipped its wings. Even though the sociopolitical structure was quite different (physical absence of royal authority, limited if not completely urban fabric in Greenland) the arrival of the new power represented by the church did not take place seamlessly. Keller views Greenland as different from other medieval societies in which the church had had all economic and spiritual power, with the traditional balance of power between royal and clerical authority. As the originator of the bulk of written source material in Greenland, the church is of particular interest to us.

## THE BEGINNINGS OF CHRISTIANITY
## IN GREENLAND

Historically speaking, Christian antecedents should be looked for in England, particularly with regard to Celtic monks. We cannot reject the hypothesis of an early Greenland Christianization that involved a Celtic presence. I believe too many research elements for have been tossed away too fast and too easily. Without seeking to take a stand on the authenticity of the documents arguing the right of the Hamburg-Bremen bishopric claim to Greenland going back to the eleventh century, I would like to briefly list the points that support these claims or at least offer some food for thought, namely:

The surprising repetition or persistence of the Hamburg bishopric's claims.
The Celtic factor in Greenland.

These two elements have never been connected before for the purpose of study. So I raise the question: Couldn't they be—in light of the ecclesiastical sources cited below—two faces of the same reality: the very early Christianization of Greenland?

Several ancient documents refer to a pre-colonial Christianization of Greenland. They were a subject of controversy and even deemed to be fakes, because the copies are often more recent and vary from one another. Let me list them quickly: there is a document from 831 saying that the Germanic emperor Louis the Pious claims the establishment of the Hamburg bishopric with Saint Anschaire as the metropolitan bishop of the Nordic countries including Gronlandon.[2] In the year 835, Pope Gregory IV is supposed to have confirmed the emperor's stated wishes. In 912, Pope Anastasius III confirmed the Hamburg-Bremen archbishop's jurisdiction over Gronlandon.[3] The papal bulls and various church documents that pushed back this bishopric's jurisdiction to Saint Anschaire persisted for several centuries as Pope Nicholas in 1448 referred to this period as the beginning of Greenland's conversion to Christianity. Authors like Rafn and Gaffarel have spoken of a later addition. Despite the evidence of the interests involved, the persistence of these claims at such a high level seems troubling.

There are several striking and very real elements concerning a possible Celtic factor. In light of ecclesiastical elements couldn't what has long been interpreted as a Celtic influence in Greenland actually be seen instead as a Celtic *presence*? Let me summarize my position.

The oldest style churches, the little churches of the Qorlotoq type accompanied by a circular cemetery, show traces of more than likely Celtic influence (see figs. 2.2 and 2.3). Keller points out that circular cemeteries were unknown in Norway, a point made earlier by Poul Nørlund. Their origin should rather be sought in the British Isles. Irish monasteries took the form of a stronghold with a surrounding wall made of earth or stones, bordered by a moat on the outside. The most important building inside the walls was the church, which was rectangular. It was made from oak planks or wattle and daub. There is no possible confusion between the appearance of these monasteries and the linear continental models. This Celtic model endured and spread. At this stage, there is no longer any trace of Romanesque architecture, and this is also the case with Celtic Christian cemeteries. This is the point where Greenland and Iceland come into the story. The resemblance with the first generation of churches (Qorlotoq) is striking. They would even belong to an even more highly evolved church style. This tradition had the advantage of blending in more easily with ancient pagan practices, such as the sacred circle that separates the sacred from the profane. It has existed in Brittany for at least three millennia. Quite often this kind of Christian church stronghold was built atop a pagan site dating from the fifth or sixth century. These churches were ideally suited for the little communities scattered across the British Isles, as well as in Greenland and Iceland.

Similarly, the churches with a choir narrower than the nave are probably a copy of the English and Irish model, in which the choir was a more recent addition to the rectangular church. This development would have begun in the eighth century. Evidence of a Celtic Christian style is generally accepted. This begs the question: Couldn't this style symbolize the Celtic faith? I would personally even say a Celtic presence. Hence the importance of the sources cited above concerning Greenland's Christianization starting from the ninth century, and their authenticity.

In fact, it seems there were Christians among Greenland's first colonists. For example, the *Landnámabók* mentions the presence of Christian colonists, such as Herjólfr and their links to Celtic regions: "With him there was a man on the boat, a Christian from the Hebrides."* The bulk of the colonists were descendants of Ketil Flatnose (Flatnefun), a Norwegian who had conquered the Hebrides, where he inevitably encountered Christian civilization.

In the twelfth century, there was a clean break in the monastic and clerical style of the Irish church following its submission to Rome and Canterbury. It is therefore fairly unlikely that the original style of the Celtic church survived, and it, too, was subject to Roman style. I believe this is more or less in line with Nørlund's thinking with regard to churches with a narrow nave. It has been suggested that several Celtic cultural elements had been omitted or censured by the Icelandic scribes.[4] The sagas speak of Irish thralls, but we are familiar with the more pertinent existence of Celtic priests, the *papae*. I have little doubt that the Nordic scribes sought to laud Scandinavian colonists and overlooked

---

*Með honum [Herjólfr] var á skipi Suðureyskur maður kristinn.*

any others, and that the Celtic population doomed to disappear or be assimilated suffered the same fate in the historical records written by these same Icelanders.

Keller emphasizes the very relevant rarity of pagan remnants in Greenland,[5] which I see as confirmation of my Celtic hypothesis. We know that only a few examples of Thor's hammer have been found, which helps substantiate the presence of Christian colonists at the beginning of colonization.

In addition to the concrete examples provided by archaeology, other illustrations of Celtic influence can be found, particularly in the domain of church administration. The first Nordic Christian kings copied ther religious administrative system on the English system, in other words a society and church of similar structure, typical of newly formed kingdoms. Everything points to a greater Anglo-Celtic influence than previously believed possible, perhaps one even stronger than that of the Hamburg-Bremen bishopric. We should recall that Celtic and Nordic societies possessed similar structures, in which kinship and chiefdoms were the principal elements of social organization. This presumably helped facilitate incorporation of the new religion. Contrary to the evangelical efforts of the Hamburg-Bremen bishopric, this one circulated through internal elements of Scandinavian society—namely, the minor chieftains who had warred in the British Isles. On their return to Scandinavia or Greenland, they offered a kind of "family-style" conversion, a trump card the German bishops couldn't play. So it was no accident that the new Norwegian kingdoms turned to their British counterparts. It has even been possible to see some parallel features between the Icelandic tithing system and that of Celtic Brittany. This gives me the basis I need to introduce my conclusion concerning the Celtic presence and the conversion of the north to Christianity. In Norway, all this cannot be simply boiled down to the role of Olaf Tryggvason. Just like in the sagas, the version of history presented by the Icelandic copyists here again shows proof of bias. History seems to have often been reduced to practical outlines that were easy to incorporate or defend—sword in hand, if necessary—to the advantage of those individuals who included scribes among their faithful servants. We must thus revise our entire idea of Nordic history. Keller offered a clear analysis of Norway's conversion that then echoed through iceland and Greenland. He divides it into four phases:

> Circa the ninth century, a pioneering phase of evangelization by Celtic and Anglo-Saxon missionaries, which he calls a cultural mission (accidental contacts and proselytyzing missions).
>
> A phase of royal mission starting from the tenth century, which includes conversion by the sword.
>
> A phase of royal administration starting from the eleventh century when the church was under royal authority. Clerical and secular administration were probably the same. This phase shows a string Anglo-Saxon imprint. Norwegian kings appealed to British bishops to organize the church and preach the gospel throughout the land.
>
> A phase of clerical adminstration starting from midway in the twelfth century. The church became independent. We shall see that Iceland and Greenland followed the same pattern with a certain time lag. The first phase including the activity of Celtic missionaries was probably quite early, not only limited to the eleventh century, if we can place our trust in Irish tradition. Nevertheless, this long concealed phase would explain the presence of these particular Celtic features in Greenland and would also encompass Erik the Red's first colonists. Olag Tryggvason's Christianization would correspond only to the royal mission second phase. It clearly seems that the existing written accounts are attempts to increase this individual's glory if not to simply reduce Greenland's medieval Christian history to this phase alone and to this lone Norwegian player. As Keller notes, "Most written accounts of the clerical administration of the early time seem to refer to a royal administration stage."[6]

We will see that the last phase of clerical administration was quite late in Greenland, and I would even describe it as laborious. The great

Scandinavian precursor is the Norwegian king Olag Tryggvason. He is responsible for the Christian laws of the year 1000 that were approved in Iceland. It was during his reign that the Norwegian church and other Norse churches of the west were put under the supervision of the Hamburg-Bremen bishopric. One of the oldest written sources, mentioned by Adam of Bremen and naming Greenland, would be a papal letter of 1053. It concerns the archbishopric of all the northern countries, as well as two bishops responsible for Greenland: Adalbert and Meinhard.* Almost exactly two years later (1055) there is also the October 29 papal bull issued by Pope Victor II.[7]

We have a reference that is twenty-three years older in which it would seem that Pope John XIX placed Greenland under the jurisdiction of Archbishop Unwan. Greenland's Christianization would have been very early, and contrary to assumptions, would not have started as a result of Olag Tryggvason's policy. We should see two—if not three with the Celtic recollections—different waves of evangelization. The approaches were totally opposing. If we accept Adam of Bremen's version, the Germanic approach was gentle and Greenland had even requested it. The Roman approach was much more problematic and sufficiently contentious to require more detailed study later.

The kinship between Vikings and Germans, a more or less common way of thinking, as well as closer forms of social organization and lifestyle must have played a role. Archbishop Adalbert of Bremen showed himself to be intensely active from the time he took up his duties in 1004, sending emissaries to the Scandinavian sovereigns to win their friendship while lecturing these churchmen to go "to the ends of the earth" to protect the faith. "He sent his instructions throughout Denmark, Sweden, and Norway, and even to the ends of the earth, urging his bishops to defend Christ's Church with faith and to fearlessly go about converting the pagans."[8]

One interesting detail we pick up here is that rich Frisian merchants mounted a voyage of exploration in the Far North in 1040—a detail that would become important in medieval cartography. This

---

*See the summary list of the historical-religious events connected with Greenland.

relationship between faith and commerce would be expanded later, as well as their simultaneous progression.

Despite Bishop Adalbert's proselytizing and the Greenlandic infatuation mentioned above, Greenland's Scandinavian colonists had already inspired mixed feelings in the Catholic hierarchy as their vacillating faith had already been noted in their bishopric. Adam of Bremen summed it up, saying: "The folk of this country call themselves partly Christian, although they have no faith, confession, or baptism. They can even be Christians and still invoke Jupiter and Mars (Thor and Odin)."[9]

Even the zealous Adalbert had noted the singular nature of the Scandinavians, but he preferred to detour around the obstacle rather than confront it, to coax rather then bother, a policy that appears to have been successful judging by Adam of Bremen's enthusasm. "Archbishop Adalbert persisted in encouraging the conversion of the pagans tirelessly and never complaining, which was the most appropriate way of dealing with these people."

Starting from the eleventh century, we can already feel the first stirrings of what Viking-church relations would be in the centuries to come. The problems mentioned by Adalbert resurfaced in the thirteenth, fourteenth, and fifteenth centuries. Among his complaints we find that the bishops were selling their blessings and the people did not want to pay their tithes, as well as the generally debauched nature of the Scandinavians.

The flock's response to their shepherd: his bishops would not attend the synod he planned, with the support of the pope and the Danish king. He was forced to cancel it. In the same vein, a century later we find the same awkwardness among the clergy and the same reluctance of its members to assume their posts in Greenland.

In the story of Einar Sokkason* we have the example of the Norwegian clergyman Arnaldr being named the bishop of Garðar by

---

*The story of Einar Sokkason found in *Grænlendinga Þáttr* and *Flateyjarbók* tells of the establishment of the Greenland bishopric in Garðar during the twelfth century under the reign of King Sigurðr Jórsalafari. In this saga, the opposing interests of the bishopric and the secular authority clearly appear in legislation concerning ownership of shipwrecks, which ended up causing bloody retaliations.

Archbishop Azder of Lund in 1124. His response is noticeable for its lack of enthusiasm. "Einar answered that he was little tempted to undertake that [expedition] for he would then have to deal with a quarrelsome people [the Scandinavians]."[10]

Two centuries later, the situation remained the same, as we shall see later in detail with Jón Skalli's nomination in 1343. In a broader Scandinavian context, Christianization did not occur smoothly. There is no need to recall the policy of Olaf II Haraldsson, and the accounts of the Icelandic or Greenlandic situation point to the fact that Christianization of the Norse dependencies—with a few small variations—took place with no indulgence. For this reason I reject the notion of a problem-free Christianization described by J. Berglund. I am striving to cast a new light on the unknown and fundamental development of Greenland and what is probably one of the keys to Norse history. The early existence of a cathedral and diocese in Vestribygð is still clouded by obscurity. In fact, the Steiness church reappears in medieval source materials often as an episcopal residence. For example, Theodore Torfeus quotes Ivar Bårdsson: "There is a large church in Vestribygð, that of Steiness, which for a time was a cathedral and episcopal see." Björn Jonssön of Skardså in his description of Greenland corrected by Theodore Thorlak[11] places this church in Straumfjord. There is a bay called Straumfjord in the western colony, and I think it was on this bank that the Holy See of Straumnes was located."

The disappearance of this See seems to coincide with Bishop Erik Upsi's departure for America and the rise of Garðar.

## DISTINGUISHING FEATURES OF THE NORSE CHURCH

In several respects, the Icelandic model illustrates Greenlandic reality well, and the organization of the church does not escape this rule. Gunnar Smedberg describes the Nordic church system particularly well in his book *Nordens första kyrkor* (*The First Nordic Churches*). The organization he depicts spilled far beyond Scandinavia as it is found in England and the Orkneys.

The essential difference between the Nordic Church and the "mother" Church resides in the fact that the walls of the church were private property and all that implies. A critical reader can easily imagine the repercussions of a situation like this. Churches were built by the community, which required a preliminary condition: a society of free peasants. This was an unthinkable situation in regions of economic feudalism.

The church as private property system was dominant during the early Middle Ages, and even during the time of the Carolingian Empire. From the perspective of the Roman Church, this was not only unsatisfactory but downright irritating. Smedberg even gives an example of Icelandic Catholics of Skáholt and Holar working on a privately funded building.

This distinctive feature of the Icelandic church was pointed out by Jette Arneborg: "The religious buildings were constructed on rural lands where the owner did not only own the church but also had the right to collect its revenues."[12]

Vera Henriksen, picking up the threads of Keller's work, is also in agreement about the conflict of customs that put church and colonists in opposition. The property right of the church walls was a source of discord for a long time during the Middle Ages. It was not necessarily the rule that the institution of the church owned its buildings. Until a later time (1300), several churches were *owned* by private individuals in Iceland, the Faroe Islands, and probably Greenland.

As Arneborg noted earlier, Henriksen stresses that in material terms the clerical taxes (tithes, for example, which will be looked at later) went to the church owners who could be a merchant, or a group that joined to build the church. It is therefore obvious that this went against the church's own interests causing great friction. This kind of privilege must have caused a good deal of gnashing of the teeth.

It is just as unthinkable that the church did nothing, that it did not use every means in its possession—a glance at the summary list strengthens my opinion as well as union with royal authority—to regain possession of its walls and dividends. Smedborg draws a distinction between two categories of Icelandic churches:

The "individual" churches* (*privat kyrkor*) constructed for the use of a single family. During pagan times, the dead were buried around the farm. The building of a church and adjacent cemetery had to have been a natural consequence of this practice. Later these churches served as chapels.

The churches with owners (*egen krykor*) built for a community larger than a parish. These churches were private property. In other words, their owner received the community's tithes and could do with them as he liked. It could be said that this kind of construction was a very good investment.

Keller is also a valuable source. He informs us that during the Middle Ages, the parish was essentially an economic concept. According to canon law, only bishops could organize parishes and define their borders. The parish church appears as a church with a priest and a cemetery. The tithes of the parish were paid to him. This church could be private property. Cathedrals and monasteries were often not part of the parish system. Exceptions existed, though, which is why their size in Iceland often varied.

In Norway, they could contain nine to ten farms.

In Iceland there was considerable variety and the church owners received Heimatiunt (tithes). Cleasby describes this as "home tithe, the tithe of the estate on which the church is built, to be paid to the lay landlord."

The "semi-churches" did not have resident priests. Some had the right to perform funerals.

The annual tithe was introduced into Iceland in 1096 to 1097 and represented 1 percent of total properties. The revenue was not based on current real revenue but on the value of the property based on a fixed interest rate of 10 percent. This practice was unknown in other countries. It originated in the Carolongian tithe in Saxony. Some people see

---

*Keller translates this as "Farm churches," which I find a bit vague.

a parallel here with the tithe of Celtic Brittany. Keller and Smedberg see the parish system as a result of the tithing system.

The owner benefited from numerous advantages while the parish priest "owned" the parish. Smedberg believes it was the case of the person who "owned" the office, in which the priest was described as the one who "owns the benefits."

Possession in the Scandinavian sense of the word *eiga* was seen in a very broad sense, designating both rights and privileges. This use of the word is more in keeping with Germanic law than Roman law.

Thanks to this description of the clerical administrative system, Keller and Nørlund interpret Ivar Bårdsson's description as that of a parish system. In concrete terms private ownership of a church was a good investment, reflected by a certain affluence that crowned the Greenland Church. Indeed, it has nothing to do with poverty if we go by the descriptions of the church's possessions,* other sources (the wedding at Hvalsey Church in 1408), and first and foremost, archaeology. The buildings were generally larger than those in Iceland and in the same lineage as those of Norway. Garðar is impressive: the natives dubbed it "Igaliku," which literally translates as "big cooking place." Hvalsey had respectable proportions with regard to the limited number of the faithful. Several of the sixteen churches even had a wooden wall, practically nonexistent in Greenland.

We should recall, however, that the inspiration and the architects came from Norway, just like the bishops, as Berglund showed convincingly in 1982. Beauvois considers the twelfth century to as the most prosperous period for the Greenland Church although it only represented one-third of an ordinary bishopric. Keller adds the thirteenth century to this prosperous period for both these centuries were quite active in church construction. Garðar was expanded after 1225, and Keller views this as a sign of economic prosperity. We could perhaps add the fourteenth century, given the assiduous foreign presence, which was surely not there for solely altruistic motives. Nevertheless, we should not underestimate a weakening of Scandinavian authority.

---

*See the Eystribygð map (fig. 2.7) with the church's possessions based on Ivar Bårdsson's text.

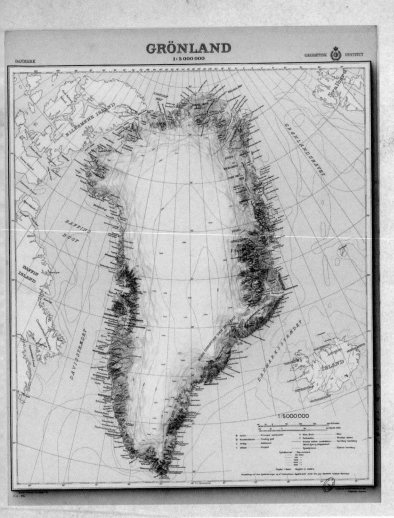

**Plate 1.** Map of Greenland, 1937
*Courtesy of Danish Geodata Institute*

**Plate 2.** Greenland, Brattahlið ruins: this is at the spot known as "the steep slope," where Erik the Red settled as leader of the Norse colony at the very start of the colonization in 985. One notable historical irony: the current inhabitants are pursuing the same kind of farming activities as the Viking-era inhabitants.
*Photo by J. Privat*

**Plate 3.** Reconstruction of the Brattahlið church (Qassiarsuk today): with its low circular surrounding wall it is strongly reminiscent of the Celtic influence discussed in chapter 9. It is consistent with the first generation of churches with its incorporation of an insulating layer of peat.

*Photo by J. Privat*

**Plate 4.** Greenland, reconstruction of the Tjodhild church: Tjodhild, the wife of Erik the Red, converted to Christianity. The main entrance looks out over the fjord. Notable is the extreme simplicity of the building (Qorlotoq type), which contrasts greatly with the development of more impressive religious constructions (Garðar, Hvalsey) inspired by continental models.

*Photo by J. Privat*

**Plate 5.** Brattahlíð: Reconstruction of a typical Viking longhouse completely covered with a layer of a natural insulating material. We also see here a traditional Viking characteristic, an overhang with a bird's-eye view of the entire fjord for obvious defensive purposes.
*Photo by J. Privat*

**Plate 6.** Reconstruction of the interior of a Viking house with a central hearth. This loom reminds us that the heavy Norse homespun cloth was extremely sought after throughout Europe, and even served as currency.
*Photo by J. Privat*

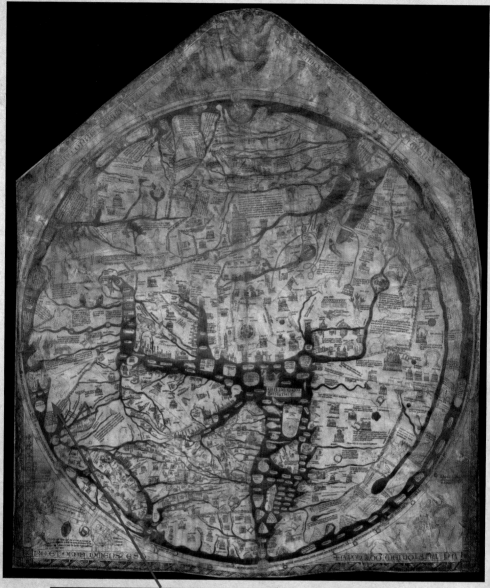

**Plate 7.** The Mappa Mundi
of Hereford, 1289
*Wikimedia Commons*

**Plate 8.** A detail of the Mappa Mundi
of Hereford, 1289
*Wikimedia Commons*

**Plate 9.** A detail from Martin Behaim's globe, 1492, which talks of an "Eisland" whose inhabitants are Christians of imposing appearance
*Private collection, original Germanisches National Museum, Nuremberg*

**Plate 10.** A detail from Martin Behaim's globe, 1492. This would be one of the first definitive depictions of the North American continent.
*Private collection, original Germanisches National Museum, Nuremberg*

**Plate 11.** Greenland: icebergs in Eriksfjord (Tunulliarfik). This was the magnificent landscape that greeted the Norse colonists of Dyrnæs. Archaeological excavations have revealed an Inuit presence in the region. Today this is the site of the small village of Narsaq.
*Photo by J. Privat*

**Plate 12.** A dragon's head that is highly reminiscent of those sported as figureheads on the prows of the famous "drakkars" (Tenerife).
*Property of Per Lillieström, photo by Lars Peter Amundsen*

Plate 13. Sixteenth-century gargoyles in Tenerife (Icod de los Vinos, Santa Cruz) that are oddly reminiscent of pagan Viking art. In Icod de los Vinos, they are found in the former lower-class neighborhoods of the plantation slaves.

Plate 14. A detail of the 1547 French world map known as the "Dauphin" from the cartography school of Dieppe illustrating the Roberval expedition. Canada is on the left, where we can read upside down "The Land of the Laborer," an obvious reference to the Norse and their farming activities.
*Wikimedia Commons*

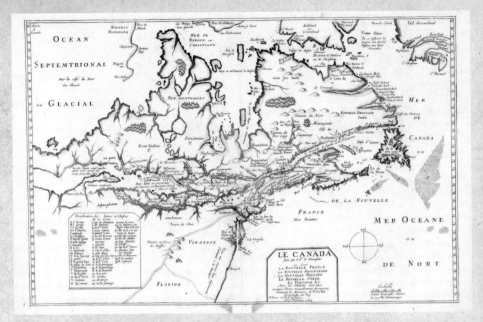

**Plate 15.** The 1664 map of Champlain (based on a 1612 original). Note at the top to the right the traditional Greenland presented as "old Greenland," across from its twin in America: "Greenland or Estotiland." I believe this to be an obvious reference to one same people who had abandoned the original Greenland. Norumbega is adjacent to New England.

***Wikimedia Commons***

**Plate 16.** Portolan by Diego Homen testifying to the tragic fate of medieval Scandinavian Greenland, which it presents as "desertibuzos Terra agricole" (deserted farmland).

Portolan on the East Coast of America, *London, 1558; original in the British Library*

Keller also notes a concentration of churches around Garðar during the final periods of construction. This may possibly be seen as a consolidation of clerical power. However, Keller adopts a slightly more reserved position that doesn't view this Greenlandic luxury as a sign of power. Personally, I would take a more nuanced position and say that this power was later and more precarious. We cannot deny though a sign of wealth objectified by commercial involvement with foreigners. Keller can only underscore it: "The parish churches (or their owners) owned considerable properties that are not mentioned in Ivar Bårdsson's description, for example farms, or parts of farms."[13]

There is a semi-obvious link between social status and church ownership in Greenland. Nørlund sees them as going hand in hand: "The large churches were built near the farms of the great leaders."[14]

This did not prevent the existence of churches in smaller settlements. Keller sees Bårdsson's description in his 1360 document as that of a diocese. He simply describes *the parishes and zones of tithes,* which would explain the lower number of churches mentioned in his report in comparison of those found by archaeology. We should also note that, quite ironically, Herjolfsnes doesn't appear although it was considered to be a "wealthy church."*

Did this church avoid tithing? (This seems very inconsistent for what could be considered as the primary commercial port of medieval Greenland.) This text seems to be more in agreement with a similar Icelandic document that is filed in the *Máldagi,* a kind of church inventory that lists the properties, funds, and revenues of its parish churches.

An example similar to Bårdsson's work can be found in Iceland. This

---

*Berglund considers this absence rather as an omission by the scribe, for according to the excavations, the Herjolfsnes Church was used until the fifteenth century. Another element may have played in favor of this omission: the fact that Ivar Bårdsson wrote that the Aros Church in neighboring Ketilsfjord now owned everything ("*quod templum ab exteriori parte omnia ad Herjolvsnesum usque possidet, insulas, scopulos, marisque ejectamenta ab interiori parte omnia ad sinum usque Pétri . . .*" For Berglund, the Herjolfsnes Church was not a "land owner" but drew its wealth from the sea, fishing, hunting, and commerce. This could explain its absence from Ivar Baadsson's list.

is the *Kirknotra* of Bishop Pål Jónsson circa 1270 describing the fjords and churches of Skálholt Diocese: "The *Máldagi* was a church document (a list or inventory) indicating to whom the church was dedicated, the list of church properties, and generally everything it contained."[15]

Keller leans toward a dual use of Bårdsson's description, in other words, a census of churches and *Máldagi*. The description of Greenland could have been copied from documents like these, either by Ivar Bårdsson or someone else on his return to Norway: "In all cases, Ivar Bårdsson brought this information back to Norway, either in the form of original documents or in the form of extracts from such documents."[16]

Another distinctive feature is that the private ownership of churches not only had material implications but spiritual ones as well. In plain English, although not a member of the clergy, the church owner had a say in religious matters, so to speak. "The Icelandic leaders and the Greenland Vikings held considerable religious power until the thirteenth century reformation of the Church, and probably for longer in Greenland."[17]

Keller discusses the considerable influence on spiritual issues held by those who controlled or "owned" the local churches. As Greenland and Icelandic society were quite singular, a free peasant could own a church, something that would have deeply shocked a southern cleric. Keller gives an example of religious authority held by church owners circa 1164 to 1180: "If a man needed last rites and the priest of the faith could not come, the person owning the parish church should then anoint [the dying man]."[18]

Smedberg similarly tells us that some "half-churches" (without resident priests) had the right to perform funerals, and it was common for the church owner to ordain himself as priest.[19] "The owner of a church [in Iceland] did not always need to hire a priest. He could always ordain himself. According to the saga on Iceland's Christianization, the majority of the powerful men—*virdigamenn*—received a teaching or were ordained as priests."

The celibacy rule was also quite fluid: "Church officials often had families and were as involved in the secular community as in other countries."[20]

All these elements helped the elite (primarily) amass considerable religious and political power. Seen from another angle, this ensured that the church had a very weak position. The elite's power formed an obstacle to a strong and independant church that had few means of pressure at its disposal. The bishop's maneuvering room was quite limited:

> Refusal to consecrate a church. It can be seen that many churches of the earliest period of Norse Christianity were not consecrated. This infers a strong majority of church owners and makes it easier to grasp the keen opposition the claims of the Roman Church aroused.
>
> Excommunication, the refusal of sacraments or communion. This second alternative seems it may have played a decisive role in Greenland as some texts seem to refer to Greenland and Canadian colonists as excommunicated.*

In a broader context, if we consider its neighbor Iceland, a rapid scan of its history reveals the church's dependency on its allies. Only sole clerical executive power was restricted. To sum up, it is safe to say that as opposed to southern Europe, the church did not wield economic or spiritual power during its first years in Greenland, much, if not too much, to the displeasure of the Catholic hierarchy.

An indirect consequence is that this distinctive feature of Nordic clerical administration allows us to get a glimpse of the structure in Greenland and how it developed. Strengthened by this information, Keller advances the possibility of a preservation of the sociojudicial structure similar to that of the twelfth to fourteenth centuries (thus the private property church and all its consequences).

A confirmation could be found in the small size—or rather the persistence of the same size—of the Brattahlið churches II and III, despite the presence of a larger congregation for the latter. Keller concludes from this that the size of the church reflects an earlier sociojudicial structure.

---

*Recall the theories of Thalbitzer, Gini, and Fægri discussed earlier, but more importantly the Roman Church's own admissions (summary list, chapter 9—years 1278 to 1279).

Eugène Beauvois concludes that Nordic tithes were not very profitable. Half went to Avignon, the other half to the King of Norway as collection and travel expenses: "This is not the lone example that shows the pontifical impositions were neither heavy nor ruinous and did not give the advantages that have been described to the pope's treasure."[21]

Often these tithes were never paid. This is surely the angle from which this issue should be approached: not the clerical taxes actually paid by the colonists but those they were asked to pay. According to the documentation cited throughout this chapter, the demands were many.

The six-year tithe was a tax to finance the Crusades. Pope Gregory X established it in a letter addressed to the archbishop of Nidaros on September 20, 1274, in Lyon. Vera Henriksen summarizes the clerical taxes of Greenland and explains how the tithe worked. This tax was divided into quarters: one-fourth going to the bishop, one-fourth going to the parish church, one-fourth going to the priest, and one-fourth to the region's poor.

This tax—according to Henriksen—was introduced by Bishop Arnald in 1126. She believes it would be difficult to make a case that this was the origin of the Greenland uprising a century later. The tithe of the year 1327 is quite well documented because two papal envoys, J. De Serone and B. Ortolis, crisscrossed Scandinavia to collect tithes and Peter's Pence (*Denarius Santi Petri*). Using the *Regesta Norvegica*, Keller drew up a table of comparative tithes.

| THE 6-YEAR TITHE OF 1327[22] | |
|---|---|
| Oslo | 5,002 marks |
| Nidaros | 4,207 marks |
| Bergen | 2,700 marks |
| Hamar | 1,571 marks |
| Stavanger | 1,132 marks |
| Orkneys | 768 marks |
| Greenland | 254 marks |
| Total | 15,634 marks |

Keller notes that Greenland's payment is only 1.62 percent of the total tithe, 5.08 percent of Oslo's payment. Greenland would therefore be the country that contributed the least to this six-year tithe of the entire kingdom of Norway. Keller notes pertinently that this is not necessarily due to the poverty of the Greenland economy but could just as easily reflect the colonists' reluctance to pay this tax. In 1270, a new tax was introduced into Greenland: Peter's Pence, or *Roma skattr* (Roman tax). Norway had been paying it since 1152 or 1153. It was applied to Iceland in 1275. The time lag of its application to Greenland more than a century after Iceland is quite noticeable. During this time period, isolation or navigational problems were not an issue. Henriksen argues that this minuscule amount could not have sparked such problems. Every man or woman possessing three silver marks, weapons, and frock coat had to pay one penny a year (the weight of a mark was about 214 grams; 240 pennies was equal to one mark, although Keller claims it was 216 and also points out that the papal envoys even suggested 192 pennies for a mark). The poor were exempted from paying this tax.

| PETER'S PENCE FOR THE YEAR 1327[23] | |
|---|---|
| Oslo | 53.52 marks |
| Bergen | 30 marks |
| Nidaros | 27 marks |
| Stavanger | 10.67 marks |
| Hamar | 10 marks |
| Greenland | 6 marks |
| Skáholt | 5 marks |
| Faroe Islands | 1.125 marks |
| Total | 143.315 marks |

Keller views the Greenland payment as surprisingly high compared to the other dioceses. In comparison, Greenland's percentage of the six-year tithe only represented 1.71 percent of the total, not including the

Orkneys. Greenland's payment of Peter's Pence represented 11.21 percent of that collected in Oslo, whereas the same tithe climbed to 5.08 percent. This tax could help us better evaluate the Greenland colony's as it corresponds to the sum paid by each family: "Each family of Sweden and the entire Norwegian kingdom paid a penny as filial tribute, or Peter's Pence to the sovereign Pontiff."[24] Using the exchange rate provided by Keller, of one mark equaling 216 or 192 pennies, we get:

6 marks × 216 pennies = 1,296 pennies/or families; one five-member family would give us 6,480 inhabitants

6 marks × 192 pennies = 1,152 pennies/or families; 5,760 inhabitants

Keller expresses reservations as these figures surpass by two or three times the number of ruins that have been found. It is quite likely that the pence tithe of 1327 combined several years (sporadic contact), equaling:

1,296 pennies over six years = 216 pennies/families, with an arbitrary average of five members = 1,080 inhabitants

1,296 pennies over three years = 432 pennies/families = 2,160 inhabitants

1,152 pennies over six years = 192 pennies/families = 960 inhabitants

1,152 pennies over three years = 384 pennies/families = 1,920 inhabitants

These figures could leave out sites that were too remote to pay the tithes. What we have here is a minimal evaluation if we consider the size of Nordic families. De Roo (1900) suggests another calculation, referring to the unit of the families' payment as "skillings":

1 mark = 8 aurar

1 aurar = 144 skillings

Thus 6 marks paid in the year 1327 = 48 aurar; 48 × 144 skillings = 6,912 skillings

6,912 skillings over six years = 1,152 families, with an average of five members/ family = 5,760 inhabitants

6,912 skillings over three years = 2,304 families = 11,520 inhabitants

Berglund analyzes the clerical taxes as determinants. In his opinion, the tithes and taxes for financing the Crusades divided Greenland society even further. Berglund also sees this policy as part of a vast movement encompassing the whole of Europe. He insists on the combined and harmful effect of clerical claims and Norwegian royal authority. Greenland would be more dependent—at least in theory—on the faraway metropolis. The earlier customary relationship between Icelandic families and their Greenland cousins would take a completely different turn.

## THE CHURCH TAKES CHARGE

I have repeatedly underscored the annoyance the unique nature of the Nordic Church must have inspired among the highest authorities. On this theme, Krogh makes clear that the existence of the church as a private property system in Greenland and Iceland could not be tolerated by the Catholic Church over the long term.

The church's attempts to restore order were many and a long-term undertaking. In a broader context, Pope Gregory VII had begun his reform in the first part of the tenth century. His intention was to free the Church of all secular influence, both spiritually and materially. Gregory VII's conflict with Emperor Henry IV is well known. His reform would lead to a compromise. Instead of an owner, a church could have a patron that supervised it and made use of its resources while the priest took care of the spiritual side.

This arrangement was introduced in 1152/1153 in Norway. It would be another century before it made its way into Iceland (1253), where canon law was accepted although Roman law and Germanic law were at odds. Again, a distinction must be made between introducing a change and its acceptance—this also is a matter of time.

Keller merges the period of 1152 to 1153 with that of 1261 to 1264 with all its laws and prescriptions introduced by the Norwegian kings to try to bring clerical reform to Iceland and Greenland, after this country became part of the Norwegian crown.

In theory, the law of the church had to prevail over that of the country. In 1190, the archbishop Erik of Nidaros forbade the *godar*

(Icelandic judicial district chiefs) to be ordained as priests in order to prevent a blend of clerical and secular administration. An apparently trivial event actually illustrates quite well the change in course. It is worth noting that at the beginning of the twelfth century, political authority moved from Brattahlið—cradle of Greenland colonization— to Garðar, the seat of the bishopric.* This is very well depicted in the story of Einar Sokkason in which the quarrel between Bishop Arnald and several Norwegians concerning a shipwreck and its goods was judged by the Thing at Garðar.

The thirteenth and fourteenth centuries would be the stage of a trial by strength between these two diametrically opposing interests. Of all Scandinavia, Norway was the first to return to the fold of the Roman Church. After a long dispute, canon law triumphed in 1152/1153, free-ing the church from secular administration and control. This put an end to the construction of privately owned churches in Norway. The process was then initiated for the private churches on Iceland and Greenland.

In 1246, Olaf was ordained as bishop of Greenland. In 1247, he arrived in Greenland bearing the new laws and new taxes of King Håkon Håkansson.

Starting from the 1260s, Iceland and Greenland fell into Norwegian control, and the organization of the church became a royal matter. Greenland's subjugation by Norway in 1261/1262[25] only aggravated the situation there. Norway established or tried to establish a monop-oly there on commerce and external relations. Berglund views this as a decisive factor: "This burden seems to have represented more than (Greenland) society could tolerate."[26]

Bishop Olaf of Garðar attended the coronation of Jon Raude in Nidaros in 1267 (he returned to Greenland in 1271). Keller thinks that, given the simultaneous presence of his Icelandic colleague Bishop Árni, who was particularly noted for his efficiency, Olaf could have had the same mission in Greenland. Although material proofs are lacking, it is hard to imagine a different clerical policy from the one being imposed in

---

*Just as at the end of colonization, during the decline of the church in Greenland, the Thing returned to Brattahlið.

Iceland and Norway. To the contrary, the presence of Greenland's Bishop Olaf during this crucial period of taking charge reinforces this hypothesis.

Henriksen connects Árni's journey to Norway (1262) to the opposition of some Greenlanders to Norway's supervision; this would explain the detour to Iceland to contact his colleagues, and possibly Earl Thorvaldsson (1208/09–1267), an eminent leader, as well as King Magnus the Lawmender's man. Henriksen only raises part of the problem for, as we shall see later, serious difference of opinion opposed Garðar and the colonists, so serious it led to the excommunication of some of them.

Between 1268 and 1282, Archbishop Jon Raude tried to introduce a new ecclesiastical law in the spirit of the Gregorian reform into Norway. One of the new bishops of Skáholt's directives was to end the private ownership of churches, which sparked fierce opposition.

Royal fines and threats of excommunication rained down. In the end the Norwegian law (Járnsida) was accepted in 1271 to 1273 thanks to Bishop Árni Thorlaksson. It would be replaced by the *Jónsbók* in 1281.

In Iceland, in 1275, a new ecclesiastical law appeared on the request of Bishop Árni (half of the tithes should go to the priest and to the church), but it only applied in Skáholt. It would not be accepted in Hólar until 1354.[27]

Similar opposition appeared in the Faroe Islands circa 1300, culminating with the expulsion of Bishop Erlund (the same conflicts also occurred on the Isle of Man).

In Norway, King Magnus Håkonsson and Archbishop Jon Raude found a compromise in clerical and secular rights with the Tønsberg concordat in 1277. However, harmony was not universal. Violent reactions continued to brew, forcing the archbishop to flee to Sweden in mid-September of 1282. The agreement was rescinded. On the death of King Magnus Håkonsson (in 1280) the original owners of the properties renewed their demands.

The year 1297 marks an important date, with royalty and clergy placing their interests in common. This was the *saettergerd um stadamál* accord (an agreement ending with the sharing of roles), obtained with the help of King Erik Magnusson, regarding the divvying up of church property.*

This was formally the end of the private ownership of churches system. Keller places this concordat between King Magnus Håkansson and Archbishop Jon Raude of Nidaros in the year 1277. According to him, the archbishop no longer had any authority in the selection of the king and the king no longer had any right to meddle in church affairs as defined by canon law. This agreement met stiff opposition and was never completely effective.

Nevertheless, a good number of Icelandic churches continued to be "private property" during the entire Middle Ages, for as we have seen earlier, the economic implications were not trivial. This property system allowed the local "elite" to increase their power and their budgets as the majority of church owners believed that the tithes and revenues of the church were free for them to use as they chose.

The year 1297 appears to be a pivotal date. As the case of Iceland was—in theory—settled, the pressure applied to Greenland became stronger. However, Greenland resistance was stubborn and more enduring than that of the Icelanders, judging by the complaint lodged by Bergen's Bishop Håkon, the 1342 note, and numerous other claims. The new ecclesiastical law was heartily defended by Archbishop Raude (1268–1269). Recent revelations corroborate the hypothesis of a large wave of clerical reforms throughout Scandinavia.

According to Icelandic sources of uncertain origin, a book of laws, the *Jónsbók,* was introduced in 1281 by Jón Lagman, also known as *Gjalderi* (the treasurer). Keller believes it is most likely that Bishop Olaf also tried to introduce the *Jónsbók.* The *Grønlands Historiske Mindesmærker* cites as one of its original source texts, the lost saga of King Magnus the Lawmender. Finn Magnussen gives us a glimpse of a very old copy of anonymous annals based on an even older original: "In 1280, death of King Magnus, the same year he sent Jón Lagman, who

---

*Smedberg (1972). It should be noted that Keller, citing numerous sources, places this concordat in 1277. This was no defeat for the church as the archbishop retained the right to coin money and obtained recognition and expansion of the church's jurisdictional rights, as well as its right to levy fines and to have its property nonliable to taxation.

was called *Gjalderi* with a (new) book of laws to Iceland. People say this book was also brought into Greenland."[28]

The same thing can be read in Lyschander's *Greenland Chronicle:* "Then Jón 'Gelker' wrote the Icelandic law . . . in intelligible letters and books. It is said this law was also sent to Greenland."[29]

The fourteenth century was particularly rich in events involving the church as we saw in the chapter on Norse written sources. This is the century that witnessed the culmination of all the clerical efforts to craft a policy for socioeconomic and religious reorganization. Here are a few examples:

In Nidaros, Archbishop Pål Bårdsson (1333–1346)—no relation to Ivar Bårdsson—was very active in the reestablishment of clerical authority. One year after his coronation, he held a synod on September 22, 1334, in which a six-point document was issued, specifying namely:

The ban on lay people obtaining administrative positions in the church.
The ban on selling church properties.
The cancellation of earlier sales.

The consequences of this latter point for the owners of Iceland or Greenland churches are easy to assess. I will also note the dates when he officiated that fit very well with the written sources and this active, effervescent period from 1340 to 1360, which we looked at earlier: for example, Ivar Bårdsson's journey understood in this slice of time. His passport issued in 1341 falls into the same context. This prompted Keller and Arneborg to connect his journey with some motifs that are quite different from the generally accepted notion of hunting for Skrælings. "Bårdsson acted on his own behalf on economic matters, probably connected with missing payments."[30]

Arneborg "thinks that the Greenlanders [Scandinavians] at a given moment during the middle of the fourteenth century, refused to fulfill their obligations toward the bishop and the Roman Church, and that this was interpreted in Skálholt as a denial of God and the Holy Church."[31]

It should be noted that Philip de Roo a century earlier had placed emphasis on Bårdsson's important position: "Through his office, he was next in dignity to the bishop, equal to abbots, and superior to barons," and also giving him credit for his role as principal officer during the expedition to Vestribygð. Returning to Arneborg's hypothesis, it is far from being an exaggeration if we consider a similar example from the same time during the pontificate of Innocent VI (1352–1362), a strict pope if ever there was one.

Here it is not simple common folk of a remote colony who are being threatened but the King Magnus Eriksson Smek directly. The pope sent him the tax collector, J. Guilaberti, charged with determinging the state of health of the Swedish and Norwegian churches following the Great Plague. "The king was threatened with excommunication. The entire kingdom of Sweden/Norway including Greenland was ordered to con-tribute to cover the pope's debts."*

In 1456, Guilaberti received the full authority needed to back the funds quickly. Finally, King Magnus was excommunicated because of this debt to the pope. These claims by the church are not isolated incidents, as there is also the matter of expeditions into Finland and Russia. All of this stems from the fact that the church's coffers were empty after this troubled and difficult time that left Norway literally decimated.

The series of events and measures concentrated on this period can-not be the work of chance nor can the 1343 nomination of Bishop Jón Skalli of Greenland during the mandate of another bishop (Árni) be interpreted as anything but an attempt to install a loyal man in the Garðar bishopric during a critical period. Jón Skalli would incidentally go on to inherit the bishopric of Hólar in Iceland where he was viewed as a man of the Roman Church.

In 1351, a new measure was taken; the pope requested the Swedish and Norwegian clergy to tax all revenues every four years. Berglund sees this as totally altering the political face of Greenland from that of a peasant aristocracy to one where the church held all power. "Toward the middle if the fourteenth century, it clearly appears that (Greenland)

---

*K. Prytz (1990). We should note that in our case, the archbishop Jon Raude had no prob-lem excommunicating the powerful Norwegian barons for young king Erik (II) Magnusson.

society had been 'feudalized,'* the Church being in fact the real owner of all lands and authority."[32]

Berglund backs Bårdsson's description by maintaining that practically all of Eystribygð belonged to the church. He believes that here the church ideal, the *Civitas Dei* (City of God) had been realized. Berglund stands out from some of the other researchers we've looked at concerning the church question in the sense that he sees this transfer of power as gentle. I would express my reservations about this, given the abundance and emphasis of the exchanges of missives during the pivotal years 1340 to 1360. (These include the two letters dated 1340 of Bishop Håkon of Bergen on the colonists' fiscal insubordination, Ivar Bårdsson's passport date of 1341, the 1342 text on apostasy, the 1345 letter concerning the refusal to pay the tithe, and one earlier duly documented precedent from about seventy years earlier, 1276 to 1279.)

The transfer process took about two hundred years in the form of compensations and indemnifications for tax debt balances and inherited assets. Personally, without rejecting this procedure, I would simply say, bolstered by the facts, that this process could not have taken place without prompting strong reservations. The earlier cited documents (from the years 1340 to 1360) are a direct consequence. The repeated occurence of litigious situations lends strength to my claim of a serious dispute between the Roman Church and the Greenland colonists. It is doubtful that a disagreement with the church—during the heart of the Middle Ages—would not be laden with consequences, and even more so when these disagreements were recurring. For example, between 1276 and 1279, we have at least four exchanges of letter between Archbishop Jón of Nidaros and the (several) popes in Rome. In a letter probably sent before 1276 to John XXI, the archbishop asked the pope's advice on collecting the tithe. We only learn with Pope John's answer dated December 4, 1276,† the reasons for this request for advice. "As the archbishop has notified us of his impossibility to go to

*Keller, when comparing Greenland and Iceland, speaks of the development of a quasi-feudal economy in Iceland.
†The *Grønlands Historiske Mindesmærker* interprets this as a permission to go to Greenland granted to the archbishop. He in fact seemed little inclined to go there.

Garðar during the first five years in order to collect the tithe for the Holy Land, he was given orders to send trustworthy men to receive the tithe of this bishopric."[33] Two years later, in 1278, the archbishop sent Pope Nicholas III a petition in which he reiterated the difficulties in getting to Garðar. During this time, Greenland was not isolated. Was the Little Ice Age solely responsible for these difficulties? I doubt this is the case, for what follows is quite instructive concerning the specific problems in Greenland. We learn, in fact, that the archbishop "recently sent a trustworthy man [to Garðar] to collect the tithe, and *to absolve of excommunication* and exempt from all irregularities those persons who had not paid the tithe. Request is addressed to the Pope to recognize these arrangements."[34]

The conflict was not so much spiritual or even bellicose, but as so well shown by Keller, Arneborg, and others, was of an economic and financial nature. This was not any less serious as it could boil down into opposing the will of the church. In other words, the Greenland colonists were more than reluctant to pay their tithes. We have here in the request of Archbishop Jón a superb confession of the problems encountered by the church, coming from a highly placed member of its hierarchy. Worse, these facts were confirmed a year later (1279) by the supreme authority, Pope Nicholas III. This is his response dated January 31, 1279:

> The archbishop is granted permission to send [people] to collect the tithe over there [Garðar] and in other islands, as well as to lift the excommunication and excuse [the colonists] of any irregularities for matters related to this collection.*

---

*Reg. Vat., folio 126, year 2, n° 39; Reg. Norv. 2, doc. 218. We should point out this sentence in the Dipl. Norv. 1, n° 66, which directly concerns the Greenland clergy: "*Et sub spe nostre ratificationis concessisti eidem, ut **clericos ab excommunicationis sententia,** quam pro eo quod huiusmodi decimam in statutis super hoc terminis non solverunt, incurrerant, absolveret, et cum eis dispenseret super irrgularitate, siquam proindre forsitan contraxerunt.*" Rome January 31, 1279. It is likely that the colonists and the clerics of the colonies were struck by this sentence.

As is easily seen, the condemnable facts are serious, repeated, and not confined to Greenland as implied by the information "in other islands." They confirm, for me, the serious divergences opposing the Greenland colonists and the church. We have here a proven case of sanctions against the Scandinavians, and it seems to me that it would be extremely unlikely that other Norse rebellions in Greenland and Canada were not followed by punishment. We can longer speak of the harsh condemnation by the clergy as a hypothesis as Gini and Fægri did in the 1950s and 1960s. This is a fact and duly noted in the papal archives. Even if Berglund does not appear to agree on the form, seeming to see a peaceful transition that all the elements refute a priori, he is in agreement with the major point—namely, a radical transformation of Greenland society. In fact, he includes in the sphere of authority the church granted itself the total domination of the administration of Greenland society. This was accompanied by the nomination of the men representing the law and the predominant role of Garðar, the episcopal seat but now also the civil and administrative seat.

This analysis matches well Keller and Arneborg's assessment. I would add that this development was, historically speaking, fatal, knowing that the church monopolized all the components essential to power: property ownership, wealth, and—let me say in passing—learning. The majority of written sources that we possess were written by clerics. We have to believe that the Vikings were generally deprived of their ability to fully evolve with history and that after the greatness of the early colonization period the wealthy farmers and local chieftains were overtaken by the multiform power of the clergy.

It should be noted that this same phenomenon of being surpassed appears on the technical level, when the *knörr* and the *langskip* lost their supremacy over the seas, supplanted by Frisian ships (the cog), then Portuguese and Spanish ships of a more commercially profitable tonnage. Greenland society, like Nordic culture in general, gave more weight to the oral, to oaths, to agreements made before witnesses as seen in countless sagas. The major decisions at the Thing were similar.

Returning to the shortcomings of Greenland society in comparison with the efficacy of the clergy, Finn Gad notes that even among the Greenland elite no seal has ever been found. Two worlds, two completely opposing notions came face to face during this time. Before what seems to be akin to a situation of clerical omnipotence in Greenland, Berglund notes that a centralized power in Garðar needed "relays" in the local areas. I noted earlier that a concentration of churches appeared in Garðar's vicinity. I would refer the reader to Berglund's own study with the title "Church, Hall and (Social) Status," which will make it possible to better grasp the extent of the complete change of elements, the large church choir symbolizing quite well the transition to a higher, clearly elitist echelon of the church, a synonym of luxury in Garðar as opposed to the private peasant church that was yet a sign of social distinction. This clearly illustrates the now dominant and prestigious role of the church.

The oral or written tradition of a people can offer great lessons. We have seen this with Inuit culture—it is no less true for Norse culture.

*The Story of Einar Sokkason* confirms that relations were far from idyllic in Greenland between the Scandinavians and the clerical administration. We see here first and foremost a superb illustration of the conflict-of-interest theory with the difference of opinion on property ownership dividing Bishop Arnaldr and the colonists. Arnaldr asked Einar for his support: "I want Einar to swear me this oath, that he will help and uphold the rights of the bishop's see and those properties which are given to God, and chastise those that trespass against them, and be the defender of all things pertaining to the see."[36]

This saga offers a good illustration of the tense climate reigning in Greenland. The noticeable virulence of the text is revealing and goes hand in hand with the almost total silence of the church about its Greenland subjects. This saga is a good reflection of the animosity that ruled between the clergy and the local populace. Here the locals are merchants and peasants. Private and clerical interests were at odds.

A remark made by Bishop Arnaldr is even particularly violent and revealing. It seems completely out of place in this spot lost "at the ends of the earth" and seems like a caricature of the Inquisition in the land of the Inuit. Arnaldr threatens Einar: "I will brand you as a perjurer if you do nothing about it."[37]

Even in faraway Greenland, the church wasn't joking. Recall, if need be, that a certain Kolgrimr was burned at the stake in Greenland in 1407 for using witchcraft to seduce Steinunn Rafnsdottir according to the writ of accusation. We can see here, indirectly, that the clergy's power was well established in Greenland in the fifteenth century. In fact, among a population with a reputation for being cantankerous (according to Bishop Árni's own words)—if not hostile—the church could allow itself the luxury of condemning someone to the stake. I would interpret this indication of the church's existing power. While it didn't have the means to send back all the tithes, it could still crack the whip.

In this context and seen from the viewpoint of the church taking charge, the question raised by Keller concerning Bårdsson is quite pertinent. Why was this inventory created? Was it at the request of the bishopric or was it written in connection with a church reform like that being led during that same time in Norway and Iceland?

The status of churches as private property was in fact a major obstacle to this reform in Iceland. Did Ivar Bårdsson's description share the same intentions?

Keller believes one element would go in this direction: the ownership change at Foss Church. This had been the king's property but was no longer at the time of Bårdsson's description: "The king doesn't own this church, only the collection of benefits."[38]

This transfer process was known in Iceland where the former owner became more or less "responsible" for the same church. Echoing this evolution, we learn that in the middle of the fourteenth century (thus still in the period of clerical effervescence: 1340 to 1360), the bishop of Bergen was responsible for a portion of the administration of royal resources and quite likely the material advantages they offered.

Before looking at the reform attempts, then the transformations strictly speaking, it is necessary to emphasize the considerable repercussions this involved. We have seen that the entire sociojudicial structure as well as the economic infrastructure were deeply enmeshed in this typically northern system. Any change in the clerical organization would automatically bring about a change of social organization, hence the Vikings' fierce opposition. It is this opposition that earned the Scandinavian colonists a solid reputation as pagans. Confirming this theory, Jette Arneborg notes that the changes in the clerical administration brought about the ruin of numerous major families in Iceland, which consequently guaranteed the total control by the Roman Church.

## GREENLAND'S REACTIONS

For contemporary Scandinavian researchers, there can no longer be any doubt about the colonists' attitude. Far too much evidence (both clerical and royal source texts) reflects the obvious ill will of Iceland and Greenland to accept the church rules followed by those of royal authority. Christian Keller suggests the rejection of the 1270 reforms was highly likely after Greenland was made subject to Norway. Just like Vera Henriksen, he nonetheless notes that this rejection was not total; according to a Vatican document, Greenland paid its ecclesiastical taxes (the tithe) by sending five hundred walrus tusks corresponding to six years of taxes, in 1327.

We know that conflicts were numerous in Iceland. Arneborg rightly states that the "private" churches were only "restored" in 1297 in Iceland. If we consider all the "literature" that was produced concerning Greenland, we have to believe resistance was longer and more tenacious there (for example, the 1340 letter of Bishop Håkon of Bergen, Bårdsson's expedition in the 1340s, and so forth).

Keller also connects the contact of Bishop Olaf of Garðar with Archbishop Jon Raude during the first years of his coronation (1267) with the difficulties encountered in Greenland. Bårdsson's description is similarly connected with the church's attempt at a reform. (Arneborg made this same connection in 1988.) The opposition of the Greenland colonists was therefore rather persistent: "It is likely that the hesitation of Greenlanders to abolish the private property system of churches, to pay taxes, and to obey the rules of canon law was the major obstacle."[39]

The examples provided earlier, all duly documented, along with other more insignificant ones, have been gone over with the magnifying glass of contemporary research, giving a completely new and interesting view. But we are soon going to look at the situation even more closely.

## The Revolt of Greenland

The year 1264 could correspond to Bishop Olaf's "improvised" departure date when faced by the protest of the Scandinavian colonists. Sources are discreet on this subject; all we know is that the colonists refused to pay the King of Norway's tax and that Olaf had little enthusiasm for maintaining his presence in Greenland as he pulled off the feat of being absent from his See for nineteen years.

The rhymed chronicle of Claus Lyschander, although later (1608: *Greenland Chronicle*) seems to revisit this event. Beauvois is highly critical of Lyschander as a literary source. Vera Henriksen, on the other hand, is quite positive about his sources, who are none other than Snorri Sturlusson's nephew, Sturla Thordarson.

> *When he [Bishop Olaf] returned to the land*
> *Animosity arose among the populace*
> *Who boldly rebelled.*
> *They wanted no Norwegian taxes.*
> *The boats returned [to Norway] empty.*[40]

In short, we could have here a fictional illustration of the ill will displayed by Greenlanders in response to the church's demands, and what's more, was followed by action. The rest of the chronicle tells us that King Magnus the Law Mender reacted quite aggressively to this, which the source dates as taking place in 1273.

How much of Lyschander's work was borrowed from fantasy and how much was inspired by reality? It clearly seems that there was, if not conflict, at least serious disagreements between the Norse colony and the central authority. Let's recall again the dates of 1278 (raising of the ban of excommunication of the Greenland colonists, which was confirmed by Pope Nicholas III) 1345 (refusal to pay the tithe), and 1355 (King Magnus Eriksson Smek decides to have a Knörr equipped by Powell Knutsson to restore order in the colony). Were troops truly sent to Greenland? In any case, it still served as a source of inspiration for Clause Lyschander.

> *There, the Greenlanders saw*
> *the sparkling swords.*
> *They heard the drums.*
> *The uproar of an entire expedition*
> *Began to show . . .*[41]

The chronicle then says the colonists submitted in the face of such arguments, and the bishop "did what he had to do." We would still like to know a little more.

We have here a fine example of the discretion of the church noted earlier. Henriksen sees the threat of excommunication here along with the threat of the refusal of holy sacraments and burial. According to the chronicle, it was King Magnus's brother-in-law, King Erik Klipping, who sent troops to Greenland at the request of Magnus. After this service, everything was restored to order.

> *They [the Greenlanders] then had to swear an oath,*
> *to pay their taxes as previously agreed*
> *and to acknowledge King Erik Glaepping*
> *As Lord and suzerain . . .*
> *He [probably Olaf] imposed each as was meet.*
> *The boats were laded and set sail.*[42]

The matter was thus efficiently carried out. A rapid glance at my historical summary of the church at the end of the chapter shows that all these facts fit with the period of the church's reorganization at the time when royal authority was precisely becoming a rival again.

If we consider 1270, the year the new clerical tax was introduced, Peter's Pence, we can conclude that by 1278 reluctance toward the new tax had grown rapidly. Rumors of the Greenland revolt circulated in Scandinavia either in 1264 or 1273. The second date seems to conform better to the context. Similarly, Bishop Olaf of Greenland returned .

there in force in 1271 (a year after the new tax). Before 1276, Bishop Jón of Nidaros wrote to the pope (probably Gregory X) about the problems collecting the six-year tithe for the Holy Land. On December 12, 1276, Pope John XXI answered and ordered the Nidaros archbishop to send some trustworthy men to Greenland to collect the tithe. Keller credits this action to a Greenland revolt during the 1270s, which he saw as a protest of the large church property owners against the clergy's attempt to "deprivatize" the churches.

The year 1340 offers other duly dated examples. There are two letters from Bishop Håkon of Bergen intended for King Magnus Eriksson Smek. Håkon complains that the Greenland subjects refuse to pay their taxes directly to him. Keller and Arneborg give credence to this source. "He [the bishop] did not have complete control over the countries imposable revenues because the contributors only recognized their debt to the king."[43]

Speaking plainly, the Greenland Vikings did not want to pay their taxes to anyone but the king and therefore posed a challenge to the bishop's authority as a tax collector. We know that toward the middle of the fourteenth century, the bishop of Bergen had obtained a part of the administration of royal resources. Obviously, the Greenland colonists had a completely different opinion in the matter. Events then seem to fall into place one after another in a beautiful design with a perfect logic:

**1341:** A year after sending his complaint to the king, Håkon issues a passport for Ivar Bårdsson. Keller believes his departure was on August 11, 1341.

**1342:** A note tells us that the Greenland colonists have abandoned the Christian faith.

**1343:** Jón Skalli is named bishop of Greenland (while Bishop Árni was still alive). I share Jette Arneborg's analysis of these events: "There is an indication that something serious was taking place in Greenland involving the Catholic Church."[44]

Concerning 1341, given the absence of other documents, we can only speculate about Bårdsson being issued a passport. However, 1342 and 1343 have been the focus of studies and pertinent observations I plan to touch on below.

Among the most extreme reactions of the Scandinavian colonists, I must mention the apostasy, which is certainly not the most unlikely hypothesis. Corrado Gini has focused on this point emphatically. He pertinently points out that *this mass apostasy was admitted* by the Catholic Church. In fact several sources refer to the Scandinavian colonists as "apostates." This cannot help but bring us back to Thalbitzer's theory about the *Excominquois.*

Gini points out that the church forbade any relationships between Christians and native pagans, and clerical authorities would either deny or hide transgressions of this nature. In favor of his argument, we must acknowledge that no source texts tell of any cases of Vestribygð refugees entering the southern colony. So, the Vestribygð colonists made no attempts to continue their traditional lifestyle.

As Fægri views it, rather than typical apostasy (renunciation of the faith) it could be a case of excommunication levied by the church for anyone any one adopting an indigenous lifestyle. This would be akin to renouncing the values of Western civilization, and consequently apostasy. This is completely plausible. Corrado actually concedes: "It is unlikely that the union of Scandinavians with the Eskimos was not followed by the apostasy of the Scandinavians."[45]

I would like to share a personal hypothesis concerning the Norse defection in 1342. The rebellion of the western colony could be summed up this way. This colony had the privilege of concurrently rejecting the clerical administration, and the royal authority and administration. This could be described as a rupture with Christian civilization. Let's not forget that Vestribygð disappeared completely, as if the colonists wished to cut their bridges with the rest of the world, which can be considered as the consequence of the earlier points.

Information concerning this "apostasy" is found primarily in Lyschander's *Greenland Chronicle* (1608) and in the *Icelandic Annals* of Bishop Gisli Oddsson of 1630. I would also like to cite the important texts used by the *Regesta Norvegica,*[46] dated 1278 and January 31, 1279, respectively.

In light of the poor track record of Scandinavian/Church relations, I would like to advance another more anecdotal hypothesis concerning Ivar Bårdsson's expedition. If we follow the arguments made by Arneborg, Keller, and others, who see Bårdsson's expedition as a punitive or coercive operation mounted by the administration, the anecdote of the livestock brought back to Eystribygð could take on a whole new meaning, purely and simply representing the seizure of the goods of those "unruly subjects," the Vestribygð colonists.

Concerning 1343, I would like to first note that this question could be inserted in the following paragraph. It depends on from what angle the events are viewed. I lean toward a Norse reaction against Jón Skalli. We know that he took a rather long time to make his way to his see. In addition, his presence in Garðar was hardly a shining example (nineteen year absence).

Even just a few decades ago, this state of things was quickly blamed on Greenland's isolation and poor communications (this is erroneous). The shock of Jón Skalli's nomination was explained away due to the reasons listed above.

Here again, Arneborg provides a pertinent analysis of the facts that is worth lingering over. In fact, she categorically refutes this interpretation, rejecting the theory of Greenland's isolation as one that is insufficient to explain something so serious as the nomination of a second bishop (Jón Skalli) for the Garðar See while Bishop Árni was still officiating during this same time: "We would rather expect that the archbishop named a new bishop after receiving certain information that such a step was necessary."[47]

Arneborg connects this nomination to the note of 1342 (on apostasy) and sees it as even a direct consequence of it. Bårdsson's receiving a passport follows in the same line and also comes from the same author: the bishop of Bergen, Håkon. These three events combined (1341, 1342, 1343) reveal the worry the high authorities felt about Greenland.

This country was a western dependency subject to taxation. As we've seen in the two letters of 1340, the colonists were refusing to pay their taxes to the bishop. In this context of great agitation, the journey of Ivar Bårdsson and the nomination of Jón Skalli take on their full value, dismissing among others the hypothesis that Skalli was nominated by mistake. It was completely intentional; it was a consequence of these two letters. A discreet remark on the absence of Greenland' new bishop there after his nomination supports this theory: "But he [Skalli] cannot go there [Greenland]."[48]

Jón Skalli's delay has nothing to do with Greenland's isolation or a lack of communication (they were regular until the fifteenth century), or even climate change. Quite simply, the Vikings of Greenland wanted no part of him.

I agree with Arneborg's reasoning, the nomination of Skalli and Bårdsson's journey in fact reveal the colonists' opposition to the Bergen bishopric's demands. What I find particularly interesting here is their refusal to abandon their bishop, Árni, whom they seem to have adusted to comfortably. This would explain why Skalli found it "impossibile" to go to Greenland.

There is also the possibility that Håkon didn't wish to send him but I find that a little illogical as once Skalli was nominated—which already spoke of their disapproval of the Greenland colonists—it would be hard to back pedal without appearing ridiculous in Norway. The sequence of events seems to bear out the Danish researcher's reasoning. In fact, in 1348, Bishop Árni was sent away to the Faroe Islands, which seems like a punishment to me.

Similarly, the nineteen-year vacancy of the Garðar See can be interpreted in two ways: the colonists had rejected Jón Skalli or else they were punished by having no bishop for almost two decades. The two hypotheses are perhaps not devoid of all foundation or are not contradictory, for the result is there, an ecclesiastical void lasting quite a long time. Skalli's own attitude shows little enthusiasm for filling his post in Greenland after Arni's expulsion. I believe it gives substance to the notion of a climate of revolt against the Church. Here is a rapid overview of his absences.

**1349:** Skalli attends the ordination of a bishop in Bergen.
**1351:** He sits in council at Nidaros.
**1354:** Present in Oslo.
**1356:** Present in Avignon.

**1357:** Leaves for Rome to request a transfer to Hólar (this gives the impression he did not have much enthusiasm for Greenland). This is also the conclusion of the *Grønlands Historiske Mindesmærker:* "He (the archbishop of Trondheim) consecrated Jón Skalli bishop of Greenland, but this churchman quickly lost all desire to go to his bishopric."[49] As for the reasons, as the sources remain unfortunately mute, I credit that to the explanations given before. Jón Skalli arrived in Hólar in 1358, but both the clergy and the laymen refused to obey him, considering him bishop of Garðar and not Hólar. He had to return to Rome to get a bull from the pope before finally being accepted. He died in 1390.

**1345:** Fiscal insubordination.

A council was held in Bergen in the archbishop's presence. An attempt was made to obtain a reduction of the tithe. The origin of this initiative is not clear, but the remote western dependencies are germane if we consider that during this same council it was said that Greenland and the Faroe Islands were not sending their taxes. The text is quite ambiguous while it clearly reports this dereliction it gives no reasons. "The Provincial Assembly Council has discussed this request (the request to levy a three-year tithe made by Clement VI) and notes the impossibility of fulfilling this request."[50]

Just as I earlier rejected the maritime isolation of Greenland as an alibi for these numerous derelictions, I reject the argument of the colony's poverty. In fact, a year later the *Icelandic Annals* tell us that "the Greenland knörr arrived overflowing with cargo."[51] If this was so, it is difficult to claim penury. It can be presumed that the church still present in Greenland was aware of this abundance and all the more put out by the colonists' ill will.

If the reader still entertains any doubts about Greenland insubordination, Beauvois tells us that in connection with this council, Greenland and the Faroe Islands stood out from the other Scandinavian countries by abstaining from paying the churchman's travel expenses. The pope's response to the Nordic claims was obviously negative but it was never recorded that the archbishop was able to obtain his taxes.

To sum up, I will recapitulate Arneborg's scenario concerning this critical time and add a few dates:

**1340:** Complaint lodged by Bishop Håkon of Bergen to King Magnus Erikson Smek, following the refusal of the western dependencies to pay their taxes.

**1341:** Passport issued for Ivar Bårdsson for an expedition to Greenland (the connection with the complaint seems quite clear). Likely departure that year according to Christian Keller.

**1342:** Alarmist note from Skáholt concerning the Greenland colonists' abandonment of the faith.

**1343:** Nomination of Bishop Jón Skalli, man of the Roman Church although Bishop Árni was still performing these duties.

**1345:** The tithe was not paid by Greenland and the Faroe Islands.

**1348:** Bishop Árni was sidelined to the Faroe Islands.*

**1414–1424:** Two Icelandic source texts that passed "unnoticed" could, in view of the tense context, be interpreted differently than they have been until now. They are known to figure among the last accounts of the Eystribygð colony and both involve a wedding celebration.

Although the marriage of Digrid Björnsdottir and Thorstein Olafsson (in 1408 in Hvalsey) displayed all the religious guarantees with the presence of Bishop Eindride Andreasson's representative, as well as the seal and blessing of the priest Paul Hallvarsson, and fulfilled all the religious regulations at the Hvalsey Church, a confirmation still proves necessary. In fact, six years later in Iceland, all the witnesses had to swear that "everything took place in conformance with the divine law of the Holy Church." In concrete terms, trust of the Greenland clergy seems to have been limited as their actions were verified by their Icelandic colleagues, if we except Jón Jonsson, who officiated in Greenland.

---

*I have added these last two dates to the scenario presented by Jette Arneborg in the magazine *Hikuin* for it seems that all these events are connected. We could even add 1355 with the mission ordered by King Magnus, and 1360, approximate date when Bårdsson's description appeared.

Sixteen years later (1424) the same scenario took place again: another participant in the wedding, Saemund Odsson, had to give the same testimony, which seems a lot for a simple formality and confirms (as far as I'm concerned) that not only was the Greenland colony distrusted but *its clerical administration* as well.

These two letters could illustrate a certain skepticism of the Catholic hierarchy about accounts of Greenland colonists concerning the requirements and laws of the Roman Church and reserved trust about its own church members. We may ask if the Greenlandic protest may not have contaminated them?

Concerning the wedding question, Arneborg reminds us that marriage banns and the wedding were part of the requirements that the Roman Church imposed on Icelanders during the long religious conflict. The marriage law was introduced in Iceland in 1275 and the banns were established in 1290.

### 1492: Pope Alexander VI's Papal Brief

A controversial letter discovered by Dr. Luca Jelic in the Vatican Archives alludes to the abandonment of the faith by the Greenland Vikings (there are those who maintain this document is a fake). Its author was none other than Pope Alexander VI, a member of the House of Borgia (1492–1503), who was in a position to know. He presided over the famous arbitration between the Portuguese and the Spanish over the divvying up of the New World that culminated in the 1494 Treaty of Tordesillas, which split these lands between those two powers. We shall see that this source document, on the cartographic level—and surely at other levels—is of major importance.

This brief is in response to the monk Mathias, who wished to be named bishop of Garðar, after a long description of the religious vacuum in Greenland for the past eighty years. The late date this was written (1492–1493) stands out. In it the highest religious authority shows his enthusiasm for naming Greenland bishops seems to substantiate a later inhabitation of Greenland, as is reflected by the summary list at the end of the chapter. Here is a revealing extract:

Because of the remoteness of Catholic priests, the majority of the diocese's inhabitants are again refusing—alas—baptism.

To end this section, I would like to cite a text by mathematician Jacob Ziegler, printed in Strasbourg in 1536, but is surely connected as it's title *Schondia* (Scandinavia) is a copy of an older text from the archbishop of Nidaros. Keller, who cites it, opts for Erik Walkendorff. It mentions the same events and the colonists' return to paganism.

> As our Mother Church only looks on the status of the faith of these lands (Greenland) with a carefree attitude, the people there have almost fallen completely into pagan ways, and in addition to their fickle mood, they are particularly drawn to witchcraft. It is said that they brew storms at sea with malefic chants thereby placing foreign ships in great peril, in order to be able to pillage them. They use *skin* craft that fear neither wave nor rock. . . . with which they *attack* the other boats.

The second part is even more disturbing. Not only is there the matter of abandoning the faith (thus apostasy) but also native techniques. Could there be confusion at work here caused by Claudius Clavus's Type B geographical maps? The *Grønlands Historiske Mindesmærker* follows this hypothesis, seeing there an amalgamation with the Sami (or Laplanders). Or is what we have here a description of those Northmen who have embraced the native lifestyle, to the point of mastering the famous *umiaq,* the skin boat mentioned in Greenland tales? Or should we be thinking directly of the kayak as Olaus Magnus clearly did in his famous engravings?

The fact remains that the frequency these allusions occur—namely, to Scandinavians using indigenous techniques or looking like them—is disconcerting and should inspire deeper investigation.

## *The Denouement*

One element that needs to be taken under consideration when we cast a glance at these remote lands is the overall situation and political context of Europe. Although they were quite far away, the islands in the Western Atlantic still suffered their consequences to a varying degree. We have seen that the church's policy in Greenland was part of a vast plan to reorganize the entire Nordic Church. On the political level, we have seen that Greenland was made subject to Norway in 1262. It is certain that policies vary from one king to the next and that the agreement enacted between the royal authority and the church in 1297 under Erik Magnusson would have even greater influence on the course of events in Greenland.

From a geographical perspective, we have been obliged to look away a little from Greenland given the scope of the clerical process in the north. I am not going to attempt to present the history of Scandinavian kingdoms. We should also note the strained relations with the counter-power of the Hanseatic League, which should not be underestimated. Norway suffered greatly from this, which could explain the "distraction" that affected their dealings with their Scandinavian cousins in Greenland, and a transfer of the centers of economic interest. In short, all these factors come into play.

However, it is necessary to point out a historical detail of the fourteenth century that had indirect (negative) repercussions on the life or (fiscal) streak of luck of the Greenland colonists. One effect of the war against the Karelians and the Russians in the fourteenth century (1348–1351, with Novgorod) was to empty the kingdom's coffers. The kingdom administrator, Erling Vidkunsson, acting on behalf of the infant Magnus Smek made an arrangement with the Pope that left him half of the six-year tithe. It was paid in 1327, the intended purpose to finance the war against the Russian and Karelian pagans. The danger was momentarily averted as a peace treaty was signed with the Grand Duke of Novgorod, but this treaty expired in 1348. Magnus Smek prepared to go to war again with the Russians. He even managed to obtain a clerical tax rate from the pope, who promised him half the revenues to cover the expenses of this new war. What's more, the other half of the taxes would remain at the king's disposal as a "papal loan." The war ended in 1351.

We saw from the Nordic source materials discussed in chapter 6

that these same kin were responsible for the mission order given to
P. Knuttson (dated 1355). To this situation can be added the plague
in Bergen and problems stemming from the ever-delicate inter-
Scandinavian relations and foreign relations with Russia and the
Hanseatic League.

In this context, the slow pace of the royal administration and attitude of letting things slide (lack of respect for promises made and consequently the increasing scarcity of maritime relations with Greenland
and Iceland), everything becomes clear, but most importantly this order
of King Magnus takes on an entirely new light.

Jette Arneborg doubts that, riddled with debt as he was, Magnus
E. Smek had ordered this expedition project as a philanthropic act of
assistance to the Vikings. She sees rather a simple means of refilling the
state's coffers. In this scenario, Knutsson would have had "to receive
four years of Nordic contributions from Greenland which came due in
1355."[53] This was a punitive expedition as historian Finn Gad describes
it: "The weapons should not have been used against the Eskimos but
against the (Scandinavian) Greenlanders who by all the evidence were
not very enthusiastic about paying. We don't know if this expedition
took place."[54]

Another important element that I have stressed repeatedly is the
almost general resistance of the western islands, particularly the Faroes,
Iceland, Greenland, and the Isle of Man. The thread tying all of these
revolts together, as shown by Keller, is a Germanic law heritage at total
odds with canon law. In fact the situation was even more tangled. The
church did not only have problems with its faraway Nordic flocks but
with itself.

As Beauvois points out, the Middle Ages is the time of the Great
Schism. Two churches were competing with each other. It is legitimate
to question the neutrality of certain written sources. Were they guided
by objectivity and scientific truth, or did they reflect instead a desire to
obstruct an enemy pope?

From this perspective we have seen that the two popes appointed
rival bishops during the fifteenth century and that both churches gave
out few gifts. The *Grønlands Historiske Mindesmærker* tells us, for

example, that a certain Matheus who presented himself as bishop of Hólar and Skálholt was excommunicated by the archbishop of Norway. This did not prevent him from performing his duties.

In a context like this, we cannot be surprised at the lack of discipline on the part of church members. For example, Bishop Andreas of Garðar (1460) ignored the order forbidding him from taking care of sacerdotal or episcopal matters in Iceland, a ban issued by Matheus, who had also been forbidden from taking office as we saw earlier.

We should note in passing Bishop Andreas's scant interest in his Garðar post, as he refused and remained in Iceland in 1461 to 1462, he then left in 1466 to replace the bishop of Linköping in Sweden.

It is easy to see that the situation was quite confused. One thing is sure, the very poor relations of the Greenland Scandinavians with the church, and what is less well known, its consequences. The inevitable response to refusal to comply with the church's wishes was excommunication. "In the middle of the fourteenth century, the Greenlanders refused to fulfill their duty to the Archbishop and the Roman Church. In Skálholt, this was interpreted as a renunciation of God and the one, true Church."[55]

The church has one radical response to the economic, fiscal, and probably political quarrels that put Rome at odds with the Scandinavian colonists of Greenland and Canada, and one that we could call even commonplace in this period: excommunication, thereby transforming the colonists into apostates. This is the image of the Greenland colonists that would persist even two centuries later when they are described as "straying sheep," manufacturing "pagan idols," or as those who had to be brought back to the right path like the "prodigal son."[56]

For Keller, the idea of a Greenlandic apostasy prevailed a longtime both in Norway and among the Curia. However, despite this Norse flock's defection, bishops continued to be appointed during the entire fifteenth century, and even in 1520 with the bishop Vincentius Petri Kampe.

A priori, this makes no sense if Greenland was deserted. Given the series of nominations there is little alternative: either the Catholic hierarchy was truly ignorant, wearing blinders, and continuing to name bishops, or else there were well-founded reasons for these appointments answering a genuine need. The Greenland Vikings remained longer than has been acknowledged, which would seem to be supported by the fifteenth-century clothing Nørlund found in Herjolfsnes. In the most optimistic scenario, we can suggest until the end of the fifteenth century or even the beginning of the sixteenth century. On the other hand, I doubt they were there alone, or if the Norse presence was predominant.

I would reject the easy solution, and as proof cite the example of Pope Alexander VI that appears in our source texts from 1492. As a specialist in delicate geopolitical matters, it is hard to believe he was ignorant about Greenland. To the contrary, it seems that the church was rather well informed of world affairs and could not at this juncture overlook the presence or absence of its flocks. My question is: Just who were these faithful requiring bishops into the sixteenth century?

It so happens that there was a significant European presence in Greenland precisely during the time of the Nordic decline. I see a causal relationship between this invasive foreign presence and the disappearance of the Scandinavians. These foreigners were moreover very good Christians. I will use two significant details that confirm my personal theory of a regular European presence in Greenland in the fifteenth and sixteenth centuries, particularly Portuguese. I find these two details rather disturbing:

1. All the nominations of bishops show the characteristics of being made provisionally, meaning that the locals had no say in the matter.[57] Speaking plainly, the Norse populace had no voice in the chapter. Was this populace still large? In the context of extremely strained relations we've seen, this could even be a sanction. We have to admit that these bishops were named for parishioners that were allegedly still presence, even if the majority of bishops never made the journey to Greenland.

2. Another even more significant detail but totally unimpressive in the long list of appointed bishops, there appears a Bartholomeus of St. Ypolito (or Hippolyto on the *Series Episcoporum*)[58] with a degree in holy scriptures. He was also a brother in a preach-

ing order. He was named Greenland's bishop by Pope Eugenius (1431–1437) on September 24, 1433, according to a report by Cardinal Conti, and was consecrated at Florence on November 7, 1434.[59] We know next to nothing about him, but he is visibly not Norse.

I would lean rather to a southern churchman, a conjecture reinforced by the little information provided by the *Series Episcoporum*.[60] Bartholomeus is presented under the label O.S.D., which I interpret as Order of Saint Dominic and which brings to mind the Spanish world. The list is fleshed out with ecclesiastical nominations of southern natives for Garðar this entire decade, lending yet more strength to my interpretation. On September 24, 1431, we have Gibelin Volant of the Order of Hermits of Saint Augustine, a minorite penitent at Saint Peter's Basilica in Rome; July 4, 1432, the Franciscan father Jean Herler of Moys de Meissen, and also at Saint Peter's Basilica in Rome. It should also be noted that in 1500, an Italian named Zacharias was named bishop of Garðar.

I have trouble grasping why southern churchmen would be nominated to tend a Scandinavian flock with a reputation for being difficult. There was no lack of trustworthy clerics in Scandinavia.

Perhaps this should be seen as a kind of sanction on the Vikings and the appointment of dyed in the wool churchmen or else we should see this as confirmation of my theory of a very Christian southern presence in Greenland, which necessitated the presence of church officials with strong ties to Rome. We should also recall that Alexander VI desired to recover his power and advantages in the Far North in opposition to the Nordic crown, hence his need to post his own men there.

There is a strong chance that Batholomeus was a native of Spain or Portugal, and he was intended to take care of southern members of the church. In this case, we would see the same process of convergent interests as that of the English merchantmen working hand in hand with the English clergy, following that of the Hanseatic League and the German bishops of Greenland. Portugal followed the same rule.

To conclude this chapter and list all the players involved in the

Christianization of Greenland, all my earlier observations of Celtic influence has prompted me to revise the standard outlines of this process. It was not unilateral—which is to say, Norwegian—nor bilateral, German/Norwegian starting with the influence of Hamburg-Bremen. I have pointed out an unknown phase that involves a Southern European influence. I believe Greenland's Christianization can be summed up as "four phases plus," including a Hamburg-Bremen bishopric phase, a Scandinavian phase, an English phase, and a southern European phase. These four phases were preceded by my "plus," the Anglo-Celtic missionary activity during a very early and poorly known era, when they could have made contact with the first Scandinavian colonists.

To return to the southern Europeans, with these nominations (in addition to the many maritime maps) we have new written testimony—which comes from Rome to boot—crediting a southern presence with the blessing of the Catholic hierarchy who were using it to punish their unruly Nordic flock guilty of apostasy.

We shall soon see that the Portuguese had the "audacity" during the first half of the sixteenth century to refer to Greenland as Portuguese territory, presenting it as "Terra del rey de Portugal" (1502 Cantino map in the Estense Library in Modena, and Maggiolo's 1511 map in Madrid, and so on) and rebaptizing it as Terra de Labrador.

We should recall that the Tordesillas Treaty prepared by Pope Alexander VI cut the Western Atlantic Hemisphere in two with all lands on the west of this line awarded to Spain and all those to the east, to Portugal, which is Brazil in the Southern Hemisphere, and apparently Greenland in the Northern Hemisphere. The presence of southern European Christians in Greenland could explain these continued nominations of bishops to Greenland until quite late.

I can even imagine a more radical hypothesis. It is possible that the Catholic hierarchy did not look poorly on the Portuguese presence in the Far North and in the worst-case scenario even encouraged Portuguese expeditions—such as the Danish-Portuguese expedition of 1473 to Greenland and Canada giving the very Catholic Portuguese carte blanche and even encouraging them to cleanse Greenland of its cantankerous subjects—apostates, remember. The church would thus get its revenge on its recalcitrant sheep, who had already been excommunicated. This would explain the vague nature of the clerical source texts. We should not forget that Spain and Portugal were the world's most ardent defenders of the Christian faith at this time and that this strained relationship between Rome and the Scandinavians would come to an end with their divorce in 1530—this same time period—with the Reformation.

I believe there are too many converging elements heading in the same direction—namely, the Roman Church concerning the fate of the Greenland Vikings—for this to be only the work of chance.

## SUMMARY HISTORY OF HISTORICAL AND RELIGIOUS EVENTS IN GREENLAND

I have added these earlier (and sometimes controversial) facts from before colonization and the Scandinavian period because I believe they are significant coming as they do from the highest religious authorities of the time. They do slightly turn our historical perception around forcing me to, for example, put Erik the Red's "discovery" of Greenland in quotes.

**831–832:** Gregory IV names Anschaire legate of the Holy See of the Northern Peoples, thus Greenland.

**834:** Confirmation of his mission.

**920 (October 29):** John X ratifies Gregory IV's decision.

**982:** "Discovery" of Greenland by Erik the Red.

**985:** Colonization of Greenland.

**1015–1030:** Rule of Olaf II Haraldsson, known as Saint Olaf. Power was divided between crown and church under the Bremen archbishop's authority.

**1025:** Pope John XIX seems to have placed the Greenland Church under the jurisdiction of Archbishop Unwan of Hamburg. Is this the same Olaf figure (*Grónlandinga biskup*) who went to Iceland circa 1021 after the departure of Bishop Bernard and before the arrival of Bishop Kól in 1095(?). Beauvois cites him in his list of transiting bishops, and De Roo in 1039.

**1034:** Greenland was placed under the jurisdiction of Archbishop Adalbert of Bremen.

**1044:** Archbishop Adalbert of Bremen sends Chritian mandates to "the most northern regions of the world."[61]

**1045–1072:** Archbishop Adalbert—best known thanks to Adam of Bremen—crisscrosses the north (Denmark, Sweden, Orkneys, Greenland) to spread the faith. He attempts to free himself of the pope's control.

**1046–1066:** Rule of the Norwegian king Harald Hardråde "the Merciless."

**1052:** A certain Erik (priest or bishop) officiates in Greenland.

**1053 or 1059:** A certain Jón or John appears as bishop on the American continent.

**1054:** Emissaries from Greenland and Iceland arrived in Bremen to discuss religious matters—namely, to ask for priests and bishops.

**1055:** Archbishop Adalbert sent an individual named Albert (or Adalbert) as bishop to Greenland. Victor II's papal bull confirmed the Hamburg Archbishop's jurisdiction over Iceland and Greenland . . . and repeated the similar decrees of his predecessors (Leo IV in March 848, Nicholas I on March 31, 858 or 864, Agapet II on January 2, 952, Benedict IX in 1044 or 1045).

**1056:** Archbishop Adalbert anoints Isleif Gissursson bishop of Iceland, and gives him mandates for the Greenland parishes. He was one of Iceland's most energetic preachers.

**1073:** Pope Alexander II (1061–1073) confirmed archbishop Liemar of Hamburg's jurisdiction over the islands of the north.

**1103:** The seat of the archbishopric of the Nordic countries and kingdoms was transferred to Lund. Adalbert lodged complaints against this decision as being disrespectful of his rights. In 1133, Pope Innocent II would settle the matter.

**1104:** Confirmation of Pope Pascal II's (1099–1118) decision. Bishop Azder of Lund received the pallium that year of 1106. He was still head of the entire North in 1122.

**1112–1121:** Bishop Erik Upse/Gnuppsson, descendant of Ørlyg

Roppsson of a family of large Icelandic landowners, left for Greenland (1112). Crowned by a certain notoriety, he left to explore the northern lands and Vinland. He was a member of the 1121 expedition to "Kroksfjardarheidi" who left a very interesting written account.[62] He died in Vinland.

**1123:** A decision was made during a Thing to create a permanent diocese in Greenland and to achieve this Einar Sokkason was sent to Norway. One particularly significant detail is that this Thing took place in the absence of Erik Upse in Vinland or the North Lands, and made an extremely important decision. It seems clear that the Scandinavians knew their bishop had perished in those remote lands and was not coming back. This implies decent communication between Greenland and the lands to the West, and thus weakens the theory of extreme isolation. Pope Calixtus II restored (partially) the authority of the Hamburg-Bremen bishopric.

**1124:** Coronation of priest Arnald of Lund as bishop of Greenland by Archbishop Azder.

**1125–1150:** The reluctant Bishop Arnold only arrived in 1126, introducing the tithe. He was relieved of his duties in 1150.

**1133:** After numerous complaints from the bishop of Hamburg, Innocent II gave his support to Adalbert's complaints.

**1148:** The construction of the Nidaros diocese.

**1150:** Jón I succeeded him (also known as Knutr, Kutr, Kavttr, Krari, and Knari). He would occupy his post for thirty-seven or thirty-eight years. It is possible that he had one or two coadjutors as the names of Eirik and Harald appear between those of Jón I and Jón II in the *Flateyjarbók*.

**1152 or 1153:** The seat of the bishopric was transferred to Nidaro II under Pope Eugene III (1145–1153).

**1158 (March 16):** Emperor Frederik I confirms the jusridiction of the Hamburg bishops over Norway, Greenland, and so on.

**1177–1198:** Rule of King Sverre Sigurdsson.

**1186:** Presence of Bishop Jón Knutr at the Icelandic Thing while en route to Norway, where he died.

**1188:** Jón Arnason, a.k.a. Jón Smyrill (the black falcon* in *Rimbegla*) was anointed bishop of Greenland (1188 for Beauvois and Henriksen, 1190 for the *Grønlands Historiske Mindesmærker*). He traveled to Rome by way of Iceland in 1202, and it is unclear if he returned to Greenland. He died in 1209.

**1194:** The eastern coast of Greenland, commonly called Svalbard in the Middle Ages, was explored by colonists around Scoreby.

**1212:** Arrival of the new bishop, Helge, son of Ógmund Rakafoll. Died in 1230.

**1217–1263:** Rule of the powerful Håkon IV Håkonsson. A period of stability and close collaboration with the church. Norwegian authority over the western dependencies (Iceland, Greenland, Orkneys) was strengthened.

**1234:** Consecration of Nicholas as Greenland's bishop. He died in 1239 according to the *Grønlands Historiske Mindesmærker* and 1240 according to the *Flateyjarbók*. According to Langebeck and Gams he did not arrive until 1239.

**1246:** Olaf was consecrated bishop of Greenland by Cardinal William of Sabina, Norway during the coronation of King Håkon Håkonsson (cf. the *Flateyjarbók*). He left a year later (1247) for Greenland with a mission from the elder king Håkon to bring the Greenland colonists under the sway of the Norwegian crown. He died in 1280. According to Vera Henriksen, he was the last bishop of Garðar. It is possible that a certain Bokki (*Bochus* in Latin) could have held an interim position or it could be an honorific name (the powerful one) attributed to Thord.

**1253:** Pope Innocent IV (1243–1254) confirms Canon Sörle of Hamar (Norway) as archbishop of Greenland, Norway, and so on.

**1260s:** The organization of the church became a royal matter.

**1262:** Greenland became subjugated by Norway.

**1263–1280:** Rule of King Magnus "laga boetir."†

---

*Keller maintains the translation is incorrect (1989, 90): *falco columbris,* or "merlin" (E. Beauvois, 1902, 15, fn 3).

†Cognomen of King Magnus, meaning an amender of the laws, generally rendered today as "the lawman."

**1264 (or 1273):** Rumors of revolt in Greenland. There could be a connection between Bishop Olaf's departure from Greenland (a Greenland uprising?) and his return in force in 1271. Olaf would thus have been absent for seven years.

**1266:** Greenland priests equip a polar expedition ship to search for Skræling settlements.

**1270:** The appearance of a new tax: Peter's Pence.

**1276:** Pope John XXI orders Archbishop Jón of Nidaros to send trustworthy men to Greenland to collect the tithe.

**1278:** Archbishop Jón of Nidaros asks Pope Nicholas III to lift the ban on excommunication (for nonpayment of the tithe) targeting Greenland colonists.

**1279:** Pope's acceptance

**1280:** Death of King Magnus the Lawman and Bishop Olaf of Greenland.

**1280–1299:** Rule of the Norwegian king Erik, enemy of the clergy and therefore called Erik "presthatare."

**1280–1288:** Post left vacant.

**1281:** Icelandic law (*Jónsbók*) was introduced into Greenland.

**1285:** The two priests Adalbrand and Thorvald, sons of Helge, discover the new lands west of Iceland (Duneyjar). In fact this quest was more of a flight from the Norwegian king, Erik's energetic measures especially his right to review the nominations of Greenland bishops.

**1288 (February 22):** Thord consecrated in Nidaros; he leaves in 1289 for Greenland. He will hold the post for twenty years (1309) before returning to his parent's home in Norway. He died in 1314.

**1288–1290:** King Erik of Norway organizes three successive expeditions in which he sends Rolf to Iceland then to the "new lands of the West." In 1288, Rolf receives orders to obtain money and sailors in Iceland. The real reason for the expeditions appears to be the hunt for two fugitive priests, Thorvald and Adalbrand, which resulted in Thorvald's arrest in "America" (Aldabrand had died there in 1286) and deportation to Norway. They had taken

Skálholt's bishop Arnar Thorlaksson's side in his conflict with Iceland's civil ruler Rafn Odsson.

**1314:** Árni anointed bishop of Greenland. He left Norway in 1315. He died in 1349.

**1319:** Death of King Håkon V Magnusson.

**1319–1343:** Swedish-Norwegian union. Conflicts.

**1325:** Consecration of Alfus.

**1327:** Pope John XXII's envoy, Bertrand d'Ortoli collects the tithes from Greenland in Bergen.

**1328:** In accordance with the pope's decision, he gave half the tithes to King Magnus of Sweden-Norway.

**1332:** Consecration of Barthold.

**1333–1346:** Intense activity on the part of Archbishop Pål Bårdsson (Nidaros).

**1340s:** Expedition of Ivar Bårdsson during the mandate of Bishop Arne on orders of Bishop Håkon of Bergen (in 1341 according to the *Grønlands Historiske Mindesmærker,* August 11, 1341, according to the *Regesta Norvegica*).

**1342:** Rumors of apostasy in part of the Norse colony of Greenland and their departure to "America."*

**1343:** Nomination of Jón Skalli (during the lifetime of Bishop Árni), who showed little haste to take on his duties. He only reached Greenland six or seven years before Árni's death to then try to take possession of a See in Iceland that was not handed on to him. He died in 1391.

**1345:** During an official council in Bergen, Greenland (and the Faroe Islands) did not pay their tithe to the pope.

**1346:** The knörr from Greenland arrives with a rich cargo.

**1347:** A Greenland vessel coming from Markland arrives in Strömfjordr, Iceland.

**1348:** Transfer (equivalent of a sanction) of Bishop Árni to the Faroe Islands.

**1349:** The "Black Plague" rages in Norway with particularly

---

*According to the seventeenth-century text of Gisli Odsson.

devastating effects in Bergen, main site of commerce with Greenland, the Faroes, Shetland, and the Orkneys. Its ravages were substantial and shook Norway (economically and politically) to its core. It is one of the probable causes for the decline of maritime relations with the Western dependencies.

**1349:** Confirmation of Jón Skalli Eriksson's nomination as bishop of Trondheim. He seems to have spent more time abroad than in Greenland (1356 in Avignon, 1357 in Rome, 1358 in Iceland where he claimed to replace Bishop Orur). He was therefore away from Greenland for nineteen years. (Death of Bishop Árni in Greenland.)

**1350:** King Magnus Eriksson Smek surrenders rule of Norway while keeping that of Shetland, the Faroe Islands, Iceland, and Greenland.

**1355–1380:** Rule of Håkon VI, last king of independent Norway.

**1355:** King Magnus Eriksson decided to fit out a knörr for an expedition to Greenland to halt the decline of Christianity there.

**1365:** Brother Alf (Alfuir or Alfus) of the Benedictine Monastery of Saint Michael in Bergen was anointed bishop of Garðar. He only arrived in Greenland in 1368 where he died in 1378. News of his death would not be known for another six years.

**1369:** Pope Blessed Urban V officially confirms the See of Hólar, Iceland to the former Greenland bishop Jón Eriksson Skalli.

**1374:** Death of King Magnus Erikson Smek.

**1378–1417:** The Great Western Schism with competition between the two churches. Circa 1400, several bishops were simultaneously named for Garðar. This is why Bishop Henry's title was contested by the antipope of Avignon, Clement VII, who named another postulant on April 7, 1389, the minorite friar Peter Staras, overturning the agreement made with Nidaros. Clement VII also named a certain Gregorius earlier.

**1379:** Skræling attack against a Scandinavian group (probably during Nordrsetur expeditions) leaving eighteen dead. Two children were taken captive.

**1379 (exact date uncertain):** King Håkon Magnusson sent one or more ships against the Skrælings, returning with two skiffs made from skins.

**1384:** King Olaf Håkonsson of Norway complains about the presence of foreign ships and trade.

**1385:** The Icelandic governor of Vatnsfjördur Björn Einarsson (known as Jorsalfari), was shipwrecked in Greenland, where he stayed two years but turned down the high judge post he was offered by the colonists. He was one of Iceland's richest men.

**1385:** Henry was anointed as Greenland's bishop but hardly gives any impression of being eager to make his way to Garðar as he is mentioned on several different occasions as being in Scandinavia (Nyborg, Denmark in 1386 and the Oslo diet in honor of Queen Magarethe in 1388). According to Beauvois, Henry wasn't recognized "neither by this or that side, but continued to be in the eyes of the archbishop of Trondheim." If Lyschander's chronicle is correct, he was stripped of his seat in Kirkwell in the Orkneys and went to Garðar. The Roman texts see this as merely an exchange of posts with Jón of the Orkneys on March 9, 1394 (*Archivium secret. Apostol. Vaticanum. Regestum Laterense*).

**1388–1412:** Rule of Queen Margarethe of Denmark-Norway.

**1391:** Bishop Henry of Greenland replaces a certain Vigfus Floason (Icelander).

**1393:** Pillage of Bergen by the German supporters of King Albrecht.

**1397:** Union of Kalmar combining the kingdoms of Sweden, Denmark, and Norway under the aegis of Queen Margarethe of Denmark (1397–1410).

**1401:** Bull of February 25, 1401, of Roman Pope Boniface IX, naming the Franciscan Berthold to succeed Bishop Alf, some twenty-three years after his death (Beauvois, 1902, 37). Garðar Cathedral would remain vacant nonetheless until January 23, 1402.

**1402 (January 23):** Boniface IX names Peter, Bishop of Strangnäs (Sweden), for the Garðar See. He declined the offer and stayed at his post where he died in 1408 (*Archivium secret. Apostol. Vaticanum. Regestum Laterense*).

**1402 (September 16):** The Bergen bishop was charged by Boniface IX with collecting the church revenues, including those of Greenland.

**1406:** Archbishop Eskild of Trondheim confers episcopal rights on a certain Anders in order to replace Henry of Garðar. According to Beauvois, it is not known if the latter was still alive and identifies Anders as Eindride Andreasson, a Greenland official who signed the Hvalsey wedding banns in 1408 with Paul Hallvardsson. It seems in fact that Anders/Eindride was only a vicar general, responsible for administrative work (Wetzer & Welte, *Kirchen Lexikon*, page on Grönland).

**1407:** A certain Kolgrimr was condemned to be burned at the stake for sorcery and adultery. Archbishop Berthold replaced Archbishop Askel of Trondheim in Greenland.

**1408:** Wedding of Thorstein Olafson and Sigrid Björnsdittir at the Hvalsey church.

Observation: this date (1408) and this event were long regarded as the last known news of Greenland. The ecclesiastical vacuum also created a void of written source material. But as the Scandinavian source texts grew increasingly rare, we find a growing number of accounts from the foreign subjects frequenting Greenland waters. I would also emphasize the chronic absenteeism of all the bishops named to the Greenland post in the fifteenth and sixteenth centuries. Let's take a quick look at the facts.

**1410:** News of the death of Eskill from Greenland: "he had been named bishop of Garðar, but we don't know in what year or by who."

**1411 (March 27):** Franciscan priest Jacobus Petri Treppe (or Teppe) was named by Pope John XXIII to succeed Eskill. He was ordered to live in Greenland and forbidden to perform his duties outside his diocese. However, Bishop Jacob of Greenland officiated as vicar general on behalf of Bishop Peder of Roskilde, Denmark (new accounts of his presence in Denmark in 1417, 1421, and 1424). He died in 1424 or 1425.

**1412:** Death of Queen Margarethe.

**1413:** Complaints from King Erik of Pomerania to the King of England regarding trade and fishing infractions in countries under Norwegian jurisdiction.

**1418:** Attack in Greenland by an enemy fleet that destroyed holy buildings in nine parishes. Numerous residents were carried off as captives.

**1420:** Account of Bishop Bertold of Garðar in Nidaros, who replaced Bishop Jens Andersson of Roskilde in 1421.

**1422 (approximately):** A certain Nicholas was named bishop of Greenland, but his existence is contested. He is said to have died around 1432.

**1424:** King Erik of Pomerania meets his brother-in-law, Prince Henry the navigator at the Emperor Sigismund's for the purpose of discussing exploration of the western lands.

**1425:** Death of Jacobus Petri Treppe (before May 25, according to Beauvois). The Franciscan priest Robert Ryngman succeeded him, named by Pope Martin V at the consistory held on May 30, 1425. It should be noted that Gams mentions a certain Nicholas as successor. According to Beauvois, we have no knowledge of any churchman who officiated in Greenland between the death of Eskill and the arrival of Hans Egede in 1721, although Catholicism was maintained there until the time of Christopher Columbus. We don't know if Robert Ryngmann resigned.

**1432 (March 19):** Gibelin Volant was given a see in Aalborg (*Roma cancellaria, Archivum consistoriale, Acta consist. Ab anno 1409 ad 1433, f°. 227 v°.*).

**1432:** Accord between King Erik of Pomerania (King of Denmark-Norway) and King Henry VI of England concerning indemnifications for *prejudicial acts suffered for twenty years,* deportations by force of populations subject to Norwegian taxes and obstruction to their return.*

---

*We see in this euphemism an allusion to their captivity (the original word *obstruction* is kept).

**1432 (July 4):** Franciscan priest Johann Herler (or Erler) of Moys/ Mouis or Monis, from the Meissen diocese in Lower Saxony received the title of Bishop of Garðar. He had a minor penitentiary theological degree from St. Peter's Basilica.[63]

**1432 (August 13):** Bishop Herler promised to satisfy the demands of the Papal Treasury and those of the Sovereign Pontiff in the following eight to fourteen months, Garðar's taxes were reduced from 2,500 florins to 64 once Rome realized the impoverished state of the diocese.[64]

**1433 (September 24):** Pope Eugene IV (1431–1447) names a certain Brother Bartholomeus of Saint Ypolito (perhaps in the south and apparently a Dominican) as bishop of Greenland. A Germanic origin is also possible as there was a Saint Hyppolyt Priory in lower Austria in Sankt Pölten. He died in 1440.

**1440:** Testimony of Bishop Gregory of Greenland in Oslo, who was present during a gathering of bishops and an international council seeking King Erik of Pomerania's help against the crimes of the Hanseatic League and the Dutch in the kingdom's coasts. The request for help was accompanied by a threat of clerical insubordination. Promoted in August 1440, he was still the bishop of Garðar in 1450.

**1444:** Strengthening of the ban on English trade in the Nordic lands by King Henry VI of England

**1445:** Icelandic leader Björn Thorleifsson and his wife, Olóf, are shipwrecked in Greenland and winter over in Garðar.

**1446:** Greenland complaints addressed to the pope concerning the destruction of churches and reports of the return of many deportees and accompanied by a request for priests and bishops to be sent seem to have reached Norway, Iceland, and England before arriving in Rome.

**1448:** Pope Nicholas V (1447–1455) requests the bishops of Hólar and Skálholt to do what's necessary for the rebirth of Christianity in Greenland by naming and ordaining upstanding churchmen.

**1449:** New treaty between King Christian I (Denmark) and

Henry VI concerning the ban on English trade in the lands mentioned above, and extension of the decree until 1451.

**1450:** Treaty of union between Norway and Denmark is signed.

**1450:** Bishop Gregorius of Garðar attends a bishop's council in Bergen. A certain Boniface was named bishop of Garðar (*Fita Fidel*).

**1451:** The decree banning English trade in the Norwegian colonies seems to expire.*

**1460:** Bishop Andreas of Garðar proclaims himself administrator or "officialis" of Skálholt (presumably with the archbishop's blessing), where he could be found in 1461 and 1462. He would replace the bishop of Linköping, Sweden, in 1466. Ten years later, he is mentioned as attending a bishop's council in Blekinge.

**1472–1473:** Danish-Portuguese expedition (officially 1476) discovers Labrador and the Strait of Anian.†

**1481 (June 15):** James Blaa, Danish Dominican, is named bishop of Garðar by Pope Sixtus IV.[65]

**1482–1483:** The Northman Didrik Pining—among others— seems to have practiced piracy on the coasts of Greenland, before becoming a trader.

**1484:** Rumors in Bergen of the murder of the last Norwegian merchants who knew the Greenland route by jealous Hanseatic League members.

**1487:** A certain Jacob is alleged to have inscribed the title, Bishop of Greenland, in his seal. According to T. J. Oleson, Pope Innocent VIII accepted the resignation of this bishop who had never done a thing for his bishopric. He was replaced by Mathias Knudsson or Canuttsson on July 9, 1492. This very poor Norwegian Benedictine was named by Pope Innocent VIII on Cardinal Borgia's recommendation.[66]

---

*I have used the same terminology as the *Grønlands Historiske Mindesmærker* that introduces some doubt as to the exact date.

†See chapter 10. According to Keller (1983, 31), an expedition mounted by King Christian I in 1472, thus probably the same one, was attacked by small craft on the eastern coast of Greenland.

**1494:** Rumors of piracy on the Greenland coasts.

**1500:** Zacharias, born in Vincenza, Italy, succeeds Bishop Canuttsson.

**1516:** Preparations made by Archbishop Erik Walkendorff for the "rediscovery" of Greenland.

**1520 (June 20):** Dutchman Vincentius Petri Kampe was named bishop of Greenland (*episcopus Thulensis*) by Pope Leo X[67] in which Greenland was described as being occupied by infidels (*ab infedelibus detenta*), but he remained in Funen (Denmark). He is mentioned several times there: 1530 and 1532 in Roskilde and the Cloister of Maribo, where he died in 1537.

**1520 (approximately):** Bishop Ogmund Paulsson of Skálholt was marooned on the Greenland coast, where he thought he saw Herjolfsnes with people and sheep.

**1520–1537:** Beginning of the Reformation in Scandinavia and the end of the nomination of bishops.

One common feature characterizes this religious history of the medieval Far North: the mystery concerning its actual origin, with the fairly serious Celtic hypothesis, and the mystery surrounding its poorly known ending. One thing is sure. This long list confirms that this long medieval religious history was far from being a long, serene river. In truth it reflected the quarrels and various tensions between the Scandinavian faithful and the Mother Church, the bishopric of Bremen-Hamburg, Rome, or Avignon. However all the nominations of bishops (whether or not they actually went to Greenland) contradicts the idea that Greenland was forgotten. It certainly was not forgotten by other nations. Moreover, isn't it said that nature has horror of a vacuum? The dark cloud of one party—the Danish-Norwegian monarchy—is the silver lining for others and offered too strong a temptation for the various Hanseatic, English, and southern appetites, which were particularly keen in the Far North. The latter could even supply us with the key to the mysterious end of the Viking colonies in the Far North.

# 10

# THE SCANDINAVIAN PRESENCE
# IN THE FAR NORTH

I believe the Scandinavian presence in the Far North is connected to the foreign presence in these same latitudes, or even inspired it. This began quite early as we can see through the parsimonious testimony of the medieval written source materials. It played a certain role in the life of the colonists. This link between the Scandinavian presence, more or less acknowledged in the north, and that of foreign nations that is much less well documented, is unbreakable. The luxury products exported by the colonists couldn't help but attract European merchants. Some very instructive archaeological finds over the past few decades have lent strength to my position. By way of example, the arm of a scales found in the Canadian Arctic reflects my theory quite well as it seems doubtful that Scandinavians would have used this weighing instrument in their dealings with the natives.

The remote Scandinavian expeditions would pave the way for the future emigration (or defection) of all or part of the Scandinavian colony of Greenland. With this intense activity of exploration and trade, we have the forerunner of the Nordic colonies in America. My use of the European maps describing this presence will again show the connection between these adventurous voyages and the consistently growing European presence.

# MYTH AND REALITY IN CARTOGRAPHY: THE MYSTERIOUS TRILOGY OF GROCLAND, GREIPAR, AND KROKSFJORD

Myths and reality often tightly overlap, one feeding the other. Removing a mythical source is not without risk of losing an important element of research—this is very true of Inuit source material—as a seed of truth quite likely gave birth to the myth. The mysterious land or island of Grocland* illustrates this problem quite well. This mythical northern island haunts numerous maps and tales. On the east, Grocland borders the Asiatic country, *Bergi regio*. The work of the Venetian traveler, Marco Polo, can be seen here. These regions are home to pygmies. We are able to place Grocland far back in time as a mysterious figure, the mathematician, astronomer and monk from Oxford, Nicholas of Lynn, mentions it in 1360 in connection with a Swedish-Norwegian expedition toward the pole, which he accompanied. As it happens, a letter of the French pope Etienne Aubert, a.k.a. Pope Innocent VI, dated September 13, 1360, calls Queen Bianca of Sweden-Norway "queen of the Swedish," and the Flemish illustrator Gerard Mercator would draw on Nicholas of Lynn's sources, as did the German Martin Behaim and many others.

**1569:** Mercator recycles the work of Nicholas of Lynn almost in its entirety, alluding to this expedition in the sidebar appearing in the mysterious island named Grocland: "The island whose inhabitants are Swedish natives."[†] By all evidence this sidebar clearly refers to the Northmen but is flawed by its delayed updating. Magnus of Sweden was also King of Norway (1319–1355) but had lost the Norwegian crown five years before the expedition's departure, hence this confusion and a slight error pointed out by Prytz. His Grocland, alias Devon Island, is located a degree too far to the south, at 73°.

---

*This name appears under different orthographs, with variations including Groclandt and Krocland.

†Literally *Insula ciuo incolae Suedi sunt origine,* see fig. 7.1.

Grocland would be picked up by all the following cartographers, geographers, and explorers, summarized below:

**1570:** Ortelius, Flemish cartographer (Latitude 75 × Longitude 340).

**1578:** Martin Frobisher, famous English explorer.

**1582:** Michael Lock, English cartographer (Latitude 72 × Longitude 330–47)

**1587:** G. Mercator, Flemish cartographer and geographer.

**1592:** Present on the globe of Irish cartographer Emery Molyneux, all the Greenland and North American place-names are English and no longer Nordic.

**1593:** Dutch cartographer Cornelius de Jode's map shows Grocland clearly drawn but not named.

**1597:** Cornelius Wytfliet, Flemish historian and geographer.

The agreement on Grocland's placement is immediately noticeable among all these different individuals. It is rare to find unanimity like this.* Taken separately, the mysterious Grocland would yield us little information, but restored to a Nordic mythical context, it takes on its full value. We should not forget that "Grocland" is a written transcription of a completely Scandinavian concept. At the risk of shocking people, I would place it near "Kroksfjordarheidi." In my opinion, there is a direct connection between the two concepts: "the moors or highlands of the hooked fjord" and "the hooked land or land in the form of a hook."

The absorption of "K" into "G" is easily imaginable to a European, and everything points to Grocland and Kroksfjordarheidi being two completely inseparable entities. The value of this cartographic evidence is its neutrality: the Europeans indicating "Grocland" there where they had to have seen it (and heard it mentioned while linguistically corrupting it).

---

*By way of comparison, regions like Labrador or "Estotiland" give rise to a variety of placements (see next chapter).

C. C. Rafn presents Kroksfjordarheidi as "*a Kroksfjödr, q.o, krókr: curvatura, sinus, fjördr: brachim maris, et heidi: montana, tesqua.*" Rafn offers a logical explanation: "The ancient Scandinavians had boats for hunting and fishing. Visibly, it had to be an important fjord requiring a difficult journey of several days. The name seems to indicate that this fjord had a strange curve (*krókr*) and was surrounded by empty highlands (*heidi*)."[1]

This comparison between Grocland and Kroksfjordarheidi has never been made because the experts unfortunately shared the bias that Kroksfjordarheidi could only be located in Greenland. In this sense, the accounts of foreign sailors are more valuable as they are more objective. Because of their ignorance of Norse literary tradition, they didn't succumb to the temptation to take the source materials literally. Several experts— some of the best—were unable to avoid this and placed Kroksfjordarheidi and Greipar on Disko Island off the northwest coast of Greenland.

Their motivation may be illustrated by this explanation by Nansen: "This hunting terrain of the ancient Scandinavians should not be sought for any farther than Disko because the clinker boats used by the Greenlanders (Vikings), *which were so poor in wood and iron,* could never ever been used for a regular connection through the ice of Baffin Bay."[2]

Here we see again the too long and too often advanced theory of the "profound destitution" of the Greenland Scandinavians that I vigorously contested earlier, as it is far from being a proven fact. Also, the Nordic peoples have, as a rule, confronted and overcome much more difficult situations.

This line of reasoning conceals the Nordic trips toward the new lands of the West, rich with wood for construction, and present in their cargoes according to the sagas and Norwegian eyewitnesses. Furthermore, archaeology shows the frequent presence of iron (mainly from meteors) from the Far North in the Nordic settlements and a tendency to casually abandon various trinkets, ironwork, nails, and so forth on their sites, which the Inuit enthusiastically recovered for themselves.

A medieval Iceland source informs us that a Greenland boat (without nails) diverted to Iceland by a storm had a cargo entirely of wood from Markland. "Then a boat arrived that had lost its anchor, with seventeen men coming from Markland, but who, on their return, had been marooned here."[3]

Another observation concerning the danger of ice and the glaciation of Baffin Bay is being increasingly questioned. We know that the climate was warmer at the beginning of colonization, followed by a little ice age (from about 1200 to 1400), and the return of a warm phase around the fifteenth century. Some researchers even maintain that the climate was warmer keeping the bay free of ice. It is true, as mentioned by Gwyn Jones, that not a single Norwegian or Icelandic text mentions this sailing problem. Furthermore, as we saw in the first chapter, an *umiaq* has been found as far away as Peary Land by archaeologists (and its frame was built with Scandinavian oak).[*] So I raise the following questions: Was navigation possible at this latitude?[†] An affirmative response comes from the Portuguese who traveled around the whole of Greenland and were the sole to champion its island nature. The trip presented by Nansen and those who maintain this theory is inconceivable is a mere bagatelle compared to a voyage between Greenland and Bergen. Disko Island, which is often depicted as rich in game, is not unique. There is even less game there than in certain Canadian hunting grounds that were duly documented during the time we will soon study and described as hunting paradises, something still true today.

So, I do not feel this argument offers overwhelming evidence for identification of this site. Unfortunately, this will not cast a shadow on the bright hopes of those claiming a Greenland location. They believe that Kroksfjordarheidi would be in Disko Bay and that Greipar would be between 67–68°N, meaning between Sisimiut/Holsteinsborg and

---

[*]Carbon-14 datings give 1220 (±50 years) for the oak wood (Gulløv, 1982, 233).

[†]Based on the strength of the information gleaned from the traditional Scandinavian lore (construction of an *umiaq* by Scandinavians in *Flóamanna saga*) I wonder if the boat found in Peary Land was really Inuit. In fact, according to Jette Arneborg (1991), the *umiaq* showed traces of "repairs made with nails." This technique is not Inuit and would thus involve, in my opinion, Scandinavians who had traveled very far north. This hypothesis would also explain the geographical knowledge held by some individuals and parties. From the end of the fifteenth century, the Portuguese regarded Greenland as an island. They made a joint expedition with Denmrk to northern Greenland and Canada in 1472 to 1473.

Aasiaat/Egedesminde. However, the medieval description could not be any clearer: it is at the end of the lands in all ancient and modern sources and translations.

The "end of the lands" is used to describe Greipar, or even "the end of the habitable lands not covered by the ice inland." A medieval version of the *Book of the Settlement of Iceland,* the *Hauksbók,* tells us that "Greipar is located to the north of Greenland, at the end of the inhabited lands."* Where does myth stop and historical reality begin?

The skald Helge Thordarson who appears in the *Skáld-Helga saga* is mentioned as having visited the frontier of the inhabitable lands in 1266. "Greipar was the northernmost tip of Greenland."†

The information provided is rather clear. A copy at the royal library in Copenhagen informs us that "the skald Helge sailed along the coast of Greenland (illegible) to the north of that land (idem) of settlements named Greipum and Kroksfjordarheidi."⁴

Anton Bjørnbo mentions reasons for these voyages that completely contradict Nansen's view (which we looked at earlier). We understand better why the Norse community was not so destitute: "The (Scandinavian) Greenlanders needed . . . to sail to settlements located at the farthest borders of the country or deserted lands, to obtain both wood and game. These places are called Greipar and Kroksfjordarheidi and are located very far away."⁵

This commentary of the time gives us a confirmation of the economic value of these regions despite their remoteness. It is too often forgotten that at the dawn of "the Age of Discovery" the immense forests of North America responded perfectly to the demand for wood for building quality ships, hence the interest of the Portuguese as we shall see in the next chapter. Several confirmations of my working hypothesis can be found in this quote—namely, verification of the remoteness of these Far North regions and the difficulties in sailing there (*et difficile mare pernavigandum*) and

---

*In the Latin version it reads: *"Boreum versus in Greipas qui habitatæ Groenlandiæ ultimus terminus est,"* and in the Norse version: *"Greipar nordr Grænlands er thar bygdar spordr."*
†Rimnasafn, 1905–1912. According to its author, Finnur Jónsson, Helge Thordarsson, grandson of Icelandic colonist Ásgeir of Höfdi, must have lived at the beginning of the eleventh century.

verification of the physical geography (*et Montana Krokksffordensa*).

The geographical information given by these sources is quite precise—it involves an extreme point of the land, therefore Greenland. A literal interpretation could have been helpful, the end of the lands represented the most extreme point of Greenland. In fact, how could such veteran sailors like the Vikings have ever confused the Disko region, located right in the center of Greenland, with the border of the lands?

A quick glance at a map of Greenland dispels this hypothesis. Only a historical bias that maintained the Scandinavians were incapable of traveling farther north has prevented serious consideration of the hypothesis that Greipar and Kroksfjordarheidi are at the northernmost tip of Greenland, close to the pole. However, facts still show the contrary. The identification of this vital nerve: Greipar—Kroksfjordarheidi—Grocland, with the northern Canadian islands is almost certain. Several hypothetical locations have been suggested, either Lancaster Sound or Jones Sound (lat 76° N), or the western bank of Baffin Bay, or the Inglefield Gulf and Kane Sound on the Greenland coast (around lat 80° N).

One of the great Danish experts of the nineteenth century identified the Kroksfjord Islands with lat 74° N in Lancaster Sound early on.[6] Professors Fridtjof Isachsen and Gunnar Isachsen concluded that the center of the Kroksfjord Islands had to be Devon Island at the entrance of the Northwest Passage (lat 73°–75° N).

Prytz believes the Scandinavians had discovered a practically virgin hunting ground. The Canadian islands are located at the level of Smith Sound where all year hunting is possible for narwhals, gyrfalcons, walrus, and polar bears. I believe this fabled hunting ground could only be Kroksfjordarheidi.

Now that we have reached this stage of our analysis, we have to use the scientific "discoveries" of our time that while explaining several mysterious phenomena of the Canadian Arctic, indirectly confirm the veracity of our source material. Peter Schledermann's work is particularly rich with archaeological findings, but also important for the scientific light it casts on this part of the world.

What could appear as confabulation, a vague medieval myth is instead confirmed by science—namely, the extraordinary wealth of the fauna (seals, walruses, narwhals) at lat 75° N around Ellesmere Island. This island is only separated from Greenland by twenty-five miles. Schledermann describes it as "customarily connected to Greenland during the winter by a heavily frozen sea."

This is the obligatory passage point for the game, and consequently the hunters in their pursuit. We should also note its mountainous nature that brings to mind the mountains of the curved fjord (the literal translation of Kroksfjordarheidi): "Over the millennia, hunters and nomads passed back and forth through the mountainous terrain of Ellesmere Island through the large pass today known as Sverdrup Pass."*

This is where the fauna is precisely most abundant. The presence of muskox, seals, and walruses arriving in the hundreds from the Greenland coast can be observed. Thanks to a combination of strong currents, relatively shallow waters, and the narrowness of the bay, special conditions are formed that create what scientists call a polynia. It so happens that this particular polynia close to lat 80° N and the Bache Peninsula has a distinctive feature that Schledermann points out": "The polynia—areas of the ocean that are free of ice—appear several months before the general ice melt, but the polynia in the waters of the North remains open all year."†

The consequences of this natural phenomenon are the presence of a large fauna creating a very favorable hunting ground: "The Arctic hunters found this polynia rich in game one thousand years ago, after crossing eastward through a pass in the mountainous interior of Ellesmere Island, called Sverdrup Pass."[7]

Excavations have revealed the presence of 25 permanent Thule peat houses (winter and summer) along the Bache Peninsula. This culture was there during the Nordic presence.

---

*Peter Schledermann (1981). See the map: "probable region of Nordrsetur." This famous region was described earlier in the legendary *Inventio fortunate* after the 1360 expedition that reported strong currents and a sea that never froze over. I cannot help but think such prosperity did not pass unnoticed.
†The author describes this major natural phenomenon one year earlier as "any non-linear shaped opening enclosed in ice. Sometimes the Polynia is limited on one side by the coast and is called a shore polynia, or by fast ice, and is called a flaw polynia. If it occurs in the same position every year it is called a recurring polynia.

This surprising environment in the very heart of the Arctic, which must have been real manna for hunters, can't help but bring to mind medieval sources like Nicholas of Lynn and his mountainous islands at lat 78° N, his four trades (probably ivory, polar falcons, white bear hides, and walrus leather, several of which are mentioned on the Behaim Globe), or else the Scandinavians with their heights of Kroksfjord. One cannot help but notice the existence of an island in this same region with the very strange and evocative name of Skræling Island, which is a typically Norse name.

If we go back to the sources, we find in fact a wealth of information that is not only geographical but sociological about Viking life and their hunting customs in the Far North. The *Greenland Annals* tell us: "The men of the Nordrsetur had their cabins or shacks in Greipar and a certain few in Kroksfjordarheidi. Driftwood was found there although no trees grew there. This northern tip of Greenland receives the most driftwood and everything else the sea can carry in, coming from the bays of Markland."[8]

Speaking plainly, the Vikings left material traces of their passage through the far north. Yet another confirmation of the extreme northern location of these sites says "the northernmost tip of Greenland," which I think completely excludes the Disko region.

The listing order of the two place names (Greipar first, Kroksfjordarheidi second) and the use of the term "certain few" as a distinguishing feature seems to imply a longer distance to Kroksfjordarheidi with most Scandinavians staying in Greipar. A new place is named Markland and is connected to these two mythical settlements. Shedding some light on one of the links if this mysterious chain could help us find answers to the other riddles. C. C. Rafn provides some specific information.

> Greipar means the space between the fingers but also gorges. This name has to have been inspired by a particular resemblance to this place. It is conceivable that several mountains (maybe five) located unusually close to each other and separated by gorges gave birth to this name.*

---

*Rafn (1837). I'd like to point out that Disko has no physical resemblance to this particular feature.

There is no doubt that the author of the medieval place-name sought to describe a manual property, describing the spaces between the fingers, and narrow bits of land that imprison the sea on both sides; the verb *greipa* mans to "grab with the hand, to grip."*

The value of Peter Schledermann's work in the Canadian Far North is one we cannot ignore, as well as the resemblance to places mentioned some centuries ago.

Devon Island located at 75° north latitude responds particularly well to the physical feature of a curve or hook mentioned earlier. In addition a mountain of more than 6,100 feet stands on its eastern side.

Ellesmere Island corresponds even more to this "gripping" function from the verb *greipa*. Its four deep fjords on the western side actually give it the appearance of a large open hand. Furthermore, Ellesmere is located at the extreme northern tip of Greenland. This is clearly the message the medieval scribes were seeking to pas on with their "end of the lands."

> III/42. *Viri profectisunt boream versus in Greipas,*
> *qui habitatæ Grænlandiæ ultimus terminus est*
> Men leave for the north toward Greipas
> the most remote border *of inhabited Greenland.*
> *ibi multis in locis hominibus*
> *vacandum erat veniationibus*
> There, in these regions, many men
> have the leisure to hunt.

The *Skáld-Helga saga* mentioned earlier gives us some interesting pieces of information. J. Meldgard is of the opinion that this poem on the *Skáld-Helga* is contemporary with the *Saga of the Sworn Brothers (Fóstbrœdra saga)* concerning the first generation of colonists circa 1022.

---

*The Latin version says: "*proprio interstio digitorum deinde augustiæ terrarum. quibus mare utsinque clauditur.*" It so happens that the Melville coast looks like the flat of a hand bordered by a mountain rebaptized "the devil's thumb."

This means that Inuit and Norse contacts occurred quite early.

Out of a desire for authenticity and to avoid any misguided interpretation based on my sense of the importance of this information, I will quote the original Latin here:[9]

(33) *Glacialum montium terram*
*et Eiriksfjordum*
*cagnoverunt cuncti;*
*expeditio strenua,*
*nave in* falgeirsvika
*portum nacta, finivit.*
(33) The land of frozen mountains
And the Eiriksfjord,
All know them,
energetic expedition;
Toward *Falgeirsvik* they sail
finding a port for the boat
V/44. *Continuo ventus in carbasa involavit*
*ut lintea distinerentur;*
*tum funes et scalmi tentati sunt:*
*remigarunt et velificarunt boream,*
*versus in Greipas*
In the sails, the wind rushed ceaselessly
So hard that the canvas tore
Oars and rigging broke apart:
They rowed and set sail toward the north
In direction of Greipas.

## Observations

The riddle of the "Greipar, Grocland, Kroksfjordarheidi" trilogy may be found in this poem. Here also in the Skaldic poetry (verse 3, line 42), Greipar is located in the north as the border of Greenland. The skald Helgi believed Greipar was still in Greenland, whereas the works we shall study below tend to place it across from the border of Greenland. It also gives us an indirect confirmation of the value of these remote lands (presence of numerous hunters); such a voyage is not undertaken for pleasure. We should note that the *Grønlands Historiske Mindesmærker*[10] casts doubt on the information provided by Helgi the Skald and views it instead as poetic exaggeration. Verse 33 confirms a point that will be developed later, the wealth of the Arctic suggested by *Falgeirsvika* (Falcon Bay). And would "Eiriksfjordum" be the more southern fjord of Eystribygð, baptized by Erik the Red?

Erik the Red never claimed to have visited the extreme north of Greenland, but we do know that a Bishop Eirik Upsi visited these remote latitudes. Could this be due to a scribe's confusion? Not necessarily. It is easy to imagine that a religious figure of his rank would have been tempted to leave his name on a remote—but wealthy—northern fjord. I note this because one element of this poem *Falgeirsvik* intrigues me. It is presented in connection with the Eiriksfjord. It so happens that this bay doesn't appear in any written source concerning Eystribygð if the poem is referring to this colony. Verse 35 (not cited) speaks of Solarfjell where the skald and his retinue were staying. Could Eystribygð have been such an ideal haven for the gyrfalcon that a bay was named after it? This also seems somewhat illogical for why undertake these long trips into the north if this highly sought-after product could be found two steps from the southern colony? it is also possible that the skald simply used a poetic image completely at home in this kind of composition. In this case, this would explain this place-name's absence in medieval source material.

Another dilemma is given to us as in his introduction Rafn strays from the text. Did he overlook something or make too quick an interpretation? Rafn in fact says: "The men left for the North toward Greipar. This was the far end of the *Greenland bridge*."

First off, this interpretation doesn't appear in this version of the *Rimnasafn*. Nor do we see *the bygdr spordr* anymore, the end of the settlements (or inhabited lands) of the poem but *bryggju spordr,* the end of a bridge,* or a jetty. Björn of Skardsaa and Torfeus[†] also make

---

*The *Grønlands Historiske Mindesmærker* gives two definitions of *spordr*. 1.) fish tail or snake, 2.) expanse, country, or extremity of a figure. The first meaning (bridge) is rare.
†Original text: *den yderste ende af en brygge eller skibsbro*" (the most extreme end of a bridge, or the bridge of a ship or even a pier).

this second interpretation (*bryggju spordr*), which they maintain describes "the most extreme point of a bridge/a pier." In this case the meaning of the poem would change: "North of Greipar was the end of the Greenland bridge." We have the same meaning in Rafn's modern translation: the end of the Greenland bridge (*Grønlands brygge ende*).

What might appear to be a trivial detail is important because throughout the Middle Ages—and beyond—the notion of a bridge connecting the continent was quite dominant. A bridge was supposed to have connected Greenland and Norway as we saw earlier, and another bridge connected Greenland to North America. This concept allows us to corroborate the dates, as goes far back in the medieval imagination. It belongs to the Norse geographical vision of a sea closed at the north as seen, for example, in the Konungs skuggsjá (*The Royal Mirror*) dating from about 1250. In it, Greenland is a landmass connected to another one. This vision persisted through several centuries. The best mapmakers never failed to reproduce this concept. Let's look at them:

**1502:** In Cantino's map, the bridge doesn't appear physically for the upper portion has been cut off. Greenland is nonetheless presented as *A Ponta d* [Asia—missing part].* The map's sidebar helps us fill this gap as it tells us: "*segum a opiniom das CosmoSricos se créé Ser a ponta d'Asia.*"

**1508:** Johan Ruysch, Flemish geographer.

**1537:** Gemma Fricus: Flemish mathermatician and astronomer.

**1541:** Gerard Mercator (who corrected it in 1568 and 1587).

**1545:** Gaspar Vopell: German cartographer.

**1570 (+1587):** Ortelius, Flemish geographer.

**1590:** Steffansson an Iceland bishop, also adds a bridge to the east.

**1605:** Hans Poul Resen, Icelandic bishop.

---

*What we have here is clearly the typical notion of that time of the Far North as a free passage (*pontus* can also mean "passage") westward to Cathay, which would inspire a rush to the north. We should not overlook the fact that all the discoveries in the West (America) were initially considered to be a stage on the road to China or "Cathay."

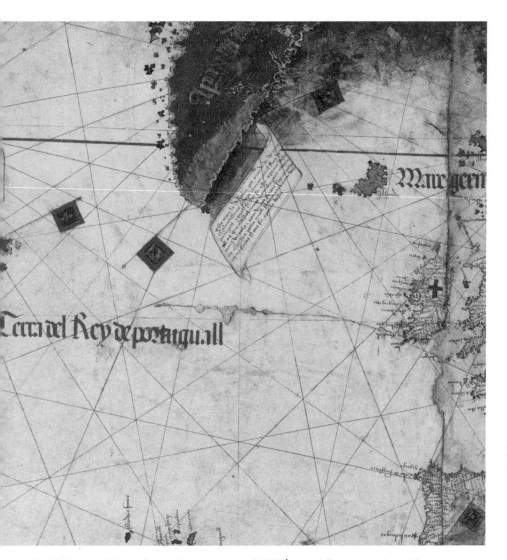

Fig. 10.1. A detail from Cantino's planisphere of 1502 (original Estense Modene Library, Milan) depicts a portion of Greenland (center top) that is relatively well drawn in comparison to the existing maps. The northern part was left out—or censored? The truncated text over Greenland is revealed in the text box off its southeast coast: A Ponta d'[Asia]. Noticeable are the Portuguese coat of arms on a territory that was a dependency of Denmark. The text box reads: "This land discovered on order of his excellency Prince Don Manuel king of Portugal is an end of Asia (esta a Ponta d'Asia). Those who made the discovery didn't land but saw the country and nothing else than steep mountains. Therefore it is considered according to cosmographers to be an end of Asia."
**Wikimedia Commons**

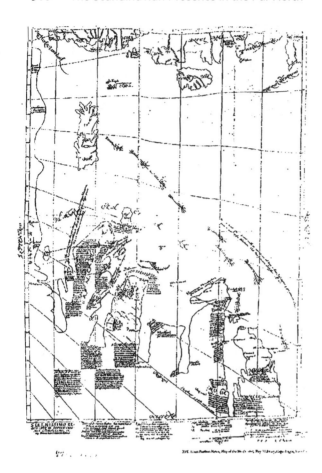

Fig. 10.2. 1605 Map by Scandinavian bishop, H. P. Resen. The fairly realistic position (for this time period) stands out, and more importantly, the relatively correct placement of the eastern colony on the western coast. *Courtesy of the Royal Library, Copenhagen*

This view would continue during the seventeenth century. The idea of a bridge to the west is less farfetched than that of a bridge to the east of Greenland. It is enough to consider the distance separating Greenland from Ellesmere Island. The poetic medieval image of a bridge connecting the tip of Greenland to Greipar is quite illustrative of this ice-covered region.

Rereading all the source materials even the poetic ones is not without value as they reveal a thread of truth. Axel Anton Bjørnbo in his essential book on the cartography of these regions Cartographia Groenlandica and the *Grønlands Historiske Mindesmærker III*[11] cites the account of the priest Halldór in 1266, confirming the clergy's interest in these remote regions and, more importantly, its presence in these places.

The priests then sent a boat northward . . . while they sailed out from the mountains of Kroksfjord until the coast vanished. . . . But when the bad weather cleared . . . they saw many islands and all kinds of games, seals, whales, and many bears. They came right into the bay and there, the entire landscape opened to them, the land to the south and the glaciers, but there were also glaciers to their south as far as the eye could see.

The region described is strongly reminiscent of the northern islands of Canada. The archipelago depicted here seems to clearly correspond to the many islands extending west from Ellesmere (Melville Bay, for example) and heading straight south toward the American continent. Here we see the same physical phenomenon described earlier: the polynia and its abundant game. Bjørnbo went right past this identification for he was unfortunately under the sway of the theory then in vogue that maintained Kroksfjordarheidi was purely and simply in Greenland. The great abundance of game in these regions only confirms that they are identical to the Norse trio of "Greipar, Grocland, and Kroksfjordarheidi." We must keep in mind the excessive sums (mentioned in chapter 3) connected with Hanseatic trade in ivory and falcons. It is easy to understand why so many foreign nations were present here.

As we saw earlier, economic and religious interests were often combined. Where wealth was to be found, the clergy was not far behind. In his chronology of the Norse presence in America, Rafn cites the presence of Garðar churchmen in the Kroksfjord: *"Sacerdotes Gronlandici, qui ad montana Kroksfiordensia, et inde boreum versus terras explorandi causa, profecti erant, hoc æstate Gardos revertuntur."*[12]

This is confirmation of the presence of churchmen who had traveled from Garðar into the Far North for commercial reasons. As I stated earlier, these journeys of trade and exploration come back to their home base. Everything is in agreement, even the testimony of Inuit art. Another medieval Icelandic source text tells of the Icelandic bishop Eirikr traveling in the western lands in 1121: "Eirikr, bishop of Greenland left in search of Vinland."[13]

This hypothesis is gaining increased acceptance among contemporary researchers as this quote from Canadian G. M. Rousselière shows: "The clergy personally organized expeditions into the North. Other signs exist of the Church's presence far to the north of the two colonies. Some archaeologists have identified a ruin on Nuussuaq Peninsula as that of chapel or church."[14]

The regular presence of Vikings in the polar region led some Nordic researchers like Jette Arneborg to advance a new hypothesis about the motivations for Inuit-Scandinavian contacts. Were their meetings by chance or intentional? Arneborg also cites Halldór's text: "It appears in Halldór's 1266 account that Vikings were deliberately looking for Skrælings, probably for the purpose of trade. That would mean that it was impossible to establish those contacts in Disko Bay."[15] We don't know if this impossibility was due to the absence of natives or the absence of products to exchange. Nevertheless, we see in this observation a confirmation of what I'm postulating, namely the absence of abundant polar game (polar bears, walruses, and so forth, and a northern location). Even if these animals could be found on Disko Island, which they can't—based on my knowledge and according to all my sources—in the kind of concentration described by Schledermann in the polynia of the Far North.

This deliberate search for commercial purposes is valid for both populations. Trading between Vikings and the natives was well known. The financial motivations we touched on earlier oblige us not to underestimate this factor. The advantage of this commercial practice is that it requires few people and—if that practice existed on a large scale—it did not deprive the Norse community of manpower during the brief Arctic summer. For this reason we should imagine the Nordrsetur as scattered settlements generating isolated journeys and not massive expeditions. No written source vouches for the latter. Moreover, their agrarian economy would not permit it, nor their social order—only the elite went to this El Dorado.

Scandinavian researchers taking their hypothesis even further as they are establishing a direct link between these intercultural contacts and the movement of Inuit migrations toward the south, accomplished by the Inussuk culture, the culture most marked by Norse influences (could this be merely a coincidence?). So the natives were seeking to make contact with Norse culture; this appears in the numerous Inuit stories cited earlier, and fits very well with their long custom of seasonal migration for the purposes of hunting or trade.

All the sources of this era are very vague on this matter. This vagueness has been interpreted as an admission. I'll quote the *Greenland Annals* based on the *Hauksbók:* "When they reached certain islands south of Snafell ('the snowy mountain') they found some vestiges of the Skrælings. They then sailed south steering toward Kroksfjordarheidi, a good day's row away."

They were sailing southward, a good day's row (because of the ice?), which could correspond to the western coast of Ellesmere a.k.a. Greipar, across from the archipelago of islands with the exceptional amounts of game and possessing a mountain more than 6,000 feet high, Mont Heiberg. Rafn cites another piece of information that could prove important in identifying this site: "People think that this should be the shortest way for them (the natives) from where they are coming."[16]

It is the total ambiguity of this text that gave birth to this notion of a deliberate search. Why were the Vikings looking for traces of the Inuit presence? Why were they so concerned with their route? A simple bellicose motive is not enough. There were Inuit in Greenland then (1266) and no need to try to mount a raid upon them elsewhere.

Let's study more carefully the information from the Inuit route. If we take Devon Island as being the Grocland that borders Kroksfjordarheidi, this gives us one verification of the priest Halldór's information. This is actually the shortest route for the natives coming from any direction, whether it is Ellesmere in the north, Baffin in the south, or the entire complex of islands to the west and southwest.

Devon Island (a.k.a. Kroksfjord or more precisely Grocland) is placed where all these routes intersect. It is a vital and negotiable crossroads that is first and foremost nourishing. It is easy to understand why both the Inuit and Scandinavians found it so important. These polar islands were therefore highly sought after because they were a source of wealth (and quite different from the cliché of desolate lands devoid of value). Theodore Thorlacius in his 1668 map wrote this about them:

"It was in these places that the Greenlanders (Vikings) in the past went especially for fish, particularly during the summer."[17]

Thorlacius's last, rather trivial observation again allows us to dismiss the theories placing the Nordrsetur farther south and strengthens my contention that its location was in the north. Fishing is possible for longer periods at the lower latitudes including both colonies and (farther north) in Disko. If fishing was not pursued, I can only see two explana-

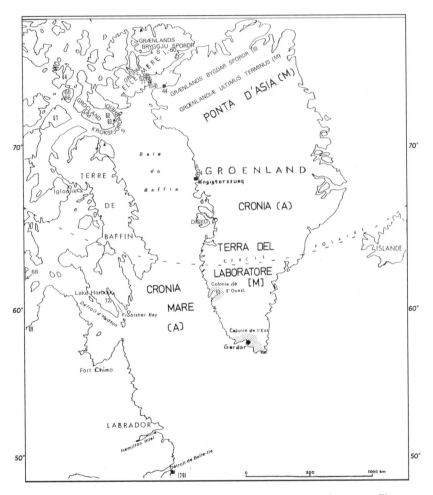

Fig. 10.3. Myth and reality, the Norse sphere until the sixteenth century. The identifications I suggest were found using southern sources (M), Scandinavian sources (S), or even ancient (A) ones. A certain number of archaeological sites or Inuit statuettes cited in chapter 4 also appear.
*Image by J. Privat*

tions, either an appreciable distance for the Norse colonies (that all the sources mentioned imply) or it was quite simply made impossible by a natural climate change due to its higher latitude (the ice didn't melt, and so on).

The value of these polar islands is again confirmed. There was a cause-and-effect connection, in fact, between these rich hunting grounds of Greipar, Grocland, and Kroksfjordarheidi, and the affluence of the wealthy farmers of South Greenland. We saw in the *Hauksbók* cited by Rafn and Bjørnbo that "all the major farm owners owned large boats for hunting purposes during the Nordrsetur expeditions."[18]

The polar islands were a veritable El Dorado at this time for hunting, fishing, ivory, and falcons. Their importance assumes its full weight when we see its traces in the cultural legacy of the Inuit, Scandinavians, and other European nations. This is where the study of the foreign presence on the medieval Arctic becomes highly significant.

## FOREIGN ACCOUNTS: A GERMAN GLOBE FROM 1492

A globe produced in 1492, therefore reflecting pre-Columbian geographical knowledge, had provided a very close description of our sources concerning these islands and their riches. The value of this information has practically gone unnoticed as one of the many geographical errors of this time depicted Greenland as an extension of Lapland. Hence the widespread confusion between the Sami (commonly called Laplanders), Karelians, and the Inuit that appears in the work of numerous medieval authors.

Concerning this globe, contemporary research restored Greenland to its rightful place, whereas it had been drawn and presented earlier as extending the Scandinavian/Lapland landmass as it appears on this globe.

If we consider the overall correct placement of Iceland, and that to the west there is a strait that has some resemblance to the Bering Strait, we have to conclude that the lands located between these two locations would correspond to Canada, which amounts to saying that here we have one of the first conclusive depictions of America, as all the lands on Earth are represented, and all the islands have a very high latitude. Here we see again the traditional 75° N latitude. Its author confirms the Inuit and Norse sources on highly sought game (a polar bear and falcon are clearly cited, or even better, drawn), so no doubt is permissible. A large island the size of a continent near the pole bears the mention: "Here the white falcons are caught."[19]

This place was therefore not completely unknown to Europeans. This German commentary confirms the interest of the Hanseatic League here and their monopoly on its trade. This large island (or continent confused for an island as occurred quite frequently during the middle ages), is separated from another northern land at its western end about which is said: "This country is inhabited during the summer."*

I have compared this narrow channel separating these two lands to the Bering Strait, for the allusion to Siberia is fairly blatant in my opinion. Skelton, Marston, and Painter have rightly pointed out a reference to Marco Polo. The long commentary on the globe describes the fur-bearing fauna, the Arctic summer, the seasonal migrations of the natives by sled (this is one of the rare sources to mention this particular transport) leaves no doubt: "In summer, the sun shines all night long, similarly, when the Russians want to have valuable furs, they have to travel *by sled that is pulled by large dogs because of the deep snow and water.*"[20]

A commentary located near Iceland is also surprising for while it concerns why the country's spelling had changed, the description it gives cannot help but bring to mind the poorly known Arctic countries: "In the land of ice there live a handsome people who are Christian. There it is customary to sell dogs for a high price and to abandon children to merchants so that they will feed them out of love for God."[21]

I am all too familiar with the (often intentional) confusion that governed the cartography of this era. If it was Iceland, why first change its spelling and then stress the beauty of its inhabitants or their Christian religion, which was no secret to anyone and went back several centuries. It seems that Behaim wanted to stress the unexpected

---

*"*Das Land ist bewont im Sommer*" taken from Marco Polo's Pipino version, chaps. 48–49, book 3.

characteristics that testify to the same surprise and commentaries of later explorers like Cartier or Verrazano who speak of beautiful natives who used the cross. One detail sticks out in particular: the lucrative sale of dogs that would be surprising in reference to Iceland, and for what purpose, besides? Now if it is a country where the use and utility of dogs was well known, it is clearly in the Arctic. The Inuit attained perfection in their use of dogs, but as Behaim is speaking of whites—Christians to boot—I have to conclude that they learned of the use that could be made of dogs in the Far North, which would be a major argument for positive contacts between these two peoples and a pertinent example of the borrowing of a traction technique. I am frankly stunned to find no mention of sleds, a technique that should have stupefied his contemporaries. For example, accounts of unsinkable boats—the kayak—are not lacking (for example, Olaus Magnus and the Zeno brothers). Based on my earlier observations of the Inuit people, I feel that the Northmen encountered Dorset people who had no large sleds but used dogs to pull small sleds.

This long analytical approach of every element of medieval Arctic geography now allows me to glue back together all the pieces of this gigantic puzzle, while respecting their sources. We have here a clear depiction of the "falcon islands" located to the east of Asia as conceived during the Middle Ages. Oleson mentions them, for example: "The islands of the eastern Canadian Arctic were depicted, like the islands of falcons, separated from the coasts of Asia."[22]

Oddly enough, Oleson doesn't make the comparison with the globe's description. Furthermore, he is too quick to advance (in my opinion) identification of the bear island (see below) with Greenland because of its physiognomy. Yet its shape was unknown at that time— with the likely exception of the Portuguese who spoke early on of *Illa verde,* and of Rome.

This notion that Asia neighbored this region unleashed the famous rush to the Northwest Passage leading to "Cathay." Here we can see not only echoes of the ideas of Marco Polo (a long strait separating Asia from a new land over which towered a northern range of mountains, the Bergi region) but also those of Nicholas of Lynn, reintroduced by

Jacob Cnoyen, that were even given credence by the illustrious Gerardus Mercator. This is how we find the polar islands and an allusion to four commercial regions with two clearly identified here: Falcon Island (an immense island the size of a continent, separated by a strait [Bering] from Asia), and the equally large Bear Island, surrounded by an archipelago. This brings to mind the description provide by the priest Halldór in 1266.

Two other islands are missing, probably the one for walrus ivory and leather, and the one for the "tooth" of the narwhal (or unicorn in the medieval imagination). The benefits that could be drawn from them represented substantial revenues in this era. The large sea mammals could also have been considered, but up to now I haven't found any confirmation written at such a late date, and the intensive exploitation of whales would only come later, hence my reservations.

## Bear Island

Because of its shape and position, it was long confused for Greenland, which was already marked, albeit incorrectly, on the globe. This error, though, allows us to authenticate my source, as this error was predominant at this time. Furthermore, the actual shape of Greenland would not be known for still some time (the nineteenth century). Bear Island cannot therefore in any case, during the medieval era and because of a morphological resemblance, be incorporated into Greenland. This observation is also valid, if only in passing, for the overly perfect configuration of Greenland in the "so-called Vinland map." Even the later existence of maps combining both concepts (A and B) on the same map don't convince me. Bear Island appears on this globe as entirely deserted and any fifteenth-century geographer or sailor knew that people lived on Greenland.

Bjørnbo clearly suggested a Norse presence and confirmed that hunting for bears took place. A drawing shows an archer taking aim at a bear, but he didn't make the connection with Canada. In his defense, he was just a decade shy of being sure of the Norse identity of the archer (in Canada). In fact Nørlund's excavations in Herjolfsnes/Ikigait in 1921 unearthed the greatest collection ever discovered of practically

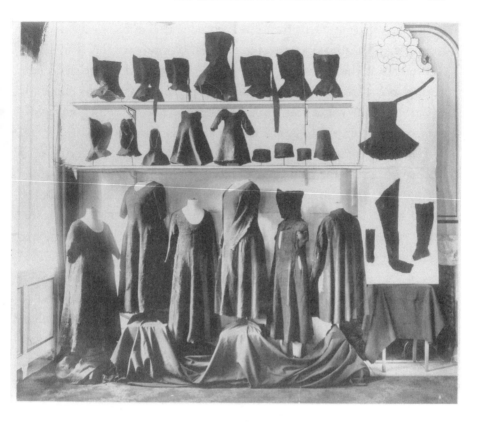

Fig. 10.4. Medieval Norse clothing found in the 1921 Greenland excavations of Poul Nørlund in Ikigait/Herjolfsnes. This is the largest collection of medieval folk garments (fifty pieces of men's, women's, and children's clothing) found intact in the permafrost. We can recognize here the long hooded garment of the archer depicted on M. Behaim's globe as well as those of some of the Inuit statuettes discussed in chapter 4.
*Photo courtesy of National Museum, Copenhagen*

intact medieval folk clothing. This clothing closely resembles that of our archer hunting a bear. We can recognize the long robe and hood,* which also bring to mind the Inuit artistic depictions of these same people. This source could only come from Nicholas of Lynn (through Jacob Cnoyen) and probably Ivar Bårdsson.

Inuit statuette no. 11 strongly evokes this outfit. Its location, the Canadian island to the south of Baffin Island in Okivilialik, is

---

*See photo from the National Museum of Copenhagen (fig. 10.4).

consistent with my identification. I would also like to point out that during the Herjolfsnes's excavations several crosses were found in some of the coffins that were dug up. Some, very simplified, were of Celtic inspiration, which led Nørlund to compare it with the Scottich and Irish style. This could confirm a Celtic influence at the beginning of the Greenland colonists' conversion to Christianity.

Polar bears could be captured alive thanks to stone traps that can be recognized by their fairly substantial sizes. The example found on the Nuussuaq Peninsula in the Disko region measures 1.15 meters by 2.28 meters. The entry tunnel was 1.5 meters long and 0.55 meter wide at the entrance and 0.47 at the location of the trap. These bear traps are also found in the Canadian regions of John Sound, Lancaster Sound, Smith Sound and even on Melville Peninsula, all typical Nordrsetur regions with strong Scandinavian connotations by virtue of the various archaeological, artistic, and mythical evidence. Oleson believes these traps are evidence of an extended Scandinavian presence, an opinion I share, as traps require maintenance of these locations and remaining there a certain time to harvest the fruits of this hunt. Oleson also cites the traditional Inuit lore according to which they were the work of the "Tuniit."

All of these elements are consistent with the Nordrsetur, illustrating their economic significance (capturing luxury game) and confirming their northern location. They also clearly identify their authors: the Vikings. Armed with this information, the famous 1360 voyage becomes a little more coherent. The source material of Nicholas of Lynn and Jacobus Cnoyen appear in a different light further removed from their mythical aura and more as a pure product of their medieval contemporaries. Nicholas of Lynn was a mathematician and astronomer, after all, and partial to the exact sciences. With the Skaldic poem mentioned earlier, this globe is the second key to understanding the Scandinavian voyages to the north or to America. In passing it also gives us confirmation of Iceland's nonisolated status: "On the island of Iceland, cod is fished that is then brought to our country."[23]

Here we have another piece of information that weakens the theory of the great isolation of the northern dependencies. These lands were well known to their European contemporaries, particularly the Germans and members of the Hanseatic League. This knowledge appears in the cartography of the time and various texts pertaining to the European presence in these regions (for purposes of trade and piracy). As a point of interest, I might add that this knowledge circulated rather well. I have pointed out the importance of certain details, and this confirms my claims: the creator of the globe, Martin Behaim was married to the daughter of the nobleman Joost de Hurtere of the Azores, and she was also the sister-in-law of João Vaz Corte-Real, a member of the 1473 joint Danish-Portuguese expedition that visited Iceland, Greenland, and the eastern coast of Canada. These are all members of high society, so it is easy to grasp the quality of their information.

## ARCHAEOLOGY'S TESTIMONY

As early as 1943, Vilhjalmur Steffanson used archaeological excavations and Inuit folklore to advance the hypothesis of a Norse presence very far north and that Scandinavians had gone as high as lat 79° N by way of the western slope of the Smith Sound. Thirteen locations with remnants were recorded in the Canadian polar islands in 1991, two in Hudson Bay, and obviously the site of L'Anse aux Meadows. Ellesmere Island has eight locations bearing traces of a Scandinavian presence. I will mention here the list of sites with the same numbers given by the Danish researcher,[24] and depict them on our maps, like those of the Nordrsetur. I have added a few additional elements that were not necessarily part of standard archaeological digs but whose evidence deserves mention: these are cairns and nest boxes the Scandinavians would have left behind. The 1997 excavations of Deby and Georges Sabo that unearthed a statuette that most likely depicts a Nordic churchman doesn't appear in his list.

### Washington Irving Island (61)
These excavations made in 1875 are relatively old. This expedition led by explorer Sir George Nares is said to have detected two cairns at the top of the island located on the eastern coast of Ellesmere (lat 79°35' N, long 73° W, near the coast of Grinnell Land). Their description and

the vegetation covering them revealed the age of these works, inspiring the hypothesis of a Norse origin probably during a hunting expedition (the famous Nordrsetur). Prytz describes this site as a prime hunting ground for walrus and Kane Basin as teeming with narwhals. Schlerdermann and McCullough visited this site in 1970 but did not find these cairns. Schlerdermann, however, believes he identified what could be the base or remains of one of them.

### Southern Side of Ellesmere, Longitude 88°–89° W (61 bis)

Two other cairns were discovered during the second expedition of the polar boat *Fram* of 1898 to 1902 led by a companion of Fridtjof Nansen, Otto Sverdrup. Lieutenant Gunnar Isachsen was responsible for the cartography of these unknown regions. The two cairns seen at long 88°–89° W in the western part of Jones Sound were interpreted as evidence of a Scandinavian presence by Fridtjof and Gunnar Isachsen, and later by T. J. Oleson: "Their construction was by all evidence not Eskimo and their date was definitely medieval."[25] One interesting detail: the south part of Ellesmere Island at this longitude is described as having lush plant growth and an abundance of animal life. This location put us smack in the middle of our medieval identification of the mythical perimeter of Greipar (southern side) across from Grocland/Devon, known for its abundant game during the Middle Ages.

### Ruin Island Thule Region (44)

The excavations in Inuarfissuaq here were made by Holtved in 1936.

Objects found: a little piece of coat mail, a piece of wool clothing dating from 1270 (±50 years), and two iron blades. Arneborg also mentions two pieces of oak dating, respectively, from 880 (±80 years) and 930 (±100 years). Holtved interprets this site as the result of a later Thule migration from Canada to Greenland in the fourteenth century (the phase specifically labeled the Ruin Island phase). After the invention of carbon-14 dating, J. Meldgaard suggested the site was inhabited about 900 to 1100. Using dates from marine samples, Jordan and McCullough gave more recent dates, the last half of the thirteenth century and circa 1200, respectively.

## Skræling Island, Buchanan Bay, Ellesmere Island (54)

Excavations were made in 1978, 1982, 1987, and 1990 by Peter Schledermann and Karen McCullough. Scandinavian tools were found in twenty-three houses. These authors don't say if they are Inuit, but Schledermann tells us that all are Thule houses dating from different eras. The majority of Norse objects are connected to the period of Inuit inhabitation of Ruin Island near Inglefield Land in Greenland. This phase is strongly represented on Skræling Island with twenty-six houses. The Scandinavian objects are mainly metal fragments, a weapon point carved from a Scandinavian rivet, iron nails, several iron rings, pieces of copper, a knife blade, two cloth remnants spun from wool dating from 1250 (±50 years) for Gulløv and from 1280 for Schledermann, a plane without a blade, and a piece of carbonized oak that Arneborg dates to 860 (±110 years). This living place was deserted about 1300 to 1350 according to McCullough. This confirms for me Scandinavian contact with Thule culture mainly and not Dorset culture. Using carbon-14 dating, Schledermann places these direct contacts between the Inuit and Viking circa 1300 (±50 years) in the Smith Sound or Baffin Bay.

## Eskimobyen, Knud Peninusla, Ellesmere Island (56)

Excavations made by Schlederman and McCullough in Eskimobyen in the northern end of the Knud Peninsula during the period of 1978 to 1982, and 1990. The objects found: remains of a pail bottom decorated with concentric circles, pieces of oak coming from a box dated 1390 (±60 years), a piece of copper, nails, and several imprecise pieces of iron and copper. The Norse objects belong to this phase. I would add that in the same region (Bache Peninsula) an Inuit ivory statuette *depicting a Scandinavian* was found. The Bache Peninsula region offers *the largest number of Norse object in North America.*

## Ellesmere Island (58)

Excavations made in 1977 under the direction of Patricia Sutherland in settlements located about 200 kilometers from Skræling Island and the Sverdrup site.

Objects found: a *scale arm of Norse origin* according to R. McGhee.

In fact, it can't help but bring to mind the scales that are used to weigh precious metals. It is valid to question its presence so far north. It would be more appropriate in exchanges with Europeans than Inuit.

### Cape Silumiut, Keewatin District, Hudson Bay (68)

The excavations were conducted by P. McCartney in 1969.

Objects found: a fragment of an iron knife blade of southern European origin (according to metal analysis). It would still have been transmitted by way of the Norse colonies but confirms an early European presence in the Far North. The settlement is dated to about 1200 by carbon-14 dating.

### Hazard Gulf, Richmond Gulf, Hudson Bay, Quebec (69)

Excavations led by Elmer Harp Jr. in 1967 and 1970. The largest sites showing signs of habitation go back as far as the 800s and into more recent times. Carbon-14 dating places the site to 795 ± 120 years. According to the stratigraphic layers, this house is from the Dorset era.

Objects found: I would specifically mention a southern European copper amulet coming from the Hazard Gulf site, copper from the Norse colonies of Greenland. It should be noted that Hudson Bay and Ungava Bay are increasingly attracting attention from specialists, several elements (cairns, nest boxes) that we shall look at briefly later seem to give grounds for at least a temporary Scandinavian presence in these regions. Examples of longhouses have also been found. Their paternity has yet to be established. A Scandinavian origin is not excluded and is supported by Oleson—for example, the longhouse called the "Ford Site" fifty miles from Pamiok Island to the west of Ungava Bay is much larger than a native dwelling. Some clues such as the absence of any Dorset presence in the area strengthens the possibility this house is of Scandinavian origin. As mentioned earlier, one of the difficulties lies in the identification of housing, especially when judging on the basis of known standards. As Gini pointed out so well, a population escaping banishment is not compelled to recreate the same structures in such a new environment like the Canadian Arctic. This is probably the criterion that created an obstacle for researchers looking for old housing models as well as tools, weapons, and so forth. Now, if the Vikings were merging more and more into the native populace, this means that this mixing would have not only biological but material repercussions. T. E. Lee notes the presence of seal oil lamps—which are typical of Inuit culture—in likely Scandinavian sites. Similarly, there is the presence of the small fire pits seen by Nørlund dating from the twelfth and thirteenth century. According to him, the Scandinavians could have adopted the Inuit technique of using seal fat for lighting, heating, and cooking. Helge Ingstad also noted a similarity between the typically Scandinavian sites such as those and Brattahlið and those of L'Anse aux Meadows. In short, we should probably start looking more often for elements of craftmanship showing signs of cultural fusion, like that of the path followed by the Scandinavian colony of Greenland. We should note that the "nest boxes," a typically Nordic technique, were found in this region, therefore adding more fuel to the Norse thesis.

Although they don't form part of the Arctic perimeter, there are two sites that need to be considered separately and not overlooked. The first one I'm going to mention is exceptional, more for the meaning than for the physical size of the discovery. The findings at L'Anse aux Meadows are unfortunately not as rich as those Oseberg or of Roskilde,* but they confirm, if proof is still needed, the real presence of the Norse in American during the Middle Ages.

### L'Anse aux Meadows, Newfoundland (70)

This site has been classified as a World Heritage Site by UNESCO if anyone is still harboring any doubts about its authenticity. It was discovered in 1960 by Helge and Stine Ingstad. The excavations were led by Anne Stine Ingstad during the period of 1961 to 1968, then under the direction of Bengt Schönbach for the period 1973 to 1976, and later (1986) by Birgitta Linderoth. The archaeological site contains three settlements that all show signs of houses, outbuildings, and even a forge, which definitively excludes an identification of this as a native settlement.

---

*Some very well-preserved Viking boats were found. The one in Oseberg, probably a funeral vessel, was richly decorated.

Relatively few objects have been found, although their number is not insignificant. If at first they are reminiscent of the objects found in the earlier sites (their value is derisory, what we have is the debris the Vikings left behind while passing through), their meaning is completely different and appears simply by listing them. The paucity of objects found confirms the uniqueness of these movements: all left relatively few traces behind them. The voyages to the Nordrsetur are expeditions for bringing back products that are very profitable commercially speaking and not intended to leave any traces behind. This is not the case with Vinland, which is more akin to a colonization— or at least an attempt at one—and what's more in a non-Arctic region, therefore outside our subject area. The problem is that Newfoundland is difficult to classify among the Nordrsetur. It barely corresponds to the descriptions left by the Scandinavians of their journeys (glaciers, snow-covered mountains, which are hard to place in Newfoundland), and it seems unlikely that hardened sailors like the Norsemen would have confused the northern latitudes with that of Newfoundland.

How should this island be classified? It has still not completely convinced all the experts who doubt that it is identical with Vinland. Let's take a quick look at the objects found there:

Iron rivets whose connection with Viking boats is easy to make.
A bronze needle of the Scotch-Irish type (heading in the direction of a Escocilant,* which we will touch on briefly later).
A glass pearl, a weaving loom weight, and other spinning items typical of Scandinavian settlements in Greenland.
A sharpening stone, a Scandinavian-type of bone needle.

Numerous remnants of wood and ironwork have also been found, as

---

*This land located just south of Hudson Bay is supposed to have been lived in by Irish and/or Scottish monks. Eugene Beauvois sees it as the Nordic *Hvitramannaland,* which has been translated as "the country of the white men," or "the land of the men in white." It has not been definitively proved whether this refers to the white chamois-skin tunic of the Naskapi people or the Nordic people.

well as a pig bone.* The archaeologists also pointed out the presence of the traces of saunas. All these elements authenticate the Norse identity of the site. The value of this site deserves its own separate study, but it doesn't fall within the scope of this work. I would simply note that its difference from all the other sites we've looked at is the presence of several women's tools for spinning. So what we have here is a completely different sort of site, one I would call more stable. The existence of a forge and the remnants of a boatyard confirm this relative stability. This site is akin to a relay station, I might say, for boats sailing to or from Greenland, thus more like a settlement of temporary colonization. Although this may stray close to euphemism. According to the written sources, the presence in Vinland was never very long as the Vikings were in direct competition with the Skrælings, who were much more dangerous than the populations they had encountered in Greenland or the Far North.

In total, "133 carbon-14 datings have been performed on this site."[26] They reflect a brief Norse presence here circa the year 1000. This presence may have lasted several years. The hypothesis of a short presence is based on the modest amount of trash (mainly domestic) left by the Scandinavians, which seems to be an important element in overall estimations concerning any peoples' presence.

Anne Stine Ingstad sees a brief Scandinavian presence in L'Anse aux Meadows. She notes the lack of traces of any intense activities such as mining or canals compared to settlements in Greenland, which would have left their mark on the site. "By all evidence the Nordic settlement was too small and inhabited too briefly to have left any mark on the vegetation."[27]

The wood and metal debris have been interpreted as evidence of boat repairs, leading to the conclusion that L'Anse aux Meadows was primarily a temporary base for Norse voyages of exploration where they could winter over and repair their boats, a kind of stopover on the Vinland route. We should also remember that according to the most optimistic sagas on Vinland, the number of colonists went from 60 to 160 in Thorfinn Karlsefni's expedition in the *Saga of Erik the Red.*

---

*This animal didn't exist in America during the Middle Ages.

## *Naskeag Point, Penobscot Bay, Maine (71)*

These excavations were made by amateur archaeologists in 1958 at an indigenous site on Naskeag Point in Penobscot Bay. Unfortunately, they did not have the benefit of professional precision and no real analysis of the location was made. There was no study of the stratigraphic layers, and the objects were only turned over to the Maine State Museum later.

All of this is truly a shame because a severely damaged coin was found there. It was identified as a Norwegian Olaf Kyrre coin, struck during the period of 1065 to 1095. I would like to point out the concordance of these dates with those of the site of L'Anse aux Meadows and the very early eleventh-century dates that support the direction of my hypothesis: Scandinavian voyages to the west and to the north began very early. This is even more regrettable when we consider how this region, particularly the Penobscot River and thus its bay, was often associated with a typically Scandinavian site: Norumbega but we will revisit this matter in greater detail as it deserves our full attention.

This site is one of the least certain from a scientific perspective. I would also like to point out that this is the sole known case in Far North where a coin has been found. Not a single coin has been discovered in Greenland, and this after a Norse presence of at least five centuries.* Nor is there any written source material that mentions coinage, hence the quasi-certitude of an economy based on barter. This is confirmed by the clerical taxes (St. Peter's Pence and other taxes for the Crusades) paid by the Scandinavians in goods, most often in ivory.

On the other hand, this coin could be the result of another European presence. Let's not forget that the 1492 globe is German, that German bishops visited Greenland, that Hanseatic League members went to Iceland, and that they used Norwegian money.

I would unhesitatingly compare this with the scale arm found

---

*We find an indirect confirmation in the response from Pope John XXI to Archbishop Jón of Nidaros dated December 12, 1276. Even in Norway, use of money was quite limited and all the more so in the faraway northwestern islands. "Norwegian money is so restricted that it has almost no value abroad. Furthermore, in some parts of the kingdom, it is not customary to use money. On these areas, wheat doesn't grow. The people live on milk and fish." Original *Reg. Vat.* John XXI, folio 23; *Reg. Norv.* 1276, doc. 158.

during Patricia Sutherland's digs (site no. 58) in Ellesmere, for we know that the Vikings were skilled merchants. To be clear, we have here confirmation of the mercantile significance of the Nordrsetur, but we have inherited another brain-teaser:

Knowing that the colonists bartered with the natives the presence of Norwegian money (which could have been brought by foreigners), and a Nordic scale (according to the archaeologists) used to weigh* valuable metals or objects, are difficult to explain in these lands. Here we find another confirmation of the presence of foreign nations in the Scandinavian Arctic. We should note here R. H. Holand's rather interesting version of this as he draws a connection between it and the very controversial Kensington runestone. According to him, this is evidence of an expedition into America circa 1360 consisting of eight Goths and twenty-two Norwegians, including Nicholas of Lynn. Several observations are called for here: all these finds were found at or near Thule settlements. We know that Inussuk culture was a later phase of Thule culture and that it was the Inuit culture most heavily influenced by the Scandinavians.

The most important observation I would counter the hypothesis of a trade between Inuit and Vikings with here is that the Inuit "territories" cover the entire polar cap. We should logically expect to find, in cases of barter, all the remains of these exchanged objects widely scatter, which is not the case. Weirdly, we only find these remains in specific places, relatively close together (as can be seen on the map). This is particularly visible in the Ellesmere region which strengthens its identification with the medieval Greipar, still called the end of the Greenland bridge in Skaldic poetry. We have the same density of Scandinavian objects on Devon Island, which physically corresponds (and by its location) to Kroksfjordarheidi or to K/Grocland of the European maps. This island is located directly at lat 75° N. All these archaeological sites are located within the legendary perimeter described earlier, with the priest

---

*I have great doubt—for practical reasons—that this tool was used for Inuit products like skins, ivory, and so on that are all much too large for it. In any event, this instrument doesn't truly suit the crafty swaps of trinkets and shiny glass beads for the valuable goods of the natives.

Halldór, Nicholas of Lynn, and others. Newfoundland and Hudson Bay are unique cases that are still too poorly documented to be considered separately.

The conclusion dictated by these circumstances is that all these object remnants are rather evidence of the passage or presence of Vikings than of bartering activity. I will not revisit the insignificant values of this alleged barter. The hypothesis of Inuit attraction to these objects as curiosities is strong. Jette Arneborg[28] gives credence to contacts between Inuit and Scandinavians in these remote locations: "The Scandinavian cultural roots existing in North Greenland and the Ellesmere Island settlements in the Canadian Arctic appear to reflect *direct contacts* between Eskimos and Scandinavians *north of Melville Bay.*"

At the same time, Arneborg dismisses identification of Disko Island in West Greenland as a meeting place for Norse and Inuit cultures: "The currently existing materials offer no sure and certain confirmation of an encounter between the Inuit and Norse cultures in the Disko Bay region during the period of 1000–1100."[29]

I also support this position. I don't believe there can be any further doubt concerning the location of the Nordrsetur, Greipar, and other famous sites of the medieval Nordic north. The abundance of the fauna proves it.

Another observation to focus on is the presence of European objects in the Far North—in small quantities of course. This confirms for me the presence of these same Europeans in the Arctic or in the most pessimistic hypothesis, in Greenland where they would have bartered these objects. I think that is a very reductive view of things and not well founded. The distance separating Greenland from these rich hunting grounds of northern Greenland and Canada was quite small compared to that traveled by the English, German, Portuguese, and other sailors frequenting Iceland or the Norse colony of South Greenland. If need be, the Danish-Portuguese expedition of 1473 in Canada and Greenland's Arctic regions confirms my claim. It is difficult to believe that after completing a journey like that, they would be satisfied with a simple stay in Greenland, knowing that that stories about the western lands were beginning to spread in Europe at least among certain privileged circles.

For example, Nicholas of Lynn's account of his journey was consulted frequently along with his book *Inventio fortunatæ,* which has since disappeared. In fact, even the illustrious Christopher Columbus read it. K. Prytz even claims it was almost his bedside reading as he mentions it several times in his journal (September 25, October 3, October 10, 1492).

I have hesitated at listing the following finds among the archaeological discoveries. During Sir George Nares's expedition, the physician Dr. Edward L. Moss found on Norman Lockyer Island (lat 79°28' N, long 74°50' W) a bird shelter. During the Fram expedition of 1900, Sverdrup and Isachsen found another at St. Helena north of Devon Island (lat 76°29' N, long 89°20' W) and on Beechey Island (lat 76°29' N, long 90°45' W) numerous shelters intended for eider to lay their eggs, thereby procuring eggs and down. These devices were of foreign manufacture and have nothing in common with Inuit practices; on the other hand, they are known in Norway. These same nesting boxes were found on Washington Irving Island (lat 79°35' N) and in the area around Alexandra Fjord. Oleson says researchers are almost unanimous about their origin in medieval Iceland. Several researchers have highlighted the differences between Inuit and Scandinavian hunting customs. It is not Inuit practice to raise birds or protect them. On the other hand, Scandinavians were known for this in all parts of Scandinavia. It was even considered antisocial in districts inhabited by the northmen to kill eider ducks or destroy their eggs. Shelters were built for eider ducks to nest in, as a way to encourage them to stay. I noted earlier the other Scandinavian objects in these areas and identified these settlements as belonging to the "traditional Scandinavian perimeter." Alexandra Fjord is close to Skræling Island and the polynia known as the Flagler Bay polynia. We should recall the existence in Norse tradition of two mysterious islands that are still unidentified, Ædanes and Eisunes.

Could there be a connection between this egg-collecting activity and Ædanes (could this be comparable to *Œrfugleneset* or *edderfuglnæs*). The eider duck was particularly sought after by the Norse for its down (*edderdun*). Schledermann doesn't dismiss this possibility (at least for the Scandinavian origin of polar bear and fox traps, or at least an Inuit borrowing of this technique).

We should also note that Thomas E. Lee mentions the existence of eider duck egg nests in Ungava Bay to which he connects the Scandinavian custom (I also recall the presence of those "anonymous" longhouses). He bases his case mainly on the work of Robert Williamsson in the Payne region who compares these nest boxes to those still existing in Iceland. "They [the next boxes] were identical to ancient Scandinavian structures. His opinion [Williamsson] is that the shelters of Payne Bay have the same origin."[30]

Lee notes the presence of numerous cairns in Ungava Bay and how some could be the work of Vikings because of the precision of their construction, their placement, and significance (landmarks for navigation among other things).* The oddest one, known as "Thor's Hammer," near Payne Bay in the Arnaud Estuary strongly evokes the pagan worship of the Scandinavians which medieval clerical sources claim reappeared after they abandoned the true faith. I would like to add one more detail, according to Lee the technical difficulty involved in erecting this monument that is ten feet high and whose largest stone weighs two tons, presumes the use of tools that only the Vikings possessed among the populations that frequented this area during that time.

In conclusion, I can say that this mythical region of Greipar, K/Grocland, and Kroksfjordarheidi is probably the best documented in both Nordic and foreign source materials. It has the benefit of numerous archaeological confirmations for which P. Schledermann is quite well placed to judge: "There seems to be sufficient material to state that the Scandinavian presence in the extreme arctic regions of Canada and Greenland, in no longer simply an appealing idea but a very reasonable hypothesis."[31] However, this region was the one most overlooked by researchers, perhaps because of its remoteness and presumed lack of value (economic among others), and the desolation of its ice-covered expanses. It is true that Vinland has long monopolized attention to the detriment of other lands.

---

*Would these be the strange works that Erik Walkendorf alluded to in his 1516 list?

# 11

# THE EUROPEAN PRESENCE
# IN THE FAR NORTH

ould the Nordic isolation so heavily emphasized for so long by contemporaries and even researchers be merely a fable? This theory that remains firmly rooted in everyone's mind today had the advantage of explaining—too easily in my opinion—the vacuum in written sources concerning certain remote and troubled periods of the Middle Ages, particularly the fifteenth century. A rapid glance over this period will give us a completely different opinion. Scandinavia in general, Iceland, Greenland, and the "American dependencies" in particular, were not as isolated as we are given to think; quite the contrary. A good understanding of Greenland implies a good understanding of its immediate surroundings, Iceland among others, not only its geographical neighbor but also mother country for its colonists.

In other words, knowing the medieval relevance of Iceland can help us understand what went on in Greenland. The opposite opinion, contrary to isolation, is in my view product of a disproportionate optimism with respect to the situation of the time.

## THE HISTORICAL ROLE OF ENGLAND

The historical bonds uniting the Anglo-Celtic world with Iceland should not be overlooked or underestimated. The discovery of Iceland was the work of the Irish. The fifteenth century was known as "The

Age of England" because of the substantial, persistent English presence, based on the contemporary accounts cited below. Gudbrand Thorlaksen Eriksen describes Icelandic history as being sewn with a long British thread that extends from the discovery of the island to the present day: "An almost uninterrupted continuity goes from ancient times to ours . . . Their commerce in Iceland is almost as old as the creation of the country . . . Sometimes, the earliest ancestors of the Icelanders came from Great Britain and its surrounding islands."[1]

This foreign Anglo-Celtic presence in Iceland (by which I mean from the first Celtic inhabitants to the fifteenth century, when the English commercial presence was dominant) is rather well documented as we shall see, but several clues give us reason to believe it was not limited to Iceland alone, we should not forget that during a simple journey from England to Iceland it was easy to be blown off course and end up farther west. The very old medieval tradition of rectangular maps, like the eleventh-century Beatine map of Beatus of Liebana, and even earlier, mention a fourth continent with ties to Hibernia (Ireland). This supports the notion of the long-suspected contacts of the Celts with the western lands very early on.

Knowing these facts should inspire greater curiosity about the British source materials. There is an entire context (economic, mainly), geographical location, and array of maritime traditions that can easily explain Anglo-Celtic knowledge of the Far North as well as their presence in these regions. In light of these irrefutable historical facts, we can better grasp the presence of the mathematician and astronomer monk Nicholas of Lynn in Greenland and Canada during the 1360 expedition. His account has long been the subject of criticism and controversy. However, in connection with this voyage, Hallyut cites the privileges that would have been granted the town of Blakeney by King Edward III.

> Privileges were granted to the fishermen of the town of Blakeney [Earldom of Norfolk] exempting them from ordinary duties [to the king] because of their commerce with Iceland.[2]

These Icelandic-British connections even left literary traces, such as this British poem:

Of Island to write is little need Save of stock-fish, yet forsooth indeed Out of Bristowe [Bristol] and costs manyone Men have prac-ticed by needle and by stone . . .

ENGLYSHE POLYEYE: UNKNOWN AUTHOR, 1436[3]

Contrary to the medieval Scandinavian source texts, the "protector-ates" of the far north were far from being isolated. Oleson is very clear in this regard: "All of eastern America, and north of the Gulf of Saint Lawrence was known to medieval Europe as *Hvitramannaland* (the country of the white men). The islands of Arctic Canada were depicted as the 'falcon islands' off the coast of Asia, Vinland was sometimes con-sidered as an extension of Africa."[*]

I will keep my distance from the easy solution that is content to regard these sometimes-far-fetched notions with a knowing smile. The Middle Ages is characterized by these kinds of erroneous notions. I have there-fore incurred the risk of using—as critically as I can—all these sources in order to not miss even the smallest piece of information. It's a fact that the *Hvitramannaland*[†] of myth and legend was always identified as a land in the west by medieval people. The error is therefore relative, just like the confusion with Africa. The more or less similar climate of the islands of Central America, the populations that initially seemed no different from one another to the average sailor of that era, all this was able to easily muddle the minds of the first European visitors to these lands. Along the same lines, Asia was not supposed to be very far away.

---

[*]Oleson (1963). This amicable bedlam of knowledge, myth, and discoveries illustrates the times quite well and of course needs to be taken with a great deal of hindsight.

[†]Rafn cites the famous passage from the *Eyrbyggja Saga*: "*[people] who wore white dresses, and had poles before them on which were fastened lappets, and who shouted with a low voice. This country was supposed to be Hvitramannaland as it was called (the land of the white men) otherwise called Irland it mikla (Great-Ireland).*" This place was rather well known; the Arab geographer Idrisi mentioned it in his books from 1099 to 1175 under the name of "*Irlandah al Kabirah*" (cited in Beauvois, De Roo).

Another sign of the regularity of these contacts is the near-monopoly of Bristol on major maritime relationships, confirmed by the letters of patent that King Henry VII gave John Cabot (Giovanni Cabotto): "For their every voyage, as often as they shall arrive at our port of Bristol, at which they are bound and holden only to arrive. . . ." Citing Fernando Colombo, Prytz shares this opinion, even including Greenland: "The ship owners and merchants of Bristol became the primary commercial partners of Greenland."[4]

The vast overall movement that formed the commercial traffic between the British Isles and Iceland cannot be considered an isolated case but as a link in a mercantile chain encompassing Iceland, Greenland, and Canada, with the last two offering more than we have been led to believe. In fact, during the fifteenth century, and probably before, Bristol was a veritable hub and crossroads for commercial ventures into the north (Iceland, Greenland, and farther west) and those in the south (Portugal and Spain).

Haraldur Sigurdsson mentions British merchants who owned ships going in both directions. This is an important detail because these two "antipodes" possessed the knowledge of the western lands. This is a major axis not only economically but also scientifically as we have seen with the astronomer, mathematician monk Nicholas of Lynn with his astrolabe. Generally, the sciences were of a very high level in England.

This is where the seeds for the great expeditions first took shape, which explains the presence of Giovani Cabatto or a certain Christopher Columbus in Bristol in 1477. Columbus acknowledges the role of the English in northern sea voyages and gave a very strange review of it.[5] Fernando Columbus cites his father's journal in 1571: "In the month of February 1477, I sailed one hundred leagues beyond the island of Tile whose southern part is on latitude 73 degrees north. . . . And to this island, which is as big as England, the English come with their wares, especially from Bristol. When I was there, the sea was not frozen, but the tides were so great that in some places they rose twenty-six fathoms."

Columbus's voyage to Iceland is no fable as it is duly vouched for by the bishop Magnus Eyjólfsson (1477–1490?). As if by chance, a prelate was also the guardian of old texts concerning Greenland and Vinland.

The cloister where he was abbot witnessed the birth of several sagas that have come down to posterity. The Helgafells Monastery also held additional interest for the astute, young Columbus as it was the departure point for expeditions to Greenland and Vinland. His curiosity was well rewarded as the bishop tells us: "Speaking Latin with Columbus who questioned him about the lands in the West, he told him the accounts of the voyage of the son of Gudleiv Gudleigi and other Northmen."[6]

We will revisit this veritable gem that has gone largely unnoticed by the public at large. This knowledge would quickly spread, along an Icelandic-English/Bristol-Portuguese axis that would later give birth to the discoveries we are all familiar with. However, they were preceded by countless anonymous sea voyages. The sailors of Albion made deep thrusts into the Far North of Greenland and probably Canada, as is related by John James, nephew of the navigator Sandersson.

He who was close to the poles, much farther than any other Englishman, told me that he saw 20 men at the same time whose heads looked like those of dogs.[7]

Without seeking to make any kind of value judgment, the allusion to the natives of the Far North could hardly be any clearer. Two interpretations are possible. The author either carried a negative bias toward the natives, or he was referring to the skin clothing they wore, in this case with a hood made of wolf or dog skin that would easily confuse our medieval witnesses with their wild imaginations. I opt for the second solution.

## THE CONVERGENCES OF ECONOMIC AND RELIGIOUS INTERESTS

As this process where economic and religious interests converge is still little known, it is worth underscoring. In tandem with Albion's commercial domination, a clerical one was taking place. For example, Jón Jónson was bishop of Holar (appearing in the *Grønlands Historiske Mindesmærker* for the years 1414, 1424, and 1461). He made four round-trip voyages to England, thereby weakening the theory of Icelandic isolation. This bishop named another Englishman as his successor: John Williamson. "Iceland during this period had English bishops, for example Jon Jonson, bishop of Holar. In 1429, he handed the bishopric over to a compatriot, John Williamson (Vilhjámsson)."

In 1439, the Skálholt diocese inherited a bishop who arrived directly from England—namely, John Serriksen, also known as Jonas Jerechini.[8]

This convergence of interests is illustrated perfectly by Williamson's attitude in 1431, when he gave his compatriots William Bell and Edmund Smith protection in his cathedral when they were facing legal actions from the native Icelanders. In concrete terms there was a tacit alliance between the English clergy and the traders who were also pirates of the same nationality. Finn Magnussen pointed out quite relevantly that this fact must have been a crucial factor encouraging a massive, unpunished presence of Englishmen: "The bishop [Jonas Jerechini] had no less than thirty companions with him who were said to be Irish, who like him, were guilty of numerous acts of violence and extortion."[9]

Contrary to the post-medieval Nordic source materials that long argued the remote lands of the north were forgotten, the Far North had not been forgotten by everyone "Greenland, ironically, seems to have been better known than ever in Europe, if we consider all the representations of it on fifteenth-century maps. His position and contours are represented more correctly than before, for example, on the maps of Claudius Clavus and Nicolaus Germanus."[10]

If I have emphasized this convergence of economic and religious interests—something completely ordinary at this time—is because it also occurred in the remote polar lands. Without jumping ahead too far, I can briefly say that this same phenomenon will be illustrated by the Germans of the Hanseatic League drawn by the wealth offered by the north. They consolidated their interests by naming the first bishops of Greenland. This could not help but attract the interest of figures like the ambitious archbishop Adalbert of Bremen, the wealth of the Arctic could bring with it power. This convergence of economic and spiritual interests appears to have been the rule and this enables me to advance the hypothesis that the same phenomenon was true of the southern powers—I am thinking mainly of the Portuguese. In fact, their presence in Greenland and the lands to the west cannot be doubted, as we shall see. Proof exists of their repeated forays into the northern lands. On the other hand, the interest of the southern clergy is less well known. However, I suspect the same sort of convergence of interests played a role in the nomination in 1433 of a Brother Bartholomeus of Sant Ypolito, bishop of Greenland by Pope Eugene IV (1431–1437). Similarly in 1431, Gibelin Bolant of the Order of the Hermits of Saint Augustine, minorite penitent of the Saint Peter Basilica, and on July 4, 1432, Jean Herler of Moys, a minorite penitent of the same basilica, were named bishops of Greenland.

Initially, nominations like this can seem incongruous. However, they could very easily reflect the Portuguese presence in the medieval Scandinavian Arctic responding in a certain way to the spiritual needs of the Portuguese, not to mention their economic lust for the western lands. The chronic absence of all the bishops named to Greenland before the Vikings disappeared doesn't conflict with my hypothesis in any way. The important thing is the underlying intent for this nomination, and its motivations that are akin to the cases of the English and the Germans of the Hanseatic League.

## THE HANSEATIC LEAGUE
## AND THE FAR NORTH

The power of the Hanseatic League in the medieval world is well known. A particularly prosperous trade would become established between the league and the Far North. However the Hanseatic League, jealous of its prerogatives, tenaciously protected its monopoly. It was rather discreet about its activities; yet some information survives mainly in Hanseatic Leagues accounts. The falcon held an important place in medieval symbology, and the gyrfalcon was the most popular hunting bird for the nobility's most favorite amusement: falconry. The Hanseatic books tell us that the Lübeckois were taxed twelve Icelandic falcons a year. As early as 1240, the emperor Frederick II exported falcons to Italy thanks to his Lübeck merchants. At the end of the thirteenth century, Bruges became Hanseatic League's chief center for the falcon trade. The Hanseatic

League (Lübeck in particular) played a major role in the lucrative falcon trade: "The Lübeck merchants had the responsibility of bringing these birds back alive from the Arctic all the way to the tropics."[11]

This explains why cartography was booming in Lübeck, particularly round maps. This city was not the only place for this business, and the falcon trade must have made people veritable fortunes if we consider that several Hanseatic cities were involved in it. Their sources conform the substantial sums involved: "The price of twelve falcons—the same as what the people of Lübeck sent annually to the emperor—was 350 aurei. This represented the approximate value of fifty tons of grain, the equivalent of the annual reserves of 100 to 200 persons.[12] This sum was considerable for the era. Echoing my theory of a global commercial movement, we find the same situation in Greenland: "in 1396, the Duke of Burgundy sent Bayezid* twelve *Greenland falcons* as ransom for his son."[13]

Oleson places the gyrfalcon region on Baffin Island and mentions Greenland and Iceland as migratory routes for this bird. Based on Icelandic ruins or traces of their passage on this island, he concludes that the majority of the falcons of the Middle Ages were captured on this island. Without wishing to dismiss this site, I would however share my reservations based on evidence from that era that has gone completely unnoticed, the 1492 globe that is also German by chance. Its testimony seems rather clear: the falcon island described as an immense continent is far from bringing Baffin Island to mind. I have instead emphasized its connection with the neighboring continent similar to Asia and the strait separating them (Bering?).

This has a direct connection with Marco Polo's source materials as the Venitian is mentioned by name below the location of the isle of polar falcons that I have identified as one of the "trades" of Nicholas of Lynn, which is literally cited in Martin Behaim's globe. My position is also strengthened by the typical text by Marco Polo on what seems to be Siberia.

The German researcher Klaus Friesland believes the falcon trade is only the visible part of the iceberg. We also know that walrus and narwhal ivory was highly sought for its quality and pure colors (mentioned

---

*Most likely the Ottoman sovereign Bayezid 1.

by Prytz) but also particularly due to the fact that the southern route was more or less blocked by the Saracens. This must have increased the price of ivory and explains the high value of Arctic goods. The substantial number of religious objects (and others) during the medieval period offers incontrovertible proof. This Nordic El Dorado explains the presence of the Frisians, English, and Portuguese. Iceland and Greenland were far from being totally isolated after the decline of Scandinavia.

The role of the Hanseatic merchants—particularly those of Bremen—was more important than we've imagined and played a major role in the organization of Greenland: "by assuring and maintaining relations between the Arctic, Scandinavia, and continental Europe. Their contribution includes mediation, negotiation, and information."[14]

With the Hanseatic League we see the same convergence of economic and religious interests seen earlier with England. In 1040, Archbishop Adalbert of Bremen was informed of the ecclesiastical vacancy in Greenland. This fit perfectly into the plans of the archbishop known as the most ambitious man of the Nordic Church during the Middle Ages. At the request of the Vikings of Greenland and Iceland, Adalbert consecrated three bishops, one for Iceland, one for Greenland (Albert, 1055) and one for the Orkneys. A "feverish" German activity coincided with the start of Greenland colonization as shown by the *Grønlands Historiske Mindesmærker*[15] with visits to the Far North by Frisian merchants (1040) and the sending of emissaries from Greenland and Iceland to Bremen (1054).[16] Once again, church affairs and business matters worked hand in hand, whether in the south with its rich spices or in the north with its ivory, falcons, and precious furs.

# THE THEATER OF PIRACY
# IN THE MEDIEVAL ARCTIC

A substantial portion of accounts concerning Greenland were written in Iceland, and both countries followed parallel times of good and ill fortune, so I will start with the situation in Iceland. The so-called English Era of the fifteenth century witnessed the alternation between respectable trade and more often piracy. Practically every year, criminal acts would occur that sparked the complaints of the citizens or royal Scandinavian protests against the British crown, sanctions, and so forth. I would also point out the abduction of Scandinavian island dwellers and their enslavement: "In 1423, British pirate attacks were severe in the northern part of the country, particularly around Olaf Fjord where they burned down the churches of Risø and Husavik . . . stealing the chalice, the mass garments, and the holy books. In this region they stole a countless number of cows and sheep; even the inhabitants, both children and adults were carried out of the country as slaves."[17]

In short, we have the same misdeeds that the Greenland *angaqoq* (shaman) told Niels Egede about in 1770, which confirms that the fifteenth century was a very troubled time in Iceland and Greenland. We should also recall the story collected by Knud Rasmussen (see chapter 3). The traditional Inuit oral sources leave no doubt on this subject: other particularly bellicose European peoples were frequent visitors to Greenland and the Canadian Arctic. From 1411 to 1490 the abuses of the English traders/pirates can be closely followed with terrifying regularity. We also know that after an auspicious period for piracy, when the vein was almost exhausted, some English boats left Iceland almost empty but didn't hesitate to visit neighboring Greenland which was much more isolated and ill-equipped to face this kind of calamity.

We should also recall, and we should see it as more than a coincidence, that the last traces of the Vikings in Greenland go back to the fifteenth century (or the sixteenth for the more optimistic source materials). It is easy to imagine the destructive and irreversible effects of a policy like this of devastation, abduction, and enslavement on such a small community. There are accounts supporting these events. Greenland Scandinavians *were* abducted from Greenland and taken to England. They were later freed thanks to royal intervention, and returned to Greenland.*

---

*See chapters 5 and 8, and the dates 1418, 1432, and especially 1446, for there are traces there of the complaints sent to Rome deemed worthy of being noted in the annals, of the return of "Scandinavian slaves" to Greenland thanks to Rome's intervention (*Grønlands Historiske Mindesmaerker*). Graah tells us in the *Grønlands Historiske Mindesmærker* that the largest attack took place in 1418. The English were seeking sailors; after the 1433 Treaty with Denmark, they brought the abducted individuals back.

We have to think that communications by sea were not as poor as we've been led to believe. "In Greenland, churches were also burned down, and many young people abducted to be taken away as slaves. Only the remote churches were spared. The pope recounts that these slaves were freed and sent back home where they tried to build new homes among the ruins."[18]

Prytz cites other cases of abductions: "An Iceland bishop—probably the Englishman John Craxton in Holar—found young natives of Iceland and the Finmark* in Lynn and ordered that they be returned home."

We recall this port of Lynn, of which the mathematician astronomer monk Nicholas was a native, often mentioned in the same breath as Bristol. These facts confirm activity between these British cities and the countries in the North. In one very interesting case, the Englishman Hakluyt mentioned some Greenland natives brought to England who had surprisingly European features.[19] When he saw them a year later at the court, now dressed in appropriate clothing, he was unable to recognize them. I have already alluded to the role the Azores will play in this subject area. These islands represented an important stopover or departure point for voyages westward as well as to the northwest. They also seem to have played a role in the slave trade (which is more or less implied in several maps like that of the Venetian Benedetto Bordone in 1528). Here contemporary research seems to be making rapid strides. For example, Swedish researcher Per Lilliestöm believes he has found traces of Scandinavian colonists in the Azores and the Canaries. On the architectural plane, some gutter and culvert motifs were reminiscent of Scandinavian motifs, and the genetic legacy of some of the sixteenth and seventeenth inhabitants there oddly brought Scandinavian features to mind, something that has always intrigued researchers. I found several examples in different cities: Icod de Los Vinos and Los Realejos, where secular structures built during the sixteenth century are consistent with the dates of the Nordic disappearance from Greenland.

---

*The author believes there is confusion concerning Greenland attached, as we have seen, to the Finmark in the medieval imagination and cartography.

Fig. 11.1. A dragon's head that is highly reminiscent of those sported as figureheads on the prows of the famous "drakkars" (Tenerife). (See also color plate 12.)
*Property of Per Lillieström, photo by Lars Peter Amundsen*

I personally investigated the Malvasia Museum building in Icod de Los Vinos, located where the poorest neighborhoods used to be home to plantation slaves among others. Numerous gargoyle remnants similar to those that are still intact seem to indicate a fairly substantial presence of slaves of Norse descent. The examples from Santa Cruz de Tenerife (see figs. 11.2 and 11.3) never fail to surprise. They adorn several sides of a famous religious building: the Church of the Conception, also built in 1500. This pagan art found on a religious edifice in very Catholic Spain seems a bit like the pagan dragons of the wooden stave churches.

With respect to the genetic factor, the hypothesis of crossbreeding with Germans is hardly defendable according to Lillieström. He points out the sadly famous role of these islands in the slave trade. The plantations and sugar refineries of Tenerife and Madeira required a large number of manual laborers. In this regard, there are also some ambiguous

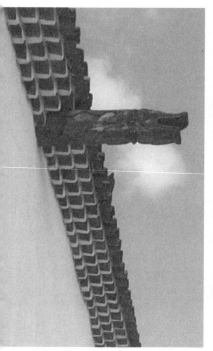

Figs. 11.2 and 11.3. Sixteenth-century gargoyles in Tenerife (Icod de los Vinos, Santa Cruz) that are oddly reminiscent of pagan Viking art. In Icod de los Vinos, they are found in the former lower-class neighborhoods of the plantation slaves. (See also color plate 13.)
*Photos by J. Privat*

medieval texts getting lost in subtleties concerning the degree of the northern people's paganism after renouncing their religion, in a more or less confessed intent to excuse slavery. In fact, the church strictly forbade the enslavement of Christians. Yet it seems clear that the Vikings of Greenland and Canada had more or less abandoned the faith but on the other hand offered the advantage of being excellent manual laborers (or "Lavrador" in Portuguese) in contrast with the Amerindians and Inuit.

At a time when qualified manual labor was sorely lacking, this deserves serious attention. Nor can I dismiss the fact that the official church had several scores to settle with its former strayed sheep. Lillieström even adopts a radical position similar to what I suggested concerning the Tordesillas Treaty in 1494. He believes Pope Alexander

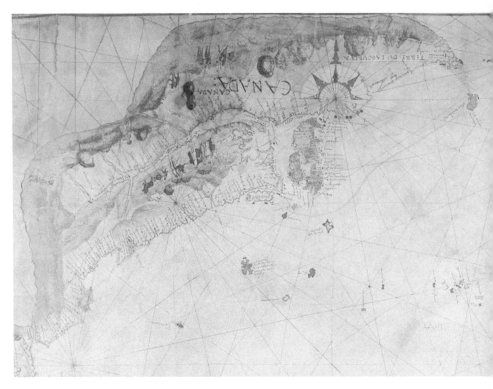

Fig. 11.4. A detail of the 1547 French world map known as the "Dauphin" from the cartography school of Dieppe illustrating the Roberval expedition. Canada is on the left, where we can read upside down "The Land of the Laborer," an obvious reference to the Norse and their farming activities. (See also color plate 14.)
*Wikimedia Commons*

Borgia made a gift of Greenland to Portugal* (Borgia's reputation needs no description, and a punishment administered by the church cannot be dismissed), which could explain the claims displayed on some Portuguese maps. Lillieström also shares the opinion that the name of Labrador attributed to Greenland is directly connected to "the products" offered by this country—namely, manual laborers (also *laborador*

---

*In my opinion, even if Greenland is not mentioned by name, all interpretations are possible as treaty stipulates: "all lands, both islands and mainlands, found and discovered already or to be found hereafter, by the said King of Portugal, toward the east, in either north or south latitude on the eastern side of the said bound . . . shall belong to the said King of Portugal and his successors . . ."

and *laboureur*—the exact translation of *lavrador* on French maps, meaning potential, very cheap, manual laborers).

## THE DANISH OVERFLOW

Denmark appears to have been completely overwhelmed by the British invasion. This can be explained by the serious situation at its own gates. The military setbacks suffered at the hands of the Holsteins carried more weight than faraway Iceland. Another reason for the lack of interest in the northern dependencies was the Danish-Norwegian reconciliation as a result of the Kalmar Union (1389), or even a kind of ignorance about the northern lands because the political maps had changed. German kings were now ruling. Erik of Pomerania was king of Denmark, Sweden, and Norway. We should also recall that Bergen was the fourth most important city in the Hanseatic League and power was slipping out of Scandinavian hands. The eyes of the Danish crown were no longer looking to the north but to the south, and its powerful Hanseatic neighbor, and later to the east, and its Swedish brother enemy after their great union shattered.

The critical situation the Danish kingdom found itself in was a godsend for the British transgressors (mainly with the Danish-Swedish conflict), and they showed no fear of any threats Danish king Christian I might utter. His authority was even flouted openly. Several significant examples will shed light on this for the reader. Attempts to restore the authority and the rights of the crown were often a complete defeat, bringing ridicule upon their authors. Here are a few examples. The royal envoys Johannes Paulson, Balthazar Van Damne (and many others) sent to the Vestmannaeyjar (Westman) Islands were taken prisoner: "The Danes were attacked by their enemies, who waged battle with banners, bows, arrows, and other weapons; they had to surrender and were given leave to go only after surrender of all their property."[20] The tax collectors for the Danish Crown were attacked and robbed of all they had collected: "The wily British had allowed the Danes to collect the royal taxes before attacking them once they were all collected."[21]

The year 1425 was particularly bloody judging on the accounts of criminal acts—various Danish, German, Norwegian, and Icelandic royal representatives were killed (note the German presence): "With reckless violence, these pirates prevented all fishing trade, destroying the boats and the fishing equipment, and based on the contents of the grievances that were filed, did as much harm they possibly could."[22]

The British presence in Iceland and Greenland is punctuated with accounts of Scandinavian plaintiffs, exchanges of demands, royal directives, treaties, and even declarations of war. I wonder how the theory of the total isolation of Greenland and Iceland could have come into being with so many documents vouching for the opposite case: in 1411 and 1413, King Erik of Pomerania forbade trade with unauthorized English merchants.

In 1431, King Erik lodged a complaint with the King of England on the damages suffered by his Danish and Norwegian subjects over the last twenty years, disrupting the exchanges between Bergen and Iceland. A flood of British royal writs is evidence of the duration and size of this chaotic situation. Let's list several dates: 1418, 1420, 1425, 1429, 1430, and 1432. Here is the text of the royal act of October 28, 1432: "The King of England through his intermediary Sir Robert Skotbroch, engages to punish his subjects having committed crimes in Iceland or elsewhere, and to return the prisoners who will also receive compensation."[23]

In 1469, the Hanseatic League declared war against England. A war at sea followed between the corsairs of several countries including France. We find additional confirmation of this British invasion in a Hanseatic intervention during the winter of 1476/1477 forcing the Danish king to halt all English commerce in Norwegian territory. The Hanseatic League would even demand the destruction of the unusually high number of boats that year. In fact, this winter was particularly mild, so much so it was noted in contemporary Icelandic source texts (let me remind you that this winter of 1477 was when Columbus landed in Iceland, then continued his journey west . . .).

The end of the fifteenth century is the dawn of a new era, the age of the "great discoveries," and all their consequences. A "redistribution of the cards," a geographical redivision would take place at the end of this century and the beginning of the next. The great loser would be the Hanseatic League, for it would lose its supremacy over northern Europe. This was the end of the role of the Hanseatic merchants in the opening of unknown Arctic routes and more or less the end of "private enterprise" as the sole player in the explorations of and trade with these unknown lands. Other nations began taking an interest in the riches of the north. The pure phase of individual exploration and disorganized trade made by audacious sailors would be replaced by national, colonial undertakings.

The first "individual" phase was quite discreet. There are several cases of exploratory voyages of the Atlantic during the second half of the fourteenth century that have been entirely passed over in silence. This silence can be explained by the discretion of their authors jealous of their secret wealth and that of their contemporaries. As the Portuguese scholar Armando Cortesoão points out, this era's chroniclers were more concerned with the kings and great lords than by the vague merchants and their long-distance trips. Literature was not neutral and often in service to the king—that is, hagiographical—not to mention the weight of the church, the veritable censor of that time ever watchful for any madman spreading ideas that did not conform to its notion of the world. The second phase would be completely different. There is a wealth of documents that are not always devoid of errors—errors that are often intentional to mislead competitors. This is the phase that would reshape the world.

## AN OUTSIDER NAMED PORTUGAL

Portugal would hold an important place in the age of the great discoveries. For a variety of reasons, this country would rule the seas. This domination would culminate with the division of the world into two hemispheres—one for Spain and the other for Portugal—by the Treaty of Tordesillas. Another element that has importance is almost completely unknown, however: Portugal's presence in Arctic regions of Greenland and Canada. This Portuguese presence in the Far North was no accident. A purely political factor that goes practically unknown to the public at large was decisive—the family ties between the Portuguese and Danish crowns. Denmark's king (Erik of Pomerania) was married to Queen Philippa (June 4, 1394–January 5, 1430), daughter of King Henry IV of England, whose cousin was the Portuguese king, Henry the Navigator.

In fact, these family ties are much older and ironically do not seem to have aroused the curiosity of historians. We find, for example, a king by the name of Waldemar chosen in 1213 and crowned in 1218, married to a certain Elenore, daughter of King Alphonse II of Portugal. He died on November 28, 1231. Let me again mention King Waldemar II who ruled from 1170 to 1241, and who in 1214 took as his third wife Berengria (Berengaria), daughter of King Sancho I of Portugal. Erik of Pomerania who ascended to the Norwegian throne on April 14, 1392, was Henry the Navigator's brother-in-law. Incidentally, he also met with him at the court of Emperor Sigismund in 1424 to look for a route from the West to China.

This long kinship, little known to most people, explains the good Danish-Portuguese relations illustrated by the repeated invitations of Danish noblemen to Portuguese expeditions. For example, there is the Danish nobleman Vallart, who was named in 1448 as commander of an expedition to the African coast. I would like to point out that Spain also practiced this policy of establishing ties through marriage with the wedding on March 31, 1258, of Spain's King Alphonso's youngest brother (Felipe) to the Princess Katrina, the daughter of the Norwegian King, Håkon the Young. Spain did not benefit from a direct collaboration on the field of explorations, but this contributed greatly to the progress of its naval construction. For example, one letter from King Henry II of Spain noted that the Spanish did not have a single ship. As it happens, the Vikings of this time were building the best boats. In exchange they got the salt and wheat they were so sorely lacking.

To return to Portuguese relations, the Dane Lolland was invited to take part in the glorious capture of Alcazar. On his return to Denmark in 1461, he was covered in honors. We should note the intense Danish-Portuguese collaboration in this fifteenth century that hosted so many discoveries and the jealous secrecy that surrounded these expeditions.

The Portuguese distrust of strangers was well-known. I need only mention their categorical refusal to Christopher Columbus when he presented them with his plans. It was just with the barest of luck that his plans did not fail completely.

The thirst for knowledge of the hypothetical lands in the West (which were Nordic possessions) explains the good Danish-Portuguese relationship, and the attitude of the latter. This is far from being negligible. One thing is sure: these ties were long overlooked by historians and Europeans in general. This is confirmed by Cortesoão: "Relations between Portugal and the countries of the North were frequent, even several centuries before Prince Henry the Navigator."[24]

The same author points out the Portuguese's good understanding of the Scandinavian cultural context: "There can be no doubt that the Immrama [Celtic sea-voyages] were known in Portugal, probably directly from their native land.[25] This knowledge seems to have been restricted to the Portuguese elite for southern source materials referring to it are rare. The consequence is a very old Portugues presence in the Far North of Greenland and Canada, as I am going to show, long before Columbus. "Contact with or via Greenland for the Markland have existed without interruption since the first Greenland voyages, followed by the English and Portuguese voyages toward these northern regions, from the end of the tenth century to the beginning of the sixteenth century."[26]

To sum up, the fifteenth century, period in which Scandinavian source texts remain silent on the Greenland situation, is witness to the diligent presence of Albion, of Germans, and of the Portuguese, which adds up to a lot for a tiny Norse population that never grew beyond— in the most optimistic figures—five to fifteen thousand inhabitants. I am only taking into consideration the surest, documented cases here, cases that cannot be denied. However, there are strong presumptions of a Basque and Breton presence. History finds it hard to be satisfied with chance and it is fairly unlikely to imagine a solely French presence in Newfoundland that ignored the surrounding areas. At the risk of repeating myself, I state that the "isolationist theory" concerning Greenland and Iceland needs to be rejected. The apparently banal familial factors of the Danish-Portuguese connection reflect the concordance of royal alliances and the political supremacy (over the sea, and militarily) of Portugal. This country seemed attract political assets, the best geographical knowledge, and the best cartography (could the Inuit story of the "map makers" collected by Rasmussen concern them?). Portugal benefited from subtle alliances in the east with Denmark and in the west with Great Britain. These two allies share a common knowledge of the far north and a longstanding presence in the area. Thanks to the play of alliances, Portugal would benefit, on the one hand, from Nordic knowledge (route to Greenland and the western lands) and, on the other, from English experience and its no less great knowledge, and its technical advances, because England shone with its scholars, astronomers, mathematicians, and so on, as well as for its military assistance against Spain.

There is a duly documented example of Danish-Portuguese collaboration in the Far North, both in Portugal and Denmark: the 1472 to 1473 expedition to Greenland and Canada.* To return to the situation of the exchange of Danish-Portuguese courtesies (in which several Danish noblemen were invited to Portugal), they would have to wait twelve years after the return of the Danish nobleman Lolland for Danish king Christian I to return the favor to his Portuguese counterpart. In December 1472, he had several ships equipped and sent to the North Sea. This fact is vouched for in a letter from the burgermeister of Kiel, Karsten Grip (here we find the old Hanseatic German actors who are increasingly playing supporting roles) to the Danish king Christian II on March 3, 1551: "The two captains Pyningk and Poidthorsth were sent with several ships by the grandfather of his majesty, King Christian I at the request of His Royal Majesty, the King of Portugal in order to seek out new lands and new islands in the North."[27]

These two "admirals," Pining and Pothorst, appear in several Icelandic source texts, sometimes as pirates (Olaus Magnus) and sometimes as royal envoys. One doesn't exclude the other because the Danish crown never disdained the services of corsairs. The main thing is that several sources conform the sending of these two individuals by King

---

*A fifteenth-century transcription error (*mil & quatrocentos & sessenta & quatro* instead of *de setenta & quarto*) has led several historians to advance the date of 1463.

Christian I at the head of several ships in search of new lands, and doing so on request of the Portuguese king. The region explored in Canada would be, according to R. H. Major, the mouth of the Saint Lawrence, which I accept with some reservations. One fact is certain, it is definitely Canada, this expedition is very well documented and appears, for example, on a globe of the Flemish mathematician Gemma Fricius, who was also teacher of the future talented cartographer, Gerard Mercator. Several pieces of information have been left illustrating this Danish-Portuguese collaboration, such as the presence of a Nordic sailor Jon Skolp, a.k.a. Joannes Scolvus: *"Quij populi ad quos Ioannes Scolvus/ Danus perverit circa annum 1476."*\*

This globe dates from 1537 and the first written account of the Danish-Portuguese expedition dates from 1476, hence the error incorporating the date of the discovery with that of publication. Numerous books would repeat this discovery as well as its dating error:

The Englishman Michael Lok in his 1582 map cites the Nordic sailor Scolvus while deforming his first name Jac(obus?). The expedition is indicated at a latitude farther north between the 75th and 80th degrees, at the same location as the mythical land we've already encountered: Grocland.

The Flemish cartographer Cornelius Wytfliet in his Ptolemaic description of 1597, mentions the countries visited: *"Secundum detectæ huius regionis decus tiilit Joannes Scoluus Polonus* [which would be a mistake for pilotus] *qui anno reparate salutis 1476 . . . navigans ultra Norvegiam, Groenlandiam, Frislandiamque, Boreale hoc fretum ingressus est sub ipso Arctico circulo, Boreale, ad Laboratoris hanc terram Estotilandiamque."*†

---

\*Oleson interprets the first term that was intriguing with its *Quit populi* as the translation of the Icelandic *Hvitir meen* (the white men) and reappears on the 1545 globe of Nancy (*quij populi*) west of Greenland.
†Cornelius Wytfliet, *"Descriptionis Ptolomaicæ augmentum."* My use of the conditional is motivated by the existence of a very troubling Polish map of the world by Jan of Strobnica (1470–1519) in Krakow dated 1512. It brings to mind a tradition of medieval maps for presenting the mystical Vinland Goá cited as an island. Poland was part of the Hanseatic sphere of influence. So, a Polish explorer?

Several mysterious lands or islands are mentioned. There is Frislandia, the mythical island that could be a "double" of the Faroe Islands or southern Greenland,* or a land lying farther west, and Estotilandia, a land always mentioned as being in the west long before Columbus. Doubt persists as to the exact location of the region visited by this expedition. Is it the mythical Grocland that Icelanders and Greenlanders knew well? Is it the Hudson Bay, which also had a long tradition of foreign contacts?

This hypothesis is more plausible as we shall see, because the globe of Gemma Fricius mentions the Terra of Bachalo close by. One final hypothesis that is equally credible: the Saint Lawrence. This expedition, which is well documented with maps or globes, is also confirmed by the rewards granted by both crowns. In Portugal, the island of Terceira was split between the two gentlemen João Vaz Corte-Real and Alvaro Martin Homem in 1474, as a royal given by act of donation February 17 and April 2 (these highly esteemed families would yield several explorers). We learn there that both these men had recently returned from a voyage to the Terre de Bachalo that they had discovered *"por mandator del Rey."*

It seems that the Northman Pining was also rewarded, if we consider his service records for King Christian I: 1478, 1481, 1482, 1483. The Danish historian Bjørnbo maintains that he assumed the duties of governor of Iceland in 1478. It is believed that the expedition took place in 1472 to 1473, but that the Portuguese Corte Real and Homem only published their journal in 1476. This same Corte Real was a relative by marriage to Martin Behaim.

The illustration of the presence of European foreigners in the Arctic goes mainly through a study of that era's cartography (including the sixteenth century) as well as several ambiguous place-names.

## *Estotiland*

This name would disappear with the coming of new southern arrivals in America. It seems to go quite far back in time, for it is frequently

---

*I would still lean toward the second hypothesis, because of the long tradition of a Frisian presence in Greenland at the onset of Scandinavian colonization and because several maps in fact place it at the southern tip of Greenland—such as Michael Lok's map of 1582.

mentioned together with other notions belonging to old Scandinavian traditional lore.

The seventeenth-century book (1669) by Theodore Thorlatius that in fact recycles a much older book by Björn Jonssön is rich in both cartographical and descriptive information. We have, for example, the map of the Holar Bishop, Gudbrandur Thorlaksson of 1606 (see pages 354–55): "The strait between the Greenland's extreme southern bank and the other continent that the cartographers call America, the strait through the Greenlanders discovered Vinland during their forays, that Pagini, through chance rather than an accurate deduction, deemed (to be) Estotiland; this same strait, the Ginnungagap of the ancients is so to speak a vast narrow pass (or gorge). We deem however that from Estotiland (if it is definitely Vinland) one can each Greenland by going straight north."*

These places are therefore closely connected to the medieval era. In popular belief, Ginnungagap was the immense ocean bordering the known world on the west. Traditional Scandinavian lore was therefore adapted to the great discoveries, which is why for Gudbrandur Thorlaksson, Ginnungagap was located between Estotiland and Winlandiæ on the west, and Greenland—the final frontier known in Nordic geography. We have to think that after the extinction of Greenland, the knowledge pertaining to these places would dissipate in the work of the Icelandic scribes. Gerard Mercator was the first to identify Estotiland with America, more specifically, Baffin Island (see the 1569 map on page 195) clearly adjoining the northern part of Hudson Bay then called *Golfam de MeroSro*. Inexplicably, Estotiland would be slow to die, for despite two centuries of foreign presence—and consequently new place-names—we still come across it.

In a period of relentless competition, we have to think that this was extremely tangible and historically founded to not vanish before the

---

*Manuscript 1669/10, Royal Library of Copenhagen. Original text: *Fretum inter Gronlandiæ oram extremam, austrum versus & aliam continentem, quam recentiones Americam v[ocant], per qvod fretum olim Grönlandi excurventes Vinlandiam invenerunt, qvam Estotelandiam Pagini, forte qvis recte existimaverit ; ipsum Hoc fretum, veteribus Ginnúngagap . . . existimamus autem [ex] Estotelandia si hæc Winlandia est versus aqvilonem in Gronlandiam recta perveneri."*

wave of foreign names. The name's persistence is intriguing, as well as the variety of its locations as if its inhabitants enjoyed a relatively extensive area. This cannot help but bring to mind the nomadic nature of the Nordic economy (hunting, fishing, and so on).

Fig. 11.5. 1606 map signed "Gudbrandi Thorlacii," the Latinized name of the Icelandic bishop of Holar, that provides a clear illustration of the notion of a land bridge in the East connecting Greenland to Norway, as well as the ample mixing of literary source with geographical discoveries.
*Courtesy of the Royal Library, Copenhagen*

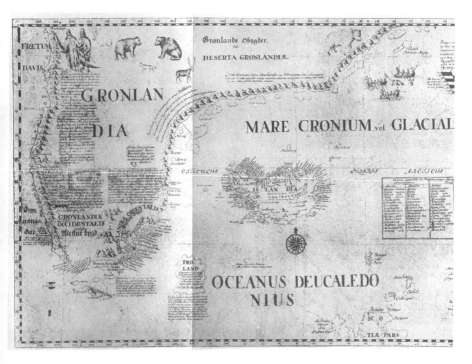

Fig. 11.6. A map from the same Holar bishop Gudbrandur Torlaksson, 1606.
It's vagueness provides an excellent illustration of the large gap separating
southern cartography (Portuguese, for example) and that of the Nordic countries
where the church held a predominant place in the diffusion of knowledge. I consider
the "mare cronium" (Cronium Sea) as inspired by the mythical Cronia of Antiquity.
*Wikimedia Commons*

**1570:** The famous Anvers geographer, Abraham Ortelius, published a map on which all the Estotiland place-names were in Portuguese.

**1580:** The map of the Englishman John Dee (astronomer, mathematician) places Estotiland between lat 60–70° N as an island.

**1593:** In the work of Clæz Plancius, Estotiland clearly borders *Terra de Labrador.* The place-names are Portuguese.

**1597:** In the first atlas entirely dedicated to America (*Descriptiones Ptolomaicæ augmentum,* Leuven), Cornelius Wytfliet calls Estotiland *laboratoris terra.*

**1606:** In *New Theater of the World,* Peder Van Aa, famous Dutch geographer and publisher—which allowed him to leave an

abundant bibliography—made the following political apportion-
ment of America:

*Estotilandia (Danis)* is attributed to the Danes.

*Terra Laboratoris (Hispanis)* to the Spanish confused with
the Portuguese, or a consequence of the Tordesillas Treaty?

*Nova Britannia (Anglis)* to the English.

*Canada Septentrionalis (Gallis)* to the French.

**1664:** Although more recent, this map of Champlain is particularly interesting because Estotiland is also called *Groenland* as
opposed to *old Groeneland,* the one we know.

Several seventeenth-century maps—particularly the French ones—
divide Greenland into Old Greenland on the east and New Greenland

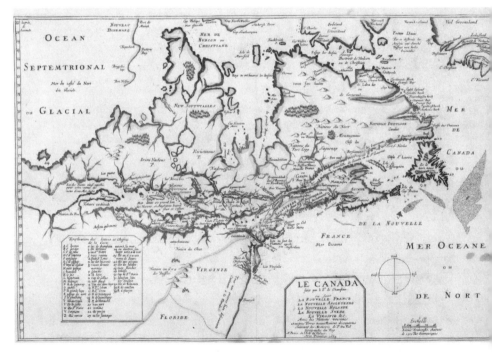

Fig. 11.7. The 1664 map of Champlain (based on a 1612 original).
Note at the top to the right the traditional Greenland presented as
"old Greenland," across from its twin in America: "Greenland or Estotiland."
I believe this to be an obvious reference to one same people who had abandoned
the original Greenland. Norumbega is adjacent to New England. (See also color plate 15.)
*Wikimedia Commons*

on the west, beyond the ocean. We know that medieval geographers imagined a land bridge connecting Greenland to America. Champlain's map seems to clearly illustrate this notion.

We also know that the same Norse population haunted both Greenland and North America, a.k.a. Estotiland, clearly indicated in this map as the northern area along Hudson Strait—a region with a strong Norse tradition that would be the object of Jens Munk's Danish expedition in 1621.

Why this region and not another, if not for the existence of a long historical consensus? This hypothesis of an old Greenland opposed to a new Greenland seems to be confirmed with a twin name we will study later: the new Labrador and the old Labrador. There could therefore be a relationship between Estotiland and Greenland. To conclude, I would like to cite, without taking any position on its soundness, the very interesting analysis of Estotiland by the Frenchman Eugène Beauvois in 1877. He situates this country south of the Saint Lawrence, identifying it with the Great Ireland/*Irland it Mikla*. Beauvois provides a particularly original explanation concerning Estotiland's etymological origin. It would be a direct allusion to the presence of the Scotch-Irish before the year 1000. There would have been confusion between the S and the T, which are very similar in fifteenth-century medieval cursive letters. Escociland would be the land of the Scottish. During the Middle Ages, the words Irish and Scottish were applied casually to both nations.

An extensive study of the old North American place-names would be very instructive when we know that one of the regions concerned was called New Scotland. It is very reminiscent of the description of Estotiland as an island, which is almost the case for this region. This direct link with the Anglo-Celtic countries seems to find confirmation in contemporary commentaries. For example, the Englishman John Dee mentioned earlier (with the map of 1580) as a mathematician and astronomer, but whose talent as astrologer of Queen Elizabeth I was no less formidable, underscored in his journal entry of October 28, 1577, the rights of the English crown over almost the entire North: "I spoke to the queen with her secretary Walsington. I declared her title to Greenland, Estotiland, and Friseland."[28]

We find additional evidence of the Norse presence with some of the Homem family maps. One member of this family took part in the Danish-Portuguese expedition of 1472 to 1473. These maps mentioned "Grænlandagno" between Boston and New York. Homem therefore drew a connection between Greenland, its Norse inhabitants, and America. Prytz reminds us that the Vikings wrote the name of their land: "Grænland."

To close this matter of Estotiland, I would like to cite the work of W. F. Ganong, who went over a large part of the post-medieval cartography concerning these regions with a fine-tooth comb. Ganong notably alludes to a Huron-Iroquois myth collected by Jacques Cartier on the presence of white men (which cannot help but bring to mind the *Hvitramannaland* of the sagas, mainly in the *Saga of Snorri the Goði*): "A kingdom in Saguenay inhabited by white men wearing wool, located between the Saint Lawrence and the Bay of Hudson, which could reflect an ancient tradition on the presence of Scandinavians around Hudson Bay."[29]

Equally interesting is Cartier's discovery of large crosses erected in various spots in Canada. His testimony is cited by Beauvois and by Rousselière: "In 1534 the natives of the Gaspay on seeing Jacques Cartier planting a cross on the shore of their country, showed him two fingers forming a cross then pointed to the surrounding countryside as if to indicate there were more like it throughout the territory."[30]

Champlain found one in the Bay of Fundy, an area that is part of a region where a Scandinavian presence is strongly suspected. According to him, the Canadian natives even possessed the rudiments of the Christian religion, the island dwellers of Cape Breton willingly made the sign of the cross, and painted it on their faces, stomachs, arms, and legs. "Chkoudoun, Sagamos or Sachem of the Saint John's River didn't eat a bite without lifting his eyes to heaven and making the sign of the cross. . . . He had crosses in all his cabins and even wore one on his chest."

## THREE TYPICALLY FOREIGN NOTIONS CONCERNING THE FAR NORTH

Here we will examine three more speculations about Greenland and the Far North.

# Illa Brazil*

The foreign presence in the Far North finds its illustration in that era's cartography. it is perfectly reflected by two concepts that we are about to look at. By all evidence they involve the Portuguese. *Illa Brasil* reflects the Portuguese interest in remote regions and has no connection with the current Brazil. According to Prytz, this name first appeared on the map by the Catalan Angelino de Dolorto concerning an island west of the English Cornwall. It seems that sailors used this term to designate the northeast coast of American during the fifteenth century. This isle was known to the British: "Since 1480 or even sooner, the merchants of Bristol regularly organized their voyages in search of the "Isle of Brasylle" to the west of Ireland using this route.[31]

It seems that the word *Brasil* refers to a kind of particularly tall, robust wood (also called "the red tree), that was highly sought after for shipbuilding. Per Lillieström identifies it with *Caesalpinia echina,* which is actually called "Brazil wood." It was already known during the Middle Ages as it would drift from the Antilles to Ireland. This Portuguese reference cannot help but bring to mind some older, Norse source materials referring to boats laden with wood coming from Markland, or else the episode from the *Saga of Erik the Red* and the famous specimen out of the west that was the object of desire . . . As we see, two totally different sources in time and origin seem to refer to the same regions; hence, the value of including these foreign non-Nordic sources in my approach that have the advantage of being fittingly external and therby relatively neutral.

During a conference on March 15, 1893 (and published the same year by Thromsen Editions in Christiana), the Norwegian historian Gustav Storm (1845–1903) gave a fairly similar explanation not restricted to its reddish color. He notes that the Spanish maps used this term to describe heavily forested islands, even without colored trees. From this he concludes that *Illa Brazil* would be no more nor less than a translation of Markland.

It is certain that certain distinctions (physical among others) that

---

*The spelling of the time varied between Brazil and Brasil.

struck the Northmen—here the abundance of high-quality wood—must have had a similar effect on other peoples. One of Homem's Portuguese maps (1516–1519) connects the Portuguese and Nordic notions: "This region [*Terra Bimenes*] of unknown position is found on the west coast; it is called the New World. It forms a border with the large country Brazil and the Norway of Corte Real; it is rich in gold and commercial products."[32]

The reference to the Vikings is obvious, and all in all normal. Their authenticated presence in Newfoundland (alias Corte Real Norwega by many mapmakers) did not slip by other visitors to the new world unnoticed. Also notable is the impertinent Portuguese territorial claim.

Knowledge of the Brazil Island was quite limited. It goes hand in hand with the period of pre-Columbian individual exploration where a policy of discretion prevailed. This is what was suggested by Professor D. B. Quinn: "both the interest of the Bristol merchants in Brasil as a 'territorial key to the fishery' and the lack of publicity about the discovery of new and extremely rich grounds."[33]

The Arctic lands and Greenland held a place of major importance in the medieval economy. In the plane of historical research, they are equally important, for they represent the link of a vital chain and serve as a landmark for other unknown lands. We have been able to see this with Estotiland, Greipar, and Kroksfjordarheidi. This also plays for *Illa Brazil* almost always mentioned together with *Illa Verde,* which is the correct Portuguese translation of the actual Greenland, which in fact is an island.

We can note in passing the advanced state of Portuguese knowledge as they corrected the Scandinavian scientific error. The Portuguese already considered Greenland to be an island.* We have already seen with the papal letter of September 1448 (referring to earlier facts, probably from 1418) that the Roman Church also knew this distinctive physical feature of Greenland. We must think that this knowledge was not widespread and that several privileged milieus benefited from

---

*As we have seen, Greenland during the Middle Ages was considered as solid land connected either to Norway in the north or to Greipar (a.k.a. the Canadian Arctic) in the west.

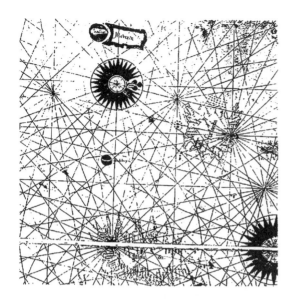

Fig. 11.8. Catalan map of
1480 (Ambrosiana Library
of Milan). One will note
that Greenland is already
presented as an island
(Illa Verde), a very rare
occurrence for this time.
Another equally compel-
ling feature is that a part
of America is described as
"Illa de Brazil."
*Wikimedia Commons*

a certain advanced level of geographical knowledge. This confirms how underestimated the role of the Portuguese has been in the destiny of the Arctic lands of Greenland, Canada, and North America.

The famous Catalan map from about 1480 (in the Ambrosiana Library of Milan) shows *Illa Brazil* depicted by a circle across from a rectangular shape representing *Illa Verde*. This geographical rela-tionship exaggerated by the author of the map could reflect the eco-nomic relationship existing between the Scandinavians of *Illa Verde*, a.k.a. Greenland, and *Illa de Brazil*/Markland(?) where the same figures—as mentioned in the medieval source texts—went to fetch their wood. The paternity of the discovery of *Illa Brazil* is often attributed to the British from Bristol.[34]

If we keep in mind the very good commercial relationship between Portugal and Great Britain, the family ties between the two crowns, separating the deeds of one from the other makes no sense. I would note that this map appeared in 1480, that is to say four years after the publication of the publication of the Danish-Portuguese expedition into Greenland and northern Canada. I would also say, in passing, that the shape given Greenland is not the worst one that appeared in that era's cartography.

## Terra Laborador

Although far from the Arctic regions, we need to consider this example. Study of the errors—geographical mainly—of the Middle Ages as I have stressed several times already (for example, with the 1492 globe) can yield much information for these errors are very revealing of the notions of the time. By examining the case of *Terra Laborador* more extensively we see that, like the isle of "Brazil," the old Labrador was completely different from the new—and current—Labrador, as displayed on the maps for around half a century.

The official explanation concerning this name would be the exploration of a certain João Fernandez, Portuguese landowner and American farmer. In 1499, he received mission letters from King Manuel of Portugal to explore the Far North. In a weird twist, he did not leave his name but his profession on the land he "discovered." W. F. Ganong, among others, is a partisan of this theory that maintains Fernandez was nicknamed "Lavrador." In support of this opinion, he cites Admiral Samuel Morison (1940): "The customary meaning of *lavrador* is farmer, peasant, worker on the land. In the Azores, according to Ernesto Do Canto, it means a small land owner who rents his lands to several people while he is busy with other affairs or traveling."

One observation immediately leaps to mind: it is not customary in the exploring tradition to baptize a land after its discoverer's profession. If despite all this we accept this explanation for *lavrador,* we are obliged to state that this is the only single case among all discoveries in America. His compatriots had no hesitation about leaving their family names on the lands they explored: *Terra Corte Reale, Terra Gomez.* Baptism based on the trade of the one who discovered it seems incongruous and goes contrary to established use and custom. *Illa Brazil* refers to a source of wealth (a tree) and *Terra de Bacalaos* (bacalhou) refers to another resource in these regions: cod. In this case, Terra Lavrador/Labrador should apply to the region's inhabitants (who had transformed "the art of agriculture" into riches worthy of being recorded in the annals) and not the explorer. Furthermore, the explanation given by Samuel Morison can not only apply to João Fernandez but other people as we shall see. From a more "pessimistic" perspective, but one I strongly suspect to be quite true, these Lavradors were the much-desired product, and subject like their counterparts in Greenland and Iceland earlier, to veritable raids.

Another argument seems difficult to explain. I have trouble understanding why the Portuguese crown that organized the 1472 to 1473 expedition in Greenland and eastern Canada (jointly with the Danish crown) would have suffered such great amnesia so soon and attribute the discovery of these lands to Fernandez a mere twenty-six years later? A glance at the various fortunes of the term Labrador in the cartography of that era can be instructive.

## Classic Labrador Through the Maps

The cartography of the era contained some long-winded accounts that were unfortunately not always perfect. Sometimes this imperfection was intentional as people would protect their discoveries with the help of false geographical data.

**1537:** The globe of Gemma Fricius mentions "promontory or cape of the farmer of Labrador." This globe was drawn by Gemma Fricius but engraved by his young student Gerard Mercator; Labrador was bordered on the west by *Baccaleurum Reggio*.

**1544:** The map of the French explorer Jean Alfonse[35] indicated a "portion of the coast of *Laboureur*" next to the island of Cape Breton. Alfonse had practical experience from exploring the country and using local sources.

**1545:** A map of Gaspar Vopell indicates *"Agricole prosen C. do Labrador."* A drawing appears to depict a knight. Ganong identifies this figure as João Fernandez. Nearby to the east of the island Corte Real, a.k.a. Newfoundland. The *Baccaleurum Reggio* is on the west.

**1569:** Mercator's map (the one already shown for Grocland) identified Labrador with the area south of Hudson Bay, rebaptized *Terre Corte Real* by the Portuguese, and first and foremost the Corte Real (probably João Vaz who took credit for its discovery after the Danish-Portuguese expedition to Canada).

**1586:** The map of the Venetian Antonio Millo clearly places Labrador on the south bank of the Saint Lawrence next to *"Nova*

*Franza"* and *"Norvega."* As we can see, several notions are placed side by side and in direct relation.

**1593:** The map of Clæz Plancius shows a different position for *Terra de Labrador* (lat 60°–65° N) compared to that of Gerard Mercator. Labrador is no longer located on the southern shore of the *Golf de Merosro* (a.k.a. Hudson Bay), but on its north shore. Estotiland sits on its northern border. Is there an intentional relationship here between the two populations?

**1597:** The map of Cornelius Wytfliet (in *Descriptiones Ptolemaicae augmentum*) is fairly disturbing. Terra de Laborador (lat 55°– 60° N) is in the same position as on the maps of Mercator and Plancius, and is also next to Estotiland, so close it seems on the verge of being incorporated. Only the two place-names provided (Angre de Ioan Maio and R. Neuado) make it possible to restore the complete Estotiland of Mercator (1569 map).

The presentation sidebar on Wytfliet's map literally merges the two geographical notions: *"Estotilandia et laboratoris terra"* and *"Laboraterris hanc terram Estotilandiamque delatus est."*

Wytfliet clearly opts for the definition of the term Labrador suggested in the introduction. His sources are Antonio Zeno (1390, and quite controversial) and Johanes Scolvus (1476) who he may have deformed in passing by presenting him as *"Polonus"* instead of *"pilotus."* The Polish historian and cartographer Joachim Lelewel (1786–1861) introduces him as Jan Z. Kolna, from a family of merchants and sailors in Gdansk. He is said to have commanded the 1476 Danish-Portuguese expedition in Canada. Therefore he would not be Danish as claimed by other sources, hence my use of the conditional. Larsen, Bjørnbo, Nansen considered him to be either Danish or Norwegian. Lelewel's theory was generally accepted.

In 1605, Hans Paul Resen's map with its *Capo de Labrador* suggests a Markland location; this map makes use of all the known discoveries. With some talent, Resen tried to establish a connection between these recent discoveries and traditional Scandinavian lore, which seems to have been a concern for many Vikings as we have seen with the bishop Gudbrand Thorlatius and his 1606 map. People will note, given the means of his time, a fairly good representation of Greenland,* and something exceptional, the Norse colony of Eystribygð is suggested in the west. This is worth highlighting as it was necessary to wait until the nineteenth century for people to realize that this colony was not located on the coast incorrectly indicated by its name but on the western coast.

*Capo de Labrador* appears south of a bay, probably Hudson Bay. Estotiland is located to the north of this bay and is bordered by Helluland that closes Warwiksound. Resen therefore opts for the hypothesis of a Labrador in the area of the Hudson Bay.

In 1677, the map of the Frenchman Champlain also opted for an identification with Hudson Bay but this time on the south shore. Here Labrador is not incorporated into Estotiland but to "Terra de Corte Real" also called "*de Labrador*" (see map).

To sum up, we have three possible locations for Labrador:

South of the Saint Lawrence (Gemma Fricius, 1537; Jean Alfonse, 1544; Gaspard Vopell, 1545; Lazaro Luiz, 1563; Antonio Millo, 1586).

North of Hudson Bay (Gerard Mercator, 1569; Theodore Plancius, 1593; Cornelius Wytfliet, 1597).

South of Hudson Bay (Hans Poul Resen, 1606; Samuel de Champlain, 1677).

The matter becomes more complicated when we consider a fourth location unknown to the public at large, which according to the dates and the experts seems older: *Terra Laborador* is located in Greenland.

It is difficult to lend support to a mistake. This was maintained as fact for almost the entire first half of the sixteenth century. Perhaps we should consider the matter from a different angle. The wandering, vague nature of the term Labrador found on the maps could easily have its origin in Greenland.

---

*I suspect he was inspired here by Sigurdr Steffansson's 1590 map on which Greenland has the same shape with Herjolfsnes located on Greenland's western coast.

The long fixation on the hypothesis of the farmer/*lavrador*/João Fernandez seems to have eluded any other explanation. Now, as suggested earlier, this word could just as easily apply to a land's inhabitants. During the medieval era, neither the Inuit nor the Amerindians of these regions worked the earth. This term can only apply to one population and one alone. This is where the Greenland name assumes its full value, as we know the Norse community practiced this "art" in Greenland and could and should have practiced it in America.*

F. Nansen believes that João Fernandez was in Greenland in 1500, and baptized it *Terra Laboratoris.* The term therefore refers to the activity of those living there and not to the discoverer's profession. (This would be *Terra Laborador* in Portuguese.) This is close to Admiral Samuel Morison's definition we looked at earlier. His depiction of a small landowner leaving to others the work of cultivating his lands while he took long trips or conducted trade elsewhere could very easily be applied to the Scandinavians. This is one of the defining characteristics of their culture and I would even say of the Nordic society of this era that spawned so many Viking voyages into the West and the East. These Northmen were simultaneously farmers, travelers, and traders, who on occasion indulged in pillaging. It would be hard to be any clearer than Cornelius Wytfliet in this regard: "The Land of Labor and Estotilandia. This last part of Indian land was first discovered in 1390 and then again by Jean Scolue Polonus, who sailed between Norway, Greenland, and Iceland in the year 1477 . . . who landed on these lands of Estotiland."[36]

The name "Greenlandic Labrador" is earlier than the American one. It confirms this way that it refers to the economy of the inhabitants and not to the discoverer João Fernandez. Hansen shares this hypothesis: "*Terra Laboratoris* is a translation of Terra de Laborador." By going farther back in time, an essential author Los Casas (*Historia de las Indias*) confirms my position: "the name of the land of the laborer

---

*We should recall that the Greenland colonists followed the Icelandic model rural economy, which itself was derived from the Norwegian model, in short ensuring a certain kind of continuity. It is totally logical that they would continue to do so in the west on lands that were actually clearly more suitable for these activities.

was invented, according to the insightful observation of the author of *The Memoir of Sebastian Cabot*, by Corte Real and the Portuguese slave traders to indicate this coast as one producing men who were singularly adept at working (al labor).[37]

## Greenlandic Labrador and Cartography
Several maps from the beginning of the sixteenth century illustrate this notion.

**1503:** An Italian map (among others) at the Pesaro Library calls Greenland: *"Terra Labrador."*

**1506:** The Italian map by King and inspired by Portuguese sources baptized Greenland: *"Terra laboratoris."*

**1527:** The map of Maggiolo gives a strange and interesting commentary that could hold the key to the mystery of the Norse disappearance from Greenland. In fact, what we read there is Groenland *"Terra de lavrador de Rey de Portugal,"* and

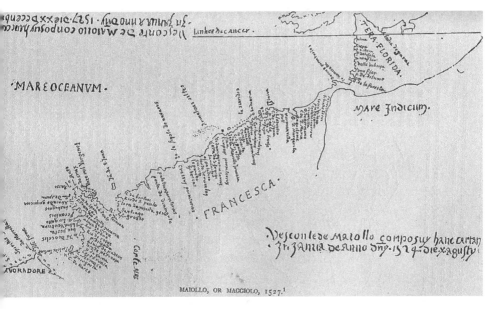

MAIOLLO, OR MAGGIOLO, 1527.[1]

Fig. 11.9. 1527 map of Maggiolo in which two place-names appear referring to the Norse that have gone entirely unnoticed. These are "Lunga villa," a reference to the longhouses of the Vikings, and "Norman villa," Norse houses.
*Wikipedia Commons*

Newfoundland: *"Terra Corte Real de Rey de Portugal."* Not only is Greenland identified as *"Terra de Lavrador,"* but worse, it appears to have been completely annexed by Portugal. A question arises: Is there purely a Portuguese pretention to Greenland sovereignty, or is this an actual statement of fact?

This cartographer's statement is important to study as it is rife with consequences. Furthermore, this claim is not an isolated case. Foreign presence, particularly that of the Portuguese cannot be doubted, it is confirmed by the source material from Inuit myth, and signed here by the people involved. We must believe that the elements at the cartographer's disposal were sufficiently conclusive (the real and regular presence of the Portuguese there and the impotence of the Danish-Norwegian crown) to advance their claims. Knowing Portugal's reputation in America and in the Atlantic in general (numerous cases of abduction of people by the Portuguese are noted) we find there many—and maybe even too many—concordant elements.

The Portuguese were feared for this practice of slavery (their need for various raw materials was great and matched by their need for manual laborers). Let's recall again the stories collected by Niels Egede and Knud Rasmussen.

According to the Inuit of the Middle Ages, they were viewed as "evil and quite belligerent." Any native involvement in the disappearance of the Vikings has never been proved.

A decisive role played by a foreign people is more than likely given the elements we possess. My investigation is now providing us with the "motive for the crime." Echoing the direction taken by the Maggiolo map is a German map by Martin Waldseemüller, who cannot be suspected of any bias.

In 1516, his "Carta Marina" depicts a Greenland named *"Terra Laboratoris"* with a Portuguese coat of arms. K. Prytz mentions a 1519 map drawn after the first Spanish landing in North America in 1513 on which Greenland bearing the Portuguese colors is called *"Labrador, Corte Realis Norwega."*

In 1528, we have another interesting case in which the Venetian

Benedetto Bordone presents a Greenland baptized *"Terra del Laboratore"* adjacent to West at *"Mŏdo nouo."* We see a strait connecting the continents. We have also seen that Groenland was considered to be *"Ponta d'Asia."*

We should note that the distinction between Greenland as "Terra de Lauoratore" and America as *"Mŏdo nouo"* is quite clear and that the Labradorian notion has yet to be granted to its western neighbor.

Following his 1542 to 1543 voyage to America, French explore Jean Alfonse mentions Greenland in his 1559 book *Voyages aventureux* in these terms: "Labrador called Laborant."

The medieval geographical notions we studied earlier will not come in handy. Canada and Greenland were connected by a land bridge for several mapmakers, and for a time, Canada was considered to a part of Greenland. This helps us better understand Champlain's map displaying an "old Greenland" east of the Davis Strait, and another "new" Greenland to the west, in America.

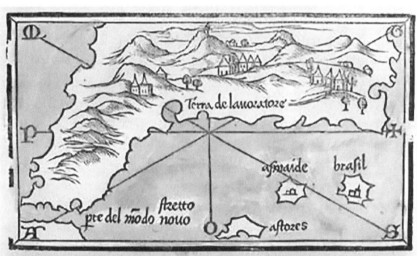

Fig. 11.10. Map of the Venetian Benedetto Bordone of 1528. Greenland, alias "Terra de Lauoratore," is separated from the modo nouo by a strait. Also notable is the reference to the neighboring Brasil Island and the equally interesting reference to the Azores (whose cape seem indicated to me) in keeping with the same line of thought I developed in the fourth part of this chapter.

*Wikimedia Commons*

This notion of a Greenland as Labrador does not seem to have lasted long, if we keep in mind the dates the classic Labrador appeared. Supporting my contention we have a 1527 map by the Englishman Robert Thorne showing the *Noua terra laboratorum dicta* well to the west (see fig. 11.11).

Curiously, Greenland lost all its identity for it no longer had a name. The position of *Noua terra laboratorum* is strongly reminiscent of the area north of the Hudson Bay. Next, the term "Labrador" would become definitively established in America. The parallel with what seems to have been the Norse migration is notable. This wandering place-name with which we are now so familiar, couldn't it reflect the journey of the Scandinavians as they advanced into America?

Here we see a parallel with Champlain's approach to Estotiland in his 1664 map (see page 356) with the old Greenland facing another (new?) Greenland across the Davis Strait. With the Terra Labrador of Greenland across from a Terra Labrador in Canada, we see the same principle and a reference to the same population. In the case where doubt could set in, a map drawn in 1558 (see fig. 11.12) by Diego Homem, grandson of the Portuguese man who took part in the 1473 Danish Portuguese expedition is quite explicit. Greenland is presented as *Desertibusoz Terra Agricole.* Had the former land of the Scandinavian colonists (Greenland Labrador) now abandoned, been replaced by a new, more prosperous land in the West? This suggests that the date it was abandoned is quite early as advanced by Prytz. This could well have been the reasoning of the cartographers of this era. I mean to assess the full value of this cartographic hoard that has been practically abandoned and left to slumber in forgotten drawers for years. It will allow me to close our triangle based on a Nordic approach that was the only approach for a longtime, an Inuit approach, overlooked until now, and a totally external approach, which interests me as much for this same reason. Portuguese, Italians, French, and so all had no stake in the quarrel pitting Vikings and clergy (authors of the source texts) against each other. Their knowledge of Nordic culture was generally limited. Attempts to compare and interpret in accordance with the known

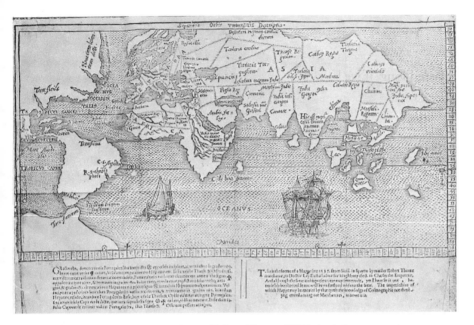

Fig. 11.11. Map of the Englishman Robert Thorne (1527) depicting a nameless
Greenland west of Iceland and a "noua terra Laboratorum dicta" in America.
*Wikimedia Commons*

Fig. 11.12. Portolan by Diego Homen testifying to the tragic fate of
medieval Scandinavian Greenland, which it presents as "desertibuzos Terra agricole"
(deserted farmland). (See also color plate 16.)
*Portolan on the East Coast of America, London, 1558; original in the British Library*

classic texts did not therefore exist for them. This can be seen in the entire stockpile of maps presented—not a single allusion to the sagas, to Vinland (with the exception of the Ortelius map from 1587), or to famous figures like Leif Erikson.

To the contrary, the Europeans with a cold methodical gaze retranscribed what they had seen into black and white (with all the expected errors of the time). What they saw was an industrious and productive people first living in Greenland, then in America. The message is simple, without any frills, errors of interpretation, or corruptions as is the case for Vinland. This finding will perhaps allow us to more easily identify the famous Vinland, or at least through elimination by identifying the Scandinavian areas like those of the Nordrsetur and others, to reduce the mesh of the net. For example, if we give more attentive examination of the interpretation Markland meaning Märchland, the borderland of the primary land of the new Scandinavian colonies, which were also identified as such by the southern explorers as Nordic lands or territories (the *Norren Bygdar*).

In fact, all the elements that I've presented in this book follow each other in a practically perfect logic. We have shown how the church had practically abandoned its responsibilities to Greenland around the second half of the fifteenth century (Pope Nicholas V's request to the "bishops" of Hólar and Skálholt in 1448) creating a dangerous vacuum from which unscrupulous sailors were able to profit.

After the Reformation, a period of disinterest and total lack of initiative set in. This occurred precisely at the time when the maps were alluding to a "new Terra Laboratoris" (1527) and a deserted agrarian land (1558). These two cartographic pieces of evidence could provide us some essential clues: the relatively precise date (a thirty-year margin seems quite minimal from the standpoint of history) of the Viking's disappearance from Greenland. This would have occurred in the interval when the colonists would have been sufficiently numerous in America to constitute the descriptive element provided by the Portuguese: "*Noua terra Laboratorum dicta*" and the one in which the writ of the death of Greenland agriculture is signed: "*Desertibusoz Terra agricole,*" as per the dates seen earlier. As the end date of the Scandinavian inhabitation of

Greenland would appear to be circa the middle of the sixteenth century.*

If the reader can still have any reservations, I would suggest it seems unconvincing to me, given what I reported on piracy and slavery earlier, that the Portuguese would have traveled all the way to a Greenland emptied of all its inhabitants for nothing.† This is something duly consigned to paper. As the principal authors of these criminal acts, they were moreover well placed to know their reasons.

## *A Mystical Case: Norumbega*

While the case of Labrador we just looked at is quite singular, the case of Norumbega beats it a hundred times over and did not have the good fortune to resist the attack of time for today, in contrast to the preceding case, it has disappeared entirely. Now we are going to understand why.

This mysterious name has not failed to cause the spilling of a lot of ink. Just like Labrador, its position is not in the north; moreover it is always placed south of this latter. Nevertheless, to conceal this land would be a mistake, for it is directly linked to the Norse colonists of Greenland. The explanation of their fate would well be hidden behind this enigmatic name, or rather that of their descendants.

Both the Spanish and the Portuguese, who were carving up the latest American "discoveries," knew of Norumbega. Its Nordic affiliation raised no objection, as it was clearly stated in Antonio Millo's 1586 map (*Norwega*) or in the map of Ortelius (*Nordvega*), which was engraved by Hogenberg Frantz in 1570 (see fig. 11.15 on page 376).

At a time when the New World was being divided up—if not being outright dismembered—the recurring appearance of this land clearly attributed to the Norse can only, in my opinion, reveal a reality. Different nations saw them and—if you follow the thread of my demonstration—traded with them, explaining the (rare) presence of Norwegian money in a Maine bay, or a scale arm in Ellesmere. Because

---

*I am basing my views on Jean Alfonse's 1542 to 1543 commentary on Greenland (among others): "Labrador called Laborant." His works enjoy a certain reputation.

†The observation is valid in the case where the Portuguese did not have the dark designs I am lending them—something I doubt strongly given all the elements assembled here—and restricted themselves to ordinary commercial exchanges.

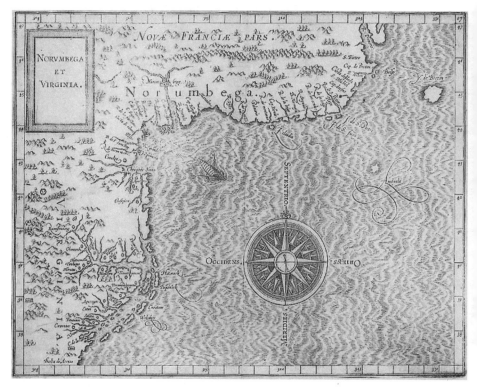

Fig. 11.13. Map of Cornelius Wytfliet from 1597, Norumbega and Virginia.
Norumbega's existence is so well established that Wytfliet created an entire map
for this region. At a time when various nations were bitter disputing control
over America, why would the attribution of this land to the Norse continually
appear if not for their actual presence there?
***Wikimedia Commons***

the place was already spoken for, the new arrivals would go elsewhere to try their fortunes, but this only lasted for a while.

In his very instructive book, *Crucial Maps in the Early Cartography,* Canadian historian and cartographer, W. Francis Ganong (1864–1941) offers a vast panorama of this reality. He quite relevantly points out a common practice of ancient cartographers—a tendency to plagiarize. According to him, Gastaldi, Descelier, and Alfonse all would have drawn from the same map. On the other hand, I will follow his reasoning with circumspection when he explains the Dieppe origin of this name, perhaps due to the "Norman" companions of Verrazano. In

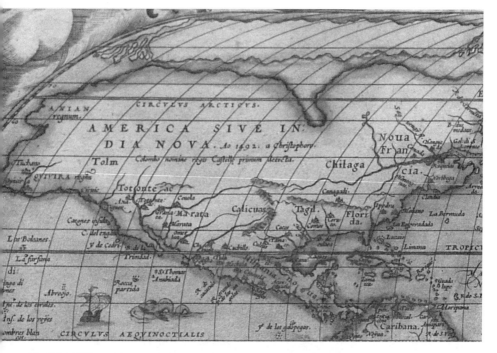

Fig. 11.14. 1570 world map of Abraham Ortelius. "Nordbega" appears as a direct reference to Scandinavians in America, similar to Antonio Millo's Norwega reference in 1586.
*Wikimedia Commons*

his book, *Cartes marines, constructions navales . . . chez les Normands,* Abbé Anthiaume adds that the word appears as *Norbegia* in Benedetto Bordone's map of 1528 and suggests a possible corruption of the word into *Norvega.* My reference to the Nordics was therefore seen then as a proven fact. Ganong places our mysterious land between Narragansett Bay and New York. Closer to our day, K. Prytz places it between north Florida and the Chesapeake Bay. I would like to cite several ancient maps and the avatars of this name (and I would even note all the abuse this place name has suffered).

**1529:** Orrambega appears on a map of Verrazano.

**1539:** The Nurumbega of the *Discorso de Rasmusio* (vol. 3, 87) based on Verrazano's date is interesting for Verrazano mentions I used by the natives to describe their country located south of Cape Cod.

**1541:** Norrumbega for the expedition of Alphonse and Roberval.

**1548:** Terra de Norrumbega in Gastaldi's work based on the *Discorso.*

**1564:** Ortelius's map shows Terra de Norumbega and Terra de Labrador, which I say were both connected to the Nordic peoples.

**1569:** Norrumbega appears in Mercator's very pretty map, but he must have taken his inspiration from his teacher Ulpius.

**1592:** Appears on Molyneux's globe.

Fig. 11.15. 1587 world map of Abraham Ortelius (new version of America suive nova orbi nova description, 1570). Norumbega clearly appears in its "traditional" location south of the Saint Lawrence adjacent to New France. Even more interesting is the Vinland of the sagas that appears corrupted in the name of "Wingandekoa," a likely alteration of "Vinland den goda."
***Wikimedia Commons***

The list is far from being exhaustive and yet is fairly revealing. Just like Vinland, its location is a subject of great controversy. Beauvois even suggests an error of interpretation: Norrumbega would not have been in the Maine region (where the famous Norwegian coin dating from the time of Olaf Kyrre was found), but in the Bay of Fundy. It responded to the impressive dimensions of what the explorers mistook for a river. Another singular feature could play in its favor, the famous tides of this bay that even Columbus describe, with a range of fifteen meters—the sole in the world according to Prytz. If we use the terms of the young Christopher Columbus sailing "100 leagues (300 nautical miles) from Tile Island" (Greenland), he would have already been wandering in the (North) American spheres as he insisted he was at lat 73° N. Don't forget that at this time the Greenwich Meridian was not the reference— it in fact passed west of Hierro Island in the Canaries. Consequently Columbus was sailing 10° west of Greenland.

Other "minor" details could help this research. Several maps mention place-names that have a clear reference to Northmen: *Norman villa* (Norman or rather Norse dwellings), and *Lunga villa* (longhouses). In the beginning fo this book we saw that they corresponded to the last stage of Nordic architecture. We find these Lunga villa, for example, in 1527 on Maggiolo's map; in 1229, Verrazano; 1542, in the globe of Ulpius I (see illustration), and always on the perimeter of the mythical Norrumbega. Let's note that Verrazano places it between Boston and Rhode Island, stating that the natives called it by this name.

These little details underscore the importance of these foreign sources that have been left too long abandoned. Their references are clear and not encumbered by the poetic interpretations typical of the sagas, riding roughshod over wine or prairies as is the case with Vinland. This meticulousness would cost the Northmen dearly, as we shall see in the conclusion, as the southern Europeans would have no trouble finding them again and sealing their fate.

One thing seems sure, Eugène Beauvois grasped the origin of this famous mystical name rather well. In 1877, he was already comparing it with the Old Norse: *Norrøn* and *bygd* (in his *Les Derniers vestiges du Christianisme . . . dans le Markland et la grande Irlande*). I would even say that he was not far off the mark. Beauvois left several pertinent works on the Nordic colonists, and I don't understand why he didn't take any interest in the genitive of *byggd, bygdar* in old Icelandic, or *bygd* (Old Norse). Norumbega can be understood easily as a corruption of Norraen *bygdar*. The confusion seems perfectly understandable for a Latin ear uninitiated to the tones of the Nordic languages.

In this case we need to understand this place-name as the installation, the settlement of the Norse (*Norrænar bygdar* or even the form *Norren bygddar*). The contemporary meaning has not changed: an inhabited or built place. Here we could have the explanation for the mysterious Norumbega.

To summarize: the intense economic, political, and religious activity of the various English, Germanic, and Portuguese nations in the Far North would be the forerunner to the spike in the development of a rich cartography as they were equally essential to each other. Ironically, Scandinavian mapmaking is rather paltry in comparison to the southern maps. This clearly reflects the decline of proficient experts, particularly the church, which held a large share of power, but also of knowledge. With respect to Greenland, the church was responsible for issuing almost all the texts and maps that I could describe as very "poetic" but hardly scientific. By way of comparison, Maggiolo's 1527 map of the American coast is more than disturbing because of all the details it offers. Despite their variety—in truth economic competition and rival interests compels this—all these maps agree on one point: a Scandinavian presence in America. They could even explain the emergence of place names like Estotiland and Norumbega that remain unexplained to this day, and even call back into question others like Labrador. More importantly, the famous map by Homem (1558) offers us written evidence for a date, or at least a serious timeframe for when the last descendants of the Vikings vanished from the eastern colony.

# Conclusion

As is easy to see, the scope of this book is quite vast, and several conclusions need to be drawn from it. The overarching idea though is that there are a number of theories or judgments concerning the medieval Scandinavian Arctic and its population that cry out for reconsideration.

The length of time Scandinavians were living in Greenland and Canada needs to be revised upward. At the beginning of the century, it was common to consider the first decades of the sixteenth century as the cut-off date (based on Scandinavian source materials). We can see that an additional half century is not unreasonable if we follow the Portuguese source materials.

The relative affluence of the Norse colonists contradicts the alarmist sources concerning their destitution. This should probably be viewed as a pretext for the resumption of contact with the former colonies. It's also confirmation, if more is needed, of the extended presence of merchant sailors or pirates in Arctic waters. We have to believe their movements were motivated. Several export products of the Scandinavians (ivory, falcons, and so forth) and basic products (iron) were found in far northern areas, which only confirms Scandanavian presence in northern Greenland and Canada.

A new look also proves necessary at the Inuit people (Kallaallit of Greenland). Any consideration of Inuit-Viking relations requires both of the following contexts:

Clear identification of the cultures involved in all Inuit-Scandinavian contact. This will emerge from various factors such as tools, dates of contacts, and so forth. As we have seen, notable differences characterize the successive waves of the Inuit inhabitation of Greenland.

An extensive approach to their traditional oral, artistic, and technical hoards. Until now, only Inuit material culture has been approached seriously (at an ethnological and archaeological level). In my opinion, the study of the two other elements stands out as a necessity, an essential diversification of the sources concerning the Far North that have been strangely overlooked until now. We should not forget that the store of traditional Inuit oral lore as a cultural legacy can have if not an historical at least informative value and that its real—truly scientific—credibility is no more susceptible to flaws than the ordinary medieval source texts, which have we have seen can contain some fantasy style writings or purposely misleading geographical maps.

The disinterest in Inuit traditional art is hard to explain as this testimony sits at another level than that of the tale. It is relatively precise, duly dated and situated. It often confirms several facts or hypotheses advanced in Scandinavian or European written sources. Knowing Inuit traditions, it seems unlikely to me that they would have taken such pains to depict an enemy population (the Vikings) and conclude from that their relations were rather peaceful if not friendly. No massacres of Scandinavian have been confirmed by archaeology. Rather, to the contrary, cohabitation seems to have been the rule in various places. The theory of war and extermination seems to have often resulted from the suggestion and vague statements—if not a simple schematization—in the clerical texts, which is also the secret of its "success." This theory indirectly exonerated the church of the coercive role it played in Greenland. To the contrary, we see the use of the subtle distinctions it introduced (the neighboring native peoples became trolls and the remote populations, Skrælings). This shows a shrewdness worthy of a cleric for de facto validation of Scandinavian colonists and native pagans. I would maintain that the first Inuit-Scandinavian contacts were much earlier than people have claimed, and I reject the idea that contacts began as late as the thirteenth century.

The subject of Inuit borrowings from the Vikings are still relevant, I would study this matter more closely than contemporary Danish research.* Based on the conclusions I presented in the beginning of the book (Inuit accounts of the Scandinavians, Inuit migrations into the south, commercial Scandinavian expeditions into the north), I believe an early contact must be considered between the two cultures, and that the differences characteristic of the Greenland Inuit with those of Canada and Alaska, particularly for Inussuk culture, should originate in the mainly peaceful contacts between the two peoples. In some cases this appears to have led to cohabitation over extended periods of time. Inuit loans to the Scandinavians are not excluded but harder to prove, although Scandinavian assimilation appears to me as the supreme example of such a thing with the Nordics in fact borrowing the Inuit lifestyle.

We should recall that serious hypotheses have been advanced on the case of Nordic boats made from skins appearing (based on the *Flóamanna saga*) at the beginning of Norse colonization that were inspired by the Inuit *umiaq,* the brace and bit (according to Leroi Gourhan), and more recently the seal oil lamp (according to T. E. Lee). This utensil was found in the archaeological layers of proven Scandinavian sites. I would like to note that the Inuit word *qulleq* strangely echoes this loan linguistically (Norse *kollek*).

Surely a new approach shoud be considered with regard to Scandinavian borrowings from the Inuit. Study of these Inuit loans should be oriented outside of the Greenland colonies, given the weight of the church and the spiritual implications of such borrowings (pagan connotations, abandonment of the faith, and so forth). These studies should no longer be restricted to typically Scandinavian or Inuit characteristics, as I believe that the mixing of the two peoples could also cause a mixing of techniques, which would seem to agree with certain ambiguous medieval source texts[†] acknowledging this, such as Olaus Magnus or Antonio Zeno mentioning Northmen in kayaks.

As well as with Canadian excavations in the Hudson Bay and

*Despite the many excavations overseen by the Scandinavians, I've been surprised at how conservative they are on the subject of Inuit borrowings.
†Others like Hakluyt seen earlier, or Cartier, seem less so.

Ungava Bay area showing the presence of typically Inuit objects or techniques in sites presumed to be Scandinavian. Recall that there is precedent for this in the eastern colony where Inussuit Inuit objects were found in Scandinavian graves.

Finally, it seems difficult to give credence to around five centuries of Scandinavian presence in the Arctic without the appearance of any influence (or inspirational motifs as H. C. Gulløv puts it). It is suggested by the existence of Inuit statuettes depicting Vikings. It seems illusory to seek to limit Scandinavian influence to this "artistic copy" as that ignores the Inuit people's abilities to adapt, and that of the Scandinavians if we turn things around. As for the latter, the sole obstacle to this kind of approach was the church. And we know that the bridges were almost certainly burned for the western colony.

The role of the church in the Arctic has been relatively obscure. The fate of Scandanavian colonists has practically never been considered in the context of their relationships with the Catholic Church. Taking into account the primary historical sources, we see that the cryptic missives from Rome, the nominations and dismissals of church authorities in Greenland, make clear that there were serious disputes between the Church and Scandanavians, especially in the Artic. Remember that the general situation was not especially stable, evidenced by the beginning of the Reformation in 1530. It is obvious that the church played several definite roles in the fate of the Scandanavian colonists:

A positive commercial role for expanding into the Far North, attracting the German and English clergy, before very likely attracting the clergy of southern Europe.

An ambiguously negative role in its stranglehold over Greenland, its tense relationship with its population having caused the departure of a certain number of them, and a very dubious role in the "divvying up of the world" following the great discoveries. What were its real implications and how should we interpret the terms of the Tordesillas Treaty concerning the lands of the Northern Hemisphere? In this very troubled, truthfully very violent time of schisms, crusades, and Inquisitions, it is hard not to see this as a blank check granted very Catholic Portugal: permission to go corrects the Greenland flock that had "abandoned the true faith."

This Greenlandic dispute, in fact, fits into a much larger quarrel with the Danish crown. In 1481, King Christian I wrote his political testament in which he stripped all power from the church (as well as from the nobles and elite of the court). For example no bishop had the right to live in a fortified castle, have more than five mounted guards, and so on. The cherry on top was that all the benefits of the church reverted to the King! It is easy to imagine Rome's anger . . .

The relationship between the Borgia pope and the Danish crown were certainly not looking rosy.

The Treaty of Tordesillas appears to me as the final word in these strained circumstances. Its effects were twofold, giving the Portuguese approval to move forward and as well as giving the Danish-Norwegian king and the recalcitrant Greenland flock a taste of their own medicine. The public at large was exclusively focused on the southern discoveries, but the drawing of this dividing line in the north was far from inconsequential. This treaty factored in the remote lands of the north and Alexander VI's clear intentions of restoring the authority of the church there and thereby benefiting from its riches. Thanks to this treaty, his very Catholic Portuguese ally got compensation for Spain and the Borgia pope settled his score with the Danish crown, giving the Portuguese carte blanche in the Far North. In this context, we better understand the presumptuousness of all these maps sporting a Greenland wearing Portuguese colors and all these new Norse lands suddenly becoming Terra de Rey de Portugal—as well as all their inhabitants.

The trail of Rome settling a score therefore finds extensive reinforcement with the "Greenland question" forming only a part of the serious liability opposing the Danish crown and Rome. I think is the most logical and well-founded explanation for the tragic fate of the Nordic colonies of Greenland and America. If anyone still harbors any doubts, recall that the gap separating the Roman Church from the Scandinavian countries would only widen irreparably with the Reformation in 1530, closely coinciding with the Norse disappearance from the Greenland-America-Arctic Canada sphere.

In fact, Greenland proved to be a much more complex matter than I imagined when starting out. To my great surprise, the deeper I dug, the newer—and quite often unknown—elements came to light. An additional problem was grated to the internal problem of "rebellion" against the administration and tax power of the clergy with bitter rivalry between the two bishoprics of Lund and Hamburg, it we study Adalbert's very real complaints (Innocent II's papal bull of May 27, 1133, for example). This state of affairs must of—if not justified—at least encouraged the unruliness of the Greenland colonists, who as we have seen, accepted German law with greater grace than Roman law.

Another thorny problem: were churchmen truly assigned to Greenland in the ninth century? Study of the documentation regarding this, and the question of its authenticity opens the path to further research. I cite them because the spirit of this book is to present all theories concerning the era.

On the other hand, we are aware of the existence of Celtic cultural elements in Greenland, which are sparingly shared in the Nordic source texts (*Landnámabók, Óláfs saga Tryggvasonar, etc.*). Should we revise our notions of Greenland's "discovery?" During this time, the sole Christians haunting these latitudes were the Irish monks, who had, incidentally, been chased out of Ireland by the same Vikings. The Church could have known very early about the existence of lands in the north and even those located more to the west. Another implication is that the Celtic monks who landed in Greenland before Norse colonization had to give it a name; which inevitably drew from the myths of Antiquity which the well-read monks surely knew. They were inspired by Plutarch's mythical *Cronia,* the land in the north where Saturn slumbers, bordered by the *Cronia Mare.* Gabriel Gravier tells us that this Cronian Sea formed a gulf as large as the Caspian Sea, and it was frozen . . .

Myth and reality became strangle interwoven in the appearance of the fabled Ogygia. Gabriel Gavier and De Roo mention Plutarch's *Ogygia:*

The island Ogygia lies at a distance of five days navigation from Great Britain; and farther in the same direction of the summer's setting sun, or west-northwest, at equal distances or 3 more days voyages, are situated *3 other islands,* in one of which Jupiter has imprisoned and chained with the bands of an everlasting sleep his antagonist, the God Saturn. Further still, at 5000 stadia from *Ogygia,* but closer to the last of the last of the other islands, is located the *Great Mysterious Continent* that encompasses the ocean. The *Cronian Sea,* which here forms a gulf as large as the Caspian Lake is so smooth and shallow, so full of mud, of sand-banks and reefs, that it would be impossible to cross it in rowing vessels. Of old, it was though, he [Plutarch] adds, that this sea was all frozen.

Gravier's identification is stupefying: "the 3 isles cited at equal distance on a line of 5,000 stadia between Ogygia and the Cronian continent correspond exactly to Greenland, the Faroe Isalnds, and Iceland. The large bay like the Palus Meotid could correspond to Hudson Bay or the Baffin Sea, the shoals and mud are reminiscent of the hydrography of the boreal ocean." Von Humbolt notes that in addition to the presence of ice, there are floating banks of bladderwrack."

After Pliny the Elder, geographers baptized all waters west and north of Iceland as the Cronian Sea. The transition (or corruption) of Cronia to Cronland or Cronia Land is not very hard. All the old document I've mentioned seem to actually refer to the country of Cronos-Cronland or Gronland. The most faithful version of the ancient spelling and spirit of the word would be that of Victor II: *Crolondiæ,* in the middle of the twelfth century. Finally, could this terminology be the result of a misunderstanding, the learned referring to the classical sources while the common folk adopted a simpler and easier term to assimilate: Grøn Land, Greenland?

De Roo makes precisely this distinction: the oldest documents say *Cronland* or *Gronland* while the more recent opt for a more "Scandinavian" *Grænland* or *Grenelandia.*

The fact remains that it is surprising to see how much the spelling of Greenland varies in the medieval source materials, and this is true even during the times when it was well known. For example, in the *series latina* dated May 27, 1133, one of Pope Innocent III's bulls speaks of Adalbert's rights over *Cronlondiœ* (Migne, vol. 179/180). Could people have been referring to two almost homophonic terms, yet distinct with regard to the cultures and interests in play? If this hypothesis proves correct, then Icelandic scribes would have clearly plagiarized ancient mythology, adapting the mythical *Cronia* to *Grønland*. We know precedents exist validation my question. As we see, the history of medieval Greenland is far from corresponding to the frozen image of Icelandic-Norwegian colonization as accepted until now—many players were involved.

I believe confining ourselves to the mythical dimension of the term would be a mistake or an extremely deceptive blindness, for it appears far too often, mainly cited by the highest authorities, in this instance those of Rome.

> **831:** When the two Benedictine monks Witmar and Anschaire returned to the general diet of the new Roman Empire of Aachen, Emperor Louis named Anschaire bishop of all the countries of the north, including Groenlandorum. We should note that the copy appearing in the *Diplomatarium Islandicum* gives the spellings I've mentioned: "*in gentibus videlicet Danorum, Suecorum, Norweon, Farriae, Gronlandon, Hallingalandon, Islandon, Scredevindon . . .*"
>
> **835:** Pope Gregory IV gives his approval. Greenland appears in several codices, that of Udalric of Bandenberg (*Danorum, Gronlandon, Islandon et omnium, . . .*), of Vicelini (*Gronlandan, Islondan, Scriderindan, . . .*), of Lindenberg (*Farriæ, Gronlandon, Helsingalandon, etc.*) May 31, 858 (or 864?)" Pope Nicholas I the Great, confirms St. Anschaire's Nordic legation, clearly naming Greenland and Iceland. Pope Anastasius does the same in 912:

*Cum illis. . . . Episcopos in omnibus gentibus Suenum seu Danorum . . . Gronlandon et universarum septentrionalium nationum*
or October 29, 920 When John X ratified the confirmation of

Gregory IV: *"Ceum illis etiamhoc tempere ad Christi fidem conversi sunt, procurante et protegente gratia Dei, videlicet Episcopos in omnibus gentibus Suenum sen Danerum, Norvegiorum, Island, Scridevinnum, Gronlandon, et universum septentrionalium nationum, nec non etiam in illis partibus Slavorum que sunt a flumine Pene ad fluvium Egidone . . ."*

Among the scholarly opponents of this early Christian presence, I would like to mention Lappenberg, Rafn, or Gaffarel, and among the supporters, Langebeck or Malte Brun. The problem is that these Germanic sources are very controversial and often labeled fakes.

The possibility of a later clerical presence also exists, or at least an obvious pontifical interest, given the continuity in the naming of bishops and the greater number of them that was known until now. The nomination of several southern bishops, among others with direct ties to Rome, reinforces my hypothesis of a desire to bring Greenland to heel. Without wanting to speculate on their absence from their diocese, the motivations behind these nominations provoke my interest. It seems that the best way for Rome to see its objectives realized was to nominate docile, trustworthy collaborators. The individuals from Saint Peter's Basilica cited in my summary list fit this criterion perfectly. Furthermore, why name bishops for a country that was supposed to be deserted at the end of the fifteenth and beginning of the sixteenth century?

Another fundamental conclusion is that the isolation of the Scandinavian dependencies in the Arctic is a deception, just as is their supposed lack of any commercial value. The presence of other European nations in Arctic waters says differently. This also has the advantage of leaving us other accounts on this topic. Eastern Canada was known long before Columbus. The Vikings were maintaining regular connections there since the twelfth century at the very latest (this is according to Bishop Eirik Upsi [Gnupson] but I would personally make it another century earlier—if not more—if we include other nations, mainly the English, who also left evidence in this regard, especially the "Celtic" sphere primarily meaning the Irish). The essential difference of these trade and exploration voyages resides in the fact that they were due first and foremost to the individual and discreet initiative of sailors and merchants, who played the role of pioneers to some degree.

The phase of the nation inspired both Spanish and Portugeuse explorations in the fifteenth century put an end to this. More seriously, it was only after the Southern powers established a presence in Arctic Greenland and Canada that all the written sources fell silent on the existence of the Scandinavian colonists.

To summarize this large book, the first—episodic and isolated—contacts between the Inuit natives and Scandinavian settlers occurred among small groups, most likely during Nordsetur expeditions. All the accounts and technical information point toward the Dorset Culture. The search for the wealth of the Arctic (ivory, falcons) couldn't help but put these two peoples into contact in the very far north. This is clearly illustrated in both the traditional Inuit lore as in the Nordic records. But the most significant contacts would seem to involve the Thule culture that was contemporary to the Vikings and whose advanced technology was in no way inferior to that of the Norse. The Thule people displayed a perfect mastery of their environment, both on land and sea, which distinguishes them from the members of Dorset culture. It is the Thule that display the most traces of contact and influence with the Vikings. The current inhabitants of Greenland are their direct descendants.

Viking colonization of Greenland went from the original Icelandic system of chiefdoms with no central authority—thus making Greenland very autonomous—toward a system under the religious than royal authority of Norway. The imposition of religious authority was a painful experience, but this was also the case with a number of neighboring islands like Iceland and the Faroes.

In tandem with this changing situation, a large number of the colonists—especially the colony of the west—remained faithful to the characteristic Viking spirit of adventure and exploration set off to take their chances in what lay just beyond their doors, the unknown lands to the west and the riches of the Far North. The first voyages took place during the eleventh century. This phenomenon was amplified by the growing deterioration of relations with the church in Rome. It excommunicated the Viking colonists of America, sealing their fate.

Oddly enough, the European presence in the Far North does not appear to have left too many traces among the Inuit except at the no less important level of safety that could explain the Inuit settlements as seen in southern Greenland not far from the Viking populations. The Scandinavian presence left its mark on their native neighbors in a variety of ways such as technological and commercial (trading), which inspired many onerous journeys. At the same time linguistic influence (there are a surprising number of word matches) and interactions of the two populations created a degree of integration noted by the last Danish colonies of the eighteenth century. Furthermore, the Norse fate is connected with the presence in Greenland of other European visitors. We can follow traces of the Viking travels in the new lands of the west followed closely by a number of different countries. It seems that these small colonies of freemen and adventurers did not measure up to this growing, invasive influx. Up to the present day, the various leads concerning the fate of the Norse in North America have not delivered any decisive argument. The relatively recent lead concerning their enslavement increasingly offers concordant elements in both the Far North and America with the geographical and linguistic fluctuations of the word Labrador, the expeditions (Portuguese mainly) to Greenland and America before Columbus, and the serious evidence for a Norse presence in the southern islands where slavery was practiced on the large farming establishments.

Portuguese cartography even seems to provide us with a *terminus ante quem** for the Nordic inhabitation of Greenland. The excellence of the southern maps is a kind of admission, testifying to their very real presence there and explaining their detailed knowledge of the area such as the fact that Greenland is an island. We need only look at Cantino's map (1502) on which Greenland appears with noteworthy contours, and again stamped "Land of the King of Portugal."

In my opinion, several responses to the questions I've raised on this medieval time period and these regions are not to be found in the north

---

*The latest possible date —*trans.*

but in the south, in some Roman, Portuguese, or Spanish archive. The historical storehouse, the cartography, the cultural heritage of certain sites (perhaps the Azores and Canaries with their gargoyles strongly reminiscent of Nordic pagan art) or survivals of Nordic traditions (like the toboggan rides in Madeira) and even genetics, could reveal quite a few surprises.

# Notes

### CHAPTER 1. THE INUIT IN GREENLAND

1. Jens Rosing, in Petersen and Staffildt, *Bogen om Grønland, Fortid, Nutid, og Fremtid,* 73.
2. Jens Rosing, in Petersen and Staffildt, *Bogen om Grønland, Fortid, Nutid, og Fremtid,* 73.
3. Jette Arneborg, *Kultur,* 994.
4. Helge Larsen, *Grønlands bogen,* 216.
5. Finn Gad, *A History of Greenland,* 167.
6. Tryggvi Oleson, *Early Voyages,* 54
7. Ernest William Hawkes, *The Labrador Eskimos.*
8. Oleson, *Early Voyages,* 57.

### CHAPTER 2.
### THE VIKINGS IN GREENLAND

1. Corrado Gini, *Extinction,* 7.
2. In *Grønlands Historiske Mindesmærker,* vol. 3, 264–392.
3. *Grønlands Historiske Mindesmærker.*
4. Helge Ingstad, *Pole Star,* 69.
5. Christian Keller, "Eastern Settlement," 136.
6. Keller, "Eastern Settlement," 136.
7. Corrado, *Extinction,* 7.
8. Keller, "Eastern Settlement," 28.
9. See chapter 6, "Prolonged Contact or Cohabitation of Inuit and Vikings," and chapter 7, "The Testimony of the Nordic Source Texts."
10. Thomas Howatt McGovern, "Thule Norse Interaction in Southwest Greenland," 177.
11. Gini, *Extinction,* 19.
12. McGovern, "Thule Norse Interaction," 178.

13. Cited in Vera Henriksen, *Mot en verdens,* 185.

14. Keller, "The Eastern Settlement Reconsidered," 28.

15. Henriksen, 281. This is the letter of April 4, 1282. It is based on the *Regesta Norvegica,* II doc. 392. Also in *Diplomatarium Norvegicum.*

16. Trvggvi Oleson, *Early Voyages,* 42.

17. *Grønlands Historiske Mindesmærker,* vol. 3, 386.

18. *Hauksbók,* cited in Carl Christian Rafn, *Antiquitates,* 273.

19. Heyerdahl and Lillieström, *Ingen grenser,* 256.

20. Robert McGhee, "Contact," 47.

21. FL CCL Corsiniana Library, Rome, Codex MS 377, f° 48 v°.

22. FL CCL Corsiniana Library, Rome, Codex MS 377, f° 49 v°.

23. Keller, "Eastern Settlement," 286.

24. Knud Krogh, cited in Keller, "Eastern Settlement," 97.

25. Ingstad, *Pole Star,* 66.

26. Ingvi Thorsteinsson, *Undersøgelser,* 97.

27. Gwyn Jones, *Norse Atlantic,* 30–31.

28. Jones, *Norse Atlantic,* 30–31.

29. Cited in Heinrich Rink, *Kaladlit,* 62–69.

30. Jones, *Norse Atlantic,* 30–31.

31. *Greenland Annals,* cited in *Grønlands Historiske Mindesmærker,* vol. 3, 513–16, and Vera Henriksen, *Mots en verdens,* 163.

32. Keller, "Eastern Settlement," 41.

33. Keller, "Eastern Settlement," 41.

34. Finn Gad, "Kildematerialet," 146.

## CHAPTER 3. THE TRADITIONAL INUIT CULTURAL BACKGROUND AS A RESEARCH ELEMENT

1. Heinrich Rink, *Eskimoiske,* 206.

2. Rink, *Eskimoiske,* 206.

3. Knud Rasmussen, *Myter og sagn,* 68.

4. Rasmussen, *Myter og sagn,* 68.

5. Hans Egede, in Niels Egede, "En kort or Infoldig," 37.

6. Jan de Vries, *Altnordisches Etymologisches,* 505.

7. Jóhannesson, *Isländisches etymologisches Wörterbuch,* 828.

8. Richard Cleasby and Gusbrand Vigfusson, *Dictionary,* 659.

9. Rasmussen, *Myter og sagn,* vol. 1, 125.

10. Erik Holtved, "Polar Eskimos," 125–26.

11. Father Petitot, cited in Jacques Privat, "Les Relations," 14.

12. Privat, "Les Relations," 14.

13. Rink, *Eskimoiske eventyr og sagn,* 71.

14. Arneborg, "Aqissiaq og Nordboerne," 213–19.

15. *Grønlands Historiske Mindesmærker,* Vol. 3, 459.

16. Christian Keller, "Eastern Settlement," 373.

17. Christian Pingel, "Antiquariske," 324–25.

18. Heinrich Rink, *Tales and Tradition,* 321; see also Rink, *Kaladlit,* 207–9.

19. Pingel, "Antiquariske," 325.

20. Rasmussen, *Myter og sagn,* vol. 3, 125–27.

21. See the recapitulative list in chapter 9.

22. *Grønlands Historiske Mindesmærker,* vol. 3, 238–44; and Carl Christian Rafn, *Antiquitates,* 465.

23. Heinrich Rink, cited in Jacques Privat, "Les Relations," 10.

24. In *Diplomatorium Norvegicum,* vol. 3, 527.

25. Olaus Magnus, *Historia,* 1555; and *Grønlands Historiske Mindesmærke,* vol. 3, 464.

26. Privat, "Les Relations," 5–20.

27. Rink, *Tales and Tradition,* 298–319; see also Rink, *Kaladlit,* 198–206.

28. Jørgensen, "Indberetning til det Kongelige Nordiske Oldskriftselskab."

29. Rink, *Kaladlit,* 1–25.

30. H. C. Rossen, *Nordboerne ved Upernivik,* 98–99.

31. Jón Thorkelsson, *Thjódsogur og Munmæli,* 61–64.

## CHAPTER 4. INUIT ART AS A RESEARCH ELEMENT

1. Hans Christian Gulløv, "Eskimoens," 226–34.

2. Peter Schledermann, "Nordbogenstande," 222.

3. Nicolas and Antonio Zeno, in Richard Hakluyt, *Divers Voyages,* C3.

## CHAPTER 5. INUIT LOANS, INUSSUK CULTURE, AND THE VIKINGS

1. Therkel Mathiessen, *Skrælingerne,* 121–22.

2. Mads Lidegaard, *Grønlands Historie.*

3. Tryggvi Oleson, *Early Voyages,* 63.

4. Finn Gad, *History,* 100.

5. André Leroi-Gourhan, *Civilisation,* 73. I have kept the spelling used by the author in the entire quotation.

6. Leroi-Gourhan, *Civilisation,* 73.

7. *Hauksbók,* cited in Carl Christian Rafn, *Antiquitates,* 274–75.

8. Leroi-Gourhan, *Civilisation,* 73–74.

9. Anne Stine Ingstad, *Discovery,* 192.

10. Rafn, *Antiquitates,* 299. This list appears in the *Grænlands Annál.* Unfortunately the date of the original, which inspired B. Jónsson (among others), is quite vague. The later date of this compilation gives us reason to think that this loan would be located at the end of Norse colonization (fifteenth to sixteenth centuries) as it notably doesn't appear in Ivar Bårdsson's list from 1360.

11. Hans Egede, *Description et histoire,* 125.

12. Poul Egede, *Dictionarium,* 277.

13. Jonsson, *Old Nordisk,* 398.

14. Leiv Heggstad, *Gamalnorsk ordbok,* 318.

15. Spelled "quaunek" by Emile Petitot.

16. Cited in Christian Pingel, "Antiquariske," 324–25.

17. Jonsson, *Old Nordisk,* 302.

18. Cited in Jan de Vries, *Dictionary of Old Norse,* vol. 15.

19. Egede, *Dictionarium,* 46.

20. Heggstad, *Gamalnorsk ordbok,* 759.

21. Heggstad, *Gamalnorsk ordbok,* 417.

22. John Davis, G. N. Bugge, and John Jane, *Tre resjer,* vol. 7, 38–51.

23. Finn Gad, 244–45.

24. Thomas Bartholin, *Acta Medica,* 73, as well as for the words that follow.

25. In Vilhjalmur Steffansson, *Greenland.*

26. Émile Petitot, *Vocabulaire,* vol. 5. I have retained Petitot's spelling, which was inspired by the Norwegian.

## CHAPTER 6. PROLONGED CONTACT OR COHABITATION OF INUIT AND VIKINGS

1. Finn Gad, *History,* 167.

2. Mathiassen and Holtved, "The Eskimo Archeology of Julianehaab District," 84.

3. Mathiassen, "Skraelingerne i Grønland, Grønlands Historie," 81.

4. Jette Arneborg, *Kultur,* 136.

5. Arneborg, 137.

6. Arneborg, 158.

7. Arneborg, 19.

8. William Thalbitzer, "Two Runic Stones." See Tryggvi Oleson, *Early Voyages,* 40.

9. Kåre Prytz, *Vestover,* 56.

10. McGhee, "Contact between Native North Americans and the Medieval Norse," 4–26.

11. Arneborg, *Kultur,* 22.

12. Claus Andreasen, "Nipaitsoq," 185.

13. Arneborg, *Kultur,* 137.

14. Arneborg, 125.

15. Corrado Gini, *Extinction,* 15.

## CHAPTER 7. THE TESTIMONY OF THE NORDIC SOURCE TEXTS

1. Knud Krogh, *Erik den Rødes Grønland,* 16.

2. Jette Arneborg, *Kultur,* 40.

3. Martin Johan Lappenberg, *Alterthumsforscher,* 851.

4. For Kåre Prytz, Hvideserk (the white shirt) is the first mountain when arriving in Greenland.

5. The large fjords of Eystribygð in Axel Bjørnbo, "Cartographia," 6; and the southern tip of the Norse sites in Prytz, *Vestover,* 61.

6. The large fjords of Vestribygð in Bjørnbo. The northernmost Norse site of Vestribygð according to Kåre Prytz, *Vestover.*

7. Prytz, *Vestover,* 61. All the contemporary distances are by Prytz.

8. *Grønlands Historiske Mindesmærker,* vol. 1, 130–31.

9. Anne Stine Ingstad, *Discovery,* 82.

10. *Grønlands Historiske Mindesmærker,* vol. 1, 130–31.

11. *Grønlands Historiske Mindesmærker,* vol. 3, 411.

12. Gwyn Jones, *Norse Atlantic,* 148.

13. Gustav Storm, *Arkiv,* see Arneborg, *Kultur,* 23.

14. McGovern, "Thule Norse Interaction," 179.

15. *Grønlands Historiske Mindesmærker,* vol. 3, 518.

16. *Grønlands Historiske Mindesmærker,* vol. 2, 206.

17. Richard Cleasby and Gudbrand Vigfússon, *Dictionary*, 641.

18. *Eadem a Septentrione regionem ignoti situs ac nominis intuetur, humani cultus expete, sed monstrosæ novitatis populis abundatem. quam adversis Norvegiæ partibus interflua pelagi seseparavit immensitas,"* Saxo Grammaticus, 17–18. In *Grønlands Historiske Mindesmærker*, vol. 3, 226–425.

19. *Erybyggja Saga*, trans. by Hermann Palsson and Paul Edwards, 128.

20. *Erybyggja Saga*, trans. by Hermann Palsson and Paul Edwards, 161–62.

21. *Islenzk Fornrit*, 1935, 261–62. English translation by Keneva Kunz from *The Sagas of the Icelanders*, 646–67.

22. Carl Christian Rafn, *Antiquitates*, 154.

23. *Grønlands Historiske Mindesmærker*, vol. 1, 243.

24. *Grønlands Historiske Mindesmærker*, vol. 1, 427.

25. *Flóamanna saga*, cited in *Grønlands Historiske Mindesmærker*, vol. 2, 108–9.

26. *Grønlands Historiske Mindesmærker*, vol. 2, 116–17. I am providing the original text because of how important I believe it to be. *"Þá herdu Þeir óp mikit; Þvar Þá kallat af Islendingar skyldu taka skipsitt; Þheir gánga út ok sjá tvær konur [tröllkonur]: Þær hurfu skjótt . . ."*

27. *Grønlands Historiske Mindesmærker*, vol. 3, 239–43.

28. *Grønlands Historiske Mindesmærker*, vol. 3, 239–43.

29. *Grønlands Historiske Mindesmærker*, vol. 3, 239–43.

30. *Grønlands Historiske Mindesmærker*, vol. 3, 239–43.

31. *Grønlands Historiske Mindesmærker*, vol. 3, 439.

32. *Grønlands Historiske Mindesmærker*, vol. 3, 459–60.

33. Original Latin: *"1342 Groenlandiæ incolæ a vera fide et religione christiana sponte sua defecerunt, et repudiatis omnibus honestis moribus et veris virtutibus ad Americæ populos se converterunt . . .existimant Ac inde factum quod christiani a Groenlandicis navigationibus abstinerent . . ."* Cited in *Grønlands Historiske Mindesmærker*, vol. 3, 459.

34. The oldest copy would be the work of Ormr Vigufsson of Eyjum who died in 1673. This is cited in the *Islandske annaler indtil* 1578, fortalen S. XXXVIII, G. Storm, 1888.

35. *Grønlands Historiske Mindesmærker*, vol. 3, 121. Also H. R. Holand, 212. Holand gives the date 1354 and translates as follows: "executed in Bergen. Monday after Simon and Judah's day in the six and XXX year of our rule [1354] by Orm Ostenson, our regent."

36. *"Veibrev frå Hakon. biskop av Bergen, for presten Ivar Bårdsson fra Bergen*

*bispedømme: Han skal reise til Grønland i biskopens og firkens ærend. Anbefales til alle.,"* in DN V. n° 152, *Regesta Norvegica* V, n° 376.

37. Rafn, *Antiquitates,* 316; Arneborg, *Kultur,* 299; *Grønlands Historiske Mindesmærker,* vol. 3, 259.

38. Original: *"Ivar Baardsson som var forstander paa Bischobsgarden i Gardum paa Grönnland udimange aar . . . var en af dennem som var udneffender aff lagmanden, at fare till Vesterbygden emod de Skrelinge, att uddrive de schrelinge udaff Vesterbygd."* in Rafn, *Antiquitates,* 316; *Grønlands Historiske Mindesmærker,* vol. 3, 259. Cleasby and Vigfússon, *Dictionary,* translate *lagmadr* as "lawyer, a man of law."

39. Rafn, *Antiquitates,* 316.

40. Fridtjof Nansen, *Nord i Tåkeheimen,* 364–65.

41. Jones, *Norse Atlantic,* 61–62.

42. Christian Keller, "Eastern Settlement," 270. The third source text written in 1360 helps us clarify this ambiguity to a certain extent.

43. Poul Nørlund, "Buried Norsemen," 250.

44. Prytz, *Vestover,* 72.

45. Cited in *Grønlands Historiske Mindesmærker,* vol. 3, 14, 907.

46. *Grønlands Historiske Mindesmærker,* vol. 3, 14.

47. *Exhibitorem presentuum Ivarum Barderi nostre dyocesis . . . quem in nostris ecclesie nostre negotiis ad Groenlandiam . . ."* from the *Grønlands Historiske Mindesmærker,* vol. 3, 888–89; *Regesta Norvegica,* vol. 5, 476.

48. Gérard Mercator, 268r Manus 150, folio 4.

49. Arneborg, "Nordboerne," 310.

50. *Grønlands Historiske Mindesmærker,* vol. 3, 522.

51. Nansen, *Nord i Tåkeheimen,* vol. 2, 269–70; see also Keller, "Eastern Settlement," 54.

52. In Lelewel, *Epilogue revue* "Ymer," 181–308, and Anthon Axel, Bjørnbo, "Cartographica," 100.

53. Mercator, 267r; see Bjørnbo 98–99.

54. Gustav Storm, "Pave Nicolaus," 9.

55. Map of Gérard Mercator.

56. *Diplomatarium Norvegicum,* vol. 6, 527, 554; Nansen, *Nord,* vol. 2, 272; Cortesoão, *Nautical Chart,* footnote 4.

57. Daniel Bruun, *Arkæologiske,* 175, and Finn Gad, *Grønlands,* 193, make this merger.

58. Keller, "Eastern Settlement," 58.

59. *Grønlands Historiske Mindesmærker,* vol. 3, 170.
60. Keller, "Eastern Settlement," 59.
60. See chapter 10 in 1452 and 1466.
61. *Grønlands Historiske Mindesmærker,* vol. 3, 518.
62. *Grønlands Historiske Mindesmærker,* vol. 3, 518.
63. *Grønlands Historiske Mindesmærker,* vol. 3, 518.
64. *Grønlands Historiske Mindesmærker,* vol. 3, 518.
65. *Grønlands Historiske Mindesmærker,* vol. 3, 518.
66. Rafn, *Antiquitates,* vol. 3, 568, and *Grønlands Historiske Mindesmærker,* vol. 3, 523.
67. *Grønlands Historiske Mindesmærker,* vol. 3, 524.
68. *Grønlands Historiske Mindesmærker,* vol. 3, 493–94.
69. *Grønlands Historiske Mindesmærker,* vol. 3, 494.
70. *Grønlands Historiske Mindesmærker,* vol. 3, 494.
71. *Arnemagnaeanske haandskriftsamling,* folio 207m, 208, 213; quarto 375, 377, 378, 408. See also *Grønlands Historiske Mindesmærker,* vol. 3, 469.
72. *Annals of the Bishop Gisli Oddson* cited in *Grønlandske Historiske Mindesmaerker,* vol. 3, 460.
73. Arneborg, *Kultur,* 152.
74. Nørlund, "Buried Norsemen," 257.
75. Keller, "Eastern Settlement," 271.
76. Keller, "Eastern Settlement," 274.

CHAPTER 8. THE DIFFERENT THEORIES ON
INUIT AND VIKING CONTACT

1. Finn Gad, *History,* 101.
2. Jette Arneborg, "Nordboerne," 302.
3. Helge Ingstad, *Pole Star,* 323.
4. Ingstad, *Pole Star,* 323.
5. Thomas Howatt McGovern, "Paleoeconomy," 174.
6. Corrado Gini, *Extinction,* 10.
7. Vera Henriksen, *Mot en verdens,* 133.
8. Gwyn Jones, *Norse Atlantic,* 65.
9. Peter Schlerdermann, "Nordbogenstande," 223.
10. Cited in Arneborg, *Kultur,* 12.
11. Schlerdermann, "Nordbogenstande," 222.

12. Schlerdermann, "Nordbogenstande," 222.
13. McGovern, "Paleoeconomy," 180.
14. Robert McGhee, "Contact," 47.
15. McGovern, "Paleoeconomy," 180.
16. McGhee, "Contact," 47.
17. McGovern, "Thule Norse Interaction," 183.
18. *Grønlands Historiske Mindesmærker,* vol. 3, 513–16.
19. McGovern, "Thule Norse Interaction," 184.
20. Eilert Sundt, *Egedes,* 161; see Frode Fyllingsnes, 1958, 56.
21. Eugène Beauvois, "La chrétienté du Groenland," 28.
22. Knud Fischer-Møller, "Norse Settlements," 80.
23. Gini, *Extinction,* 10.
24. Gini, *Extinction,* 10.
25. Gini, *Extinction,* 18.
26. Gini, *Extinction,* 10.
27. Gini, *Extinction,* 56.
28. William Thalbitzer, "Grønlandsforsknings," 16.
29. See *Meddeleser om Gronland,* 77. Table 4 and in Lescarbot, 1618: *Histoire de la Nouvelle France.*
30. Gini, *Extinction,* 25.
31. Gini, *Extinction,* 15.
32. Jones, *Norse Atlantic,* 63.
33. Tryggvi Oleson, *Early Voyages,* 75.
34. Gini, *Extinction,* 15.
35. Gini, *Extinction,* 17.
36. McGovern, "Thule Norse Interaction," 173.
37. McGovern, "Thule Norse Interaction," 173.
38. Poul Nørlund, *De gamle Nordbobygder,* 253.
39. Christopher Keller, "Eastern Settlement," 108.
40. Therkel Mathiassen, *Skrælingerne,* 123.
41. McGovern, "Thule Norse Interaction."
42. Gini, *Extinction,* 26.
43. McGovern, "Thule Norse Interaction," 181.
44. Inge Kleivan, "Grønlandske sagn," 327.
45. Kleivan "Grønlandske sagn"; see also Jens Rosing, "Nordbominder," 488.
46. Kleivan, "Grønlandske sagn," 327.
47. Keller, "Eastern Settlement," 1989.

## CHAPTER 9. THE CHURCH IN GREENLAND

1. Christian Keller, "Eastern Settlement," 275.

2. *Regesta Pontiff,* 324.

3. *Papstregesten,* 4.

4. Kirsten Hastrup, *Culture and History in Medieval Iceland,* 8.

5. Keller, "Eastern Settlement," 299.

6. Keller, "Eastern Settlement," 212.

7. Wetzer & Welte, *Kirchen Lexikon.*

8. Adam of Bremen, *Gesta Hammaburgensis,* book 3, chapter 12, 218. Cited in *Grønlands Historiske Mindesmærker,* vol. 3, 411–41.

9. Adam of Bremen, *Gesta Hammaburgensis,* chapter 26, 242.

10. Cited in Vera Henriksen, *Mot en verdens,* 109.

11. Björn Jonssön, *Grønlands beskrivelse Colligeret,* 75.

12. Jette Arneborg, "Nordboerne i Grønland," 306.

13. Keller, "Eastern Settlement," 252.

14. Poul Nørlund, *De gamle Nordbobygder,* 29.

15. Keller, "Eastern Settlement," 260.

16. Keller, "Eastern Settlement," 260

17. Keller, "Eastern Settlement," 40.

18. Keller, "Eastern Settlement," 40.

19. Gunnar Smedberg, *Nordens första kyrkor,* 110.

20. Smedberg, *Nordens första kyrkor,* 110.

21. Eugène Beauvois, "La chrétienté du Groenland," 27; Peter Munch, *Pavelige,* vol. 1, 102.

22. Keller, "Eastern Settlement," 280; see also *Regesta Norvegica,* vol. 4, 488, 493, 496, 504, 505, 506, 518–21, 532–33.

23. *Regesta Norvegica,* vol. 4, 486, 487, 495, 503, 507, 515, 522, 541.

24. *Arch. Secr. Pontif. Vaticanum, Armarium,* 25, vol. 18, folio 5.

25. *Grønlands Historiske Mindesmærker,* vol. 2, 774–79; Keller, "Eastern Settlement," 91. In fact, the process would have lasted from 1262 to 1264.

26. Joël Berglund, "Kirke, Hal og Status."

27. Smedberg, *Nordens första kyrkor.*

28. *Grønlands Historiske Mindesmærker,* vol. 3, 458.

29. Lyschander, *Grønlandske Chronica,* 66; and *Grønlands Historiske Mindesmærker,* vol. 3, 458.

30. Keller, "Eastern Settlement," 267.

31. Arneborg, *Kultur,* 709–10.
32. Keller, "Eastern Settlement Reconsidered," 311.
33. Berglund, "Kirke, Hal og Status," 276.
34. Original Reg. Vat., Jean XXL year 1, folio 23, *Regesta Norvegica,* vol. 2, 155.
35. Original Reg. Vat., folio 127, year 2, n° 38; DN 1, n° 66; Reg. Norv. 2, doc. 209.
36. Cited in Gwyn Jones, *Norse Atlantic,* 237.
37. Jones, *Norse Atlantic,* 242.
38. *Grønlands Historiske Mindesmærker,* vol. 3, 255.
39. Keller, "Eastern Settlement," 274.
40. *Grønlands Historiske Mindesmærker,* vol. 3, 455–56; Henriksen, *Mot en verdens,* 127.
41. *Grønlands Historiske Mindesmærker,* vol. 3, 120–23.
42. *Grønlandske Historiske Mindesmærker,* vol. 3, 457.
43. Based on the original: *"Hakon betvivler at fehirslen får de inntekter og den vissore den skal ha. Sidenfehirden ikke har muligheler for kontroll med dem som kommer nord- og vestfra, fordi disse sier seg ansvarlige overfor ingen annen enn kongen selv . . ."* August 8, 1340. *AM Regesta Norvegica* 5, 340, 370.
44. Arneborg, "Nordboerne i Grønland," 306.
45. Corrado Gini, *Extinction,* 25.
46. *Regesta Norvegica,* vol. 2, 209–18.
47. Arneborg, "Nordboerne i Grønland," 306.
48. *Grønlands Historiske Mindesmærker,* vol. 3, 15.
49. *Grønlands Historiske Mindesmærker,* vol. 3, 462.
50. *Regesta Norvegica,* vol. 5, doc 801, September 15, 1345.
51. Arneborg, "Nordboerne i Grønland," 307.
52. Keller, "Eastern Settlement," 273; see *Grønlands Historiske Mindesmærker,* vol. 3, 497–501.
53. Arneborg, "Nordboerne i Grønland," 308.
54. Finn Gad, *History,* 185; Arneborg, "Nordboerne i Grønland," 308.
55. Arneborg, "Nordboerne i Grønland," 309–10.
56. Absalon Pederssøn Beyer, "Om Norges Rige," 49–51.
57. Gad, *History,* 170.
58. *Series episcoporum,* 334.
59. *Archivium apostolicum secretum Vaticanum, Obligationes* n° 566, alias 65, v° 66: Eugeni IV, Nicolai IV, Calixti III, Pi II, Pauli II.
60. *Series episcoporum,* 334.
61. *Grønlands Historiske Mindesmærker,* vol. 3, 405, 413, 421, 423.

62. See chapters 1 and 10.

63. *Archivum Apostolicum Secretum Vaticanum, Armarium* XII, n° 121. *[Acta consistoriala]*, 272–74.

64. *Archiv. Apostol. Secret. Vatic. Obligationes* n° 306 [alias 55]: *Primus obligationeum Eugenii, quarti*, 1431–39, f° 39 v°, cf. ibid.: *Obligationes Collegii, Liber sub. Mart. IV, Eug. IV,* ab an. 1427 ad 1433 n° 596 [alias 64] f° 130).

65. *Archivum Lateranense Sixte IV, anno X,* lib.I, f° 17.

66. *Romae cancellaria, Archivium S Consistorii : provisionum Innocenti VIII, et Alexandri VI/ Acta Consistotialia anno 1489–1503,* folio 24.

67. *Roma Cancellaria, arch. Secr. Consistorii, Acta Consistoralia, 1492–1523,* f° 138 v°.

## CHAPTER 10. THE SCANDINAVIAN PRESENCE IN THE FAR NORTH

1. Carl Christian Rafn, *Antiquitates,* 275.

2. Jette Arneborg, *Kultur,* 153 (italics mine).

3. *Icelandic Annals* cited in Carl Christian Rafn, *Antiquitates,* 264–65.

4. Original manuscript, Royal Library of Copenhagen. Cited in Björn Jönsson, *Grønlands,* 5.

5. *Hauksbók,* cited in Rafn, *Antiquitates,* 276 and Axel Bjørnbo, "Cartographia."

6. Cited in *Grønlands Historiske Mindesmærker,* vol. 3, 881–85; as well as Peter Munch, *Historisk,* 218.

7. Schledermann, "Ellesmere Island. Eskimo and Viking Finds in the High Arctic," 58.

8. *Grænlands annál,* 1978, and *Grønlands Historiske Mindesmærker,* vol. 3, 248.

9. *Arna Magneana,* 604f. Quarto; *Rimnasafn,* 1905/12; and Rafn, *Antiquitates,* 276–78.

10. *Grønlands Historiske Mindesmærker,* vol. 3, 570, fn 56.

11. *Grønlands Historiske Mindesmærker,* vol. 3, 238–44.

12. Rafn, *Antiquitates,* 465.

13. Original: *"Eirikr biskup af grælandi fór at leita Vinland"* (extracts from *Icelandic Annals,* cited in Rafn, *Antiquitates,* 261.

14. Guy Marie Rousselière, "Exploration and Evangelization," 591.

15. Arneborg, *Kultur,* 157.

16. Rafn, *Antiquitates,* 272.

17. Björn Jonssön manuscript, 1669, note ccc. Royal Library, Copenhagen.

18. *Allir stórbændir i grænlandi hofdu skip stór. ok skütur bygdar til at senda i Nordrsetu eptir apfla med allra handa veidiskap ok telgduin viduin; ok stundum foru their sjálfir med. (sem vida verdr i frásögum getit, . . . i Skáldhelga sögu.)*

19. Original text: "*hic fecht man weissen Valken.*"

20. Original text: "*in Sommer verlieSe iSt es sunnenSchein die ganze nacht. Item als die reussen in dasselbe land wollen das köstlich fehwerk zu holen so müssen sie auf Schlitten fahren um des wesser und tie und tieffen snees willen welche von grosen hunden gezogen warden.*"

21. Original text: "*In Eislant ist schon weiss Volkh und sindt Christen. Daselbst ist gewohneit das man die hundt teler [teuer]verkauft und ihre Kinder geben sy hinwesk den kaufleuten und um gots willen auf dass die andern brot haben.*"

22. Tryggvi Oleson, *Norsemen*, 19.

23. "*In der Insel Islant fengt man den Stockfish den man in unser Landt bringt.*" Globe by Martin Behaim, 1492.

24. Vilhjalmur Stefansson, *Greenland*.

25. Fridtjof Isachsen and Gunnar Isachsen, "Hvor langt mot Nord," 78; and Oleson, *Early Voyages*, 41.

26. Arneborg, *Kultur*, 117.

27. Anne Stine Ingstad, *Discovery*, 326.

28. Jette Arneborg, *Kultur*, 149.

29. Arneborg, *Kultur*, 153.

30. Thomas E. Lee, "Payne Bay Région," 146.

31. Peter Schledermann, "Nordbogenstande," 224.

## CHAPTER II. THE EUROPEAN PRESENCE IN THE FAR NORTH

1. Cited in Finnur Magnússon, "Om de Engelskes Handel," 112–69.

2. Haklyut, 1589, "acts of King Edward III during the 2nd, 4th, and 31st year [of his reign];" Zahrtmann, "Bemærkninger," vol. 2, 26–27; Adolf Nordenskjöld, *Facsimile Atlas*, 64.

3. Zahrtmann, "Bemærkninger," vol. 2, 25–26. Just as for the poem by the skald Helge, I retained the original text and spelling.

4. Kåre Prytz, *Vestover*, 93.

5. Original extract: *Io navigai l'anno MCCCCLXXVII nel messe di Febraio oltra Tile isola cento legue, la cui parte australe è lontana dall Equinottiale settantatre gradi . . . Et a quest'isola, che è tanto grande, come l'ingleterra, vanno gl'Inglesi con le loro mercantatie, specialmente quelli di Bristol . . ."* Fernando Columbus, *Histories,* 89. Also in Bartolomé de Las Casas, *Historias de las Indias,* vol. 1, 48.

6. Original: *"Cum Colombo Latine conversans, ei, de occidentalibus terris interroganti, narrationes de itineribus Gudleivi Gulaegi filii aliorumque Borealium versimiliter retulit,"* in Carl Christian Rafn, *Antiquitates,* 24.

7. Cited in Helen Wallis, "England's Search," 466.

8. Magnússon, "Om de Engelskes Handel," 119.

9. Magnússon, "Om de Engelskes Handel," 120.

10. Tryggvi Oleson, *Norsemen,* 19.

11. *Urkundenbuch der Stadt Lübeck,* vol. 4, 307.

12. Sigurdsson, "Some Landmarks in Icelandic Cartography," 540, in *Urkundenbuch der Stadt Lübeck,* vol. 4, 307.

13. Gwyn Jones, *Norse Atlantic,* 52.

14. Klaus Friesland, "The Hanseatic League," 541.

15. *Gesta Hammaburgensis ecclesiae pontificum,* vol. 3, 406, 902–3. Original in Adam of Bremen, *Descriptione regionum vel insularum aqvilonis,* Cap XL–XLI (CCXCVII-XLVIII).

16. Original: Adam of Bremen, *Historia ecclesiæ hammaburgensis.* Lib. III Cap XXVI (CXLII). *Grønlands Historiske Mindesmærker,* vol. 3, 415, 419. See chapter 5.

17. Magnússon, "Om de Engelskes Handel," 27.

18. *Diplomatarium Norvegicum* 6, n°. 527, 09/20, 1448.

19. Helge Ingstad, *Vesterveg til Vinland,* 258.

20. Magnússon, "Om de Engelskes Handel," 141.

21. Magnússon, "Om de Engelskes Handel," 141.

22. Magnússon, "Om de Engelskes Handel," 118.

23. Magnússon, "Om de Engelskes Handel," 121.

24. Armando Cortesão, *Nautical Chart,* 76.

25. Cortesão, *Nautical Chart,* 76.

26. Oleson, *Early Voyages and Nothern Approaches 1000–1632,* 19.

27. In Louis Bobé, "Akstykker," 303ff.

28. In *Tabulae Americae, Africae, Articae et regionum intra polum articum sitarum,* 1580.

29. William Francis Ganong, *Crucial Maps,* 390.

30. Eugène Beauvois, *Colonies Européennes,* 41; see also Guy Marie Rousselière, "Exploration and Evangelization."

31. R. A. Skelton, Thomas E. Marston, and George D. Painter, *Vinland Map,* 234.

32. Prytz, *Vestover,* 172.

33. David B. Quinn, "English Discovery," 277–85.

34. Skelton, *Vinland Map and Tartar Relation,* 238.

35. Jean Alfonse, *Cosmographie.*

36. Francisco López de Gómara, *Histoire des Indes,* 125.

37. Cited in Alexander Von Humboldt, *Histoire,* 153.

# Bibliography

Adam of Bremen. *Gesta Hammaburgensis ecclesiæ pontificu.* Reprinted by Hanover & Leipzig, Hamburg-Bremen: B. Scmeidler, 1917. Translated into English by F. J. Tascham. *Adam of Bremen, History of the Bishops of Hamburg-Bremen.* New York: Columbia, 2002.

Ailly, Pierre (Petrus de Alliaco). *Imago Mundi.* 1476. French translation: *Quatre traités cosmographiques + notes of Colomb,* Paris: Maisonneuve, 1930.

Albrethsen Sven Erik. Traek af den norrøne gårds udvikling på Grønland," in Myhre et al. (eds.), *Vestnordisk byggeskikk gjennom to tusen år, Stavanger,* 1982.

Alfonse, Jean. *La Cosmographie avec l'espère et régime du soleil et du Nord " par Jean Fonteneau dit Alphonse de Saintonge.* 1544) Published and Annotated by Georges Musset. Paris, E. Leroux, 1904.

———. *Les voyages aventureux du capitaine Jean Alfonse, Saintongeais, contenant les règles et enseignements nécessaires à la bonne et seure navigation," (orig 1559) revu et corrigé de nouveau . . . à la Rochelle, par les héritiers de H. Haultin,* 1605.

Andreasen, Claus. "Nordbosager fra Vesterbygden på Grønland." *Hikuin* 6 (1980): 135–46.

———. "Langhus-Ganghus-Centraliseret gård." *Hikuin* 7 (1981): [PN].

———. "Nipaitsoq og Vesterbygden." *Grønland* 5, 6, 7 (1982): 177–188.

Anthiaume, (Abbé). *Cartes marines, constructions navales, voyages de découverte chez les Normands, 1500–1650.* Vol. 1. Paris: Éditions Dumont, 1916.

Arctander, Aron. "Ecrit d'après un journal tenu par Aron Arctander au Groenland lors d'un voyage de reconnaissance dans le district de Julianehaab pendant les années 1777–1779." *Samleren* 6 (1793): 1105–242.

Arneborg, Jette. "Nordboerne i Grønland, et bidrag til diskussionen om Eskimoernes rolle i Vesterbygden affolkning." *Hikuin* 14 (1988): 297–312.

———. "Nordboearkeologiens historie og fremtid." *Grønland* 5 (1989): 121–137.

———. "Aqissiaq og Nordboerne." *Grønland* 6–7 (1990): 213–19.

———. *Kultur mødet mellem Nordboer og Eskimoer. En kritisk analyse af kildernetil . . . kultur mødet . . . i Grønland. Vurderet in norrønt perspektiv.* Unpublished thesis, 1991.

Bårdsson, Ivar. *Grønlands beskrivelse,* in *Grønlands Historiske Mindesmærker.* Vols. 1–3. Copenhague: Finnur Jonsson, 1930.

Bacon, Roger. *The voyages and travels of Sir John Mandeville.* Cassell, France: National Library, 1883.

———. *Opus Majus.* Vol. 2. Oxford: Placenton Press, 1897.

Bartholin, Thomas. *Acta Medica.* Copenhagen: Peter Haubold, 1673.

Beauvois, Eugène. *La découverte du Nouveau Monde par les Scoto-Irlandais et les premières traces du Christianisme en Amérique avant l'an 1000.* Nancy [Press? City?], 1875.

———. *Les colonies européennes du Markland et de l'Escociland au XIVème siècle.* Nancy [Place?]: Éditions Crépin Leblon, 1877.

———. *Origines et fondation du plus ancien évêché du nouveau monde: le diocèse de Gardh en Groenland 986–1126.* Paris: Éditions Dufosse, 1878.

———. "La chrétienté du Groenland au Moyen-Âge." *Revue des Questions Historiques* Vol LXXI, 1902.

Berglund, Joël. "Kirke, Hal og Status." *Grønlands tidskrift* 8, 9 (1982).

———. "The Decline of the Norse Settlements." *Arctic Anthropology* 23, nos. 1, 2 (1986): 109–35.

———. *Herjolfsnæs.* Qaqortoq, Greenland: Qaqortoq Kommunes Forlag, 1988.

Bjørnbo, Axel Anthon. "Cartographia Groenlandica." *Meddelelser om Grønland* 48 (1912).

Bjørnbo, Axel, and Carl Petersen. *Fyenboen Claudius Clausson Swart (Claudius Clavus).* Den kongelige danske videnskab selskabs skrifter, 6 rekke, historisk & filosofisk afd. Vols. 1–2. Copenhagen, 1904.

Blair, Emma, and James Robertson. *Philippine Islands (1493–1803).* Vol 1. Cleveland, Ohio: A. H. Clark, 1903–1905.

Boas, Franz. "Eskimos of Baffin Land and Hudson Bay." *Bulletin of the American Museum of Natural History* XV (1907).

Bobé, Louis, ed. "Akstykker til oplysning om Grønlands Besejling 1521–1607." *Danske Magasin* 5, no. 6 (1909).

Le Bouvier, Gilles,. *Le livre de la description des pays.* Paris: E. Leroux, 1908.

Boye, Wilhem. "Beskrivelse af og fortegnelse over de ved Premier Lieutnant

D. Bruun i Nordboruinerne fremgravede Oldsager I: D. Bruun: arkeologiske undersøgelser i Julianehåbs district." *Meddelelser om Grønland,* XVI (1895): 438–61.

Bruun, Daniel. "Arkæologiske undersøgelser i Julianehaabs distrikt." *Meddelelser om Grønland* XVI (1898): 173–461.

———. "The Icelandic Colonization of Greenland" *Meddelelser om Grønland* LVII (1918). Also appears in *Canadian Journal of Anthropology* 2 (1978).

———. "Erik den røde og Nordbokolonierne i Grønland." *Gyldendal boghandel* 2, Copenhagen, 1931.

Bugge G. N., John Davis, and John Jane. *Tre rejser til Grønland aarene 1585–87.* Vol. VII *Det grønlandke selskabs skrifter.* Copenhagen: Gadsforlag, 1930.

Champlain, Samuel. *Les voyages du sieur Champlain, Xaintongeois.* Vol 1. Québec, Canada: Abbé C. Laverdière, 1870.

Charlevoix. P. F. *Histoire et description de la Nouvelle France.* Paris: Rolin Fils, 1744.

Cleasby, Richard, and Gudbrand Vigfússon, eds., *"An Icelandic-English dictionary."* 2nd ed. Oxford: Clarendon Press, 1957.

Columbus, Fernando. *Histories del S. Don Fernando Colombo.* Translated by Euègene Muller. Paris: Eugène Muller, 1879.

Cortesão, Armando. *The Nautical Chart of 1424 and the Early Discovery and Cartographical Representation of America.* Coimbra, Portugal: University Editions, 1954.

*Danorum Historiæ.* Libri XVI. Edited by J. Olorinus, Basilæ. 1534.

Dansgaard, Willi, S. J. Johnsen, N. Reeh, N. Gundestrup, H. B. Clausen, and C. U. Hammer. "Climatic changes, Norsemen and Modern Man." *Nature* 255 (1975): 24–28.

*Diplomatarium Arna Magnæanum exhibens Monumenta diplomatica . . .* Vols. 1–2 Havn: Grimus Johannisn Thorkelin, 1786.

*Diplomatarium Norvegicum.* Vols. 1–3. Edited by Norsk Historisk Kjeldeskrift Institutt. Christiania: P. Mailing Kommisjonen for Diplomatarum Norvegicum, 1849–1876. Reprinted. Oslo: 1970.

Duason, Jon, *Landkönnun og Landnám Islendinga í Vesturheimi.* Reykjavik: 1941–1947.

Egede, Hans. *Description et histoire naturelle du Groenland.* Translated by Jean-Baptiste Des Roches de Parthenay. Copenhagen and Geneva: Frères Philibert, 1763.

————. *Relationer fra Grønland 1721–1736 og det gamle Grønlands ny Perlustration 1741. Meddelelser om Grønland* LIV (1925).

————. "Continuation af relationerne betreffende den Grønlandske Missions Tilstand og Beskaffenhed, forfattet i form af en Journal fra Anno. 1734 til 1740 af Coloniens Christians- Haab udi Disco-Bugt Ved Poul Egede Missionair udi Grønland." *Meddelelser om Grønland* 120 (1939): 1–122.

————. *Det gamle Grønlands perlustration; eller en kort beskrivelse om de gamle norske coloniers begyndelse og undergang i Grønland, Grønlands situation, luft og temperament . . .* Copenhagen: Gelmeyden, 1729.

Egede, Niels. "En kort og Infoldig Beskrievelse over Grønland, indretted udj. Historier som af gronl: ere fortalt, saa og af mig selv erfared, og sammenskreved her paa Colonien Holsteinsborg den förste Januarij 1769 af N. Egede." Edited by H. Ostermann. *Meddelelser om Grønland* 120 (1939): 233–69.

Egede, Poul. *Dictionarium Gronlandico-Danico-Latinum.* Hafniæ: Marcus Woldike, 1750.

————. *Efterretninger om Grønland uddragne af en journal holden fra 1721 til 1788.* Vol. 29. Copenhagen: Mads Lidegaard, 1988.

*Eiriks saga rauda.* Edited by Matthias Þorðarson. Reykjavik: Islenzk Fornrit IV, 1935. Translated into French by Maurice Gravier. Paris: Aubier, 1954.

*Eyrbyggjasaga.* Edited by Einar Ól. Sveinsson. Reykjavik: Islenzk Fornrit IV, 1935. French trans. Régis Boyer, Paris: éd. Aubier: 1973.

Fabricius, Otto. *Den Grønlandske Ordbog.* Copenhagen: C. F. Schubart, 1804.

Fægri, Knud. *Omkring Grønlands bygdenes undergang.* Bergen: Naturen, 1957.

Fitzugh, William. *Early Contacts North of Newfoundland before A.D. 1600: A Review. Cultures in Contact.* Edited by William W. Fitzugh. Washington, D.C.: Smithonian Institution Press, 1985. Knud Fischer-Møller, "The Medieval Norse Settlements in Greenland: Anthropological Investigations." *Meddelelser om Grønland* 89, no 2 (1942): 84.

*Flateyjarbók.* Christiania: Gudbrandr Vigfusson & C. R. Unger, 1860–1868.

*Flóamanna saga.* In *Islendingasagnaútgáfan, islendinga sögur.* Vol. 12. Reykjavik: Gudni Jonsson, 1953.

*Fostbrœdra saga.* Reykjavik: Guni Jonsson i Islenzk Fornrit VI Vestfirdinga sogur, 1943.

French translation by Française Régis Boyer, Paris: Gallimard (coll. Bibliothèque de la Pléiade), 1987.

Friedland, Klaus. "The Hanseatic League and Hanse Towns in the Early Penetration of the North." *Arctic* 37 no 4 (1984): 539–43.

Fritzner, Johan. *Ordbog over det gamle norske sprog.* Vol. 2, Christiania, Norway: Den Norske Forlagsforening, 1891.

Fyllingnes, Frode. *Undergongen til dei norrøne bygdene på Grønland i Seinmellomalderen. Eit Forskninghistorisk oversyn.* Oslo: Middelalderforum, 1990.

Gad, Finn. *Grønlands historie I indtil 1700.* Copenhagen: Nyt Nordisk forlag A. Busck, 1967.

———. "Kildematerialet og den norrøne Grønlands tradition." *Grønland* 8, 9 (1982).

———. *A History of Greenland.* London: C. Hurst and Company Limited, 1973.

Gaffarel, Paul. *Etude sur les rapports de l'Amérique et de l'ancien continent avant Christophe Colomb.* Paris: Ernest Thorin, 1869.

———. *Histoire de la découverte de l'Amérique depuis les origines jusqu'à la mort de Christophe Colomb.* Paris: A. Rousseau, 1892.

Gams Bonifacius. *Series episcoporum Ecclesiæ catholicæ quotquot innotuerunt a beato Petro Apostolo.* Regensberg, Germany: G. J. Manz, 1873.

Ganong, William Francis. *Crucial Maps in the Early Cartography and Place-nomenclature of the Atlantic Coast of Canada.* Toronto: University of Toronto Press, 1963.

Gini, Corrado. "On the Extinction of the Norse Settlements in Greenland." *Forretningsøkonomisk Institutt* 10 (1958).

Gordon, E. V. *An Introduction to Old Norse,* 2nd ed. Reviewed by A. R. Taylor. Oxford: Clarenton Press, 1957.

Gravier, Gabriel. *Découverte de l'Amérique par les Normands au Xème Siècle.* Paris: Maisonneuve, 1874.

*Grænlands annál.* In *Grænland in midaldaritum.* Reykjavik: Olafür Halldórsson, 1978.

*Grænlandingasaga.* Reykjavik: Mathias Thordarson *Eyrbyggjasaga,* 1935 in *Islenzk fornrit.* Vol. 4. Translated into French by Régis Boyer, *Sagas Islandaises,* Paris: Gallimard, 1987 (Bibliothèque de la Pléiade).

*Grønlands Historiske Mindesmærker.* Vols. 1–3. Reprinted. Copenhagen: Det Kongelige Nordiske Oldskriftselskab, 1976.

Gulløv, Hans Christian. "Eskimoens syn på Europæeren." *Grønland* 5 (1982): 226–234.

Hakluyt, Richard, *Divers Voyages Touching the Discovery of America*. Works issued by the Hakluyt Society, London, 1850. Also on microfiche 1966, USA. Reproduction of the Zeno brother's texts collected by Rasmusio, secretary of state of Venice, 1582.

——. *The principal navigations, voiages, Traffiques and discoveries of the English Nation* . . . London: 1589. Reprinted. Glasgow, 1903–1905.

Halldórsson, Olafur. *Grænland í miðaldaritum*. Reykjavik: Sógufélag, 1978.

*Hansisches Urkundenbuch* III. Vol. 7. Leipzig: Vereinfür Hansisches Geschichte Weimar, 1876–1939.

Hastrup, Kirsten. *Culture and History in Medieval Iceland*. Oxford: Clarendon Press, 1985.

*Hauksbók*, Copenhagen: Finnur Jónsson, 1892–1896.

Hawkes, Ernest William. *The Labrador Eskimos*. Ottawa: Geological Survey, 1910.

Heggstad, Leiv. *Gamalnorsk ordbok*. Norske samlaget edition. Oslo, 1958.

Heggstad, L., Hødnebø Finn, Simensen Erik: "Norrøn Ordbog," last edition of *Gammal ordbog*, Oslo: det Norske Samlaget, 2012.

Henriksen, Vera. *Under seil mot det ukjente*. Oslo: Aschehoug, 1987.

——. *Mot en verdens ytterste grense*. Oslo: Aschehoug, 1988.

Heyerdahl, Thor, and Per Lillieström. *Ingen grenser*. Oslo: J. M. Stenersens Forlag A. S., 1999.

*Historia Norvegiæ, Monumenta Historie Norvegiæ*. Kristiania, 1880; Norwegian Reprint. *Norges Historie*. Oslo: Astrid Salvesen, 1969.

Holm, Gustav. "Ethnological Sketch of the Angmassalik Eskimo. The Ammassalik Eskimo." Edited by W. Thalbitzer, *Meddelelser om Grønland* XXXIX (1914): 147.

Holtved, Erik. "De Eskimoiske sagns oplysning, belyst ved Axel Olriks episk love." Edited by Gunnar Knudsen. *Danske studier for Universitetsjubilæets Danske samfund* (1943): 20–61

——. "Archeological Investigations in the Thule district I." *Meddelelser om Grønland* 141, no (1944a): 308.

——. "Archeological Investigations in the Thule district II." *Meddelelser om Grønland* 142 (1944b).

——. "Archeological Investigations in the Thule district III, Nugdlît and Comer's Midden." *Meddelelser om Grønland* 146, no. 3 (1954).

——. "The Polar Eskimos. Language and Folklore." *Meddelelser om Grønland* 152, no. 2 (1951).

Humboldt, Alexander Von. *Histoire de la géographie du nouveau continent. Examen critique.* Vol. 2. Paris: Éditions Librairie de Gide, 1837.

Ingstad, Anne Stine. *The Discovery of a Norse settlement in America. Excavations at l'Anse aux Meadows, Newfoundland.* Oslo, Bergen, Tromsø: Norwegian University Press, 1977.

Ingstad, Helge. *"Landet under Leidar stjernen,"* ed. Gyldendal, Oslo, 1959.

———. *Land under the Pole Star."* New York: St Martin Press, 1966.

———. *The Norse Discovery of America."* Vol. 2. Oslo-Bergen-Tromsø: Norwegian University Press, 1985.

———. *Vesterveg til Vinland.* Oslo: Gyldendal Norsk Forlag, 1965.

———. "Vinland Ruins Prove Vikings Found the New World," *National Geographic* 126, no. 5 (1964): 708–34.

Isachsen, Fridtjof and Gunnar Isachsen. "Hvor langt mot Nord kom de norrøne Grønlendinger på sine fangstferder i utbygdene?" *Norsk Geografisk Tidsskrift* IV (1932–1933).

Isachsen, Gunnar. "Nordboernes faerder til Norderseta." *Den Norske Geografisk Selskab Aarbog* XVIII (1906–7).

*Islandske annaler indtil 1578,* Christiania: Gustav Storm, det norske historiske kildeskriftfond, 1888.

*Islendingabók,* ed. Jacob Benediktsson, Reykjavik: Islendzke fornrit I, Islendingabók, Landnámabók, 1968.

Iversen, Johannes. "Et botanisk vidne om Nordboernes Vinlandsrejser." *Naturhistorik tidende* 8 (Oct. 1938).

Jeannin, Pierre. *Histoire des pays scandinaves.* Paris: PUF, 1965.

Jóhannesson, Alexander. *Isländisches etymologisches Wörterbuch.* Bern: Francke, 1956.

Jóhannesson, Jón. "The Date of the Composition of the Saga of the Greenlanders." Translated with an introduction by Tryggvi Oleson. *Saga-Book* 16 (1962–1965): 54–66.

Jones, Gwyn. *The Norse Atlantic Saga.* Oxford: Oxford University Press, 1964. Reprinted with a contribution by Robert McGhee, Thomas H. McGovern, and Colleagues, Birgitta Linderoth Wallace. Oxford: Oxford University Press, 1986.

Jonssön, Björn (de Skardsaa). *"Grønlands beskrivelse Colligeret af Izlandise Antiqvitäter ved en Curieux Mand paa Iszland ved naffn Björn JonSön paa Skarsaa. men vdSat paa DanSke ocs med nogle Marginalibus forkiaret item med adhillige mappis GeogrAphicis foröget, aff Théodore Thorlacis Isl: Anno 1669.* Gammel. kgl. Samling, Copenhagen.

Jonsson, Erik. *Old Nordisk ordbog.* Copenhagen: Det Kongelige Nordiske Oldskrift Selskab, 1863.

Jónsson, Finnur. *Flóamanna saga.* With Commentary. Copenhagen: Samfund til udgivelse af gammel Nordisk Litterratur, 1932.

Jordan, Richard. "Inugsuk Revisited: An Alternative View of Neo-Eskimo Chronology and Culture Change in Greenland." In *Thule Eskimo Culture: An Anthropological Retrospective.* Edited by A. P. McCartney, 149–70. Ottawa, Canada: University of Ottawa Press, Mercury Series, 1979.

Jørgensen, Jørgen Frederik. "Indberetning til det Kongelige Nordiske Oldskriftselskab." Julianehaabs Missionsbolig, 26.07.1837, unpublished, Nationalmuseets Nordbosamling.

Keller, Christian. "The Eastern Settlement Reconsidered." Unpublished Thesis. Oslo: 1989.

Keyser, Rudolph. *Den norske kirkes historie under Katholicismen.* Vol. 2. Christiania: C. Tønsberg, 1858.

*Kulturhistorisk Leksikon for Nordisk Middelalder.* Vols. 1–22. Copenhagen: Rosenkilde & Bagger, 1956–1977.

Kleinschmidt, Samuel. *Den Grønlandske ordbog.* Copenhagen: H. F. Jørgensen, 1871.

Kleivan, Inge. "Grønlandske sagn om Nordboerne." *Grønland* 8 (1982): 314–30.

———. "History of Norse Greenland." In *Handbook of North American Indians* Vol. 5, *Arctic.* Edited by David Damas, 549–55. Washington D.C.:, Smithsonian Institution, 1984.

———. "De Grønlandske stednavnes vidnesbyrd om vandringer og forskellige aktiviteter." Edited by Lotte Rix and H. C. Gulløv. Presented at *Vort sprog, vor kultur* in Nuuk, Greenland, Oct. 1981. Nuuk: Pilersuiffik, 1986, 77–90.

*Konungs annáll: Annales Islandorum regii,* Islandska handskrifter n.o 2087. 4.to i den gamla samlingen (kgl. lib. Copenhagen), *Diplomatarisk aftryck,* H. Buergel Goodwin, Uppsala universitet (M4 Fol) Årskrift (1906): 191–93.

*Konung skuggsiá.* Translated by Einar Már Jónsson. Paris: Esprit Ouvert, 1997.

Kornerup, Thorvald. *Aperçu des Meddelelser om Grønland, 1876–1899.* Edited by the commission directing geological and geographical research in Greenland. Translated by A. Barel, Copenhagen, 1900.

Kristjánsson, Jónas. *Eddas and Sagas.* Translated from Icelandic into English by Peter Foote. Reykjavik: Hið íslenska bókmenntafélag, 1988.

Krogh, Knud. *Kunstvandring, hemmeligheden bag Grønlandsbispens hundrede køer,* Copenhagen: Nat. Mus. Arbejdsmark, 1974.

————. *Erik den Rødes Grønland.* Copenhagen: National Museet, 1967. English Edition. *Viking Greenland,* Copenhager: Nationalmuseet, 1967.

*Landnámabók,* Copenhagen: Finnur Jónsson, 1900 (*Hauksbók, Sturlubók, Melabók*). Reprinted, edited by Gudni Jónsson, *Islendinga sögur* I, Reykjavik: Islendingasagagnautgáfan, 1953. Reprinted, edited by Jacob Benediktsson, *Islendingabók, Landnàmabók,* Reykjavik, 1968. Partially translated into French by Régis Boyer, Paris: Mouton, 1973.

Lappenberg, Martin Johan. *Hamburgisches Urkunderbuch.* Vol I. Hambourg: Voss, 1912.

————. *An die Alterthumsforscher Deutschlands und des Nördlichen Europas.* Hamburg: 1834.

Larsen, Helge, *Grønlands bogen.* Vol. 1. In *Det grønlandske Selskabs,* 205–52. Edited by Kaj Birket Smith, Ernst Meutz, and Friis Møller. Copenhague: J. H. Schultz, 1950.

Larsen, Sofus, "La découverte de l'Amérique septentrionale, 1472–73 par les Danois et les Portugais." Thesis summary. Coimbra Academia das Sciencias de Lisboa: 1922 (ed. Spéc. Boletim da Classe de Litras).

Las Casas, Bartolomé de. *Historia de las Indias.* Vol 1. Madrid: Ginesta Printers, 1875–76.

Lee, Thomas E. "Archeological discoveries, Payne Bay Région, Ungava 1966." *Centre d'études nordiques travaux divers* 20 (1968).

————. "Archeological findings, Gyrfalcon to eider Eilands, Ungava 1968." *Centre d'études nordiques, travaux divers* 27 (1969).

Lelewel, Joachim. *Pytheas de Marseille et la géographie de son temps.* Paris: Joseph Straszwicz, 1836.

Leroi-Gourhan, André. *La civilisation du renn.* Paris: Gallimard, 1936.

Leroy-Ladurie, Emmanuel. *Histoire du climat depuis l'an Mil.* Paris: Flammarion, 1967.

Lescarbot, Marc. *Histoire de la Nouvelle-France, contenant les navigations, les découvertes faites par les François ès Indes occidentales et Nouvelle France, en quoy est comprise l'histoire morale, naturelle et géographique de la dite province.* Paris: J. Milot, 1609. Reprinted in three volumes. Edwin Tross: 1866.

Lessing, F. D. *Libelle of Englyshe Polyeye.* Oxford: Sir Georges Warner, 1926.

Lidegaard, Mads. *Grønlands Historie.* Copenhagen: Schultz, 1961.

López de Gómara, Francisco, *La Historia de las Indias . . .* Anvers: M. Nucio, 1554. Translated into *Histoire générale des Indes occidentales et terres neuves,* Paris: L. Somnius, 1587.

Lucas, F. W. *The Annals of the Voyages of the Venetian Brothers Nicolo and Antonio Zeno in the North Atlantic Ocean.* London: D. B. Quinn, 1898.

Lyschander, Claus Christoffersen. *Grønlandske Chronica.* Copenhagen: Kungl. Lib., 1608.

MacCartney, A. P. and D. J. Mack. "Iron Utilization by Thule Eskimos of Central Canada." *American Antiquity* 38 no. 3 (1973): 328–38.

MacCullough, Karen M. "The Ruin Islanders: Early Thule Culture Pioneers in the Eastern High Arctic." *Archeological Survey of Canada. Mercury Series.* Vol 141. Hull: Canadian Museum of Civilization, 1989.

Major, Richard Henry. *The Life of Prince Henry of Portugal Surnamed the Navigator and its Results.* London: Asher & Co, 1868.

Marcussen, Björn. *Sogupættir Islendinga.* Holar: Bjorn Marcussen, 1756.

Mathiassen, Therkel. *Skrælingerne i Grønland, Grønlandernes Historie.* Folkelæsning n°. 364: Copenhagen, 1935.

McGhee, Robert. "Contact between Native North Americans and the Medieval Norse: A Review of the Evidence." *American Antiquity* 49, no. 1 (1984): 4–26.

———. "The Relationship between the Medieval Norse and Eskimos between Greenland and America Cross-Cultural Contacts and Environment in the Baffin Bay area." 51–60. Arctic Centre, University of Groningen, Netherlands: 1987.

McGovern, Thomas Howatt. "The Paleoeconomy of Norse Greenland. Adaptation and Extinction in a Tightly Bounded Ecosystem." Unpublished diss., Columbia University, New York, 1979a.

———. "Thule Norse Interaction in Southwest Greenland: A Speculative Model." In *Thule Inuit Culture: An Anthropological Retrospective,* edited by Allen P. McCartney. 171–88. Ottawa, Canada: University of Ottawa Press, 1979b

———. "Cows, Harp Seal, and Churchbells. Adaptation and Extinction in Norse Greenland." *Human Ecology* 8, no. 3 (1980).

———. "Settlement and Land Use in the Inner Fjords of Godthaab District, West Greenland." *Arctic Anthropology* 19, no 1 (1982).

———. "A Study of the Faunal and the Floral Remains from Two Norse Farms in the Western Settlement." In *Arctic Anthropology* 20, no 2 (1983).

Magnússon, Finnur. "Om de Engelskes Handel og færd paa Island i det 15de Aarhundrede, især med hensyn til Columbus formeentlige reise dertil I Aaret 1477, og hans beretninger desangaaende." edited by Det Kongelige

Nordiske Oldskrift Selskab. *Nordisk Tidskrift for Oldkyndighed* II (1833): 112–169.

Mathiassen, Therkel. *Archeology of the Central Eskimos 1: Report of the Fifth Thule Expedition 1921–24. The Danish Expedition to Arctic North America in charge of Knud Rasmussen.* Vol. 4. Copenhagen: Gyldendal, 1927.

———. *Archeology of the Central Eskimos, 2: The Thule Culture and its Position within the Eskimo Culture,* Copenhagen: Gyldendal, 1927.

———. *Eskimoerne i nutid og fortid.* Edited by P. Haase. Copenhagen, 1929.

———. "Eskimo finds from the Kangerlussuaq region," *Meddelelser om Grønland* 104, no. 9 (1934).

———. "Contribution to the Archeology of Disko Bay." *Meddelelser om Grønland* 93, no. 2 (1934).

———. "Skrælingerne i Grønland, Grønlandernes Historie." *Folkelæsning* no. 364: Copenhagen, 1935.

———. "Inugssuk a Medieval Eskimo Settlement in Upernivik district, West Greenland." *Meddelelser om Grønland* 127 (1936): 147–340.

Mathiassen, Therkel and Erik Holtved. "The Eskimo Archeology of Julianehaab District." *Meddelelser om Grønland* 118, no. 1 (1936).

Meldgaard, Jørgen. "Nordboerne i Grønland." *Søndags universitet* 62 (1965).

———. "The Prehistoric Cultures in Greenland: Discontinuities in a Marginal Area." In *Danish-Netherlands Symposyium on Development in Greenlandic Arctic Culture, Arctic Centre, University of Groningen, Netherlands* 19–52, 1977.

———. "Inuit-Nordbo projektet arkeologiske undersøgelser i Vesterbygden i Grønland." In *National Museet Arbejdsmark.* Copenhagen: 1977b, 159–69.

———. "Om de gamle Nordboer og deres skæbne. Betragtninger over Helge Ingstads bog: Landet under Polarsjernen." *Grønland* 3 (1961).

———. "Settlement and Land Use in the Inner Fjords of Godthåb District, West Greenland." *Arctic Anthropology* 19, no 1 (1982).

Mercator, Gérard: 1577, see Nicholas of Lynn.

Migne, Jacques Paul. *Patrologiæ Cursus, series latina.* Book 131. Paris: 1831.

———. *Det Norske Folks Historie.* Vols. 1–7. Kristiania: 1852–63.

Morison, Samuel Eliot. *Portugese Voyages to America in the 15th Century.* Cambridge, Mass.: Harvard University Press, 1940. Translated into Portuguese by Lu. M. Maia Varcla. *As Viagens portuguesar à America,* 1988.

Mørch, Johan Christian. "Tanker om Grønlands Østerbygd i anledning af Herr Cancellie Raad V. Eggers Afhandling. Julianehaab den 8 Ianuarii 1799. Norges Svalbard og Ishavs undersøgelser." *Meddelelser* 52 (1942): 17–59.

Müller, Peter Erasmus, *Saga Bibliothek*. Vols 1–3. Copenhagen: Schultz, 1817–1820.

Munch, Peter Andreas. *Pavelige nuntiers Regnskabs og dagbøger førte under tiende, opkraevingen I Norden 1282–1334*. Christiania: 1864.

———. *Historisk, geografisk beskrivelse over Kongelig Norge i Middelalderen*, Christiania: 1849.

Nansen, Fridtjof, *Nord i Tåkeheimen*. Vols. 1–2. Christiania: Bjørn Ringstrøms Antikvariat, 1911. Reprinted. Oslo: 1988.

Nicholas of Lynn, *Inventio Fortunatæ*, lost book, 8 saved pages appear in a letter from G. Mercator to John Dee (Brit. Museum, MS. Cott Vitell C VTI. *ff* 264–268). Sources used here Manus. 150 fol. IV Univ. Bibl Oslo: 264v–268v, G. Mercator letter dated 1577. Also in T. J. Oleson, *Timarit Thjodraeknisfelags Islendinga*, vol. 44, 1963.

Nordenskiöld, Adolf Erik. *Facsimile Atlas to the early cartography with reproduction of the most important maps printed in the XV and XVI centuries*. Stockholm: 1889. Reprinted. NY: Dover Books, 1973.

Nørlund, Poul. "Buried Norsemen at Herjolfsnæs." *Meddelelser om Grønland* 116 (1924): 1–270.

———. *De gamle Nordbobygder ved Verdens Ende*. Revised Edition. Nationalmuseet, Copenhagen, 1967.

———. *Vikings settlers in Greenland and their descendants during 500 years*. Translated by W. E. Colwert. London: Cambridge University Press, 1936.

Nørlund, Poul & Mårten Steinbenzer. "Brattahlid." *Meddelelser om Grønland* 88, no. 1 (1934).

Odsson, Bishop Gissli. *Annalium in Islandia farrago*. In *Islandica*. Vol. 10, Ithaca: 1917.

Olaus Magnus, *Historia de gentibus septentrionalibus*, Rome, 1555. In *Grønlandske Historiske Mindesmærker*. Vol. 3. 464 ff. Reprinted in Swedish. *Regesta Norvegica. Historia om de Nordiska folken*. Stockholm, 1909–1951.

Olearius, Adam. *Beschreibung der Muscowischen und Persische Reyse*. Schleswig: Johan Holwein, 1656.

Oleson, Tryggvi. *The Norsemen in America*. Ottawa: The Canadian Historical Association Booklet, 1963.

———. *Early Voyages and Nothern Approaches 1000–1632*. New York: Oxford University Press, 1964.

Olsen, Olaf. "Nordboforskning." *Grønland* 5–7 (1982): 141–43.

Ortelius, Abraham. *The Theatre of the whole world.* London, 1606. Reprinted, Amsterdam: Theatrum Orbis Terrarum Ltd., 1968.

*Papsregesten.* Harald Zimerman (J.F. Böhmer Regesta Imperii,II.S) Vienna – Köln – Graz: Böhlan, 1969 DM 196.

Pederssøn Beyer, Absalon. "Om Norges Rige." In *Historiske topografiske skrifter om Norge og Norske landsdele, forfattede i Norge i det XVde Aarhundrede,* Kristiania: G. Storm 1895. Second edition, Norwegian University Press, 1968.

Petersen, Hjalmar and Erik Staffildt. *Bogen om Grønland, Fortid, Nutid, og Fremtid.* Copenhagen: Politikkens forlag, 1978.

Petersen, Robert. "The Greenland Tupilak." *Folk, Dansk etnografisk* 6, no. 2 (1964): 73–102.

Petitot, Émile. *Vocabulaire Français-Esquimau.* Paris: Ernest Leroux, 1876.

Pingel, Christian. "Antiquariske Efterretninger. Grønland." *Nordisk tidskrift for Oldkyndighed* 2 (1833): 313–43.

Plumet, Patrick. "Les Vikings en Amérique." *La Recherche* 18 (1987): 1160–68.

Privat, Jacques. "L'art inuit au Groenland." EHESS, Unpublished thesis. Paris: 1988.

———. "Les relations entre Inuit et Norrois au Moyen-Âge, un faux mystère?" *Il Polo, Rivisto trimistrale dell'Istituto Geografico Polare* 4 (Dec. 1991): 5–20.

Prytz, Kåre. *Vestover for Colombus,* Oslo: Aschehoug, 1990. Translated into French. *Christophe Colomb n'a pas découvert l'Amérique,* Lausanne: Livre ouvert, 1992.

Quinn, David B. "The Argument for the English Discovery of America between 1480 & 1494." *Geographic Journal* 127, no. 277 (1961): 85.

Rafn, Carl Christian, *Antiquitates Americanæ, sive Scriptores septentrionales rerum ante colombianarum in America, Samling af de i Nordens Oldskrifter indeholte efterretninger om de gamle Nordboers opdagelsessreiser til America fra det 10 de til det 14.de aarhundrede . . .* Edidit societas regia antiquariorum septentrionalum, typis officinæ Schultzianæ Hafniæ. 1837.

———. *Americas (Arktiske landes) Gamle Geographie efter de Nordiske oldskrifter.* Copenhagen, 1845.

———. *Fornaldar sögur Nördrlanda* Vol. 3. Copenhagen, 1829–1830.

Rasmussen, Knud. *Myter og sagn fra Grønland.* Vol. I. Copenhagen, Kristiania, Berlin, London: Østgrønlandeme, 1921.

———. *Myter og sagn fra Grønland.* Vol 3. London, Berlin, Copenhagen: Cape York distriktet og Nord-Grønland, 1925.

*Regesta Norvegica.* Vols. 1–9. Edited by Erik Gunnes. Oslo: Kjeldeskriftfondet, 1978–1983.

*Regesta Pontiff.* Publication 1885, 324. Lipsæ Veit et Comp. edit. Philippus Jaffe, editor Augustus Potthasl. Berolini 1874–1875.

Resen, Peder Hansen, "Grønlands beskrivelse." Edited with a German Glossary. Greendland: J. Kisby Møller, 1685.

*Rimbegla Sive rudimento computi ecclesiastici veterum Islandorum.* (Collection of arithmetic treatises based on a Twelfth century Icelandic manuscript.) Edited by St. Bjornonis. Copenhagen: Royal Library of Copenhagen, 1780.

Rimnasafn, I. *Samling af de ældste islandske rimer.* Copenhagen: Finnur Jónsson, 1905–1912.

Rink, Heinrich, *Kaladlit okalluktualliait-Grønlandske folkesagn.* Vols. 1 and 4. Godthaab: 1860. Reprinted, Tønder: 1972.

———. *Eskimoiske eventyr og sagn.* Edited by C. A. Reitzel. Copenhagen: 1866–1871. Reprinted with foreword by Helge Larsen. Copenhagen: 1982. Reprinted in English. *Tales and Tradition of the Eskimo,* Edinburgh-London: 1875.

Robbe, Pierre, "Existence et mode d'intervention des sorciers (Illisiitsut) dans la société inuit d'Ammassalik." *Etudes inuit* 7, no. 1 (1983): 25–40.

Roo, Philip de. *History of America before Columbus.* Philadelphia & London: J. B. Lippinicott, 1900.

Rosing, Jens. "Nordbominder fra Angmassalik." *Grønland tidskrift* n° 11 (1958): 438–39.

Rossen, H. C. *Nordboerne ved Upernivik.* Copenhagen: Det Grønlandske Selskabs Aarskrift, 1915–1916.

Roussell, Aage. "Farms and Churches in the Medieval Norse settlements of Greenland." *Meddelelser om Grønland* 89, no. 1 (1941).

Rousselière, Guy Marie. "Exploration and Evangelization of the Great Canadian North: Vikings, Coureurs des Bois, and Missionaries." *Artic* 37, no. 4 (1984).

Sabo, Debby, and Georges Sabo. "A Possible Thule carving of a Viking from Baffin Island." *Canadian Journal of Archeology* 2 (1978).

Sawyer, Peter. "Dioceses and Parishes in Twelfth Century Scandinavia." In *St. Magnus Cathedral and Orkneys Twelfth Centure Renaissance.* Edited by Crawford Barbra, 36–45. Aberdeen: 1988.

Saxo Grammaticus. *Gesta Danorum.* Copenhagen: Jorgen Olrik in Danmarks Riges kronike, 1970.

Schledermann, Peter. "Notes on Norse Finds from the East Coast of Ellesmere Island. N.W.T." *Arctic* 33, no. 3 (1980): 454–63.

———. "Polynias and prehistoric Settlements Patterns." *Arctic* 33, no. 3 (1980).

———. "Ellesmere Island. Eskimo and Viking Finds in the High Arctic." *National Geographic,* 159, no. 5 (1981): 572–601.

———. "Nordbogenstande fra Arktisk Canada." Translated by H. C. Gulløv. *Grønland* 5–7 (1982): 218–25.

*Series Episcoporum Ecclesiæ Catholicæ.* Pius Bonifacius Gams/ Graz: Akademische Druck U. Verlaugsaustalt, 1957.

Sigurdsson, Haraldur. "Some Landmarks in Icelandic Cartography down to the end of the XVIth Century." *Arctic* 37, no. 4 (1984).

Skelton, R. A. *Vinland Map and Tartar Relation.* New Haven, Conn.: Yale University Press, 1965

Skelton R. A., Thomas E. Marston, and George D. Painter. *The Vinland Map and the Tartar Relation.* New Edition, New Haven, Conn.: Yale University Press, 1995.

Smedberg, Gunnar. *Nordens första kyrkor, en kyrkorättslig studie.* Upsala University, dissertation. Lund: Gleerup, 1973.

Snorri, Sturlusson. *Heimskringla,* Reykjavik: Islenzke Fornrit, XXVI–XXVIII, 1979.

Stefansson, Vilhjalmur. *Greenland.* Garden City, N.Y.: Doubleday, Doron & Company, 1942.

Steinnes, Asgaut. "Ein Nordpolsekspedition år 1360." *Syn og Segn* 64 (1958): 410–19.

Storm, Gustav. *Monumenta Historica Norvegiæ.* Kristiania, 1880

———. "Om biskop Gissle Odsson annaler." *Arkiv for Nordisk Filologi* 7 (1889–90): 351–57.

———. "Den Danske geograf Claudius Clavus eller Nicolaus Niger." In *Ymer.* Edited by Svenska Sällskapet for Antropologi och Geografi, Stockholm, 1891, 13–17.

———. "Columbus på Island og vores forfædres opdagelser i det nordvestlige Atlanterhav," *Den Norske geografiske Selskabs Årbog* 4, Kristiania: 1893.

———. "Et brev til Pave Nicolaus den 5ᵗᵉ. Om Norges beliggenhed og under," Kristiania: ed. det Norske Geografiske Selskabs Aarbog 9, 1897–98, 1, 3, 1898.

Söderberg, Sven. "Föredrag i Filologiska sällskapet i Lund, Maj 1898." *Sydsvenska dagbladet Snällposten* 295 (Nov. 30, 1910).

*Sturlunga saga.* Copenhagen: K. Kålund, 1906–1911.

Sundt, Eilert. *Egedes Dagbok i Udtag.* Oslo: 1860.

Thalbitzer, William. "Eskimoernes kultiske Guddomene." *Studier fra sprog og oldtids forskning* 43 (1926).

―――. "Fra Grønlandsforsknings første dage." *Festskrift udg.* Af Kobenhavns universitet, 1932, 5–107.

―――. "Powell Knuttssons rejse. En forsvinden færd til Grønland og Markland?" *The Greenland Society Yearbook,* Copenhagen, 1949.

―――. "Two Runic Stones from Greenland and Minnesota." *Smithsonian Miscscellaneous Collection* CXVI. no. 3 (1951).

Thorallesen, Eigil. *Efterretning om Rudera eller Levninger af de gamle Nordmænds og Islaenderes Bygninger paa Grønland Vester-Side, tilligemed et Anhæng om deres Undergang sammesteds.* Copenhagen: 1776.

Thorkelsson, Jón. *Thjódsogur og Munmæli.* Reprinted, Reykjavik: 1956.

Thorlacius Théodore. See Jonssön, Björn.

Thorsteinsson, Ingvi, *Undersøgelser af de naturlige græsgange i Syd-Grenland 1977-1981,* Upernaviarsuk, Greenland: Landbrugets Forskningsinstitut & Forsøgstationen 1983.

Thuren H. "On the Eskimo Music." *Meddelelser om Grønland* 40 (1911): 1–45.

*Urkundenbuch der Stadt Lübeck.* Vol. 4. Lübeck, Germany: Verein für Lübeckische Geschichte und Altertumskunde, 1843–1932.

Vebæk, Leif Christian. "The Church Topography of the Eastern Settlement of the Benedicte Convent at Narssassuaq in the Unartoq Fjord." *Meddelelser om Grønland, Man and Society* 14 (1991): 81.

Vries, Jan de. *Altnordisches Etymologisches Worterbuch.* Leiden: E. J Brill, 1961. Perger, Rev. "Greenland" 6. In Wetzer & Welte. *Kirchen Lexikon.* 1898.

Wallace, Birgitta Lindroth. "The l'Anse aux Meadows site, I." In Jones, Gwyn. *The Norse Atlantic Saga,* 285–304. Second Edition. New York: Oxford University Press, 1986.

Walkendorff, Erik. In *Grønlandske Historiske Mindesmærker* Vol. 3, 492–95. Copenhagen: 1838–1845.

Wytfliet, Cornelius. *Descriptiones Ptolemaicae augmentum.* Louvain: 1597. Reprinted, Amsterdam: N. Israël, Meridian, 1964.

Wallis, Helen. "England's Search for the Northern Passages in the 16th and Early 17th Centuries." in *Arctic* 31, no. 4 (1984).

Zahrtmann, Christian Christopher. "Bemærkninger om de Venetianerne Zeni tilskrevne Reiser i Norden." In *NordiskTidskrift for Oldkyndighed*. Vol. 2, 1–35. Det kongelige nordiske oldskrift selskab Edition. Copenhague: 1833.

Zoéga, Geir T. *A Concise dictionary of old Icelandic*. London: Oxford University Press, 1910. Reprinted. Oxford: Clarendon Press, 2004.

# Index

Numbers in *italics* preceded by *pl.* refer to color insert plate numbers.